THE CHURCH IN RESPONSE TO HUMAN NEED

TOM SINE, Editor

Missions Advanced Research and Communication Center

Library of Congress Number 83-50051

Copyright © 1983 by Tom Sine

All rights reserved.

Published by
Missions Advanced Research and
Communication Center
919 West Huntington Drive
Monrovia, California 91016 USA

ISBN 0-912552-39-5

Printed in the United States of America

CONTENTS

INTRODUCTION

Tom Sine

Anticipation is beginning to build as we approach
Wheaton 83. We are coming together as brothers and sisters
in Christ from all over the world to explore how we can be
much more a part of God's mission to that world. One track
will examine the mission of global evangelism, another the
mission of the local church, and our track, Consultation 83,
will focus on mission to global human need. Efforts will be
made during the conference to explore how our work in global
evangelism, church planting, and development can be more
closely integrated, both theologically and programmatically.

The purpose of Consultation 83 is to enable those Christians involved in responding to human need to:

(1) analyze the underlying value assumptions implicit in
    our development programs;

(2) articulate some new biblical principles to enable us
    to respond more biblically to the growing needs of
    those with whom we share this planet;

(3) utilize those new biblical principles that come out of
    our study and discussion to create some practical new
    ways of responding to human need;

(4) explore ways that we can work more cooperatively in holistic mission with those involved in evangelism and church planting;

Beyond the Consultation itself, we are designing a follow on process to develop curriculum on a more holistic approach to the mission of the church.

Consultation 83 was born out of a concern expressed in the unit on Ethics and Society of the World Evangelical Fellowship. Under Ron Sider's influence this concern grew into a Consultation.

In this pre-conference publication you will find papers that have been prepared to both help us analyze the value assumptions off which we are currently operating and suggest some new biblical principles that could lead to the creation of some fresh new approaches to responding to human need. (Regrettably some of the authors were unable to complete their papers for this publication.)

It is expected that every participant, in preparation for the conference, will not only read and study these papers, but also list:

(1) new insights you've derived from the papers;

(2) questions or areas of disagreement;

(3) implications of ideas and principles within the paper on present development theory and practice;

(4) ideas of creative ways that biblical principles within the papers could find expression in imaginative new approaches to working for social transformation;

(5) suggestions on how we might be able to work more cooperatively with those involved in ministries of evangelism and church planting.

Your notes will be extremely useful to you when the issues raised in the papers will be discussed in small groups during the conference.

Special thanks to Kathy Boyadgis for supervising the production of this pre-conference publication, to Mary Thomson for typing all the papers, as well as the help from the support staff in Ed Dayton's and Wayne Bragg's offices.

Ed Dayton's assistance was essential to the completion of this publication, as was input from Consultation 83 Steering Committee under the leadership of Vinay Samuel and Art Beals.

Please join us in prayer that God will use the entire process to help us discover both a new vision of His mission and a new power to carry out that mission in a world of expanding need...that "His Kingdom will come and His will be done on earth."

DEVELOPMENT: ITS SECULAR PAST AND ITS UNCERTAIN FUTURE

Tom Sine

INTRODUCTION

"We are appalled to know that about 800 million people,
or one fifth of the human race, are destitute, lacking the
basic necessities for survival, and thousands die every day.
Many more millions are without clean water and health care,
without opportunities for education and employment, and are
condemned to eke out a miserable existence without the possibility of self-improvement for themselves or their families.
They can only be described as "oppressed" by the gross economic inequality from which they suffer and the diverse economic systems which cause and perpetuate it....All these are
rooted in the profound sinfulness of humankind, and they demand from the people of God a radical response of compassion..
In addition to worldwide evangelism, the people of God should
become deeply involved in relief, aid, development, and the
quest for social justice and peace." [1]

As we prepare for Consultation '83, we strongly affirm
the commitment of the CRESR Report to larger mission of the
church in both evangelism and social responsibility and to
the particular concern expressed for the poor with whom we
work.

PURPOSE

The purpose of this paper is to help us to begin to more
fully understand the context within which we work with the
poor, not only today but tomorrow. In a world of rapid

change it is essential that those of us who work in development learn to anticipate the new needs, constraints and opportunities before they arrive, so that we have time to create new forms of response.

However, this paper is not only written to help us more thoroughly understand the rapidly changing context in which we will be doing development in the future, but to more critically evaluate the philosophical and theological premise of our development activities in the present.

If we hope to articulate a more biblical premise for a Christian response to human need, we must first understand the secular origins of the term "development." And then we must reflectively assess to what extent those secular assumptions have crept into our understandings as Christians of how to work with those in need.

It is hoped by broadening our context to focus not only on the needs today but the global challenges we are likely to face tomorrow and examine our premise to assess to what extent we may have unwittingly bought into some secular notions of development....We will be better able to articulate a biblical premise for our work with those in need.

This paper is really two papers in one, looking at both development's uncertain future and its secular origin. Of course, as an American, I am writing from my own context, but I have attempted to raise questions with which the church in all nations must struggle...as we together seek to advance His kingdom.

DEVELOPMENT: ITS UNCERTAIN FUTURE

"Suddenly--virtually overnight when measured on a historical scale--mankind finds itself confronted by a multitude of unprecedented crises: the population crisis, the
environmental crisis, the raw materials crisis, just to
name a few. New crises appear while the old ones linger on
with effects spreading to every corner of the earth until
they appear in point of fact as global, worldwide crises..."[2]

These global crises signal the reality that we have entered a period of dramatic planetary change. We can no
longer predict the future by studying the past. Nor can we
any longer assume the future will simply be an extension of
the present...as long range planning tends to do. It is essential that those of us working with the poor for the kingdom learn to anticipate tomorrow's challenges before they
arrive. To the extent we are able to anticipate even a few
of the emerging challenges, to that extent we have time to
create new ministry responses, even though attempting to
forecast the future is very difficult and sometimes uncertain,
the only other option is to be surprised by change.

The best example of anticipatory planning I have found
was completed by the Philippine Council of Evangelical
Churches. They analyzed the economic, social and technological trends in the Philippines between now and the year 2000.
Their forecast led them to conclude that the continuing high
rate of inflation would have a particularly negative impact
on most Christian families, who are on subsistence incomes.
They immeiately saw the implications of this economic trend.
It means that mothers will be forced to join the labor market for the families simply to survive, "leaving children
unsupervised, thus weakening the home."[3]

In response to this anticipated challenge the Philippine
Council of Evangelical Churches is creating some economic development projects to enable women to earn the supplemental
income they will need, while they stay at home and take care
of their children. But you see, it never would have occurred
to them to create the supplemental income projects for women
in their own homes if they had not first anticipated the need.

Recently I worked with World Vision International to help
them redesign a long range planning context to enable them to
more effectively anticipate the context in which they will be

ministering in the next ten years. Essentially in this document we outlined a few social, economic, political and technological trends to enable them, in their five year planning
process, to more effectively address tomorrow's challenges
as well as today's needs.

It is essential that those of us working with the poor
critically examine both the theological assumptions on which
our Christian development programs are premised and our assumptions about the future. Only as we learn to anticipate
the needs, threats, and opportunities of tomorrow's world
do we have any hope of mobilizing resources and directing
ministry to those areas of greatest need.

Let me outline a few of the challenges that are likely
to confront those working in global mission during the last
two decades of the twentieth century. I will sketch out some
of the questions these trends raise for us theologically and
relationally, as well as suggesting some new ways we might
respond programmatically.

FUTURE OF OUR GLOBAL ECOLOGY

The United States Office of Technological Assessment predicts that the projected levels of combined economic and
population growth will seriously threaten the carrying capability of our finite planet through massive pollution of air
and water, deforestation, creation of deserts, elimination
of natural areas of wildlife habitats, depletion of fish
stocks, progressive simplification and homogenization of nature. They concluded that these pressures on global systems
will create escalating rates of inflation, which will take
their greatest toll on the poorest of the poor. [4]

In many parts of the two-thirds world, the major energy
crisis is the firewood crisis. Seventy percent of the timber
cut in these regions winds up under the cooking pot, creating
deforestation and erosion of croplands.

This means those of us working in the two-thirds not only
need to focus on human needs but also on the ecological context. We need to monitor those geographical areas that are
threatened with destruction by human growth and try to find
ways, in cooperation with others, to reverse those trends.
Failing our biblical responsibility to be "earth keepers" and
stewarding the ecological context within which we live and
work, our efforts at economic development may be pointless.

FUTURE OF THE GLOBAL POOR

Approximately 70 million people are in imminent danger of starvation, 400 million are chronically malnourished, and fully one billion don't get enough to eat. Two billion, or almost half the world's population, make less than two hundred dollars per person per year.[5]

West Berlin Chancellor Willy Brandt in his *North South Report* predicts the plight of the planetary poor will only worsen as we approach the year 2000. In fact, he is deeply concerned that the growing global inequity between North and South threatens world peace and stability. That is why he has called for a major international program by industrialized nations to help the poorer parts of the planet to become self-reliant.

The Global 2000 Report, published recently by the U.S. Government, essentially states that the world's poor are in a growing state of jeopardy: "the world in the year 2000-- more crowded, more polluted, and, even less stable ecologically, and more vulnerable to disruption than the world we live in now, unless the nations of the world act quickly and decisively to change current policies."[6]

The problem is that neither the nations nor private voluntary agencies are acting decisively. Some experts are predicting we will have twice as many hungry people by the year 2000 as we have today. But because those of us in Christian organizations aren't paying adequate attention to these signals, we aren't mobilizing an adequate response to address the growing issues of hunger and poverty in our world tomorrow. How can the church be motivated to mobilize its resources to much more fully respond to this growing challenge?

FUTURE OF GLOBAL URBANIZATION

Perhaps one of the most urgent signals that must be addressed in the very near future is the unprecedented urban explosion this planet will face between now and the end of the century. Today there are six hundred million landless poor in Africa, Asia, and Latin America. By the end of the century, it is predicted that there will be one billion. These rural people who own little more than their own bodies can stay on the land only as long as they are strong enough to work it. Erik Eckhelm forecasts that "conflict rooted in the inequality of land ownership is apt to become more acute in country after country."[7]

Millions of landless people, those who have given up hope for the land, are flooding into the cities of the two-thirds world. "By the end of the century, three quarters of all Latin Americans and one third of all Asians and Africans will be living in cities."[8] By the year 2000, Latin America will be more urbanized than Europe. The largest city in the world by the century's end will be Mexico City with thirty-two million people. São Paulo, Brazil, will be second with twenty-five million.[9]

Again very few public or voluntary agencies are paying attention to this critically important trend. To avert a potential human holocaust in these critically over-populated corridors, action must immediately be taken in the areas of land retention and rural and urban development. Evangelical agencies have historically worked intensively in the areas of rural development but have had very modest involvement in programs of land reform. Only in the last several years have a few agencies, like World Vision and World Concern, begun to consider the area of urban development. However, if we in the church, in concert with others, are to effectively respond to this anticipated urban challenge, we must: (1) not only do much more in rural development, (2) we must initiate programs to return land to the landless, and (3) begin creative new urban ventures to enable these in the exploding cities to become self-reliant in meeting their basic survival needs.

FUTURE OF GLOBAL REFUGEE MIGRATIONS

In addition to monitoring and responding to the unprecedented urban migrations of our common future, we also are called upon to be much more effective in anticipating and responding to the emerging refugee movements of tomorrow's world. Refugee movements are a by-product of political destabilization,and political destabilization is likely to increase in the future as well. Therefore we need to identify these politically unstable regions of the world and analyze where the next refugee flows are likely to come from. In cooperation with the United Nations and government agencies, new refugee programs need to be developed in advance of new refugee movements.

FUTURE OF GLOBAL ECONOMICS

Of course the issues of world hunger, global ecology, and large scale human migrations are inextricably connected to global economic and political structures. Some of the most difficult challenges confronting the church in the future are economic, political, and ethical.

Richard Barnet predicts, "There are enough resources in the world to support a decent life for the predicted global population of the year 2000, but not to support lopsided opulence or continual ecological plunder"[10] (that characterizes our world today).

In the seventies we abruptly awakened to a new image of our planet as both a finite and a shrinking pie. Unquestionably, a major contributing cause to the rapid depletion of non-renewable resources and their escalating costs has been the dramatic economic grown of countries in the northern hemisphere. Robert Heilbroner points out that until recently the industrialized North has been growing at a rate of about 7% a year, or doubling about every ten years. If that rate continued for another 50 years, we would require a volume of resource extraction thirty-two times larger than today.[11]

We in the North have assured ourselves and those with whom we share the planet that our trajectory of high economic growth is not only good for us, but the benefits will trickle down to all the earth's inhabitants. Recent evidence seems to raise serious question as to whether our high growth benefits or penalizes those with whom we share this finite planet. Alvin Toffler has charged that those of us in the North have treated the rest of the world as though it were our "gas pump, garden, mine, quarry, and cheap labor supply."[12]

In spite of the failure of "trickle down economics" and the growing concern among many North and South regarding economic justice, there is little evidence of serious change of international economic structures. The call for a new economic order in 1974 by two thirds world countries has virtually been ignored in terms of the proposals it raised. Even though the issue of Third World debt is a growing concern to the economic capitals in the North, little is being done to resolve this issue. Therefore, we can expect the gap between rich and poor nations to continue to widen as we approach the year 2000.

"Under the influence of the U.S. Government, World Bank
had fundamentally changed directions. These changes will
probably influence its activities through the Eighties. The
World Bank is becoming more of an umbrella agency through
which private investment is channelled to the Third World.
Essentially, under the new focus, instead of the bank being
a cushion against the Market, the bank will now be the Market,
tying interest rates to the market. It seems likely that
these changes will have a negative impact on the poorest
countries."[13]

The changes at World Bank reflect a dramatic change in
foreign policy by the Reagan administration. As we move into
the Eighties, there is a growing disparity between the interests of the United States and Two Thirds World countries. Of
primary policy concern to the U.S. at this point in time is
"National Security." And the entire planet is seen by American policy makers in the context of U.S.-Soviet relations.
Mr. Reagan has taken a more ideological approach to both domestic and foreign policies than any U.S. president in fifty
years.

At the Cancun Summit, he lectured the poorer nations to
follow the U.S. example and pull themselves up by their own
bootstraps. Even though the U.S. is offering some private
sector assistance, U.S. foreign aid to poorer nations is declining, and one wonders how resource poor nations are supposed to pull themselves up in a global economy rigged in favor of the rich and influential nations and against the poor.[14]

Even though most industrialized nations have in the wake
of a global recession experienced a slowing of economic
growth, the engines of growth are beginning to start up again.
As Christians, we must ask if the North begins to experience
a higher rate of economic growth, who will benefit and who
will lose? Should we really leave the future of the poor to
Darwinian economic theories? Do the church and Christian relief and development agencies have any responsibility to influence government policies in our respective countries, or
is our only responsibility to patch up those victimized by
unjust economic structures?

In view of prophetic warnings from Isaiah to Amos regarding God's judgment coming against those who live affluently
at the expense of the poor, biblical Christians must come to
grips with the issue of social justice as it relates to the
use of planetary resources and global economics. I am not

suggesting we try to curtail growth in the North but advocate
a policy of more equitable growth that insures justice for
all those that share this finite planet.

Within the church we need a new theology of stewardship that is both more biblical and more responsible in a
finite, interdependent world. Nowhere in the New Testament
is the tithe normative for stewardship. Following Christ
was always a whole life proposition. We need to affirm again
that "the earth is the Lord's." Therefore for a biblical
people, it is never a question of "How much do I have to give
up?" If "the earth is the Lord's," the question is "How much
of God's do I get to keep?"--in relationship to all those
with whom I share this planet. That means before we build a
multi-million dollar church in America, we check to see if a
church in Bolivia can afford a metal roof. It means before
we buy a luxury item for ourselves, can a family in another
part of the world afford to feed their children? We need to
begin stewarding all our personal and institutional resources
of time, education, money and facilities as though they belong to God and His church international. The International
Fellowship of Evangelical Students promotes one model. Their
Executive Committee is comprised of twelve members, eight of
whom are from the South. Even though financial resources
come largely from the North, this committee has authority to
determine their use in ministry.

This means in practical terms that relief and development
agencies in the North need to consider bringing brothers and
sisters in the South into full partnership in the use of resources that belong to the international body of Jesus Christ,
and it suggests that northern agencies need to international-
ize their leadership. It calls all of us in the North and
South to streamline our agencies, cut the frills, and significantly reduce overhead so that a much greater share of the
resource gets overseas. Two new agencies in the U.S., Harvest, in Phoenix, Arizona, and Good Deeds, in Seattle, Washington have found ways to reduce overhead by simplifying opera-
tions and finding non-traditional ways to raise money for
overhead cost. As a consequence, they are able to send 100%
of designated gifts to the field.

And it calls all of us working with the poor to significantly reduce our own lifestyle costs, living much more simply
so that more of God's resource is available for the work of
His kingdom among those in need. Unless we authentically
incarnate the values of the kingdom in lifestyles of simplicity, how can we work with the poor in integrity? (Increasingly

evangelical relief and development agencies' policies in this
area are becoming more visible. See "A Giver's Guide," *The
Other Side,* March, 1983.)

FUTURE OF GLOBAL POLITICAL CONFRONTATION

Closely related to the larger issue of economic justice
is the issue of political freedom and world peace. In the
last two years there has been a dramatic escalation in the
nuclear arms race and cold war between the super-powers.
Christians and others concerned for peace in western Europe
and the U.S. have challenged this build-up, calling for a
multi-lateral nuclear freeze on the production and deployment
of nuclear weapons.

Unless the Soviets and the U.S. agree to freeze production and deployment of nuclear missiles and begin actually
reducing their nuclear stockpiles, they will not have the
moral clout necessary to persuade nations without nuclear
weapons to sign a nuclear non-proliferation treaty. Failure
to secure signing of a nuclear non-proliferation treaty will
mean that forty nations will develop nuclear weapons by the
year 2000. And the forecast is very high that some of those
weapons will be used.[15]

Is it possible for Christians, churches, and Christian
agencies to labor to save the lives of the poor from the ra-
vages of hunger and economic injustice and not speak out
against the ultimate violence--nuclear war? In working for
the kingdom, is our sole task to run ambulance service at the
bottom of the cliff, treating the victims of injustice and
violence, or do we have a responsibility to challenge the
forces that push the innocent off the cliff? Should we, for
example, speak out against human rights violations in Russia,
Iran, and El Salvador? Should we seek to stop the flow of
arms into the Middle East or Central America, or should we
leave the policy issues to others? Since the Bible calls us
to work for peace and reconciliation, what does that mean in
our world today and tomorrow?

FUTURE OF THE GLOBILIZATION OF CULTURE

The global expansion of weapons of destruction is only
one form of human control and intimidation. Less visible but
perhaps more pervasive is the introduction and often imposi-
tion of Western values into traditional cultures. Someone
has written that America has become the image of the better
future for many in the Two-Thirds World. Unfortunately this

observation appears to be accurate. Through transnational
marketing by multi-national corporations, we appear to be
creating a global consumer society in which everyone listens
to the same kind of music, drinks the same soda, and buys into the same individualistic, materialistic values.

A communication industrial complex is being formed by
Western interests to gain control of communication networks
in the South. From satellite television to laser radio, advanced communication systems are apparently being used to
promote a new global culture, changing local customs, tastes
and values through media.[16]

Increasingly Two-Thirds World countries are in response
pushing for "a new information order." Christopher Nasciemento, a Cabinet member in Guyana, argues that the West dominates and controls the direction, flow, management, and content of information internationally. The creation of "a new
information order" could fundamentally alter consciousness
all over the planet. Not only might this slow the "Westernization" of the world, it might very well raise some consciousness among those in the One-Third World as well.[17]

Those of us involved in global mission need to ask to
what extent are we unconsciously promoting westernization of
traditions and cultures, and to what extent are we working
for Kingdom agencies that are trans-cultural? Should Christian development projects ever seek, as a conscious planning
goal, to help people preserve and augment those traditional
values they want to keep in the face of growing westernization? Should Christian organizations help nationals to gain
greater control of media and information systems within their
own countries in response to this growing challenge?

FUTURE OF GLOBAL CHRISTIAN FAITH

Closely related to the issue of the future of culture is
the issue of the future of religion. "Presently, some 1.433
billion people consider themselves Christian and are affilia-
ted among over 20,800 distinct denominations. The percentage
of Christians to the total world population has been slowly
declining: from 34.4% of the world's population in 1900 to
32.8% in 1980. Massive gains in the Two-Thirds World countries are offset by growing apostasy in the One-Third World."[18]
Of course the most rapidly growing edge of the church throughout the world are the Pentecostals and Charismatics. We need
to learn from those that God is evidently blessing.

Not only is the rate of Christian growth globally slowly declining, there is a significant shift in the demographics of the church. By the year 2000 over half of all the Christians are going to be in the Two-Thirds World. We are witnessing a fundamental shift, not only in demographics, but potentially in the leadership of tomorrow's church, according to Buhlmann in his book *The Coming of the Third Church*. It means that those of us in the One-Third World will have to listen more and talk less. We will find it is essential to read theology from our brothers and sisters in Africa, Asia, and Latin America to be informed.

As we plan our development strategies for the remainder of the twentieth century, we need to ask what the implications will be of working in true partnership North and South, freely sharing leadership with those who are the growing edge of the church? It will mean that the dying church in the North will be forced to turn to the growing church in the South for renewal and revitalization. It will mean that churches in the Two-Thirds World will play an increasingly aggressive role as missionary sending agencies, not only to the unreached, but in relief and development work. And in view of the mounting challenges discussed in this paper, it will be essential that Christian agencies set aside their competition and conflict and work much more cooperatively--North and South increasingly under Two-Thirds World leadership--witnessing our unity in Jesus Christ.

In view of the unprecedented global challenges confronting the church in the last two decades of the twentieth century, it is essential that those of us working with the poor learn:

(1) to more effectively anticipate the needs, challenges, and opportunities that are likely to be a part of tomorrow's world;

(2) to identify the implications of those anticipated challenges to the church and its biblical mission to the world;

(3) to create imaginative new ministries to more effectively respond to the anticipated challenges in each part of the world in which we are working;

(4) to more justly and conscientiously steward the resources of time, education, and money God has entrusted to us in our personal lifestyles and institutional

programs--freeing up much more for the work of the
Kingdom and using it in partnership with those in
the Two-Thirds World;

(5) to set aside all competition and conflict, and cooperatively join together in our common mission to
the poor, increasingly relying on the leadership and
vitality of the church in the Two-Thirds World--and
receiving their ministry to us.

(6) to articulate a theology of biblical mission to human
needs that is responsive to the context of a very
rapidly changing future;

(7) to pray as we have never done before that "God's
Kingdom will come and His will be done on earth"
through His church, in response to the escalating
challenges of tomorrow's world.

A business-as-usual approach to these anticipated chal-
lenges--simply doing 3% next year of what we did last year--
will not make any significant difference. We must mobilize
our constituencies and organizations to a much greater commitment to global mission in the 80's and 90's in both proclaiming the love of God and demonstrating His love in a lifestyle of justice and service. And in Consultation '83, we
need to examine our theological assumptions within the context of a rapidly changing future.

DEVELOPMENT: ITS SECULAR PAST

Before we attempt to articulate a biblical premise for
working with the poor, we not only need to more effectively
anticipate tomorrow's challenges but more critically analyze
the secular origins of Western "development." It is important to not only understand the secular origins of "development" but the secular values implicit in Western "development"
to determine to what extent those values have unwittingly become our values in Christian development programs. To what
extent have the secular values of Western development crept
into our values as we have sought to work with those in need?

In order to surface these implicit values the following
questions will be asked of western development. What are the
implicit images of: The Better Future? God and His Universe?
The Nature of Persons? The Pathway to the Achievement of
that Better Future?

What is the Implicit View of the Better Future in Western
Development?

Western development is a child of the European and American Enlightenment. It is based on the implicit belief that
human society is inevitably progressing toward the attainment
of a temporal materialistic kingdom. In fact, the certain belief that unending economic and social progress is a natural
condition of free persons has become the secular religion of
the west.

Somehow the millenial expectation of the inbreaking of a
new transcendent kingdom was temporalized and secularized into the expectation of a future of unlimited economic and technological growth. In Francis Bacon's book *The New Atlantis*
we are shown the first vision in western history of a technological paradise achieved solely through the instrumentality
of man.

Implicit in this progressive view of the future was the
firm conviction that economic progress would automatically result in social and moral progress. Here then is a view of the
better future that is primarily economic focusing largely on
human activities of production and consumption. Not surprisingly, the "good life" became synonymous with self-seeking and
one's ability to produce and consume ever increasing quantities
of goods and services.

The expansive nature of the Western dream of progress motivated westerns to go beyond their own national boundaries in search of both resources and markets as the Industrial Revolution began. The realization of the American dream was made possible by the appropriation of enormous areas of land and the resources from Native Americans. The great leap forward of industrial and economic growth in the west would not have been possible without the abundant relatively inexpensive resources acquired through colonization of countries in the southern hemisphere.

One of the realities that we as Christians must realize is that "missionary activity has gone hand in hand with colonization for almost two millenia. No matter how we interpret the underlying relations between the two orders, it is self-evident that political expansion and the church's expansion in the world have covered the same ground, geographically and chronologically."[19]

Since the church's expansion went hand in hand with western economic and political expansion, the question with which we must struggle is: To what extent have the values of secular western development permeated a Christian view of development?

As a point of information, Marxist ideology was born out of the same Western ferment and also sees society moving towards a temporal future that is singularly economic and political. The intention of the Marxists is to ensure that all peoples participate in this future and they believe in its inevitability.

As we enter the eighties, virtually no one any longer believes in the inevitability of economic, technological and social progress other than Marxists. The events of the seventies have sounded the death knell for the Enlightened belief that humankind could achieve a utopia here on earth. In spite of this new sobering awareness, the essential image of the better future implicit in contemporary development has not significantly changed since the beginnings of western expansion. At the very core of contemporary development is a notion that the better future is synonymous with economic growth. The "better life" of persons is really defined principally in economic terms. Nations which have experienced major economic and technological growth are described as "developed;" those which haven't are characterized as "underdeveloped." In spite of the growing awareness of the negative human and environmental consequences of unrestrained growth, the "developed" world has become a showcase of the "ideal" future for the "under-developed" world. The apparent superiority of the "developed" image of the ideal future has directly influenced the defini-tion and goals of contemporary development. Thirty years ago the primary goal of western development in the Third World was "maximization of GNP per capita." Today the goal has been broadened to increasingly focus on "basic needs" to raise the economic level of the world's poorest people.[20]

John Sommers argues that "it has become increasingly clear that economic well-being is not sufficient goal and the measuring of development on the materialistic basis of per capita gross national product is inadequate and often mislead-ing."[21] He goes on to advocate that development should be de-fined in spiritual and cultural terms as well as economic. There are some non-Western models that are based on a broader understanding of the scope of development.

For example, Gandhi had a very different vision for the future of his people than the one that is implicit in the western model. "The future lay in imitating the industrial technological society of the west. India's salvation, he ar-gued, lay in 'unlearning what she has learned in the past 50 years.' He challenged almost all of the western ideals that had taken root in India. Science should not order human val-ues, he argued; technology should not order society, and civilization was not the indefinite multiplication of human wants, but their limitation so that essentials could be shared by all."[22]

Gandhi's image of the better future for India was a nation of 600,000 decentralized villages which were highly self-suf-ficient units, in which traditional culture, religion, and family life were strengthened. While longing to see grinding poverty ended, he opposed development which would create ma-terial affluence, because he was convinced that affluence would lead to cultural erosion and moral bankruptcy. His vi-sion for the future gave primacy not to economic development, but to the development of the inner spirit and the reinforce-ment of positive values and reconciled relationships within traditional culture.

What is the Implicit View of God and His Universe in Western Development?

Western views of development are not only tied to singu-larly secular notions of the better future, but secular views of God and His universe as well...that have their origins in

the Enlightenment. In sixteenth century England, Francis
Bacon drew a historic line between the "words of God" and
the "works of God." By that act he gave major momentum towards a new dualistic view of the universe. Essentially all
in the natural order that can be experienced through the
senses was lumped into the "works of God." The revelational
and spiritual aspects of existence were pigeon-holed under
the "words of God."

Not only was the Creator seen as passive, but His creation was also seen as a passive realm, a grab bag of physical
resources available for the taking. This dualistic view of
God and His universe has resulted in a desacralization of His
creation, freed from the purposes and presence of God. Westerners learned to think of the world around them as nothing
but passive resources to be exploited to enable them to a-
chieve their materialistic dreams for the future.

Jeremy Rifkin asserted, "Faith in the liberating power of
materialism carries with it one critical assumption, the belief the earth possesses unlimited abundance. The formulators
of liberalism, the men of the Age of Reason and the Enlightenment, had no doubt that the earth would yield more wealth than
could possibly be used...In the 1600's the new world, the
greatest frontier known, was just opening up for exploitation.
By the beginning of the next century, industrialism had begun.
Wherever people looked, it seemed that the world held more--
more wealth, more prosperity, more productivity, more knowledge to be used in the service of humanity. The obvious contrast with the unchanging order of the Middle Ages was proof
to all persons of reason that the new age was superior to all
that had come before."[23] This secularized view of God and
His universe was foundational to the economic growth and expansion of an age of western development.

The dualism of Bacon and his followers has borne its fruit
in our age. In contemporary development as in much of western
culture, there is no belief that God lives and acts in history.
The world and its future are perceived to be solely in the
hands of man. Contemporary development theory is premised on
a thorough-going secularization of the natural and human orders. In reading contemporary development literature, not the
slightest consideration is given to the possibility that God
is, or that He has any influence on human affairs. In fact,
the literature tends to deny even the existence of any realm
beyond sensory experience. It is assumed in development theory that "developed" peoples have the responsibility through
rational, development planning, to enable as many of the

"underdeveloped" people as possible to join the inner circle
of economic growth and prosperity.

The massive exploitation of global resources has brought
us to a new reality. The *First Report to the Club of Rome*
in 1973 called to everyone's attention that new reality--that
the earth is not infinite, it is finite. This new reality
more than any other contemporary insight has put to rest the
western belief in both the inevitability and indeed the possibility of all people fully participating in the western
dream.

Far from being simply a passive malleable resource as
Bacon had suggested, we have recently discovered that for
every act we take against God's world, it seems to have a
capability to counter-punch. We can no longer thoughtlessly
exploit the natural order. We are being forced to consider
the consequence of every act we take. We are being forced
to perceive ourselves as stewards not of passive resources
but of a vast, active, fragile planetary system. Recent development literature is beginning to belatedly reflect this
new view. Unfortunately transnational corporations are often
slower to espouse this new awareness.

What Is the Implicit View of Persons in Western Development?

Closely related to the image of God and His universe,
implicit in western development is the image of humanity.
When Francis Bacon divided the natural and the sacred realm
he unwittingly divided body from soul. Even as the universe
was reduced to nothing but the sum of its physical properties,
many in the west learned to view persons as nothing but the
sum of their biological core and their behavioral surface. In
a universe freed from divine presence and purpose, human beings were increasingly seen as alone. Their lives were seen
as having no sense of divine intention or innate worth.

In an essentially economic world-view, their worth was
seen as largely derivative. To the extent that the individual
contributed to the collective economic growth, to that extent
the individual was viewed as having worth. Therefore one of
the primary characteristics of persons in western culture is
the tendency to identify themselves and indeed derive significance and meaning for life from their ability to produce and
consume.

Self-interest and self-seeking became the basis of this
new society of economic progress and growth. It was widely

assumed during the Enlightenment that if individuals pursued
their own private self-interest, it would work for the common
good. John Locke was the archapostle of this new doctrine.
He condemned the American Indians for living on land filled
with abundant resources and not exploiting them in order to
live lives of personal affluence.

"With Locke, the fate of modern man and woman is sealed.
From the time of the Enlightenment on, the individual is reduced to the hedonistic activity of production and consumption to find meaning and purpose. People's needs and aspira-
tions, their dreams and desires--all become confined to the
pursuit of material self-interest."

A person's sense of meaning, identity and worth are derived from his ability to successfully partipate and compete
in an essentially economic world. Increasingly Americans
have learned to derive their very identity from what they
produce and what they consume. The more we own, the more we
are. Those in western culture not able to fully participate
in the economic rat race are seen as a threat to the entire
system. Persons are reduced in value, based on their economic
value to the larger technocratic order. Pope John Paul has
declared that capitalism reduces persons to consumptive
things and communism reduces them to economic things.

The seventies have accurately been characterized as the
"me first" decade in America. The self-seeking encouraged by
Locke and Jefferson has in contemporary western culture become an absolute mania. The good life for the individual is
strongly oriented towards acquisitive, consumptive and sta-
tus-seeking behaviour--even among Christians, using up an unjust share of limited planetary resources.

Modern development conceiving this world as primarily
an economic realm tends to talk about human personality, human activity and human goals in largely economic terms--such
as human resources, beneficiaries, etc. Therefore, modern
development activity tends to foster a reductionistic view
of human personality and activity, often ignoring the areas
of spiritual, cultural, and relational development.

*What Is the Implicit View of the Pathway to This Better Fu-
ture in Western Development?*

Even though the proponents of western progress believed
in the inevitability of the attainment of a materialistic
paradise on earth, they also believed it would only be

achieved through rational man's initiative. Human instrumentality, not the initiative of God, was essential to create
this new age.

Bacon proclaimed that he had discovered a new promethean
power that would enable humankind to fashion a new technological utopia. That power was the rational human ability to
empirically examine the natural world. Knowledge is power.
Empirically derived knowledge was new power that would enable
humankind to subdue a passive nature and create a new materialistic utopia.

Locke, believing that all human activity is based on materialistic self-interest, encouraged self-seeking as yet
another pathway to achieve this enlightened paradise. Thomas
Jefferson incorporated in the "Religion of America" the Lock-
ean life goal of the individualistic pursuit of happiness--
as a cardinal doctrine.

Adam Smith, building on the philosophy of Locke, created
a new economics of growth that became an essential pathway
to the temporal kingdom of progress. He removed any sense of
morality from economics. Essentially he postulated that individuals and organizations should have complete freedom to
pursue self-interest in the quest for economic gain. He maintained that if they were given that freedom that the invisible
hand of natural law would ensure that the common good would be
achieved through private selfishness. This is the premise of
capitalism and is based on Darwin's survival of the fittest.

"Smith championed the cause of a growing class of manufacturers who saw their interests stifled by government monopolies and the closed ranks of the mercantilists. Just as
Locke had promoted the social interests of bourgeois merchants
and traders, Smith appealed to 'natural laws' based on New-
tonian-Baconian science to legitimatize the economic interests of the new industrial entrepreneurs."[25]

Since contemporary advocates of development no longer
view progress as inevitable and since there is no God even to
lend endorsement, even greater responsibility has been shifted to human initiative to set the world right. Until recently it was believed that global development could be best
achieved through the intervention of high technology and advanced science. With the publication of Schumacher's classic
Small is Beautiful in 1973, people began to shift their attention to smaller and more appropriate technological responses to development needs in the Third World. Science and

technology are still seen as a primary pathway to the better
future. All that has changed is the realization of the importance of appropriate application whether we are talking
about community health, sanitation or agriculture.

The lassez-fair economics introduced by Adam Smith are
still alive and well and provide the foundation for most contemporary development planning. This model, based on a belief that private selfishness will secure the common good,
has, however, fallen on hard times in many sectors. During
the past 70 years a host of socialist regimes have sought to
demonstrate another pathway of planned economics--that ele-
vates the common good above private gain. Marxist ideology
opposes western economics and development planning as obscur-
ing the real problem of the overthrow and replacement of unjust structures, but Marxism often constrains civil freedoms.

More recently the disastrous environmental and human consequences of global corporate expansion has seriously challenged the premise of Adam Smith's economic model, causing
many to call for a new economic order. Even so, most western
development activity tends to accept this model of economic
growth as given, and it is seen as a primary pathway, in its
diverse expressions, to a better economic future.

As long as the better collective and personal future is
defined almost exclusively in economic and physical terms,
contemporary development has no pathways to that future
other than the appropriate application of science and technology, growth economics and utilitarian education.

*What is the Implicit Image of the Better Future Among Chris-
tians working among Those in Need?*

(1) Are we unconsciously trying to help the poor climb
    aboard the escalator of Western progress, believing
    the better future is ever increasing levels of materi-
    al consumption and economic growth?

(2) Is the better future we are trying to help people at-
    tain essentially economic?

(3) Is the good life the "individualistic pursuit of hap-
    piness" or something else?

(4) What are the images of the better future that are im-
    plicit in development projects you are working with?

(5) While we obviously need to address the urgent economic needs of the poorest of the poor, do our development projects imply that our image of the better future includes concern for the spiritual, cultural
relational dimensions of life?

(6) What image of the better future are we "showcasing"
in our own lives and values and in the organizations
we work for?

(7) What is a biblical image of the better future? What
are God's intentions for the human future, and how
should we be consciously working to promote God's intentions through our development processes? How can
we work for righteousness, justice, peace, reconciliation and love through our present organizations?

What is the Implicit View of God and His Universe in Our
Christian Development Activities?

(1) Have we unconsciously bought into the secular illu-
sion that God is "out to lunch" and the work among
the poor is really up to us?

(2) Do we see "nature" as nothing but passive, malleable
resources to be used in our development activities,
or do we see the natural order in more sacred terms
filled with the presence and purposes of God? What
is our theology of earth-keeping?

(3) Do we tend to see the world dualistically in defining
church planting, evangelism, and disciplemaking as a
part of the larger spiritual order of things and development programs as essentially secular activities--
done in Jesus' name?

(4) Do development proposals you are working with mention
the active participation of God? Do you think your
proposals would have more explicitly mentioned God's
involvement if they were focused on evangelism instead
of development?

(5) Is God seen as an active, directing,enabling presence
in your development project, or is the focus primarily
on human activity, which we presume He passively sanctions?

(6) Someone has said, "In our areas of strength, we are all practicing atheists." Do you feel those of us trained and experience in development tend to be more dependent on our own initiative than those involved in more "spiritual" ministries?

(7) What is a biblical view of the involvement of God in mission to the poor, the sick, and the forgotten? Is it possible that the high initiative of God evidenced in the life and ministry of Jesus and the early church in supernatural acts of deliverance, healing and miracles is available to the church today in our work with the poor? Should we seek insights from Charismatics and Pentecostal believers in re-examining our doctrine of the Holy Spirit in mission to those in need?

What is Our Implicit View of Persons in our Christian Development Programs?

(1) Do we unconsciously tend to think of persons as nothing but the sum of their biological core and their behavioral surface--the product of random genetic activity?

(2) Do we tend to see persons economically, with Christian development agencies focusing on them largely in terms of their economic and physical needs and leaving the spiritual and relational needs to the church?

(3) Do we tend to define persons in largely economic terms? Do we describe groups, for instance, as "developed" or "undeveloped" or persons as "beneficiaries" or "resources"?

(4) Do we tend to assign worth to individuals or groups based on their economic status--that is, their productivity and the level at which they are able to participate in the larger consumer society?

(5) Do our development activities tend to encourage the values of individualism, materialism, and acquisitive behavior, undermining community and traditional values?

(6) How do those working in ministries of evangelism and disciplemaking tend to see persons differently from those working in development?

(7) How should the biblical view of persons as made in
    the image of God, as principally spiritual, relation-
    al beings, created for corporate life, change the
    ways in which we do development?

What is the Implicit Image of the Pathway to the Better Fu-
ture in Christian Development?

(1) Do we primarily rely on our human initiative or the
    initiative of God in our work with those in need?

(2) Is our confidence in the "can do" capability of West-
    ern science and technology in our efforts to help the
    poor? Do we begin with felt needs or God-given dreams?

(3) When we leave a successful development project, are
    the people more dependent on Western science and
    technology or on God?

(4) Do we place our confidence in Western economic models
    to bring people to a better future, assuming that the
    pursuit of private self-interest will work to the com-
    mon good, or are you working from another philosophy?

(5) What seem to be the primary pathways to the better
    future implicit in the development project you are
    involved with? How are they integrated with mini-
    stries of church planting, evangelism and disciple-
    making?

(6) What is a biblical image of the pathway to achieve
    the future intentions of God and how drastically
    would its implementation alter our existing Christian
    development activities?

(7) In the New Testament, the mission of church isn't car-
    ried out through individual human initiative working
    through institutional structures, but through organic
    fellowships of believers empowered by the Holy Spirit.
    How could we create methods of Christian development
    that flow organically out of Christian communities of
    shared life empowered by the Spirit of God, to advance
    His kingdom in response to the challenges of tomor-
    row's world?

As we have examined "Development: Its Secular Past and Uncertain Future" we are confronted by a rapidly changing world

to which we need to respond, and a secularized view of development that needs to be altered by fresh biblical insights. I am confident that Consultation '83 will provide those insights. Against this backdrop, we conclude with a challenging commission from Orlando Costas:

> Let us therefore mobilize all our resources--manpower, finances, talents, imaginations, contacts and opportunities--to meet this open door the Lord puts before His church in this hour of history. Let us give ourselves to be a prophetic, priestly, and royal community...Let us proclaim, teach and witness to, without reduction or apologies, the whole gospel of the kingdom to the whole man in the whole world. Let us strive for the integral growth of the church, to the end that all peoples on earth must experience God's salvation in Jesus Christ in their struggles for hope and life everlasting, reconciliation and forgiveness, inner brokenness and guilt, solidarity, justice and dignity."[26]

TOM SINE is author of *The Mustard Seed Conspiracy*, consultant in futures planning and Third World Development, and Coordinator of the Consultation 83 process.

FOOTNOTES

1. *Evangelism and Social Responsibility*. Report from CRESR 82. Lausanne Committee and World Evangelical Fellowship.

2. Mihaljo Mesarovic and Eduard Pestel. *Mankind at the Turning Point*. (New York: E.P.Dutton & Co. 1974) p.1.

3. Augustin B. Vencer. *1980 Annual Report*. (Manila: Philippine Council of Evangelical Churches, 1980) p.15.

4. United States Office of Technology Assessment. *Technology and Population*. (Washington, D.C. 21 August 1978) p.2.

5. Michael Harrington. *The Vast Majority: A Journey to the World's Poor*. (New York: Simon & Schuster, 1977) p.14-15.

6. "Global 2000: A Warning," *Agenda*. September, 1980.

7. "Study Urges Crop Reform," *Christian Science Monitor*. 2 July 1979. p.2.

8. Jan Tinbergen, Coordinator. *Reshaping the International Order*. (New York: E.P.Dutton & Co., 1976) p.31.

9. "Hemisphere Trends," *Americas*. January 1979 (p.17).

10. Richard Barnet. *The Lean Years: Politics in an Age of Scarcity*. (New York: Simon & Schuster, 1980) p.309.

11. Robert Heilbronner. *An Inquiry into the Human Prospect*. (New York: W.W.Norton Co., 1975) p.47-48.

12. Alvin Toffler. *Third Wave*. (New York: William Morrow & Co., 1980) p.345.

13. Robert Manning. "The World Bank Feels the Pinch," *South*, March, 1982.

14. Roger D. Hansen. *U.S. Foreign Policy and the Third World: Agenda 1982*. (New York: Praeger, 1982) p.*vii-xii*.

15. Ruth Legger Sivard, "World Military and Social Expenditures." Background Paper 21. (Washington, D.C.: Bread for the World, February 1978)

16. Cees Hamelink. *The Corporate Village*. (Rome: IDOC International, 1977) p.135-137.

17. Christopher Nasciemento. "A Third World View of the New Information Order," *Christian Science Monitor,* December 18, 1981.

18. "Status of the World." Unpublished research paper. MARC Monrovia, 1982.

19. Walberg Buhlmann, *The Coming of the Third Church* (New York: Orbis Books, 1977). p.42.

20. Morawetz, David. *Twenty-Five Years of Economic Development*. (Washington, D.C., World Bank, 1977) p.7.

21. Sommers, John, *Beyond Charity: U.S. Voluntary Aid for a Changing Third World* (Washington, D.C.: Overseas Development Countil, 1977) p.3.

22. Collins, Larry and LaPierre, Dominique, *Freedom at Midnight* (New York: Simon Schuster, 1975).

23. Rifkin, Jeremy and Howard, Ted. *The Emerging Order: God in the Age of Scarcity*. (New York: G.P.Putnam's Sons, 1979) p.25.

24. Rifkin, p.33.

25. Rifkin, p.34.

26. Orlando Costas. *The Church and Its Mission: A Shattering Critique from the Third World*. (Wheaton, Ill: Tyndale House, 1974) p.284-285.

BEYOND DEVELOPMENT

Purpose. My purpose is to examine four current major approaches to "development" and their basic assumptions, in order to understand the strengths and weaknesses of each. This, then, should help guide us, as the church, toward a more adequate approach that is beyond the current conceptualizations and practices of development.

...Rather than seeking an ideal doctrine of development on social transformation and then trying to fit the approaches to it, I will begin with praxes and seek to formulate criteria against which we can measure and test any conceptualization or definitive social change.

Modernization. Modernization theory assumes that:
   (1) traditional societies are underdeveloped;
   (2) modernization is inevitable;
   (3) production equals development;
   (4) benefits will trickle down to the most needy;
   (5) nation to nation aid fosters development.

The very existence of tribes, hunters and gatherers is being threatened by modernization. Traditional culture is being displaced and the global ecological systems have been placed in serious jeopardy by modernization.

Dependency and Under-Development. Dependency and under-development theory assumes that:

   (1) neo-colonialism prevents indigenous capital development;
   (2) centers grow at the expense of peripheries;
   (3) dependency is perpetuated by the domination of the center;
   (4) economic development is the most important;
   (5) capitalism causes the ills of dependency;
   (6) dependency is a one-way street.

Global Reformism: The New International Economic Order.
   Global Reformism assumes that:
   (1) The assumptions of modernization are valid, and reform would help the poorer countries catch up;
   (2) world resources are infinite;
   (3) poorer nations can remain united in their call for reform;
   (4) the Western model of development is the ideal model;

(5) Trickle down economics really works;
(6) International economic reform will enable dependent
    countries to control their own destiny with honor.

Self-Reliance: An Alternative Development. Self-reliance
attempts to create...a harmonious cooperative world in which
each part is a center, living at the expense of nobody else,
in partnership with nature and in solidarity with future
generations. Self-Reliance assumes that:

(1) self-reliant development can be ideologically neutral;
(2) a strong political state is a precondition;
(3) local people have enough consciousness to work for
    their own self-reliance;
(4) people are conformable, rational and non-egoistic;
(5) a community has a degree of self-sufficiency in terms
    of capital and production.

Transformation. Transformation is intended to:
(1) enable persons to become fully human;
(2) change social and economic principles to conform to
    the Kingdom principles of peace, justice, and love
    manifested in the community of God;
(3) transform both the material and spiritual dimensions
    of life as a joint enterprise between God and man.

The characteristics of transformation are: (1) providing
life-sustenance, (2) equity, (3) justice, (4) dignity and
self worth, (5) freedom, (6) participation, (7) reciprocity,
(8) ecological soundness, (9) hope, (10) spiritual transformation.

WAYNE BRAGG is the Director of the Human Needs and Global
Resources (HNGR) Program at Wheaton College, Wheaton, Illi-
nois.

BEYOND DEVELOPMENT

Wayne Bragg

Rain clouds began to mask the equatorial sun above the
high plateau of Western Kenya. Inside the thatched house
Rev. Shadrack Opoti and wife were meeting all day with their
church leaders to discuss evangelism and social programs for
their people. Outside, millet was spread on a cow-dung
drying area.

Afternoon rain began spattering the dust and we broke up
the meeting to help sweep up the millet. We stashed the
millet sacks, holding a season's food, into the crowded room.
I sat on sack one listening all afternoon to the musical Luo
language but understanding nothing except Shadrack's occasional interpretation. A girl brought a bowl of steaming
cornmeal ugali; another water and a towel for our hands.
After washing, we passed the bowl around and scooped out
handfuls to eat, sharing the daily bread. After dinner Shadrack leaned back and everyone looked at me. "We want to hear
from you about development," he said.

What could I say to convey my feeling of solidarity with
these dear stranger-friends? We had so much in common - the
same human condition and Christian commitment - and yet we
were so culturally removed. I was suddenly aware of the
silence as they looked at me across the kerosene lamps on the
table. What could I say about development? What is the

Christian Church's role in human need? Is it merely bringing the benefits of Western technology to the Third World? To what degree?

"You have heard of the United States?" I paused. (Translation.) Nods.

"Doubtless you think of the United States as a very advanced country where everyone is rich, with tall buildings and cars, like in Nairobi?" Nods.

"And happy?" Nods and smiles.

"What would you think of a place where people can live next to other families and never know their names?" A murmur.

"And never talk to neighbors, because they live inside houses with everything brought in - water, gas for cooking, telephones, lights, and even the news and cinema on television? A place where people can live and work alone and never need anyone else in the community?" Murmurs and glances.

"What would you say about that kind of life?" I insisted.

A rapid crossfire of dialogues in Luo ensued. After ten minutes, Shadrack turned back to me and said, "They don't think they would like to live like that."

I continued, "Some of my people think they have the best way of life in the world and think others are underdeveloped, but frankly I think you have a good way of life, even without those things, and maybe even better. You could teach us how to relax together, work together and share. How to talk with and trust each other."

They laughed and nodded, exchanging meaningful glances.

I had been impressed by the traditional values, family cohesion and community ties of the Luo. Any child could go up to any adult and be held and talked to. All members have roles and a sense of belonging and sharing. Cultures like this could teach the industrialized West a great deal about more humanized living. E.F. Schumacher (1973) speaks of modern man "creating a system of production that ravishes nature and a society that mutilates man." I could have told my new village friends about the great social cost of this

kind of development in the United States: child abuse and
child pornography, a million run-away youths each year,
violent crimes - rape and murder - every 24 seconds, property
crimes every three seconds, the homeless 5,000 "street"
people in Chicago, the one million Americans who live primarily on pet food, the 40 percent unemployment of black men,
the poisoned environment - acid rain and polluted waters, or
the millions of "ordinary people" in suburbia who live
uptight on alcohol or Valium. Most of us are as Denis Goulet
noted, blind to our own cultural and human under-development,
our domestic misery, structures of privilege, and exploited
masses (Goulet, 1971:11).

The elders in Soy were painfully aware of the human needs
around us that warm Kenyan evening, as was I. Yet it became
apparent as we talked about "progress" or development that
economic, material wealth does not necessarily constitute the
"good life." What they desired was a little more security -
better health care, nutrition, crops - not to give up their
way of life. Western development may, indeed, prove more
harmful than beneficial if it violates and destroys cohesive
values in a traditional society. There are trade-offs in any
change; yet, whether we like it or not, there is a great deal
of change going on today world-wide, perhaps more than in the
history of civilization. Since the advent of mankind on
earth, human civilization has been characterized by gradual
change through technological advances by discovery and innovation, allowing societies to increase their control over the
enviroment (and often over other societies). But recently,
since the industrial revolution and the advent of the scientific era, there has been an unprecedented, rapid economic
and social change that has created a divided world - a world
of extreme material wealth and one of extreme poverty. These
are the "developed" and "developing" (or "less developed")
countries, often referred to as the One-third World and the
Two-thirds World.

This situation of inequity, in turn, has created the
phenomenon of planned social change, the development programs
at local, national, and international levels. Local communities have projects, nations have Five Year Development Plans,
and international aid for development finds many avenues of
expression. Hundreds of millions of dollars are committed
yearly. [The bibliography on development is extensive: one
computer search revealed 7,485 titles on the topic.]

The Christian Church is increasingly involved in these
programs, in one way or another. Traditionally the Christian

response to human need has been one of compassion;
missionaries have taken the benefits of modernity to their
fields of service in the form of schools, medicine,
hospitals, agricultural techniques and the like. Since World
War II these spontaneous acts of mercy have become institutionalized in church and para-church agencies for relief and
development. The evangelical churches of the West alone
commit millions of dollars yearly to these programs, and
Third World church groups are also responding increasingly to
human need in their midst.

Until very recently, these agencies have done little evaluation of their programs to see how effective they are and,
indeed, if they are doing what they think they are. The
Church has not paused long enough to examine the assumptions
underlying the concept of development. It has seemingly
accepted uncritically the secular humanistic premises of
Western development which have become a secular religion. As
Tom Sine indicates (1981:72), this carries an

> ... implicit belief that human society is inevitably
> progressing toward the attainment of a temporal,
> materialistic kingdom ... [and] a firm commitment
> that economic progress would result in social and
> moral progress.

THE INTENT OF THIS STUDY

This ethnocentric acceptance by the Church of the tenets
of the Western approach to development is the problem that I
seek to address in this study.

My purpose is to examine four current major approaches to
"development" and their basic assumptions, in order to understand the strengths and weaknesses of each. This, then,
should help guide us, as the Church, toward a more adequate
approach that is beyond the current conceptualizations and
practices of development. I assume, by starting from the
various *praxes* of development, that each approach contains
elements of truth, as well as distortions and evil. Since
each developmental approach arises from within a specific
socio-cultural context, and since God reveals Truth within
all cultures, through common grace, thus all societies and
systems, including all developmental approaches, contain
elements of value.

Thus, rather than seeking an ideal doctrine of development
or social transformation and then trying to fit the

approaches to it, I will begin with praxes and seek to formulate criteria against which we can then measure and test any
conceptualization or definition of social change.

FOUR APPROACHES TO DEVELOPMENT (AND UNDER-DEVELOPMENT)

This Consultation consists primarily of people who are the
product of the modern technological world; even though many
come from the Third World, they are modern as well as traditional. The main contemporary approach to development is
Modernization theory; it has contributed much to a popular
understanding of the concept of development and involves the
greatest number of programs, human resources, and amounts of
money. This is why this paper discusses Modernization at
length. The three other approaches – Dependency, Global
Reformism, and Self-reliance – are either a reaction to
Modernization or some variation on it. Dependency, as we
shall see, is really not as much a theory of development as
of under-development, which is attributed to the process of
Modernization.

MODERNIZATION

Since the modern industrial and technological era has
ushered in an unparalleled economic growth and prosperity for
the West (more correctly, the North), the idea of making its
fruits available to the rest of the world has motivated
governments, inter-government institutions, and private
voluntary organizations.

Modernization theory gained impetus after World War II as
a response to the needs of new nations and to the Cold War.
It holds that the way to development is to diffuse the Western, industrial system to these "lesser developed" countries,
for which it is also called diffusionism. The ultimate goal
is to increase production and economic growth which will
raise the standard of living and provide a "good life" for as
many as possible. Francois Perrox perceived Modernization as
the

> ... combination of mutual and social changes of a
> people which enable them to increase, cumulatively
> and permanently, their total real production
> (1964:155).

A corollary, *sub rosa*, motivation is to combat the rising
tide of international Communism. By spreading the economic

benefits of the capitalist market system, the hope is to destroy the need for socialist movements. W.W Rostow, a political adviser to various U.S. Presidents, wrote his *Stages of
Ecomonic Growth: a Non-Communist Manifesto* (1960) with this
thesis in mind. He saw the process as natural stages from
"traditional" to modern, a sort of Spencerian social
Darwinism.[1] Through the evolutionary process, societies move
from a backward stage until they "take off." The evolution
is helped, so this view says, by the transfer of knowledge –
technology – and capital from the "advanced" nations. This
transfer closes the technological gap and creates an economy
that supposedly matures until it reaches the final stage of
high production and mass consumption. Then the benefits
would trickle down to the poorer sectors from the industrialized, modern sector creating a society and economy that would
look very much like Western Europe, the U.S., or Japan. This
is the "Great Ascent," the struggle for economic development
in our time, described by Heilbroner (1963), who wrote from
an ambassadorial post in India. The ultimate stage of modernization will be eventually the post-industrial society described by David Bell (1973).

Assumptions of Modernization

    Modernization theory makes at least five assumptions, all
of which are flawed.

1. The first assumption is that traditional (rural, agrarian)
societies are underdeveloped and that the values and institutions of traditional society *cause* underdevelopment as well
as express it. "Resistance to development" came to be a perjorative criticism of any non-Western society, as though
Western development were the *summum bonum* of human existence
and these backward people didn't know enough to accept it.
This is the height of ethnocentrism. Is progress preferable
to the adaptive patterns developed over centuries? The
Maasai elder who refuses to send his son to a government
school rightly sees Western education as teaching him to
despise the ways of the fathers. Colin Turnbull (1962) and
Chinua Achebe (1974) describe the anguish of the African
young man caught between tradition and modernity. Other
writers propose that traditions can be positive forces to be
built on. We will examine the social, economic, and ecological costs of modernization further on.

2. A second assumption is that Modernization is an inevitable, unilinear process that operates naturally. Every
culture goes through the progressive stages. Besides being

too generalized a theory to explain the range of variations, the evolutionary theory fails to show the interactions between societies which modify the evolutionary sequence and cannot guarantee that random change does not operate (Roxborough, 1979:14-15). The stage theory likewise assumes that all traditional societies are alike and that "developing" countries today are similar to the "developed" countries at an earlier stage and can modernize in the same way. In actual fact the internal and external socio-economic conditions are greatly different now. Trade and the market do not operate in the same way today as they did in early capitalism. The rich countries can determine what is grown in the poorer, and the prices, due to their purchasing power, tariffs, and other rules of trade. Raul Prebisch sees the function of trade as "only benefiting the economically stronger countries," as the terms of trade decline. It takes many more bags of coffee to get a tractor today.

3. Third, Modernization Theory assumes that productivity equals development, and that large-scale capital, energy, and import-intensive systems are most productive (Sunkel, 1981). Benjamin Higgins (cited by Castel, 1971:11) counters that "productivity is not development, but merely the possibility of development." There is a qualitative aspect to development that productivity ignores. Indeed man can be reduced to a unit of production, *homo faber*, with all the anomie and alienation that goes with mass production. What may be exported along with Modernization is universal alienation and industrial bondage.[2] In Hong Kong, where the Modernization theory is working best, the multi-national corporations are exploiting 34,000 children under the age of 14, half of whom work ten hours a day (Hayter, 1981:106). There is more to development than meeting the economic needs. Man is multidimensional with psychological needs: dignity, self-esteem, freedom, participation. To reduce him to only a producer-consumer is to assume a basic materialism as the goal of life. Obviously the material human needs are necessary but not sufficient for self-realization as shown by the hierarchy of needs (Maslow 1954).

Modernization contemplates economies-of-scale as the most efficient means of production, hence the emphasis on high technology and capital-intensive production. This creates more problems, however, than it solves when the long-term benefits are considered. Large industrial plants, situated in urban centers, tend to exacerbate the rural-urban migration and create squalid squatter settlements, as well as create pollution and ecological destruction (these social

cost factors are described further on). Capital-intensive
production not only creates large external debts (Brazil
approximates $80 billion now) but also in most cases destroys
the smaller local companies. Further it worsens structural
unemployment and underemployment by destroying traditional
sector jobs, especially agricultural, creating a pool of
cheap labor (Sunkel, 1981:98). The latter state of the rural
labor force is worse than the former as jobs are destroyed
and they cannot go back to the land. Obviously, as well, the
local market is vulnerable to the fluxes of the international; in Buenos Aires Ford Motor recently fired 600 men,
all from San Fernando, an urban squatter town. This is the
price of articulation into the international capital market
system.

4. A fourth assumption, commonly held, is that the benefits
of the system trickle down to the most needy, the poorest of
the poor. The infusion of capital at the top supposedly
creates jobs and ultimately the "economic pie" grows and
everyone gets a slice. This neo-classic economic theory is
alive and well (in the U.S.) in the "supply-side" theory,
over which so much debate has recently arisen. I can only
briefly illustrate the inadequacy of this simplistic and
reactive formulation which assumes conditions of a previous
era of capital formation. The phenomenal rise of
multinational corporations (MNC's) or, better called
transnational corporations, has altered the rules of the
international game. With "maximization of profits" as the
primary goal, the MNC's use their mobility to create a
"neo-mercantilism" that only serves their ends, not the ends
of the host countries and peoples. Barnet and Muller's
Global Reach (1974) describes the contradictions between
national interests and the MNC's interests. The favorable
conditions for MNC's in lesser developed countries have
created a new "comparative advantage" which works for the
MNC: cheap labor, looser controls on pollution, fewer safety
regulations, longer work days, better labor discipline,
little or no trade union protection of workers, and higher
profits (Hayter, 1981:45 ff). The power of these
corporations is explored by Abdul Said and Luiz Simmons in
The New Sovereigns (1975).

A case history of MNC's in Brazil is well-documented by
Peter Evans (1979) in which he concludes:

> One of the implications of my analysis is that
> the industrializing elite alliance (of local,
> multinational, and state capital) that currently

holds sway in Brazil is inherently incapable of
serving the needs of the mass of the population.

The real purchasing power of the salary has dropped 235% in
Brazil during the period of the "economic miracle." The poor
are worst hit. In Seoul, Korea the work week is often 84
hours, seven days a week, and in São Paulo the poor workers
may travel four to six hours a day on buses to work (Hayter,
1981:107).

Furthermore, the jobs created are volatile. When wages
rise, companies move. In Hawaii, Castle and Cooke (founded
by missionaries!) closed down their pineapple production and
took to the Philippines where peasants are being forced out
of their land. This is the trickle-down effect? The poorest
are at the mercy of the transnational corporations, which are
aided by the modernizing elite of the country. Since the
demise of colonialism, international agencies such as the
World Bank and the Inter-American Development Bank have
replaced colonial governments as the main promoters and
financiers of rural development, according to Gavin
Williams, whose study (1981) shows that the World Bank
continues to propagate the old Modernization theories of
increased production in agriculture, despite its rhetoric.
Robert McNamara theoretically shifted the World Bank from a
policy of benefiting governments (which redistributed wealth
to the rich) to a policy aimed at the poor, especially the
rural poor. However, the World Bank, according to Williams,
continues to benefit the large-scale commercial farms and
rich farmers while excluding the poor peasant farmers. Rural
development is a big business. It benefits contractors and
consultants, experts and bankers, chemical manufacturers and
seed producers, officials and extension workers (Williams,
1982:17). He argues cogently that the World Bank policies
increase the dependence of producers on production for the
market and subject the peasants further to private and state
monopolies.

> Agro-industrial corporations have benefited in
> all these cases. Peasants have benefited in some
> cases, at the cost of increasing dependence and even
> loss of control of the land. In others they have
> impoverished and dispossessed (*ibid*:37).

5. A fifth assumption is that bilateral, nation-to-nation aid
fosters development. In the case of the United States, the
U.S. Agency in Development (U.S.AID) was conceived as a
mechanism to transfer technology and foster institutional

growth in Third World countries. In actual fact the aim of
foreign aid was summarized by Richard Nixon, who said in
1968, "Let us remember that the main purpose of American aid
is not to help other nations but to help ourselves." This
theme is expanded by Eugene Black, former President of the
World Bank:

> (1) Foreign aid provides a substantial and immediate
> market for United States goods and services. (2) For-
> eign aid stimulates the development of new overseas
> markets for United States companies. (3) Foreign aid
> orients national economies toward a free enterprise
> system in which United States firms can prosper
> (Cited by Hayter, 1981:85).

Agenda, an official U.S.AID publication indicated that some
1.2 million American jobs depend on exports to the Third
World. Some estimates show that 75% of USAID funds are spent
in this country.

What does AID money do when it gets overseas? A U.S.AID
consultant, William Paddock, toured the successful AID projects world-wide and wrote a devastating critique, *We Don't
Know How* (1973), a documented exposé of the reasons for
failure of foreign aid. *Aid As Obstacle* (Lappé *et al.*,
1980), makes a compelling argument for canceling the whole
food aid program. It concludes that by dwelling on food aid
attention is diverted from the process of how hunger is
created. Consistent with this call for an aid moratorium, a
recent AID director saw some programs as exacerbating the
plight of the poor in situations where land tenure practices
are inequitable. He went on to assert that such assistance
has only served to create or strengthen an agro-business
elite or support for a relatively few U.S. corporations
abroad (Gilligan, 1979).

Unintended Results: The Social and Ecological Costs of
Modernization

Social Costs. In addition to the social costs implied in
the economic distortions discussed above, there are several
unintended results that are critically important for the
people being "developed," and ultimately for the world.

> The estimated 200 million tribals, hunters and
> gatherers, now on the receiving end of "progress"
> are among the world's largest and most endangered
> species. Hunger, disease, development and war

are their enemies (*Newsweek*, October 12, 1981:92).

Tribal people are bearing the brunt of an accelerated pace of
Third World modernization. An unintended outcome threatens
the very existence of people whose way of life is not tied
into the money market, and therefore not seen to be important. Indeed the so-called primitive people often occupy
land that is rich in resources and very desirable for
developers. The aborigines of northern Australia began
losing sovereignty over their tribal lands when uranium was
found. American Indian groups are under pressure because of
the resources, especially oil, on the lands given to them by
treaty. The gold and strategic mineral rush to the Amazon
Basin has been added to the traditional timber rush of the
past decade, all aided and abetted by the Brazilian expan-
sionist policy. Since the European invasion four centuries
ago Brazil's Indian population has declined from between 3 to
6 million to approximately two hundred thousand today. The
Waimiri-Atroari, once a proud and vast tribe, has been pushed
back into the jungle 625 miles where they now number a few
hundred. One of the tactics used by Brazilian settlers was
to give them clothing infected by smallpox. This technique
was pioneered in U.S. Indian warfare by British General
Jeffrey Amherst. By the year 2000, all but a few of the
Amazon tribes will be eliminated, according to anthropologist
Jean-Patrick Razon (*Newsweek*, October 12, 1981:93).

In the Philippines one hundred thousand Kalinga and Bontoc
people stand to lose their ancestral grounds, including the
phenomenal rice terraces, to the Chico Dam project sponsored
by the World Bank. Enough outcry was raised to embarrass
World Bank, but the project will still be carried out in the
benefit of the ruling elite. Similar dam projects threaten
the existence of indigenous groups around the world. The
combination of international agencies and local government
policy creates a power that is hard for the voiceless tribal
peoples to resist. Survival International and other similar
groups have taken up the cause, and indigenous groups such as
the Shuar Association have banded together for survival. Two
noteworthy publications document the cultural genocide that
is taking place: *Victims of the Miracle: Development and
the Indians of Brazil* (Shelton Davis, 1977) and *Victims of
Progress* (John Bodley, 1975). When the way of life of any
group is threatened, ultimately all mankind is threatened.
As Goulet says (1971:16) the man who despises another de-
humanizes himself. The cultural aggressor demeans himself

when he demeans another. Beyond the ethical and moral questions mankind will lose the insights and knowledge of these
tribal peoples. Their knowledge of local wildlife, medicinal
plants and ecology will go with them. Barbara Bentley of
Survival International contends that it is:

> ... like destroying a library of information. A
> range of cultures enriches us all. If we get rid
> of these people we're effectively destroying a part
> of ourselves (*Newsweek*, October 12, 1981).

A similar social cost of development is less dramatic but
just as real: cultural loss. Not only those who lose their
lands and their lives are victims of progress but also those
who lose their cultures. The loss of traditional values
through the cultural imperialism of westernization is increasing. The Hastings Center Report (1977) recounts the
following: The Mayurunas, a small remote Amazon Indian
tribe, have found Western civilization so devastating to
their tribal and cultural identity that they have apparently
decided to kill their babies rather than let them grow in an
alien culture. They first encountered Western culture when
the rubber tappers entered their lands in the 1960's. When
the oil workers found them in 1972 there were 2,000 Mayurunas. Now there are about 400. The Mayurunas are now
killing their male children as well as female, according to
Paulo Lucena, a Brazilian anthropologist.

Ecological Costs. The western scientific movement is
based on a materialistic and atomistic view of nature.
Nature is to be subdued and conquered. "Man over nature" is
one of the basic themes of the North American value system,
born perhaps of the unlimited resources and the pioneer
spirit that could always push westward. By the time some of
the "outer limits" of our environment and resources were
reached, new scientific breakthroughs or new trade
arrangements provided other alternatives. This attitude
toward nature was exported with the modernization approach.
The result has been disastrous. The strain that modern
society has put on the ecosystem can be seen briefly in a few
indicators.

Modern men in modern societies consume a disproportionate
amount of the earth's renewable and nonrenewable resources.
The comparative consumptions between a North American child
and a child from India show that an American child consumes
500 times more during a lifetime than the Indian child (Ward
and Dubose, 1972:119). If indeed the " ... world cannot

afford the United States" (Taylor, 1963) then it could
certainly not support a whole world that consumes on the
level of the West.

One critical area is the degradation of the earth's fertile land. A *New York Times* article (Rensberger, 1977) indicated that fertile productive land world-wide is being
denuded and destroyed at the rate of 14 million acres a year,
resulting in desertification. Already 43% of the planet is
desert or semi-desert due partly to overcutting, overgrazing,
improper cultivation, and changing settlement patterns.
"Fully one-third of today's arable land will be lost in the
next 25 years, while the world's need for food will double,"
the article indicates. In the United States over 1 million
acres of prime farm land is being converted into parking
lots, shopping centers, and highways per year. In Latin
America Sunkel reports high-level soil erosion in three
countries: Colombia with 30% eroded, Chile with 62%, and
Mexico with 72% (Sunkel, 1981:102). Urbanization and
suburbanization has put its pressure on fertile lands.
Mexico City is the largest city in the world, and still
growing at over 5% a year, spreading itself over arable land
at the rate of 742.2 square kilometers in 1970 (Sunkel,
1981:104-105). Other great cities like Buenos Aires,
Caracas, and São Paulo follow suit.

Haiti was once a tropical rain forest that produced more
income for France than any other colony. It is now so
denuded that the government tags every large tree to preserve
it, and each tropical rain washes boulders down dry river
gulches, eroding the top soil and forcing Haitian peasants to
cultivate farther and farther up the mountainsides. Rain-
fall, except for hurricanes, has dropped 90% in some places.
This situation can be generalized to many parts of the world
where tropical or moist forests are being degraded at the
rate of 250,000 square miles each year: the massive deforestation is around 6 million hectors a year in Latin America
according to FAO. When the fragile soils no longer produce
without fertilizer, colonizers push onward into virgin
timber. Even the grasslands that replace the forests become
rapidly depleted, supporting on an average one cow to 2.5
acres at first and dropping to 12 to 17 acres per cow in five
years (Myers, 1982:II,5).

The United States now imports 10% of its beef, mostly from
Central America where pastures are replacing virgin rainforests, according to Norman Myers. His article "Cheap Beef
and Priceless Rainforests" (*ibid*) shows that from 1960 to

1980, the region's moist forests declined from 130,000 square miles to 80,000 square miles. Incidentally, the World Bank supported the cattle production conversion. These tropical forests contain a genetic treasure of flora and fauna that is worth thousands of times more than the cattle. Modern civilization is killing the goose that lays the golden egg because 50% of the drug prescriptions in the United States contain substances extracted from tropical plants. Likewise the 16 plants that produce 90% of the world's food today were domesticated first from tropical plants (*U.S. News and World Report*, 1981:83).

When the United States banned harmful pesticides and insecticides, factories kept turning out more than ever for increased exportation to the Third World. The modern export crop economy demands an ever-increasing application of pesticides, harmful to the workers, who don't know how to use the product, and to the environment, where residues build up to an intolerable level. People drink from the streams where the effluents go, wash clothes, and bathe in them. Blood samples in children in Central America have shown 50 times the safe level of some toxins.

The vertiginal growth of the automobile industry in the Third World has spewed more and more contaminants into the air. Pollution, both from hydrocarbons and from manufacturing, are the sign of "progress." The restraints on pollution in the First World, with the corresponding clean-up costs, have forced multinationals overseas. Paul Samuelson, the Nobel Prize-winning economist, wrote in the *EPA Journal* that American polluting industries should stop trying to clean up their act and simply go abroad! The U.S. and other industrial nations are exporting their pollution.

Conclusion

The elders of the Soy village in Kenya had quickly perceived that the social cost of an American-style modernization might be too high, but they, like millions of the wretched of the earth, look at the West longingly for the kind of progress that would allow them to lead longer, better, and easier lives. Modernization has provided a radical improvement in millions of lives - currently one billion - but its flaw is to assume that the only way to achieve this level is through the exportation of Modernization, without realizing its ethnocentric assumptions and deleterious social costs. But perhaps the greatest cost to the rest of the world is the perpetuation of the dependency

of the "have-nots" on the "haves." The neo-Marxist theories
have expanded this concept.

DEPENDENCY AND UNDER-DEVELOPMENT

The problem today is not one of absolute physical
shortages but of the economic and social maldistribution and misuse; mankind's predicament is rooted
primarily in economic and social structures and
behavior within the between countries. Much of the
world has not yet emerged from the historical consequences of almost five centuries of colonial control
which concentrated economic powers overwhelmingly in
the hands of a small group of nations. To this day
at least three-quarters of the world's income, investment, services and almost all of the world's research
are in the hands of one quarter of its people (Cocoyoc
Declaration, 1974).

The Dependency theory of under-development has arisen in
reaction to the continuing and increasing disparities between
the rich nations and the poor. While modernization during
the past almost 40 decades has generated considerable overall
economic growth world-wide and certainly in the developed
countries, the per capita income measures and standard of
living measures hide the inequitable distribution of this
growth. Gustavo Lagos (1981:130) compares the GNP of the
United States of 861,623 million dollars with a population of
203 million and the GNP of Latin America of 119,842 million
dollars with a population of 266 million. He goes on to
indicate that the top 5% group of income in the U.S. receives
more in dollars than all the groups in Latin America put together. Ten million privileged North Americans receive more
than the entire Latin American population! Dependency theory
is an attempt to understand this phenomenon. As we have
seen, Modernization poses that under-development is an
original state that must be changed by bringing the backward
and isolated countries into the world economy and integrating
these into the world capitalist system. Dependency theory,
on the other hand, sees under-development as part of a dialectical relationship with development, the flip side of development. The root cause of under-development is development.

André Gunder Frank's thesis of "The Development of Under-
Development" (1969) encapsulated the thinking that arose in
Latin America in the 1960's which perceived Latin America's

under-development as being a product of the colonial and neo-
colonial activities of the "centers." The centers (or metro-
poli) are the developed countries, and "peripheries" are the
under-developed satellites. The first hypothesis that Frank
sets forth is that under-development is not the product of a
country's own characteristics or structures but, rather,
under-development is generated by the development of
capitalism itself. Second, he hypothesizes that the
development of the periphery or satellite is greatest when
its tie to the metropolis is the weakest. And, third, he
argues that the regions most under-developed are the ones
which had the closest ties with the centers in the past. He
suggests that Latin America has grown more during the periods
of crisis when isolated from the U.S., as during the World
Wars. As Brazilians say, Brazil grows at night when the
politicians are asleep. Thus, development and under-
development are part of the same process. Within a given
economy the process is called internal colonialism
(Stavenhagen, 1969), which operates in favor of the urban
elite and against the Indian or rural peon, creating the
rich-poor disparity within Third World countries.

Dependency theory stresses the vulnerability of economies
that are not autonomous. Dependent countries are those whose
involvement with the world market has led them to specialize
in the export of a few primary products. This means that the
export product prices are essential to the process of accumulation of capital, while for the center countries each
product represents only a small fraction of total imports.
Since most of these products are agricultural or mineral
there is a wide variety of sources of the products which
gives an advantage to the center. Bananas mean a great deal
to Ecuador and Costa Rica, but while North Americans eat a
lot of bananas, they're not central to the developed economy.
As Evans (1979:26-27) points out, the development of the
dependent country requires a good market for its product in
the center; therefore, economic fluctuations in the center
can have severe negative consequences for the periphery. On
the other hand, an economic crisis in the periphery offers no
real threat to the centers. Thus the state of dependency
could be defined as "a structural condition in which a
weakly-integrated system cannot complete its economic cycle
except by an exclusive or limited reliance on an external
complement" (Caporaso and Zare, 1981:48). This external
reliance is also due to the foreign control of industry in a
given periphery country. Bonino (1975:28) illustrates that
41.6% of the total Brazilian industry was in the hands of
foreigners in 1975. Of these, certain industries were 100%

controlled, such as the automobile industry. Others had a
very high percentage of foreign control, such as the chemical
industry, with 94% external control, and the rubber industry,
with 82%. He concludes that Brazil has become a factory of
multinational corporations and the Brazilian population is a
reserve of cheap labor.

Another characteristic of a dependent economy is that it
demonstrates uneven growth patterns. Capitalist development
according to de Janvry (1981:1-2) is uneven because development is not linear or homogeneous and because accumulation
occurs through a sequence of periods of advances and stagnation. He suggests that development in particular regions is
associated with deformed development in other regions, therefore development and under-development are a single dialectical unit and reflect the world-wide accumulation process.
This process then only perpetuates the dependency syndrome.

Assumptions of Dependency Theory

1. Dependency theory takes as a given that neo-colonialism
prevents indigenous capitalistic development. Cardoso (1978)
argues that industrialization is being carried out in the
periphery, largely by the multinational corporations. Thus
it is possible to have a "dependent development," although
that seems a contradiction in terms. Peter Evans's study of
Brazil's development (1979) substantiates this thesis and
shows that the MNC's have changed the calculus of dependency
with the mixture of foreign, local, and state capital. He
further asserts that capital accumulation took place in the
periphery even under conditions of classic dependence and
that Brazil has been incorporated into the capitalist world
economy in a new way (10). Thus a new dependency pattern has
been created in some Third World countries.

2. This theory assumes that the centers grow at the expense
of the peripheries, which languish in dependent doldrums.
Alain de Janvry (1981) argues that, not only the multinational corporations, but OPEC and the revolutions in Africa
and Nicaragua as well as Viet Nam have altered the power of
the centers. He shows that growth is actually increasing in
the periphery and declining in the center. From 1969 to 1979
there was 26 times higher capital formation in Latin America
than in the United States, so exploitation must not be causing stagnation!

3. Dependency assumes that exploitation of the Third World
arose with colonialism and is perpetuated by international

dominance by the centers. History is replete with exploitative relationships and dominance by one class of another, one
nation by another. In Mexico the Aztecs cruelly subjugated
and exploited other tribes. In Peru, the Huancas and Aymaras
were oppressed by the Incas long before Pizarro landed (see
Tito Paredes's excellent discussion of this in his paper on
Socio—cultural Change, below.

Oppression and maldistribution likewise are not limited to
international relationships. Internal colonialism operates
to the great disadvantage of the masses in favor of the
elites. The classic contrast between the extremely rich and
the direly poor in the Third World attests to this.

4. It is important to note that Dependency theory still
assumes that the economic side of development is the most
important. Is development only one—dimensional? "It is
therefore a perversion to imagine that the discussion on
development can be limited to what is called a satisfaction
of basic material needs" (*What Now*, 1974:28). While the
basic needs are critical, man does not live by bread alone.

5. Capitalism and the capitalist market system are assumed to
cause the ills of dependency. While admitting that exploitation and dependency do go on under the capitalist system,
this is not to say that these conditions are unique to capitalism. Berger (1976:101) suggests that:

> Unfortunately relations between economically
> unequal partners are almost invariably exploitative,
> and this has nothing to do with capitalism. A
> socialist metropolis is just as capable of exploita-
> tive relations with Third World dependencies, as Soviet
> economic policy has painfully revealed ... when a poor
> country has economic dealings with a rich country it is
> almost always supping with the devil - and the devil
> has the much longer spoon.

6. Dependency theorists have assumed only a one—way dependency. In actual fact the changing world situation has made
the developed countries very dependent upon the developing.
Strategic minerals and raw materials needed by industrialized
states are located in the Third World. Heraldo Muñoz (1981)
makes a strong case for "strategic dependency." As the key
non—renewable and renewable resources diminish or are
controlled, as oil has been, the developing countries will
scramble and pay a higher stakes game in order to maintain

their lifestyles and their defense. Dependency is a two-edged sword, and as the formerly dependent countries begin to realize their power the whole geo-political game will change. This is, in fact, the leverage that the Third World is using to call for a re-ordering of the world economic system, the New International Economic Order.

Conclusion

Pastor Opoti and his people in Soy would concur with the analysis by the Dependency theorists, having lived until the early 1960's under colonial rule. They saw the best lands in the Western Highlands taken by the white expatriates until the Mau Mau revolt and freedom. They bore the brunt of an export economy while favoring the external. Kenya's political independence did not mean much for the interior people except the redistribution of land and a concomitant sense of national pride. When Jomo Kenyatta bought out the white landowners, the Kikuyu and Luo farmers had no management knowledge, tools, or capital to run their farms. Any cash crop production still flows largely to the external market, such as the tea produced in the Kericho region.

Traditional village life goes on much as it did before independence, while Kenya's leaders are still "supping with the Devil" as Berger would say.

GLOBAL REFORMISM: THE NEW INTERNATIONAL ECONOMIC ORDER

A second reaction, sparked partly by the critical analysis of the neo-Marxist dependent theorists, is a political call for equity. Perhaps it is too early to see any tangible results, especially for the poor of the earth, but Global Reformism is a theory of development that, again, would provide a corrective to Modernization.

In 1974, the United Nations Sixth Special Session of the General Assembly developed a "Declaration of the Establishment of a New International Economic Order" (NIEO) under the leadership of Third World representatives. The subsequent Seventh Special session in 1975 adopted the resolution "Development and International Economic Cooperation" based on the "Charter of Economic Rights and Duties of States." All of these documents demonstrated the dissatisfaction of the poorer dependent nations with their share of the world economic pie, and their disposition to challenge seriously

the international economic status quo. In a sense this challenge grew out of the post-World War II decolonization process and was a reaction to a growing dissatisfaction with
center-periphery dependency. The NIEO was, and continues to
be, a cry for economic interdependence rather than dependence, based on a more equitable international distribution
of wealth. Interdependence was interpreted by the NIEO
proponents, the famous Group of 77 nations, in terms of
equitable and fair trade agreements arrived at by equal and
autonomous nations rather than an interdependence characterized by poorer countries exchanging more raw goods for more
manufactured wares. In fact, the Lima Declaration had called
for an increase in the share of Third World countries in
world industry from 7 to 25 percent by the year 2000.

The NIEO proposal for global reform was based on sound
principles: autonomous control by developing countries over
their own economies and resources, international cooperation,
active aid assistance by developed countries, a greater participation in decision-making, better terms for the transfer
of technology, greater facilities for industrialization in
the Third World, food security, and changes in the monetary
system.[3] These laudable goals, however, are resisted by the
developed nations, especially the United States. The actual
status of the NIEO Programme is nebulous because of the strategies by the developed countries do delay or contain the
reforms while protecting their own interests. It is a political process as well as economic. Besides its ineffective-
ness thus far due to its political nature and due to the fact
that the NIEO is bureaucratized in the U.S. system, the NIEO
is flawed by a number of inherent weaknesses. I am endebted
to Björn Hettne (1978) for his excellent discussion of the
problems of global reformism on which some of the following
critiques were based.

Assumptions of Global Reformism

1. Global Reformism accepts all the assumptions of the
modernization/growth approach and, thus, would merely provide
a way in which the poorer economies can catch up faster with
the richer. It would open the growth spigot for a faster
trickle to run down from developed to developing economies.
The NIEO is reformism, not a radical change in the structures, and may be regarded as a typical quasi-reform rather
than true reform. Quasi-reform gives the appearance of
reform but may indeed be the antithesis of change. By calling for more developmental aid, for example, the NIEO assumes
that aid is development, which is not the case. While it may

spark economic development, its function has often been the contrary.

The functions of aid have been many: to make `weak´ economies capable of joining the international capitalist market, to make them more able to suppress internal rebellions, to link them to one or the other of the main political blocks and to facilitate the spread of the Western model of development, but rarely to give an impetus to development (Hettne 1978:25).

As far as trade goes, even under a more equitable arrangement, it may only further dependence. The NIEO Programme assumes that the route to development is more trade with industrialized countries and more Western technology, rather than alternative local solutions. In fact, increased access to high technology through more favorable trade arrangements will only exacerbate the social cost of rapid industrialization in developing countries. Brazil, for example, is now promoting a control on the importation and development of robot technology to prevent serious deterioration of employment. A "new" economic order may be only a larger Trojan horse for developing economies. It allows the developed nations to maintain control over the process of "development." This is particularly true in the case of the multinational corporations, which even the industrial nations cannot control, much less the developing countries. The MNC´s have sophisticated ways of circumventing even the proposed increased controls and policies that the host country may try to impose under the NIEO.[4]

2. The NIEO assumes that world resources are infinite. An inherent flaw in the new order concerns the deleterious impact on environments in the Third World. Not only would the increased industrialization adversely affect the pressures on the ecosystems, in terms of migration to large metropolitan centers, but also the more highly polluting industries would shift to the Third World. For unsuspecting countries the instant cure to poverty may turn out to be worse than the disease, even though most developing nations have closed one eye to the evils of pollution, deforestation, pesticides, and other ecological depredations in order to "cure" the ill of poverty. For example, Delfim Neto called poverty Brazil´s "pollution" problem.

In terms of global resources, the rising expectations and demands for consumer goods would deplete even more rapidly the diminishing supply of non-renewable resources, as well as threaten even more seriously the earth's biosphere. Besides scarce minerals and oil, normally renewable resources like humus topsoil, forests, and potable water are also on the endangered list. The rapacious Modernization assumes an unlimited resource supply, and the Global Reform approach would only shift consumptive patterns.[5]

3. Reformism idealistically presupposes both that the "have-not" countries (including formerly have-not OPEC countries) can maintain cohesiveness in their demands for equity, and resist the divide-and-conquer tactics of the "have" countries. Not only have the regional Trade Associations and/or Common Markets mostly failed, but cracks have appeared even in the OPEC solidarity. How then can a global strategy of reform hope to break the syndrome of dependence and initiate a world-wide change in the economic rules? The West quickly employed several strategies to block the NIEO proposal. Charles Ries describes the United States' strategies:

> First we have the `unilateral strategy' (Project Independence);   secondly the `alleviationist' strategy, e.g., quick actions on minor problems but no concesions on basic demands; and thirdly, the `acquiescence but delay strategy,' e.g., symbolic declarations in anticipation of the erosion of the solidarity of the Group of 77 (cited by Hettne 1978:26).

These tactics have generally prevailed as the political and bureaucratic wheels turn slowly but *not* inexorably toward change.

4. Another serious criticism concerns the assumption that development is a unilinear Western model that the less-developed world must follow. The framers of the Cocoyoc Declaration foresaw this in 1974:

> We emphasize the need for pursuing many different roads of development. We reject the unilinear view which sees development essentially and inevitably as an effort to imitate the historical model of the countries that for various reasons happen to be rich today.

It is illusory to think any country can repeat the historical growth pattern of another richer country, since resources and cultural, political, environmental, and social conditions vary. When attempted, what usually results is a mixture of the worst parts: "There is no reason for the Third World to imitate the impoverishing modes that produce one-dimensional men and women" (*What Now*, 1975).

5. Reformism assumes that the trickle-down approach works. Yet a most important weakness in the Programme lies in its inability to meet mass needs and its catering to the small minority who want to catch up with Western ways of life (Amin, 1976:393). The NIEO would further the growth of a rich "inter-nationalized bourgeoise" among and within developing countries. The beneficiaries would not be the neediest, and indeed it is potentially an accelerated under-development for the poor.

> We are still in a stage where the most important concern of development is the level of satisfaction of basic needs for the poorest sections of the population in society ... A growth process that benefits only the wealthiest minority and maintains or even increases the disparities between and within countries is not development. It is exploitation ... We therefore reject the idea of ‘growth first, justice in the distribution of benefits later’ (Cocoyoc Declaration, 1974).

The benefits of a new more just economic system ought, logically, to result in more justice for those who have suffered most under the "old" economic order.

6. Finally, Global Reformism presupposes that the Programme will enable the dependent countries to control their own destinies with honor. The palliative provided by "easy" imported solutions may further erode the capabilities a society has to deal with its problems from within with dignity, as Indian economist S.L. Parmar noted:

> A society must begin with its reality. If poverty and injustice are the main facts of economic life, the potentiality of the poor must be the main instrument for overcoming them. This would be possible if the people in developing countries discover a sense of dignity and identity within their socio-economic limitations. To assume that only when we have more, when we are nearer to the rich nations, we will have dignity and identity, is a new kind of enslavement to imitative values and structures (cited by Hettne, 1978:29).

Furthermore, this quick technological and economic "fix"
would delay any real social transformations within the Third
World. Dom Helder Camara, Bishop of Olinda, Brazil, queried,
"How can there be a new international *economic* order without
a new international *social* order?" (cited by Sommer, 1975:
142). Radical social reform is a priority in the poor
countries, if indeed "development" is more than economics and
if all of society is to benefit from any new economic order.

Conclusion

*Even if the proposed changes in the world economic system
were to reach to the village level in Western Kenya, which is
doubtful, my friends in Soy might lament the changes produced. Just as the poor in Brazil have fared worse under
an accelerated Western-style interdependent development, the
Luo would find the changes ultimately deleterious and threat-
ening to their life-style. They would see Kenya turned more
rapidly into a polluted and impoverished backyard for rich
nations and corporations, and an even greater gap between
themselves and the elite. If the politically improbable
should occur, the rural peoples of Kenya would have exchanged
their birthright for a technological fix.*

SELF-RELIANCE: AN ALTERNATIVE DEVELOPMENT

An alternative to the NIEO was proposed by the U.N. Stockholm study group that produced the 1975 Dag Hammarskjold
Report:

> The search for a new international economic order
> requires a reformulation of the basis for the overall
> system of relationships between Third World countries
> and the international system. Instead of total inte-
> gration into the international system, what is needed
> is selective participation. This proposition responds
> to the basic reality that development comes from
> within, not from without. It is based on the convic-
> tion that self-reliance is both necessary and possible.
> It also expresses the idea that if a Third World
> country is to integrate into anything, it must inte-
> grate into a collective effort of self-reliance with
> other Third World countries (*What Now*, 1975:18).

This Self-reliant approach is now examined.

An important development strategy, Self-reliance has
emerged gradually to captivate the imagination of the

developing world. The concept is rooted in Third World experiences and arose as an antithesis to the dependency syndrome. Johan Galtung (1981:173) considers self-reliance as an important political strategy of contemporary history that is seeking to undo five centuries of dependency on the West.

Early experiences in Ghandi's India and pre-1900 Japan, and, more recently, the experiences of Tanzania, China, and Sri Lanka (and partial experiences in other places) point the way to self-reliance. In 1967 the TANU party met in Arusha, Tanzania to develop strategy for that recently independent country. The Arusha Declaration spelled out the *Ujamaa* (socialist) ideal:

> In order to maintain our independence and our people's freedom we ought to be self-reliant in every possible way and avoid depending on other countries for assistance. If every individual is self-reliant, the ten-house cell will be self-reliant; if the cells ... wards .. Districts ... Regions are self-reliant, then the whole nation is self-reliant and this is our aim (1967).

Under President Nyerere's leadership, Tanzania has pursued these goals of national self-identity without depending on either the Communist or capitalist blocks. It is not as though Tanzania did not want development. Tanzania merely wanted development on different terms, namely its own, and by its own initiative. It was only by withdrawing from the world capitalist system that Nyerere perceived it possible to act autonomously. [See his speeches in *Freedom and Development/Uhuru na Maendeleo*, 1973.]

China was another example of resisting modernization, through radical self-reliance. Under Mao and the cultural revolution China took a leap backward (from the modernists' perspective) and rejected the consumer values and all of the trappings of both Soviet and Western industrialization. The universities were closed and everyone was sent to a commune who wasn't already there, and the great experiment was on. The new Chinese Wall went up around the country economically, culturally, and politically. While it may be criticized for sacrificing a whole generation, millions of people, in the purges, as well as forcing a happy and colorful people into dullness and grayness (Berger, 1976), China has been one of the great social experiments of this century. It has produced some concepts that could prove very useful to the Third

World and even to the First and Second. The concept of the
barefoot doctor with practical skills has already been emu-
lated and translated into public health models by a number of
countries and international agencies.

The social cost of the Chinese experiment was exceedingly
high. The figure of outright executions in China between
1949 and 1955 runs into the millions, during the period of
agricultural collectivization. Then there was the physical
and mental suffering of Chinese confined to the "Reform
Through Labor" camps and other programs of forced labor
(Berger, 1976:95). Berger goes on to say that it is doubtful
whether the population as a whole benefits any more under
socialist systems than under capitalism, and he sees China as
an "equality of poverty."[6]   The recent opening to the West
with the accelerated exchange of scholars program plus the
welcome that China gives to teachers of English and to the
Coca Cola Company would seem to indicate that one-fourth of
the world's population cannot be kept in isolation and in a
perpetual state of self-reliance.

However, Self-reliance is not isolationism; as the Stockholm Report noted:

> ... even if a country or group of countries may
> consider it necessary to withdraw, partially or
> momentarily from the international system, so as to
> strengthen their independence (What Now, 1975:35).

Self-reliance gives economic content to political independence, continues the Report, and makes it possible to make
decisions and enter into relationships on an equal footing
with other countries. The ultimate goal of temporary detach-
ment from the present economic system is increased, not
absolute, national self-reliance, as the Cocoyoc Declaration
manifested in 1974. Indeed, the ideal sought is:

> ... a harmonized cooperative world in which each
> part is a center, living at the expense of nobody else,
> in partnership with nature and in solidarity with
> future generations.

Cocoyoc further defined the concept of self-reliance that had
emerged on the political scene at the 1970 meeting of Non-
aligned nations in Lusaka. It is worth quoting the philosophy expressed at Cocoyoc:

> We believe that one basic strategy of development
> will have to be increased national self-reliance. It
> does not mean autarchy. It implies mutual benefits
> from trade and cooperation and a fairer redistribution
> of resources satisfying the basic needs. It does mean
> self-confidence, reliance primarily on one's own re-
> sources, human and natural, and the capacity for
> autonomous goal-setting and decision-making. It
> excludes dependence on outside influences and powers
> that can be converted into political pressure. It
> excludes exploitative trade patterns depriving coun-
> tries of their natural resources for their own develop-
> ment. There is obviously a scope for transfer of
> technology, but the thrust should be on adaptation and
> the generation of local technology. It implies decen-
> tralization of the world economy, and sometimes also of
> the national economy to enhance the sense of personal
> participation. But it also implies increased inter-
> national cooperation for collective self-reliance.
> Above all, it means trust in people and nations, re-
> liance on the capacity of people themselves to invent
> and generate new resources and techniques, to increase
> their capacity to absorb them, to put them to socially
> beneficial use, to take a measure of command over the
> economy, and to generate their own way of life (Cocoyoc
> Declaration, 1974:174).

Thus the Self-reliant approach to development is a strategy for more appropriate development, based not on external
constraints and potential dependency, but rather on internal
needs and criteria. It is endogenous rather than exogenous.
The Stockholm meeting in 1975 further defined this aspect:

> If development is the development of man, as an
> individual and as a social being, aiming at his
> liberation and at his fulfillment, it cannot but
> stem from the inner core of each society. It relies
> on what a human group has: its natural environment,
> its cultural heritage, the creativity of men and
> women who constitute it, becoming richer through
> exchange between them and with other groups. It
> entails the autonomous definition of development

styles and life styles. This is the meaning of an
endogenous and self-reliant development (*What Now*,
1975:34).

Structurally, self-reliant development would equalize and
redistribute power among nations and people, which is one
definition of development. Glyn Roberts (1979:14ff) discusses power as an important factor in development, at macro
and micro levels. Power, he argues, is the ability to control the environment or people, physically, economically, or
culturally. But without structures that allow for a demo-
cratization of power, there is no authentic development.
Self-reliance involves decentralization which would "allow
all those concerned, at every level of society to exercise
all the power of which they are capable" (*What Now*, 1975:39).
This redistribution of power is necessary for the exercise of
fundamental human rights - the right to express oneself and
the abolition of repression, the right of equal opportunity,
the right to control one's own destiny. Self-reliance seeks
to redress the inequitable distribution of of economic and
political power and to promote participation from the lowest
levels up.

Self-reliant development could also be called "appropriate" development because it is derived from local conditions and seeks indigenously oriented technology rather than
Western high technology. Since F. Schumacher popularized the
concept of small-scale decentralized technology which he discovered in India in his book *Small is Beautiful*, the idea of
appropriate or intermediate technology has taken hold in
development circles. Appropriateness in terms of cost,
employment generation, simplicity to build and maintain,
compatability with the environment (not "harsh technology"),
renewability, and effectiveness - all contribute to self-
reliance. Appropriate development uses local resources
rather than transferred high technology.

In contrast, President Reagan affirmed in his campaign
here in Wheaton that what the world needs is not aid but
American technology and tractors to solve the world food
problem. But the *U.S. News and World Report* (August 31,
1981:83) suggests that it would take $250 billion in tractors
to replace the 400 million donkeys, horses, llamas, camels,
caribous, yaks, and oxen in the world that provide animal
power for poor countries. Can the world afford the American
level of technology? President Nyerere, for one, doesn't
think so:

I've been telling my own people, 'We've got to
change, we must mechanize, we must have better tools.'
But what are better tools? Not the combine harvester.
If I were given enough combine harvesters for every
family in Tanzania, what would I do with them? No
mechanics, no spare parts ... It would be a very serious problem - unless, of course, I sell them for hard
cash. But we still have to give the people better
tools, tools they can handle, and can pay for. Americans, when they speak of better tools, are talking
about something quite different. We are using hoes.
If two million farmers in Tanzania could jump from the
hoe to the oxen plough, it would be a revolution. It
would double our living standard, triple our product!
(quoted by Smith, 1973).

Nor could the biosphere support the pressure on resources
that industrialized technology implies. Technology needs to
be conditioned by the context. This principle also applies
to appropriate health care and prevention and appropriate
education, both accessible and tuned to the people's needs.

Assumptions of Self-reliance

Although Self-reliance offers an exciting alternative to
the development dilemma of the Third World (and, importantly,
to the "over-developed world"), it also makes assumptions:

1. These theorists make the assumption that it is possible to
be neutral. Since Self-reliance was forged in an ideological
context, it can easily remain politicized despite itself.
Nyerere remarked once, "When I say, 'From China we can
learn,' they say we are going Red." The Third World is
squeezed between the polarized power blocks and any initiative to pursue its own path is viewed politically and sus-
piciously.

2. A second assumption is a corollary to the first; Self-
reliance presupposes a strong political state as a precondition. It must be strong enough to resist the political
and economic pressures and manipulations by the international
power structure. The Cocoyoc meeting described these methods
as: the built-in bias of the world market mechanisms, withdrawing or withholding credits, embargoes, economic sanctions, subversive use of intelligence agencies, repression,
counterinsurgency, and even full-scale intervention. The
political cost may be high. The state must be stable enough

to follow through on a long-term program toward Self-reliance since there is much to un-do as well as to do.

3. The Self-reliant approach presupposes a state of consciousness by the people if it is to operate at the local level. *Ujamaa* has suffered in Tanzania from being a top-down process; people who were moved into rural settings were not prepared materially nor conceptually. Self-reliance requires education and participation, or else it contravenes its own principles.

4. Self-reliance perceives people as easily conformable, rational, and non-egoist. It is susceptible to the charge of being optimistic about mankind and too utopian. It is almost too good to be true, perhaps ignoring human nature. For example, which people will be satisfied with intermediate technology when they see the fruits of high technology everywhere? Can a nation insulate itself from the market economy that promotes the "good" (i.e., consumer) life? Papua New Guinea has deliberately prohibited television for this reason. Some Third World leaders see appropriate technology as a new imperialism to keep them from achieving the standard of living enjoyed by the industrial states. They demand the right to the modern lifestyle and will pay the high social cost, as the Brazilian model shows.

5. Finally, the strategy of Self-reliance assumes a degree of local self-sufficiency in terms of capital and production. It has been described as "sweating capital out of one's own population" by Berger (1976:89). He goes on to criticize it as a system that foregoes any immediate alleviation in the condition of large numbers of people, prolonging the "maximum sacrifice" at a very high human cost. Tanzania is one of the poorer East African states. External capitalization seems a faster and more humane way to Berger, yet President Nyerere defends the longer, harder route to self-reliance:

> In fact, a reliance upon capitalist development means that we give to others the power to make vital decisions about our economy ... for such development will be foreign owned, and foreign controlled ... There can be no question about this - the foreign domination is permanent, not temporary (1973:384, 385).

Conclusion

The people of Soy would like the process of change to begin from within their context and needs, reflecting the Luo cultural heritage and lifestyle, as well as respecting the land and environment they love. Their traditional patterns would become the basis for creative improvements. Power would continue at the village level, not wielded by absentee landlords, corporate heads, or elite politicians. They would be able to manage the appropriate technological innovations introduced to help them gently harness the resources, without creating dependence. I can see these dear friends nodding and smiling at the prospect. Whether the international political conditions and the internal resource base will ever let them realize the dream is the question.

SYNOPSIS OF THE FOUR APPROACHES

Modernization has provided, for select populations, the potential for a better life by providing for basic human needs in an unparalleled way in history - food, health, shelter, transportation, communication, education, leisure, *inter alia*. Increased wealth has provided the leisure and the means for great cultural, intellectual, and even "spiritual" progress of civilization, whereas in poverty, man's energy and creativity have to be dedicated to survival. But likewise a materially wealthy society can also produce tedium, exhaustion, and desperation (Clark, 1980:24). The irony of the industrial, wealthy state is that materialism often creates often one-dimensional people. Wealth alone is not enough for true development, and the cost is high.

> The human cost of accumulation in the industrialized countries, whether market-oriented or centrally planned, has been terribly heavy even if this fact has sometimes disappeared from the memories of the descendants of the sacrificed generations (*What Now*, 1975:34-35).

Modernization overlooks one of the real reasons why under-development exists in the first place, inherent in the market economy that is not truly free, but skewed in favor of the rich nations.

Dependency theory attempts to explain the causes of under-development. In its negative reaction to Modernization, Dependency still seeks progress and modernization, but on the

basis of a socialist revolution. Structural changes are proposed to lessen or eliminate the growth of the capitalistic
centers at the expense of the peripheries, but socialist
exploitation is no less exploitative. Development is still
top-down with stronger state controls. The development proposed is just as unidimensional and materialistic as modernization; humans are seen as producers and consumers with the
state or collectivity as the supreme value. Human needs
include also the psychological and political spheres:

> Just as men have a right to food, they also have a
> social right to speak, to know, to understand the
> meaning of their work, to take part in public affairs
> and to defend their beliefs, the right to education,
> to expression, to information and to the management of
> production (*What Now*, 1975:27-28).

Dependency did, however, conscientize and prepare the ground
for the proposed Global Reform and for Self-reliant theory.

Global Reformism, as represented in the NIEO and more
recently in the Brandt Report (1980), accepts and propagates
the basic tenets of Modernization, while seeking a structural
realignment to provide a more equitable access to the fruits
of Western industrial and technological development. It is
both a political and an economic proposal that ignores the
ecological implications of the quick technological "fix" and
the potential perpetuation of selective (elite) development
at the expense of the poor. It is still a proposal, although
some nations are implementing some aspects of the agenda.

Self-reliant development positively proposes an endogenous
and appropriate style of development. It rejects the
imported technological growth model in favor of a lower-level
progress in the reach of all. It is still "progress" but an
enlightened sort, determined by the context and responsive to
the local power structures and to ecological constraints.
Self-reliance does not "buy into the system" but rather
creates many styles of development. It has potential for a
more just and satisfying level of existence for all peoples,
but it suffers from idealism and the lack of enthusiasm for
it by the current power blocks.

BEYOND DEVELOPMENT TO TRANSFORMATION

As this study shows, each of these four approaches to development contributes something to the ideal of human progress, yet contains inherent assumptions and flaws. Development is a diffuse concept that inadequately describes the goals and the processes of human and social change. It comes to mean whatever anyone wants it to mean, given whichever set of culturally-defined assumptions. For some, development connotes all the benefits of scientific and humanistic progress. For others, development is perceived as a perjorative term and is called "developmentalism." Some liberation theologians, such as Gutierrez, call for a radically different system, rather than an extension of developmentalism that only places band-aids on human misery and injustice.

What is a Christian perspective? Many theologians and Christian development workers have struggled with the limitations — the cultural baggage — of the term, but have continued to use it for lack of a better one. Others have tried (as Edgar Stoesz, 1975, and Merrill Ewert, 1975) to redefine and "Christianize" the term. Yet the negative and limited images remain. I propose, therefore, a term, a concept, that is less loaded and that is more adequate to a Christian perspective. I suggest *transformation.*

Why Transformation?

Transformation is a particularly Christian concept — to take the existing reality and give it a higher dimension or purpose: a rag-tag slave group transformed into the Hebrew nation, five loaves and fishes into a banquet for 5000, bread and wine in the symbol of spiritual unity with Christ, Jesus' human form into the glorified body. It takes what is and turns it into what could be.

It is the change from a level of human existence that is less than that envisioned by our Creator, to one in which man is fully human and free to move to a state of wholeness in harmony with God and with every aspect of his environment. The Papal encyclical *Populorum Progressio* (1967) envisioned such a "world where every man can live a fully human life." Transformation implies the restoration of the *imago dei* and the bringing into subjection of the principalities and powers ("institutions and orders" — Stephen Mott 1980:226ff) within the new order of things (I Cor. 5:17). Man, the predator is

transformed into man the co-creator, the steward. Social and
economic relationships are changed to conform with the
Kingdom principles of peace, justice, and love, manifested in
the people of God as community.

Transformation involves both material and spiritual
changes, holistically. Material progress without
transformation of the person is difficult to achieve and
maintain. Case histories abound of "development" programs
that have failed due to human greed, power play, graft,
politicking, or plain lethargy. Cooperatives depend on
people with a sharing ethic; they have usually failed. There
is no true "development" without true transformation. Even
U.S. AID recognizes that the churches and the mission
agencies are more honest and efficient at implementing
programs than government or secular agencies (Sommer,
1975:72). Conversion to God is the primary transformation and
this is explored further below.

Transformation is a joint enterprise between God and man, not
just a mechanistic or naturalistic process. It involves,
then, a tranformation of the human condition as we observe it
within each of the theories; the so-called "developed"
modernized world needs transformation to free itself from a
secular, materialistic condition marked by broken relationships, violence, economic subjugation, and devastation of
nature,and the "under-developed" world needs transformation
from the subhuman condition of poverty, premature death,
oppressions, disease, fears.

This transforming process is toward a world more in line
with God's original purposes through not only a present
amelioration of the human condition, but also a process that
moves actively and creatively toward the future, through the
mission of the church.

> This struggle of humanity towards its full dignity
> reveals that man and the world are created with a
> specific purpose, with a goal to be obtained through a
> continuous process of change and renewal. (Nissiotis
> 1975:82)

It is a process of God's continuing action in history
through His people — through the manifestation of the
present-and-coming Kingdom.

Characteristics of Transformation

As we examined the current developmental approaches, we
found that not only do they contain serious weaknesses but
also make strong contributions to human welfare. What are
these positive values and how do they contribute to the basic
criteria against which we can measure human and social
transformation? How do the four approaches contribute to a
theory of transformation? At least eleven characteristics
stand out:

Life-sustenance. Any plan for transforming human existence must provide adequate life-sustaining goods and
services to the members of the society (Goulet, 1975:94).
Basic human needs must be met. Without food, water, shelter,
clothing, life is impossible. With only minimal life-
support, existence is sub-human, afflicted by disease,
malnutrition, brain damage (protein deficiency), high infant
mortality, unemployment, ignorance, economic bondage. The
physical requirements are basic needs, the "inner limits,"
for calories, protein, and water, without which 500,000
children in the Third World die each year. Another billion
people go to bed malnourished each night.

Obviously Modernization, with its technology and scientific approach, has met these basic needs for the majority of
the population in the industrialized West (there are pockets
of poverty). It is no wonder that the Third World looks
longingly toward industrialization, even though the social
costs are high.

Meeting basic needs is a necessary, but not sufficient,
condition for social transformation. Wealth increases the
range of human choices. With improved material conditions,
man is enabled to deal with the other needs in Maslow's
hierarchy. The quantitative becomes the basis for the
qualitative ascent of human society (Goulet, 1975:333).
James indicates this when he admonishes:

> Suppose a brother or a sister is in rags with not
> enough for the day and one of you says 'Good luck to
> you, keep warm and have plenty to eat,' but does
> nothing to supply their bodily needs, what is the
> good of that? (James 2:15-16).

Even the spiritual transformation depends on the physical.
Our daily bread is essential.

The Self-reliant approach also seeks to meet basic human needs, but by lowering the standards and stressing the basics, in contrast to the growth model and luxuries of the West.

Equity. A second characteristic of social transformation is an equitable distribution of material goods and opportunities for progress among the peoples of the world. The glaring disparities between the haves and have-nots are well documented. Whatever the causes, the fact remains that two-thirds of humanity is suffering deprivation while a minority lives extremely well. On the one hand the overconsumption by the United States contrasts sharply with the poorer regions: the U.S. wastes more energy than Japan uses, spreads more fertilizer on lawns, golf courses, and cemeteries than China uses. The problem, in part, is distribution. On the other hand, within Third World countries the terribly skewed income distribution needs to be redressed. If the wealth of the upper 5% of the population were more evenly distributed, equity would be served. Land tenure is perhaps the biggest problem in Latin America, the upper dominant class holding often as much as 80% of the arable land and water, as in El Salvador.

The Dag Hammarskjold Report (*What Now?* 1975:26) states:

> There are sufficient resources to satisfy the basic human needs without transgressing the `external limits' [of the biosphere]. The question is primarily one of a more equitable distribution.

Lappé and Collins argue that the world can produce food enough for 10 billion inhabitants if the people were given access to the land, among other changes (1977:13ff). If social progress is to be valid, the advantages must reach the most needy. Modernization has failed to distribute its fruits to the poor. Over 30 million Americans are under the poverty line in the U.S. The poor nations are getting poorer and further in debt.

"The Christian favors a kind of development that is within the reach of the majority" (Taylor, 1977:13-17). An essential element of transformation is equity. All are God's children, with the needs and potentials. God has a special concern for the have-nots - the poor, defenseless, weak, marginalized, sick, and hungry. The early church shared with the needy (Acts 2:42-47). Paul, commenting on the sharing by the Macedonian church, stresses equality:

> ... it is a question of equality. At the moment your surplus meets their need, but one day your need may be met from their surplus. The aim is equality: as Scripture has it 'the man who got much had no more than enough, and the man who got little did not go short' (II Cor. 8:14-15).

Dependency theory has pointed out the inequitable distribution, and Self-reliance theoretically offers the greatest possibilities to redress the problem by stressing the needs of the poorest of poor, and a "fairer redistribution of resources satisfying the basic needs" in a "harmonized cooperative world ... living at the expense of no one else" (Cocoyoc 1977).

Global Reformism, on the other hand, falls short of a relatively equal distribution among all levels of the population, while attempting a more even distribution among nations.

Justice. Justice is correlated with equity, yet goes beyond mere redistribution. One can have a fair share of material goods and services without enjoying justice; slaves were often treated very well but within unjust relationships. Relationships and power structures need to be transformed into just ones, eliminating privileges for the few when they are at the cost of the many. The class and caste systems, institutionalized racism, the status of women, the controlling elites, and the international trade rules need transforming.

> A just vision of the transformed world is: where every man, no matter what his race, religion, or nationality can live a fully human life, freed from servitude imposed on him by other men or national forces over which he has no control (*Populorum Progressio*, 1967).

God is just, and He seeks justice above everything else.

> For the Lord your God is the God of gods, the Lord of lords, the great, the mighty, the awesome God who does not show partiality, nor take a bribe. He executes justice for the orphans and widows and shows his love for the alien ... (Deuteronomy 10:17-18).

Isaiah 58 describes in detail the justice that God would have done. Justice is one of the major themes of the Bible.

Modernization is blind to justice; the maximization of profit motive and the un-free capital market system tend to create injustices. The anchovies of Peru go into cattle feed to make marbled beef for rich palates, while Quechuan diet is protein deficient. Both Dependency and Reformism fail to address the justice issue because exploitative structures remain intact: the State on the one hand and the elite on the other.

Self-reliance does seek to redress the unjust relation-ships. It would allow every level of society to exercise local, democratic power, promote equal rights, and throw off any repression. Likewise the tribes who resist the oppres-sion of modernizers seek justice in their own way — a right to live as they always have on their lands.

Dignity and Self-worth. A fourth characteristic is dignity. It is necessary for people to have a sense of self-worth and dignity in the process of change. Many a development project has been vitiated by a donor-recipient relationship that robs recipients of dignity. The very fact that people are seen as "target groups" or "recipients" of programs creates paternalism. They sometimes internalize a feeling of inferiority or rebel against the strong/weak relationship. It is difficult to receive with dignity; people need self-esteem to be fully human. Stoesz (1975:3) put it:

> Development is people with an increasing control over their environment and destiny, people with dignity and self-worth.

Self-identity requires a good dose of self-esteem. Demeaning and condescending attitudes by the rich nations and agencies need transforming into partnership attitudes. Christ knew how to serve without condescension and how to give with dignity. His attitude even with His persecutors was one of ascribing worth to them, "They know not what they do."

Relationships within the Modernization approach have been extremely paternalistic and demeaning, and Dependency and Reformism have sought to rearrange these on behalf of the periphery. Global Reformism calls for better terms of trade and equal-to-equal arrangements between autonomous nations.

The Self-reliance approach carries this further, calling for temporary withdrawal and for a readjustment of "needs" that would remove weaker economies from under the control of the stronger. By relying on self, it "excludes dependence ... that can be converted into political pressure" (Cocoyoc, 1974). It also means trust in people and nations based on an equal footing, thus creating better self-esteem and dignity.

Freedom. One of mankind's most cherished birthrights, freedom, is a vital component of our concept. History is replete with the struggles of peoples to resist servitude, subservience, and slavery. Goulet (1975:26) sees one of the objectives of development to be men free from servitude – servitude to nature, to ignorance, to other men, to institutions, to beliefs considered oppressive. Christian transformation involves liberation of people from these bondages, and from bondage to themselves. Christ told his followers, "If the Son makes you free, you will truly be free." Freedom from oppressive systems, tyrants, customs, and freedom to be all that one wants to be; to be self-actualized, however that is conceived. Freedom to achieve all the dimensions of human potential; to realize the genetic potential endowed by God.

Concretely, social transformation for most Africans is freedom from the vestiges of colonialism and racism and from economic neo-colonialism. Nyerere of Tanzania underscores this:

> Freedom from colonialism and the preservation of
> some of our local traditions are at least as impor-
> tant as the accumulation of Western-style wealth.
> It is more important to us to be human than to be
> merely rich (Arusha Declaration).

For Latin American peasants, the desire for freedom from oppressive national policies and structures that marginalize them from their land, and freedom from police states was the birthing of liberation theology.

Dependency theory struck a blow for economic freedom from neo-colonialism, but failed to assure continued freedom under revolutionary regimes. Self-reliance does attempt liberation from the unjust international and national powers by stressing local control and participation, to ensure the people's freedom.

Participation. An important ingredient in all of this is the role that people play in social transformation. To the degree that people participate in the process, to that degree it is meaningful, effective, and lasting. The best-laid plans of "developers" have been wrecked by a top-down approach rather than participation by those involved. Local initiative and control from the beginning of any project are essential for people to "own" the program and carry it forward. Nyerere suggested, "All men who are suffering from poverty need to be given confidence in their ability to take control of their own lives" (1970 Maryknoll talk). Without this they remain untransformed.

In the economy of God, He defers to human participation in the matter of reconciliation. Man was always allowed, even required, to participate in the shaping of his own history, personal and collective. True human transformation comes about when people are able to act upon their own needs as they perceive them and progress toward a state of wholeness in harmony with their context.

In contrast to the other models, Self-reliance fosters a full participation by the people, at every level, "to invent and generate new resources and techniques, to increase their capability to absorb them ... to generate their own way of life (Cocoyoc 1974:174). The result is "endogenous development" done from within.

Reciprocity. Progress and social change result from both independent discovery within a culture and from intercultural contact and diffusion of innovation. All societies receive benefit from others. The United States has a rich heritage from many cultural influences, as do most nations. In a good sense of the word, we all depend on others. This is certainly biblical. No one is self-sufficient and certainly no society is. However, when it comes to social change and amelioration, the temptation has been for the industrial, modernized countries to assume that they have the key to success, and will use it to help the world "develop." It is easy to forget that they can learn from the poorer countries, poorer materially but richer perhaps culturally. The Dag Hammarskjold report reminds us that:

> There is a vast area for cultural cooperation which
> would help the industrial societies to recognize
> finally that the human experience is rich, and
> redefine their styles of life (1975:34).

The positive values of the traditional societies can instruct
the modern societies in many ways, if they will but listen.
Cocoyoc affirmed that they should "help the affluent nations,
for their own well-being, to find a way of life less exploitative of nature, of others, and of themselves." This
implies reciprocity and, as Goulet says, vulnerability. Are
the rich societies willing to open themselves up to learning
reciprocally? Is "aid for the over-developed West" possible?[7] Under the approach of Self-reliance, it would be.
The alienated worker, overextended consumer, ruptured family
in the West could learn some things. Invariably young people
who volunteer to live and serve in a Third World community
gain as much or more than they give, because they recipro-
cate.

   Cultural Fit. Transformation must be appropriate to the
culture which it penetrates; it must fit. Too often modernizers have ignored customs and social patterns in an attempt
to bring material benefits to the "backward." In fact they
saw traditions as deterrents to the adoption of change and
technology, without understanding the rationality of the
accumulated wisdom of a society. They did not stop to listen
to the peasant! The result has been cultural imperialism and
destruction of indigenous values, even of whole cultures.

   The Westernized elite who clamor for a new international
economic order tend to ignore the cultural heritages of their
peoples, even sacrificing them to "progress" via industrialization and exportation. The Dependency theorists have no
better record when they come to power; witness the Indian
problems in Central America or Peru under revolutionary
regimes.

   Cultures are, by extension, a part of God's creation and
He respects them all. "Thou art worthy because thou didst
create all things ... thou ... didst purchase for God men of
every tribe and language, people and nation ... " (Revelation
4:11 and 5:9). Christ honored all culture by becoming part
of Jewish culture with all its traditions (some gone bad).
No culture is pure and holy, but all have intrinsic value
that can be redeemed and used for social transformation.
When a culture is destroyed, a part of creation and a part of
all humanity dies. We are all then empoverished. In Self-
reliance, the stress on cultural heritage and the creativity
of the men and women who constitute it is strongly biblical
in tone.

Ecological Soundness. Just as any good transformation
should be culturally sensitive, it should be environmentally
sound. We live in a closed biosphere (with only solar energy
coming in) that is delicately balanced for man's existence.[8]
The pressures put on the eco-system are increasing with
population and industrialization, particularly the high and
harsh technology fostered by modernization. We have seen the
ecological costs. Unless the process is transformed into a
"gentle" technology that works with nature instead of abusing
it, our grandchildren will live (if they can) in a totally
inhospitable biosphere depleted of non-renewable resources
and choked by our own wastes, nuclear and otherwise. The
Cocoyoc Declaration urged that we have an ethic for our
grandchildren, "preserving a base of production compatible
with the necessities of future generations."

A clear theme of stewardship and the preservation of land
runs through the Bible, e.g., each seventh year the land was
to rest (Leviticus 25:4).[9] Man is to be a steward of the
natural resources.

Self-reliance stresses an ecological balance within the
natural environment, and a technology that is appropriate and
compatible with the eco-system. It would not raid the
world's non-renewable resources for a quick "technological
fix." Witness the hoe-to-oxen plough transformation called
for by Nyerere, above.

Hope. If there is one common element present in all
transformation it is the factor of hope. Without an attitude
of expectation, even optimism, change rarely occurs. Peasants or landless slum squatters will not take risks unless
there is a good chance that the change will result to their
benefit. This involves an element of hope. Pessimism,
usually born of bitter experiences in the past, is the
nemesis of positive social change.

A primordial characteristic of Christianity is hope.
God's intervention through Christ interjected a sense of
movement into history. The Lordship of Christ gives the
rationale and the responsibility to make changes which
predict the day when every knee shall bow before him (Yoder,
1977:18). There is a way out of the human predicament. God
is on the Throne. Evil will not always prevail. God hears

the cries of man. Man, through Christ, is enabled to realize
here and now something of the Kingdom's presence - "The kingdom has come near" (Matthew 10:7).

All the approaches except perhaps Dependency are optimistic about their solutions; Modernization holds out the
hope that the "good life" will trickle down and Global
Reformism, the hope of a restructured world economy. Yet
these macro solutions often give rise more to pessimism than
to hope. But the one that holds the most hope for the
"little" people of the world is Self-reliance because it
proposes small solutions at a village level and gives the
participants control.

Spiritual Transformation. This characteristic is only
implicit in the approaches studies. The core of human and
social transformation is spiritual. Without the change in
attitudes and behavior implicit in μετάνοια (conversion),
man remains a self-centered creature. Sin, both individual
and institutionalized, is a basic deterrent to social
transformation. Sin has been defined as the "social and
cosmic anti-creation" (Reuther, cited by Gutierrez, 1973:9)
resulting in injustice and exploitation; racism and
oppression; alienation and anomie. We noted from the
deleterious effects of Modernization that man has a rapacious
nature and that the existing order (*cosmos*) is distorted by
inequalities and injustices. The spiritual transformation of
man, with its break with the present system through a
transformation (renewal) of the mind, is an essential
ingredient to social transformation. Structures can be
changed by God through common grace, but the biblical model
is transformed men transforming social structures.

Thus the spiritual transformation is not only of the
individual but of society, indeed of all creation. Wallis
(1977:8) sees redemption as a "world event in which the
individual has part." The individual becomes part of the
community of believers, which is the means by which the new
order, The Kingdom, is made present in the world. Indeed,
Ron Sider muses:

> Perhaps the genuinely unique contribution of
> Christians to development is precisely the people
> of God - the Church - as a new community where all
> relationships are being redeemed (talk given at
> High Leigh, England, 1980).

As these relationships are redeemed, structures and institutions are changed, as we have seen in the historical moments when Christianity has changed society — the status of women, child labor laws, the work of Wilberforce against slavery, and the like.

The development theories examined do not explicity incorporate the spiritual change of man and society, but it is implicit in most of them, in an indirect way. The Global Reformism and Self-reliance approaches call for a more just world order and their stress on man's liberation and fulfillment reflect Christian values. Although none of the models puts spiritual regeneration as a goal or means to progress, their references to becoming "more fully human" and becoming less victimized and alienated can be given soteriological meaning as well as sociological. In fact Nyerere, father of the Self-reliant model, is a Christian. The point is that human spiritual change — regeneration and reconciliation — must accompany and condition social transformation.

FROM DEVELOPMENT TO TRANSFORMATION

No development theory adequately meets all the characteristics presented in this paper, while each reflects to one degree or another some of the essential elements of transformation. The one that comes closest to the Christian is perhaps Self-reliance. Each developmental approach has strong contributions to an adequate definition, but each falls short of a holistic and biblical perspective.

"Development" that is Christian, when these characteristics are present, is transformation of the person and social structures that frees man to move toward a state of increasing wholeness in harmony with God, himself, his fellow man, and his environment. As Samuel Escobar says, "It is not just a better life but a better way of living among men as whole persons."

To my friends in Soy, this transformed way of living among men with present and coming Kingdom values, might be expressed by Isaiah thus:

For I create the land of Kenya to be a delight, and
her people a joy -
   Luo,
    Maasai,
     Kikuyu,
      Turkana,
       Kalenjin.

I will take a delight in my people, and weeping and
  cries for help from oppressors shall never again
  be heard in the land.

There, no child shall ever again die an infant,
  nor lack food or health care.

No old man shall fail to live out his life;
  every boy and girl shall live his and her hundred
   years before dying,
  and will live out the years
   in respect and love with the family.

Men shall build houses and inhabit them,
  plant vineyards and eat their fruit,
  plant millet, ground nuts, maize and sorghum
   and eat thereof.

They shall not build for others to inhabit,
  nor plant to export for others to eat;
  justice will reign in the land.

My chosen shall enjoy the fruit of their labor and
  leisure of their efforts;
  they shall not toil in vain nor work for absentee
  landlords.

They care for the land I gave them,
  it blooms under their tender care.

They shall rule themselves and share in the decisions
  for the people as they see their own needs;
  no outsider shall impose his will or plans on
  them.

Yet nation shall learn from nation,
  and tribe from tribe;
  none shall exalt itself over the other.

*They shall not toil in vain nor raise children
    for misfortune,
    for they are the offspring of the blessed
        of the Lord,
    and their children after them.*

*Before they call to me I will answer,
    and while they are still speaking I
        will listen,
    for they are my people.*

*Their hearts are attentive to my precepts,
    they find delight in my laws.
My people hear the cries of the needy.
They release the yoke of the oppressed.*

*The man I care for is a man downtrodden and
    distressed,
One who reveres my words.*

*I will send peace flowing over Kenya like a river,
    and the wealth of nations over her like a
        stream in flood.*

*The Lord shall make his power known among his
    servants,
    for see, the Lord is coming in fire with
        his chariots like a whirlwind,
The Lord will judge by fire,
    with fire he will test all living men.*

*I myself will come to gather all nations and races,
    and they shall come and see my glory.*

*For, as the new heavens and the new earth
    which I am making shall endure in
        my sight,
    says the Lord,
        so shall your race, and your name endure,
    and week by week on the sabbath,
        all mankind shall come to bow
            down before me,
                says the Lord.*

[Based on Isaiah 65 and 66]

NOTES

All Scripture references are quoted from the NEW ENGLISH
BIBLE, 1976, Oxford Study Edition. (New York, Oxford
University Press).

1. An excellent brief description of modernization theory as
    it applies to Latin America is found in J. Samuel Valen-
    zuela and Arturo Valenzuela (1981). See also Ian Rox-
    borough's first three chapters in which he deals with the
    transition from traditional to modern society, from a
    social theory perspective, and its replicability (1979).

2. Ivan Illich, a Catholic scholar from the Centro Inter-
    cultural de Documentacion in Cuernavaca, Mexico, in his
    article "Outwitting the Developed Countries" (1969)
    defines under-development as a state of mind. He sees
    underdevelopment occurring "when mass needs are converted
    to the demand for new brands of packaged solutions which
    are forever beyond the reach of the majority ... the
    ruling groups in these countries build up services which
    have been designed for an affluent culture; once they
    have monopolized demand in this way they can never
    satisfy majority needs." He attacks the automobile as
    anti-transportation and hospitals as anti-health. "Every
    dollar spent in Latin America on doctors and
    hospitals costs a hundred lives. Had each dollar been
    spent on providing safe drinking water, a hundred lives
    could have been saved." His book *Deschooling Society*
    (1970) is a call to make education a social process
    rather than a commercial package that benefits the few.

3. The full text of the NIEO Programme is also found in the
    appendix of *Beyond Dependency*, Erb and Kalleb (1975).

4. See Galal A. Amin's "Dependent Development" in
    Alternatives, 1976:4 where he examines the
    multinationals' power and the NIEO.

5. The 1975 Dag Hammarskjold Report addresses the ecological
    "outer limit" concept and concludes: "Assuming that re-
    sources are limited, a rigorous discussion must first
    identify who consumes the resources and for what purposes
    they are being used. The industrial market economies,
    with 18 percent of the world population, consume 68 per-
    cent of its nine major minerals (oil excepted), while
    the Third World (China excepted) with 50 percent of the
    population is consuming 6 percent. Clearly, the pressure
    upon resources, which is real and complex, has little to
    do with demographic pressure in itself. At most, it sug-
    gests that the style of consumption of the industrialized
    countries would be unbearable if 4 billion or 10 billion
    human beings all sought to adopt it, although this is an
    argument for a change in the industrialized societies'
    consumption styles rather than one in favour of advising
    the poor to reduce birth rates" (*What Now*, 1975:36).

6. Peter Berger in *Pyramids of Sacrifice* (1976) describes
    the Chinese experience in terms of the human costs. On
    pages 163-179 he describes the achievements of the regime
    and the costs, and concludes, "Perhaps the weight of
    human pain to be accounted to Chinese communism can be
    summarized as follows: this regime has succeeded in
    making one of the liveliest peoples in the world walk the
    streets without noise and without laughter." He
    contrasts the Brazilian modernization approach with the
    Chinese approach and concludes that neither serves as an
    adequate model.

7. *Aid to the Overdeveloped West* is a book by Bob Goudz-
    waard (1975).

8. Only recently in history has the Western world begun to
    realize the precariousness of nature, with Rachel Car-
    son's book *The Silent Spring* (1962) and Barbara Ward and
    René Dubos's book *Only One Earth* (1972). More recent
    works include *The Seventh Year* by W. Jackson Davis
    (1979).

9. A good treatise on stewardship of earth is *The Earth is
    the Lord's*, edited by Mary Evelyn Jegen and Bruno V.
    Manno (1978).

BIBLIOGRAPHY

Achebe, Chinua
   1974   THINGS FALL APART. (Greenwich, CN: Fawcett).

Amin, Galal A.
   1976   Dependent Development,in ALTERNATIVES.

Arusha Declaration
   1967   In FREEDOM AND SOCIALISM/UHURU NA UJAMAA,
           Julius Nyerere. (New York: Oxford University
           Press).
           [See Julius Nyerere]

Barnet, Richard J. and Ronald Muller
   1974   GLOBAL REACH: THE POWER OF THE MULTINATIONAL
           CORPORATIONS. (New York: Simon and Schuster).

Bell, Daniel
   1973   THE COMING OF POST-INDUSTRIAL SOCIETY.
           (New York: Basic Books).

Berger, Peter
   1976   PYRAMIDS OF SACRIFICE: POLITICAL ETHICS AND
           SOCIAL CHANGE. (Garden City, New York: Anchor
           Press).

Bodley, John H.
   1975   VICTIMS OF PROGRESS. (Menlo Park, California:
           Cummings Publishing Co.).

Bonino, José Miguez
   1975   DOING THEOLOGY IN A REVOLUTIONARY SITUATION.
           (Philadelphia: Fortress Press, Confrontation
           Books).

BRANDT REPORT
   1980   A report on World Poverty and Affluence set up by
           Willy Brandt. West Germany Government.

Caporaso, James A. and Behrouz Zare
   1981   An Interpretation and Evaluation of Dependency
           Theory, in FROM DEPENDENCY TO DEVELOPMENT: STRA-
           TEGIES TO OVERCOME UNDERDEVELOPMENT AND INEQUALITY,
           Heraldo Muñoz, ed. (Boulder: Westview Press).

Cardoso, Fernando Henrique and Enzio Faletto
    1978   DEPENDENCY AND DEVELOPMENT IN LATIN AMERICA.
            (Berkeley: University of California Press).

Carson, Rachel
    1962   THE SILENT SPRING. (Boston: Houghton Mifflin).

Castel, Helene (ed.)
    1971   WORLD DEVELOPMENT: AN INTRODUCTORY READER. (New
            York: The MacMillan Co.).

Clark, Kenneth
    1980   CIVILIZAÇÃO: UMA VISÃO PESSOAL, Martins Fontex,
            ed. (Brasília: Universidade de Brasília).

Cocoyoc Declaration
    1974   Declaration by UNCTAD/UNEP Expert Seminar.
            Cocoyoc, Mexico, UN General Assembly. Published in
            DEVELOPMENT DIALOGUE, No. 2 (1972), pp. 88-96.

CRIME IN THE UNITED STATES, Uniform Crime Reports 1980.
            (U.S. Department of Justice).

Dag Hammarskjold Report
    1975   [See WHAT NOW? ANOTHER DEVELOPMENT].

David, W. Jackson
    1979   THE SEVENTH YEAR: INDUSTRIAL CIVILIZATION IN
            TRANSITION. (New York: W.W. Norton & Co.).

Davis, Shelton H.
    1977   VICTIMS OF THE MIRACLE: DEVELOPMENT AND THE INDIANS
            OF BRAZIL. (London: Cambridge University Press).

Day, Terence L.
    1981   Foreign Aid: No Bundle of Cash, in AGENDA
            (November) (Washington: United States Government
            Printing Office).

de Janvry, Alain
    1981   THE AGRARIAN QUESTION AND REFORMISM IN LATIN
            AMERICA. (Baltimore: John Hopkins University
            Press).

Erb, Guy F. and Valeriana Kallab
    1975   BEYOND DEPENDENCY: THE DEVELOPING WORLD SPEAKS
            OUT. (Washington: Overseas Development Council).

Evans, Peter
  1979   DEPENDENT DEVELOPMENT: THE ALLIANCE OF MULTI-
         NATIONAL, STATE AND LOCAL CAPITAL IN BRAZIL.
         (Princeton: Princeton University Press).

Ewert, Merrill
  1975   HUMANIZATION AND DEVELOPMENT. (Akron, PA:
         Mennonite Central Committee).

Foster, George
  1973   TRADITIONAL SOCIETIES AND TECHNOLOGICAL CHANGE.
         (New York: Harper and Row).

Galtung, Johan
  1981   The Politics of Self-reliance, in FROM DEPENDENCY
         TO DEVELOPMENT: STRATEGIES TO OVERCOME UNDER
         DEVELOPMENT AND INEQUALITY, Heraldo Muñoz, ed.
         (Boulder: Westview Press).

Gilligan, John
  1979   AID POLICY ON AGRICULTURAL ASSET DISTRIBUTION:
         LAND REFORM. PD.72 (January 16) (Washington: U.S.
         Agency in Development).

Gouzwaard, Bob
  1975   AID FOR THE OVERDEVELOPED WEST. (Toronto: Wedge
         Publication Foundation).

Goulet, Dennis
  1971   That Third World, in WORLD DEVELOPMENT: AN INTRO-
         DUCTORY READER, Helene Castel, ed. (New York:
         MacMillan Co.).

  1975   THE CRUEL CHOICE: A NEW CONCEPT IN THE THEORY OF
         DEVELOPMENT. (New York: Atheneum).

Gunder Frank, André
  1968   DEVELOPMENT AND UNDERDEVELOPMENT IN LATIN AMERICA.
         (New York: Harper and Row).

  1972   The Development of Underdevelopment, in DEPENDENCE
         AND UNDERDEVELOPMENT: LATIN AMERICA'S POLITICAL
         ECONOMY, James Cockcroft, André Gunder Frank, and
         Dale Johnson, eds. (New York: Anchor Books).

Gutierrez, Gustavo
    1973   A THEOLOGY OF LIBERATION. (Maryknoll, N.Y.:
            Orbis).

Hastings Center Report
    1977   (February)

Hayter, Teresa
    1981   THE CREATION OF WORLD POVERTY: AN ALTERNATIVE VIEW
            TO THE BRANDT REPORT. (London: Pluto Press).

Heilbroner, Robert L.
    1963   THE GREAT ASCENT: THE STRUGGLE FOR ECONOMIC
            DEVELOPMENT IN OUR TIME. (New York: Harper and
            Row).

Hettne, Bjorn
    1978   CURRENT ISSUES IN DEVELOPMENT THEORY. (Stockholm:
            Swedish Agency for Research Cooperation).

Illich, Ivan
    1969   Outwitting the "Developed" Nations,in NEW YORK
            REVIEW OF BOOKS, No. 13 (November 6).

    1970   DESCHOOLING SOCIETY. (New York: Harper and Row).

Interamerican Foundation
    1977   THEY KNOW HOW. (Washington: United States
            Government Printing Office).

Jegen, Mary Evenly and Bruno V. Manno
    1978   THE EARTH IS THE LORD'S. (New York: Paulist
            Press).

Lagos, Gustavo
    1981   The Revolution of Being: a Preferred World Model,
            in FROM DEPENDENCY TO DEVELOPMENT, STRATEGIES TO
            OVERCOME UNDERDEVELOPMENT AND INEQUALITY, Heraldo
            Muñoz, ed. (Boulder: Westview Press).

Lappé, Frances Moore, Joseph Collins, and David Kinley
  1977   FOOD FIRST: BEYOND THE MYTH OF SCARCITY. (New
          York: Ballantine).

  1980   AID AS OBSTACLE: TWENTY QUESTIONS ABOUT OUR
          FOREIGN AID AND THE HUNGRY. (San Francisco:
          Institute for Food and Development Policy).

Maslow, Abraham
  1954   MOTIVATION AND PERSONALITY. (New York: Harper and
          Row).

Mott, Stephen C.
  1980   Biblical Faith and the Reality of Social Evil, in
          CHRISTIAN SCHOLARS' REVIEW. (1980. Vol. IX, No.
          3), 225-240.

Muñoz, Heraldo
  1981   The Strategic Dependence of the Centers and the
          Economic Importance of the Latin American
          Periphery, in FROM DEPENDENCY TO DEVELOPMENT:
          STRATEGIES TO OVERCOME UNDERDEVELOPMENT AND
          INEQUALITY, Heraldo Muñoz, ed. (Boulder: Westview
          Press).

Myers, Norman
  1982   Cheap Beef and Priceless Rainforests, CHICAGO
          TRIBUNE (January 3).

NEW ENGLISH BIBLE,
  1976   Oxford Study Edition. (New York, Oxford University
          Press).

Nissiotis, Nikos A.
  1975   Introduction to a Christological Phenomenology of
          Development, in A READER IN POLITICAL THEOLOGY,
          Alistair Kee (Philadelphia: Westmininster Press).

Nyerere, Julius
  1967a   Arusha Declaration, in FREEDOM AND SOCIALISM/UHURU
          NA UJAMAA. (New York: Oxford University Press).
          [See Arusha Declaration]

1967b   EDUCATION FOR SELF-RELIANCE. (Dar Es Salaam:
        Government Printer).

1970   Talk to Maryknoll missioners (Maryknoll, N.Y.).

1973   FREEDOM AND DEVELOPMENT/UHURU NA MAENDELEO. (Dar
        Es Salaam: Oxford University Press).

O'Brien, Philip J.
1975   A Critique of Latin American Theories of Depen-
        dency, in BEYOND THE SOCIOLOGY OF DEVELOPMENT:
        ECONOMY AND SOCIETY IN LATIN AMERICA AND AFRICA,
        Ivan Oxaal, ed.   (London and Boston: Rout-
        ledge and Kegan, Paul).

Paddock, William and Elizabeth
1973   WE DON'T KNOW HOW: AN INDEPENDENT AUDIT OF WHAT
        THEY CALL SUCCESS IN FOREIGN ASSISTANCE. (America:
        Iowa State University Press).

Parmar, Samuel L.
1975   Self-reliant Development in an Interdependent
        World, in BEYOND DEPENDENCY, Guy F. Erb and
        Valeriana Kallab, eds. (Washington: Overseas
        Development Council).

Perkins, John
1982   WITH JUSTICE FOR ALL. (Ventura, CA: Regal Books).

Perroux, Francois
1964   Le Notion de Developpement, in L'ECONOMIE DE XXe
        SIECLE (Paris: Presses Universitaires).

Phillips Anne
1977   The Concept of Development, in REVIEW OF AFRICAN
        POLITICAL ECONOMY, No. 8 (January-April).

Pope Paul VI
1967   POPULORUM PROGRESSIO ("Development of Peoples")
        March 26. (Vatican City).

Rensberger, Boyce
1977   14 Million Acres a Year Vanishing as Deserts Spread
        Around the Globe, THE NEW YORK TIMES (August 28).

Roberts, Glyn
    1979   QUESTIONING DEVELOPMENT. (Alverstoke, Hampshire:
            The Alver Press).

Rowstow, Walt W.
    1960   STAGES OF ECONOMIC GROWTH: A NON-COMMUNIST
            MANIFESTO. (Cambridge: Cambridge University
            Press).

Roxborough, Ian
    1979   THEORIES OF UNDERDEVELOPMENT. (Atlantic Highlands,
            New Jersey: Humanities Press).

Said, Abdul and Luiz Simmons
    1975   THE NEW SOVEREIGNS (Englewood Cliffs, NJ: Prentice
            Hall).

Schumacher, E.F.
    1973   SMALL IS BEAUTIFUL: ECONOMICS AS IF PEOPLE
            MATTERED. (New York: Harper and Row).

Sinclair, Maurice
    1980   THE GREEN FINGER OF GOD. (Exeter: Paternoster
            Press).

Sine, Tom
    1981   Development: Its Secular Past and its Uncertain
            Future, in EVANGELICALS AND DEVELOPMENT, Ronald
            Sider, ed. (Philadelphia: The Westminster Press).

Smith, William Edgett
    1973   NYERERE OF TANZANIA. (London: Gollancz).

Sommer, John G.
    1975   U.S. VOLUNTARY AID TO THE THIRD WORLD: WHAT IS ITS
            FUTURE? (Washington, D.C.: Overseas Development
            Council).

Stavenhagen, Rodolfo
    1969   SOCIAL CLASS IN AGRARIAN SOCIETIES. (Garden City,
            New Jersey: Doubleday).

Stockwell, Edward G. and Karen Ann Laidlaw
    1981   THIRD WORLD DEVELOPMENT PROBLEMS AND PROSPECTS.
            (New York: Nelson-Hall).

Stoesz, Edgar
    1975   THOUGHTS ON DEVELOPMENT. (Akron, Pennsylvania:
            Mennonite Central Committee).

Sunkel, Osvaldo
    1981   Development Styles and the Environment: an Inter-
            pretation of the Latin American Case, in FROM
            DEPENDENCY TO DEVELOPMENT: STRATEGIES TO OVERCOME
            UNDERDEVELOPMENT AND INEQUALITY, Heraldo Muñoz, ed.
            (Boulder: Westview Press).

Taylor, John V.
    1975   ENOUGH IS ENOUGH: A BIBLICAL CALL FOR MODERATION
            IN A CONSUMER-ORIENTED SOCIETY. (Minneapolis,
            Minnesota: Augsberg Publishing House).

The Vanishing Tribes, NEWSWEEK. (October 12, 1981), pp.
            92-97.

Turnbull, Colin
    1962   THE LONELY AFRICAN. (New York: Simon and
            Schuster).

U.S. NEWS AND WORLD REPORT. (August 31, 1981).

Valenzuela, J. Samuel and Arturo Valenzuela
    1981   Modernization and Dependency: Alternative Perspec-
            tives in the Study of Latin American Under-
            development, in FROM DEPENDENCY TO DEVELOPMENT:
            STRATEGIES TO OVERCOME UNDERDEVELOPMENT AND
            INEQUALITY, Heraldo Muñoz, ed. (Boulder: Westview
            Press).

Wallis, Jim
    1977   The Vehicle for Vision, in SEEDS OF THE KINGDOM
            /SOJOURNERS.

Ward, Barbara and René Dubos
    1972   ONLY ONE EARTH. (New York: W.W. Norton and Co.,
            Inc.).

Williams, Gavin
    1981   The World Bank and the Peasant Problem, in RURAL
            DEVELOPMENT IN TROPICAL AFRICA, J. Heyer, ed.
            et al. (New York: St. Martins Press).

WHAT NOW? ANOTHER DEVELOPMENT
    1975   The Dag Hammarskjold Report on Development and
            International Cooperation, Special Issue of
            DEVELOPMENT DIALOGUE (Uppsala) 1975, No. 1/2.

Yoder, John Howard
    1977   The Biblical Mandate, in SEEDS OF THE
            KINGDOM/SOJOURNERS.

CULTURE AND SOCIO-CULTURAL CHANGE

Purpose. The purpose of this paper is to discuss relationships between culture, social transformation and mission praxis.

A Holistic Dynamic View of Culture. Culture is derived from its biological, environmental, psychological and historical components of human existence, and, as such culture is learned, structured, dynamic, variable, divided into aspects, can be studied scientifically, and culture provides an individual both the means to adapt himself to his situation and express himself creatively.

Dimensions of Culture. Culture has the following dimensions:

(1) ideological dimension, (2) social dimension, (3) technological and economic dimension, (4) time dimension.

Reflections on God, Culture, the Fall and Liberation of Man, and the Created Order. In the final analysis, God is responsible for culture. In all peoples and in all nations there is something good as well as there are many things that are evil. Only the Good News of the Kingdom, the power of the Gospel will make the good of cultures be even better.

Developmental Change and the Rise of Cultural Relativism and Functionalism. Functionalists see society as stable and favor preserving the status quo. Church growth advocates such as McGavran and Wagner seem to have a "neutral attitude" towards social struggle and they don't discuss whether they are bad or good or under the judgment of the Gospel. Their viewpoint seems to have been influenced by the functionalist and relativist approach to social structure. Even in some of Wagner's recent modification of his position, his bias appears to be functionalist, in favor of preserving the status quo.

Conflictive Approach. While functionalists tend to see equilibrium in cultural systems, conflict theories see structural change everywhere. These theories constitute the legacy of Karl Marx. Instead of seeing society as essentially stable like a functionalist, it sees struggle and tensions which can be used to bring about revolutionary change.

The Latin American Theory of Dependency. The failure of reformist approaches and the deteriorating conditions in Latin
America since the late 60's have created a new theory which
is tied to Marxism. The dependency theory postulates that
the main reasons for underdevelopment of the Third World is
its condition of dependency on the developed capitalist world.

*Conflictive Dependentist Approach in the Mission of the
Church.* While this approach has sensitized us to the inequities and the contradictory forces at work in the world,
it also could lead us down a road to conflict that could
threaten the future of our world. The church has another
mission.

Towards a Holistic View of Socio-Cultural Change. We see
God's creation, culture and development integrally related,
focusing on the material, spiritual, social, personal needs
of man, while seeking to change structures. Holistic development is "movement towards that freedom and wholness in
a just community which persons will enjoy when our Lord returns to bring the Kingdom in its fulness."

     TITO PAREDES is an anthropoligist working through an
institute with the Andean People and particularly the Quechua
Indians in Peru. His focus is in helping these people in the
cultivation of their culture.

CULTURE AND SOCIO-CULTURAL CHANGE

Tito Paredes

1. INTRODUCTION

The purpose of this paper is to discuss the relationship between culture, social transformation and mission praxis. I will first attempt to discuss the concept of culture and provide an outline of the basic components of culture. I will also try to discuss some basic approaches to the phenomenon of socio-cultural change and its influence upon some mission praxis of considerable influence today. Finally, I will conclude with some reflexions on the theme from a Latin American Christian perspective.

2. WHAT IS CULTURE?
Towards a Holistic and Dynamic View of Culture

2.1 Culture in Its Limited and Narrow Sense

One of the contributions of anthropology to modern society has been to make us all aware that the concept of culture should not be confined only to its narrow sense, which implies that a limited group of people have privileged access to selected aspects of their culture. By this I mean that culture should not be confused with knowing and listening to classical music, reading the classical literature of one's country, or to have formal usually high-level education. This limited view of culture excludes the great majority of peoples of the world who have not had access to formal educational

systems connected with the western tradition. However, it
should be clear that this does not make these people "uncul-
tured" or devoid of a cultural tradition.

Anthropology has helped us to understand that all the
peoples of the world, regardless of whether they know how to
read or write, regardless of whether they have access to
formal western-types of education, are depositories of rich
cultural traditions that they have developed through hundreds
and even thousands of years, and therefore they should not be
belittled just because they do not fit our own conceptions of
what culture is.

2.2. *Culture in Its Inclusive Sense*

As I mentioned before, the field of anthropology has rescued the term "culture" to be used and applied in a wider and
more inclusive sense, that is to refer to the ways of life
and thinking of peoples everywhere. It is true that the definition of culture is not an easy task or one on which everybody agrees. It is not an exaggeration to suggest that there
may be as many definitions of culture as there are anthropologists. In 1952, anthropologist Kroeber discussed and collec-
ted 161 definitions of culture (1). The Willowbank report (2)
on "Gospel and Culture" defines culture in the following way:

"Culture is an integrated system of beliefs (about God or
reality or ultimate meaning), of values (about what is
true, good, beautiful and normative), of customs (how to
behave, relate to others, talk, pray, dress, work, play,
trade, farm, etc. etc.) and of institutions which express
these beliefs, values and customs (government, law courts,
temples or churches, family schools, hospitals, factories,
shops, unions, clubs, etc.), which bind a society together
and give it a sense of identity, dignity, security, and
continuity." (p.7)

This definition in my opinion is a good start, but it is
not inclusive enough. More and more it is being realised
that culture has several dimensions that cannot be ignored.
Anthropologist Herskovits (3) says the following about culture.

1. Culture is learned.
2. A culture is derived from its biological, environmental, psychological and historical components of human
   existence.
3. Culture is structured.
4. Culture is divided in aspects.

5. Culture is dynamic.
6. Culture is variable.
7. Culture presents regularity which allows for analysis
   through the methods of science.
8. Culture is an instrument by means of which the individual adapts himself to his total situation and provides
   him with the means of creative expression.

Herskovits' definition is a more inclusive view of culture,
which I prefer.

2.3. *Basic Dimensions of Culture*

In the following paragraphs, I will briefly present an outline of what in my opinion are those aspects of culture that
need to be accounted in any discussion of culture and development. I will make a diagram which will illustrate the most
important components of culture and then briefly explain what
I mean by the different components of what I will call "towards
a holistic and dynamic model of culture."

TOWARDS A HOLISTIC AND DYNAMIC MODEL OF CULTURE (4)

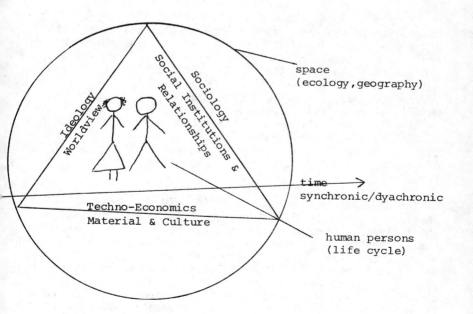

Any approach to the study of the socio-cultural reality of
a people or society must take into account the elements illustrated on the previous page. I realise that a serious study
of a society that pretends to cover all the aspects of the
diagram will take a lot of time and paper. I also realise
that not everyone is interested in studying in depth all those
aspects of a total society. There are some students of society who are only interested in some dimensions like the economic or ideological ones. This is particularly true nowadays
when the excessive especialisation of the social sciences
makes certain social scientists concentrate only on some aspects of the phenomenon of culture, or on certain sub-cultures
or classes of a given society. However, recognising this
limitation and these considerations, it is important that any
study that is done on a culture, even though it is very spe-
cialised, be situated within the historical-socio-cultural
context of the above diagram.

The idological dimension - is composed of ideas, beliefs,
knowledge expressed in articulate speech or another symbolic
form, and includes mythologies, theologies, legends, literature, philosophy, science, folk wisdom and common sense
(White 1949:364:365).

The sociological dimension - is made up of interpersonal
relationships expressed in patterns of collective, as well as
individual, behavior. It includes social, kinship, economic,
ethical, political, military, ecclesiastical, occupational,
professional and recreational institutions (White 1949:365).

The technological and economic dimension - includes the
material, mechanical, physical and chemical instruments, together with the techniques of their use by means of which people interact with their natural habitat. Here we find the
tools of production, the means of subsistence, the materials
of shelter and the instruments of offence and defence (White
1949:365).

The ecological dimension - has to do with the natural-
physical environment in which a people live and carry out
their lives. There is a relationship between the environment
and a given society. The physical environment is the fountain
of resources that allows the group to survive and live. Just
as the environment conditions the culture of a people, similarly man exercises an effect upon the environment. Man can
misuse the environment and exploit it irrationally. But, on
the other hand, man can also use it carefully. We cannot

study a people unless we understand the ecological dimension
in which they live and its interrelationship with the other
aspects of culture.

The time dimension - all peoples have developed not only
in a given natural space, but also they have developed in
time. People, as we observe them today, have a historical
past that has conditioned the present. We can refer to syn-
chronic time when we talk about societies in the present time.
On the other hand, we can refer to diachronic time when we
talk or study peoples, taking into account the historical
past, that is to say taking their historical development
seriously. A society today cannot be understood adequately
unless we make reference to its historical past. We cannot
ignore today the historical past of peoples. (5)

Culture and the Human Being.

We would only be talking in abstractions and come to a
socio-cultural determinism if we do not take into account the
human person. A person is a concrete reality whose behavior
and life-cycle are observable in time. Culture conditions a
person and enables him to function and behave within it. But
the human being is not a robot or a computer which has been
programmed to behave in a certain way without its being able
to do anything about it. The human person learns the acceptable behavior within his culture, and he can choose to behave
within those constraints or prefer not to do so and pay the
consequences. The human person is a conscious being. He is
aware of many of his acts and behavior, and therefore we need
to take this human person and his peculiarities into account
in our studies.

People are born, they grow, they become adolescents, adults,
old people, and finally they die. This process in the life of
a human being, anthropologists call "life-cycle." During the
life-cycle of a human being, there are many changes that in
some way or another, affect the society and the culture of the
individuals. Human beings create and modify cultures. We cannot ignore them in the study of culture or development.

The Issue of Cultural Determinism

According to one's point of view, one of the aspects of culture described above, may be the basic and determinant aspect
of a society. For example, for Leslie White

"the primary role is played by the technological system.
This is, of course, as we would expect it to be, because

it could not be otherwise...the technological system is
therefore primary and basic in importance. All human
life and culture rests and depends on it" (White 1949:365).

In contrast to White, Weber places the emphasis on ideological factors and this is exemplified in his classic *The Protestant Ethic and the Spirit of Capitalism*.

Emile Durkheim (6) may be an example of sociological determinism, and the Marxist approach may be a determinist view not
only of history but also of economic and technological aspects.

My own position is that it is fruitless to talk about the
determinism of one or other of the aspects. As far as I am
concerned, it is a very sterile debate, similar to the debate
of "what comes first, the chicken or the egg." It is possible
to arrive and establish what may be the important conditioning
factors of a given social phenomenon or of a given culture,
only after very serious study and analysis. Rather than talking about determinisms, I think we should talk in terms of
regularities and tendencies within a given society. Furthermore, we need to give due role and place to the different variables at work within cultures (7).

2.4. *Reflexions on God, Culture, The Fall and Liberation of
Man and the Created Order.*

In this section it is not my intention to provide an elaborate theological treatise on the biblical perspective of culture, but rather to point out certain, what to me are biblical, perspectives on culture.

I would like to start by saying that it is God who in the
last analysis is responsible for the creation of culture. The
Bible tells us that God created not only the universe, the
heaven and the earth, but also He created men and women in His
image, in His likeness. Man is a creature of God, and the
Bible clearly tells us that it is God who created man in His
image and likeness. Although this is not the place to treat
this theme in depth, basically the meaning of this is that man
was created to live in communion and fellowship with God and
outside of God, man cannot become what he was intended to be.

As Samuel Escobar says, "Man comes from God and because of
this he encounters his destiny and he is able to realize all
his possibilities only in Jesus Christ who is also man and
God" (Certeza No. 42:33).

The social sciences, particularly cultural anthropology, have provided evidence that all peoples of the earth have some kind of religious orientation. All peoples have an orientation toward the supernatural beyond the human individuals themselves. This wouldn't be possible unless God had created man with that necessity of God. And in this sense it is very true when Pascal concludes that within all men there is a vacuum that only can be filled with the Lordship of Jesus Christ.

God gave man the physical, moral and social and spiritual capabilities. God created man with the creativity and the potential to create culture.

In Genesis 1:26-28 and in Genesis 2:15, we find that man is situated by God in a special relationship over creation. He is placed as the administrator, as the caretaker and cultivator of the whole earth and of the whole universe. God expected man to use the capabilities that He put in him to interact creatively not only with God and other men but to interact also with his environment. In other words, man was expected to elaborate, to adorn, to mold, to produce culture.

The fact that as soon as God ordered Adam to take care of creation he began to give names to the animals of the created order leads us to conclude that Adam was beginning to put to work that capacity to create culture, to work creatively with the created order.

In conclusion then, we affirm that in the last analysis God is responsible for culture. When He created man, when He created the universe and all that there is in it, He intended a special communion between God and man, a special relationship free from sinfulness between man and man and between man and the cosmos. But this was not so. Something terribly wrong took place in the history of man.

The Bible tells us and the history of the world evidences that sin and evil were introduced into the created order, and it speaks in Genesis 3 and 4 of the activity of Satan, the power of sin and the effects of the fall of man on not only man's relationship to God, man's relationship to other men, but also speaks of man's relationship to the earth as being damaged. The whole created order of the earth was cursed as a result of man's rebellion against God.

Adam and Eve disobeyed God and since then all of our labors and works are accompanied by sweat, by conflict and tiredness (Genesis 3:16-19; Romans 8:19-22). Selfishness, pride and

ethnocentrism are part of the human history of peoples and
nations, and this is the basic cause for the struggles of
peoples, families, and nations throughout the history of mankind.

But in spite of the fall of man and of his irrefutable
need of redemption, the peoples from the created order still
reflect in some way the grace and the likeness and image of
God, the Creator. In all peoples and in all nations there is
something good as well as there are many things that are evil.
There are many things that can be either for good or for evil.
The Bible says that the rain and the sun benefit not only the
just but also the unjust. The land produces for all. There
are many people who have a sense of justice, a sense of beauty,
who are able to express kindness and creativity. This in many
ways reflects the Creator. However, people, no matter how good
they may appear, no matter how capable, or how beautiful their
works are, are still in need of salvation, and still in need
of liberation, liberation that can only be found in Jesus
Christ.

The world, peoples, families, cultures, nations do need
the Gospel, the Good News of the Kingdom of God. Only the
good news of the kingdom, the power of the Gospel will make
the good of the cultures be even better. It will make the
good citizen a better citizen, a good student or professor a
better student or professor. That which is evil the Gospel
will transform and will change, and that which is indifferent
or neutral will be made useful and good.

In summary then, once again, the fall of man, the activity
of Satan, the sinfulness that was introduced into the created
order brought about a drastic change in the relationships between man and God, between men and other men, and between man
and the created order. This fallen situation of man and the
created order made it imperative that the new man, the new
creation, be brought about, and God set Himself the task of
providing the means for this new created order of creation and
of man. So, the work of Jesus Christ--His saving work, His
liberation--is capable of bringing about this new order of
things for man, nations, and the whole of creation.

3. *Socio-Cultural Change in the Anthropological Tradition
   Developmental Change in the 19th Century*

The 19th Century was characterised by special concern over
the origin and development of things, the origin and development of man's biological dimensions, human relationships, socio-
economic institutions, and even on ideological and religious

origins. In Darwin, (8) we observe an obsession for the
biological origin of man and its biological development
through time from the lower forms of biological life. In the
British Anthropologist, Taylor, (9) we find an interest in the
origin and development of religion. In L.H.Morgan, (10) we
find an interest in the development of property, government
and the family. Following Morgan, Marx among others was
also interested in the development and origin of society. This
interest was greatly motivated by the search for laws of progress which were thought to be applicable to all peoples in
all times and in all places. Thus societies and cultures
were conceived as organisms that function through laws. Therefore, if one was able to determine the stages of development
of a people, this was expected to be applicable to the whole
world.

Behind this search for the origins and development of man,
there was the assumption that mankind was on a road to perfection, and this perfection was seen not only in its economic,
social and ideological aspects, but even in its moral aspects.
People, at the time, assumed that the ideas of the degenera-
tion and the fall of man were contrary to the evolutionary
discoveries of the 19th Century science. This search and obsession for the origin and development of society led to the
establishment of a hierarchy of who or what societies were the
most and least developed in the evolutionary scale. Today we
know that the 19th Century social scientists had a built-in
ethnocentrismo in their system that made them look upon their
societies as the highest society in the cultural development
of mankind, and usually those "other" societies were on the
lower scales of cultural development. Thus, European and
North American man and society were seen as the model of
development that all mankind was bound to follow. This western
ethnocentrism nourished much of the philosophy behind Development, as Tom Sine correctly asserts:

"Western development is a child of the European and American Enlightenment. It is based on the implicit belief
that human society is inevitably progressing toward the
attainment of a temporal materialistic kingdom. In fact,
the certain belief that unending economic and social progress is a natural condition of free persons has become the
secular religion of the west....

"Implicit in this progressive view of the future was the
firm conviction that economic progress would automatically
result in social and moral progress..." (*Development: Its
Secular and Its Uncertain Future*). (11)

*Developmental Change and the Rise of Cultural Relativism and
Functionalism.*

The 19th Century evolutionary climate soon found its opponents and critics. Many anthropologists, at the end of the
19th Century and the beginning of the 20th Century, began to
realise that much of the data of the 19th Century evolutionists
was shaky and unreliable. They also began to realize that the
assumptions on which their evolutionary schemes were built
were more conjectures and speculations about society and men,
which solid field data was not able to support. As a result,
there arose a reaction to evolutionary thinking, and this
response took different forms.

Two of the schools that arose in reaction to the evolutionary climate of the 19th Century include the Diffusionists and
the Historicists. (12) In general, these approaches and their
variances criticised the evolutionists for their unilinear
schemes, for their poor handling of the cultural data, for
their ethnocentrism and for what they considered to be their
conjectures and speculations about the origin and development
of society and their institutions. They proposed a more careful use of data, together with more specific and rigorous
study of specific cultural areas, instead of devising grand
scale theories applied to the whole world.

It is not my intention to go into these theories that reacted against the evolutionary climate, but suffice it to say
that these contributed to the rise of the functionalist-relativist approach to culture.

Cultural relativism proposes the idea that any cultural
system should not be seen from the framework of another cultural
system, but rather wihin its own framework, and it should not
be judged whether it is high or low on the scale of development, but rather on its own peculiarity. Societies were said
not to be superior or inferior, lower or higher, better or
worse, but rather just different to other societies. Under
this new tide of thinking, there was strong feeling that judgment should be withheld and that societies should not be compared with others. With the rise of cultural relativism, the
concept of development in terms of unilinear growth, advancement, passing through fixed stages of development, etc., was
devalued.

Concurrent with the rise of cultural relativism, we see the
rise of the functionalist school of thought. The functionalist school within anthropology, in very simple terms, meant

that society was looked upon as a biological organism made up
of many parts, each part inter-related with the other parts,
and each part functioning for the maintenance of the whole
society. There is a tendency to see equilibrium and harmony
in this approach. Change, although recognized, is not accounted adequately, especially when this change is swift
change. The functionalist tradition within anthropology has
contributed to a careful description and analysis of social
groups and cultures within its own framework of reference.
It has helped us to understand how cultural systems work.
However, at the same time, the limitations have been that
since there is a preference for analysing small scale societies, oftentimes these studies have not taken into account
the larger context in which these societies live. For example, a native society in the jungle of Peru may not, under
this approach, be studied with a very careful look at the
national context in which the society lives! Thus the interactions between this society and the other societies around
may not be looked at and analysed adequately. The cultural
relativist position and the functionalist tradition both have
contributed to viewing societies as cultural systems that have
a genius of their own that may devise their own development
programs which, although from a western perspective may not
make much sense, may be adequate and appropriate in their own
context. So this functionalist relativist tradition needs to
be carefully taken into account in any talk and action on social transformation, particularly its bias for preserving the
status quo.

*The Functionalist-Relativist Approach in Some Missionary Prac-
tices.*

How is this approach worked out in the missionary task? We
find a very clear example of this orientation in missionary
work in the following quote from Smalley about social structures:

> "There is nothing intrinsically moral or right and wrong
> about social structure as such. The many different social
> structures as found today in the world are simply many dif-
> ferent ways of organizing group behavior into useful chan-
> nels and of making life more valuable to the participants
> in the society. The missionary's role in relation to this
> as in relation to other cultural matters is to let history
> take its course and to concern himself with more important
> issues." (1958:23)

Smalley's perspective on society appears to underline that there is no need to change the social structures because they are assumed to be amoral. Furthermore, social change should not be a concern of the missionary, since there are other more important things that he is supposed to do. From a Biblical perspective, we cannot accept this assumption.

All the social structures are under the judgement of God. Our world today is one in which the rich are getting richer and the poor are getting poorer. This situation reflects unjust and sinful relationships not only within a country, but this is also manifested at the world level. The indiscriminate exploitation of natural resources and the pollution of the physical environment are often motivated by the love of money and the desire to satisfy or create artificial needs. All of these are evidences of the manifestation of sinfulness at the structural level. Therefore, we cannot conclude that the social structures of our world are amoral. We have to point out that there is a lot of injustice, that there is a lot of discrimination, a lot of indiscriminate exploitation of the environment and a lot of human exploitation also. The manifestations of sin and evil are concretely expressed not only in the individual sinner but also in the structures of society. When the Bible denounces the exploitation and domination of the poor, when the Bible denounces the injustice, the corruption and the idolatry of Israel in the Old Testament, the Bible is judging not only men who are committing this act, but the Bible is also judging the human inter-relationships that manifest this structural and relational sin.

Another example of the non-critical acceptance of the functionalist approach to social structure we find in Peter Wagner's book *Look Out the Pentecostals Are Coming*. In this book, among other things, Wagner argues that:

"...This is a book whose theme is the growth of the Pentecostal Churches in Latin America. What must or must not be the social posture of these Churches is a very fascinating theme, but it is one that must be debated in another place. Here, we are basically interested in knowing whether the socio-political position of the Pentecostals in Latin America, in general, contribute or are an obstacle to the growth of the church." (1973:157)   (13)

Wagner appears to be saying that in the growth of the church it does not really matter much whether the social structure is good or bad, or whether the Gospel has something important to say to it. The only important thing appears to be whether

these structures contribute or not to the numerical growth
of the Pentecostal Churches.

The thought of Wagner about social structures reflect in
part the thinking of Dr. Donald McGavran. In his book *Understanding Church Growth,* McGavran has a chapter which he has
entitled "The Social Structure and Growth of the Church." In
this chapter, McGavran lets us know clearly that his major
concern about the social structures is not whether these are
bad or good, but rather how they contribute to the growth of
the Church. McGavran suggests that the *"great obstacles to
conversion are social and not theological."* (1970:191) In
the same work, but in Chapter 11, which he has entitled "Without Crossing Barriers," he concludes that *"...men like to become Christians without crossing racial, linguistic or class
barriers."* Also McGavran adds:

"It takes no great acumen to see that when marked differences of colour, stature, income, cleanliness and education are present, men understand the Gospel better when
it is expounded by their own kind of people. They prefer
to join Churches whose members look, talk, and act like
themselves."   (1970:198)

For McGavran as well as for Wagner, the proclamation of the
Gospel, which includes the judgement of the social structures
in which one lives, does not appear to have major importance.
Whether the social structures are bad or good is a very fascinating theme, it is worthy of being discussed, but one on
which the Gospel and the growth of the Church have very little
to say. What is important, or what is most important, is
whether a given social structure is causing numerical growth
in the Church. Whether this is a good or bad or an unjust
structure, even though it could be discussed at the secondary
level, it does not have the most priority.

The above is not to say that McGavran does not recognise
in social action a very legitimate activity of the Christian.
However, this activity must be subordinated to evangelism,
which is understood in terms of the reconciliation of man with
God and the numberical growth of the Church:

"A multitude of excellent enterprises lie around us. So
great is the number and so urgent the calls, that Christians
can easily lose their way among them, seeing them all equally as Mission. But in doing the good, they can fail to do
the best. In winning the preliminaries, they can lose the
main game."   (1970:32)

McGavran concludes:

"A chief and irreplaceable purpose of mission is church
growth. Service is good, but it must never be substi-
tuted for finding."   (op.cit.)

From this, we deduce that McGavran tends to dicotomise and
prioritise the evangelization against social action. In a
similar fashion, he appears to understand the mission of the
Church exclusively as procuring numerical growth of persons
who are getting reconciled with God.

From my point of view, this approaches a "neutral attitude"
towards social structure, which gives no priority to the evils
of social relationships. It is, in fact, influenced by the
functionalist and relativist approach to social structure.
Both Wagner and McGavran are influenced greatly by this anthropological school of thought. This, in my opinion, reflects a
non-critical attitude of the premises upon which the social
sciences have been elaborated. Also, this attitude reflects
a tendency in the Western world to dicotomise the material and
spiritual dimensions of reality, as well as to make priorities
of the spiritual over the material, rather than integrating
them and looking at them holistically.

Since I wrote the above paragraphs, I have come across the
latest book of Peter Wagner *Church Growth and the Whole Gospel*.
This book is put forth as a response to current criticism of
the Church Growth Movement and supposedly presents a break-
through "position paper" on the relation of contemporary social ministries to Church Growth teaching. There are some
initial comments on this book that I would like to point out:

Wagner himself recognises an uncritical approach regarding
social structures, justice and social action by the Church
Growth Movement when he says:

"...evangelicals during most of the twentieth century chose
to concentrate largely on soul saving. Wes Michaelson is
correct in his observation that the evangelical heritage
has been 'dominant individualism,' with its great emphasis
on 'converting,' while assigning a peripheral status to
'questions of discipleship, justice and the shape of the
church.' The Church Growth Movement, firmly located in
the evangelical camp, uncritically, and somewhat innocent-
ly, participated in this ethos."   (1981:3)

Wagner very forcefully and clearly tries to argue that although the above is a thing of the past, thanks to the Movement's critics, Church Growth is mending some of its deficiencies regarding the cultural mandate. Over and over, Wagner
insists that "neither the cultural nor evangelistic mandate
is optional for men and women who belong to the community of
the King and for whom Jesus is Lord." This new view of Wagner
may be the "change of mind" that Wagner says he has undergone
(1981:xii).

Wagner also points out that although in the past he confined Mission to the evangelistic mandate, now he accepts
that Mission includes both the cultural and evangelistic mandate (1981:91). He points out, however, that McGavran continues to confine Mission only to the Evangelistic mandate
(p.106).

There appears to be an obvious modification of position on
certain issues in Wagner's thinking that one cannot deny. For
example, his view of Wholistic Mission is one that includes
both the Evangelistic and Cultural mandates. On this basis,
I would have to soften my view of Wagner's position on social
ministries (to use his term) that I drew up in part on the
basis of his book *Look Out the Pentecostals Are Coming* and
other works.

From my perspective, however, much of Wagner's efforts at
persuading his critics that the Church Growth Movement is really serious about the cultural mandate fall down when he forcefully continues to insist on the priority of the Evangelistic
mandate. Wagner pleads that "...the evangelistic and cultural
mandates can be differentiated one from another, but they must
not be polarized...." However, the dichotomizing between the
two is evident in Wagner's thinking. This further becomes
clear when he makes his distinction between social service and
social action, and at the same time affirms his preference for
social service against social action, since social service and
not social action contributes to Church Growth (p.37).

Wagner defines social service as

"the kind of social ministry geared to meet the needs of
individuals and groups of persons in a direct immediate way.
If a famine comes, social service will provide food for
starving people...social action is the kind of social ministry geared toward changing social structures...by definition, involves socio-political change."   (p.36)

I would like to suggest that this tendency to approach social structure "statically" is not only a reflexion of their
particular theological reading of Scriptures, but also a reflexion of what Costas has called an "anthropological- functionalist syndrome" (Costas 1971:15).

As I have pointed out before, there is in functionalism an
inbuilt tendency to see societies as orderly mechanisms in
state of equilibrium. Although Wagner argues that "Church
Growth Theory recognises and promotes culture change" (1981:
155), on closer examination one observes that this is true at
best so long as change is slow and religious ideologies
change:

"The Church Growth Movement which leans toward the functionalist camp advocates minimal cultural change and concentrates mostly on religious change." (1981:155)

This influence is also manifested in the lack of church
growth studies that give adequate accounting of the socio-
economic dimensions of a people. The emphasis is mainly on
the ideological variables. Furthermore, the homogeneous unit
principle is also a reflexion of the functionalist approach
that tends to treat small, primitive cultures, societies as
homogeneous groups that are isolated from each other. In
this process, the dynamic inter-relations of the group under
study with other groups is lost sight of. The idea of "consecrated pragmatism" (1981:69-86) also reflects functionalist
ideology.

Wagner himself recognises that the Church Growth Movement
has been greatly influenced by cultural anthropology, which
in turn has been greatly influenced by functionalism:

"Cultural anthropology has been the social science most
influential on the Church Growth Movement, particularly
as it has touched the field of Missiology, it has brought
an orientation toward the anthropological school of thought
called functionalist." (1982:153)

The practical outworkings of the functionalist bias of
Wagner is the support of the existing social structures of
society; this fact is particularly clear when he argues, as I
pointed out before, that social service (feeding the hungry)
is preferable over social action (changing social structures).
Thus, he is reflecting unconsciously his functionalist bias
for the preservation of the status quo.

It would be unfair to say the Church Growth Movement is
only functionalist-orientated. Wagner is right in pointing
out that:

"besides functionalism, they are drawing on ethnohistory,
cognitive anthropology, symbolic anthropology and other
methodologies "   (p.163, note 18).

However, it is not too much to say that there is a functionalist priority in the methodology of the social sciences
of the Movement.

Conflictive Approach[14]

While functionalists tend to see equilibrium in cultural
systems, conflict theories see structural change everywhere.
These theories constitute the legacy of Karl Marx. Dahrendorf
points out that:

"For Marx, society is not primarily a smoothly functioning
order of the form of a social organism, a social system, or
a static social fabric. Its dominant characteristic is,
rather, the continuous change of not only its elements, but
its very structural form. This change in turn bears witness to the presence of conflicts as an essential feature
of every society. Conflicts are not random; they are a
systematic product of the structure of society itself. According to this image, there is no order except in the
regularity of change." (Appelbaum 1970:82)

For Marx, change and conflict are the engines of history and
civilization - "the history of all societies up to the present
is the history of class struggles" (loc.cit.). For Marx, the
key to understanding structure and conflict at any period lies
in the relations of production--relationships created between
persons in their production of goods from raw materials and
between workers and those who control their productive efforts.

The conflict within a given society is between the haves
and the have-nots, between groups which control the means of
production and those who labor in the modes of production.
There is thus a perpetual conflict between social classes--
one trying to gain ascendancy, the other trying to maintain
it.

For Marx, there are three great historical periods which
stand in a dialectical relationship: the primitive Communism
stage, the mercantile and capitalistic stage and the developed

Communism stage. PRIMITIVE COMMUNISM is characterized by its
community labor through the participation of family members
where the interests of the community rather than individuals
are of importance. There is a lack of any kind of economic
exchange and the diverse activities of hunting, fishing and
weaving are social functions whose fruits are given and taken
freely to the community--the family. The individual work activities act as a part of the collective family or community
labor and form essentially a distributive system (Dognin
1973:2). During this stage of history, although people are
free, this freedom is incomplete, because all are chained and
enslaved to nature. Although the division of labor, classes
and class conflict are absent, the freedom is dull and pur-
poseless--not complete; this will only be realised during the
developed Communism stage (Appelbaum 1970:87).

     The second stage is a negation of the first. It is charac-
terized by the introduction of the division of labor, private
property and an exchange economy based on individual labor.
This stage constitutes the dissolution of community property
and labor. Feudalism and present-day capitalism, characterized
by individualism, are antitheses of primitive communism (Dognin 1973:3). During this period, technology develops which
exercises an increasing control over nature. But people become alienated, because the essential mechanism for this control is the division of labor, and this is alienated labor.
Division of labor and private property create relations of
domination and subjection, class formations and class struggles in ever-changing patterns (Appelbaum 1970:87).

     Modern capitalism, which is the developed form of the se-
cond stage, introduces into this exchange economy great contradictions that become unbearable. Out of these contradictions the cleavage between the proletariat and the bourgeois
becomes so great that the struggle between these two forces
issues in the classless society by virtue of the victory of
the proletariat. This--developed Communism--is characterized
by a return to Communism, but not a limited and inferior one
such as that of the first stage, rather a superior Communism
which benefits from the advances of technology and progress.
Only in this stage can people realise themselves as free beings:

     "In Communist society, where nobody has one exclusive
     sphere of activity but each can become accomplished in
     any branch...society regulates the general production and
     thus makes it possible for me to do one thing today, and
     another tomorrow, to hunt in the morning, fish in the

afternoon, rear cattle in the evening, criticize after
dinner, just as I have a mind, without ever becoming
hunter, fisherman, shepherd or critic." (ibid:89)

To Marx, contradictions, conflicts and struggles are constantly present in any society--especially modern capitalist
society. It is this conflict which moves human history from
primitive Communism to capitalism and eventually to Communism.
A Marxist analysis of any society tends to major on the existing conflicts between the proletariat and the bourgeois. So
instead of seeing stability like the functionalist, it sees
struggle and tensions which can be exploited or used to bring
about revolutionary change. A Marxist point of view will not
be satisfied with simple reforms or community development ap-
proaches--since these would only be considered distractions
from the real task of bringing about the revolution.

The Latin American Theory of Dependency[15]

The failure of the Alliance for Progress and the inability
of reformist approaches to do something significant about the
deteriorating social conditions of Latin America have contributed since the late '60s to the emergence of what has become
known in Latin America as the theory of dependency. Its ties
with Marxist thought are significant, and it may also be viewed
as a Latin American expression and application of Marxism. According to Murge:

"The Theory of Dependency is part of the theory of imperialism and colonialism, and all these theories are deriva-
tives of Marxism." (1971:4)

The dependency theory postulates that the main reasons for
the under-development of the Third World is its condition of
dependency on the developed capitalist world. The developed
world carries out its socio-economic activities in its own
interest, while the under-developed world--tied to the international capitalist system through a long historical process
of interactions with it--follows along, passive and powerless.
The "metropolis," the center of power in the developed world,
has a position of dominance over the "periphery," the under-
developed world. The economy of the under-developed world
depends upon and moves around the interests of the developed
world. This dependency situation is sometimes called neo-
colonialism or external colonialism. Dependency is perceived
not only in economic terms, although this is basic, but also
in its socio-cultural, political and ideological ramifications.

This analysis is also applicable to the national context
of indigenous societies. Anthropologist Varese tells us:

"In different kinds of degrees, through long historical
processes, all the ethnic minorities find themselves in
a situation of domination. They are victims of that national economic, social and cultural structure which has
been defined as internal colonialism." (1975:45)

Varese further adds that through these dynamic processes
tribal communities that were autonomous and self-contained
have been incorporated into a net in which they are in a dependent and nonsymmetrical relationship. They respond to a
pattern of conquest and colonial expansion that has taken
place through Latin America   (ibid:45-48).

From this perspective, social studies or mission approaches
which do not take seriously the dynamic complexity of the relationships between the developed and underdeveloped world are
at best faulty and at worst irrelevant and to be completely
rejected. The same goes for studies that do not take seriously the context of a nation or a region. From this perspective, communities cannot be studied as isolated units devoid
of their larger contexts and historical developments. People groups must always be studied in historical relationships
to other people groups, classes and national and international
interests.

*The Conflictive Dependentist Approach in the Mission of the
Church.*

In the "Final Document of the International Ecumenical Congress of Theology" which took place in Sao Paolo, Brazil, from
the 20th February to the 2nd March 1980, we find an example
that may be classified as a Conflictive Dependentist Approach
in the mission of the Church to social reality:

"The situation of suffering, misery and exploitation of
the great masses of people which are concentrated especially, but not exclusively, in the so-called Third World, is
so obvious as well as unjust...However, the most important
historical process of our time begins to be carried out by
these peoples...Their oppression has its roots in the colonial exploitation of which they were a victim for centuries.
Their fight for life, for their cultural and racial identity which was denied by the foreign dominator, is as ample
as the domination itself..." (p.3).

"As the popular movement develops, the fundamental question put forward is the formulation of a historical project which basically is a critique of capitalism and imperialist domination..." (p.4).

It is evident that the document, when it affirms that the oppression of the poor "has its roots in the colonialist exploitation of which they were victims for centuries" is limiting the concept of oppression almost exclusively to a social, economic and political manifestation. In the case of our Latin America this implies, according to the document, that the situation of oppression began when the Spaniards arrived in 1492.

It is true that the Bible speaks to us of a structural oppression where sin reigns. It also speaks against injustice and the exploitation of men by men (Exodus 3:8-10, Isaiah 58:3-12, Jeremiah 6:13-15). Against this kind of oppression, the Lord raises his voice of protest and denouncement (Isaiah 58:6-8). In the experience of the Exodus of the Hebrew people, we see the liberating action of God from this type of social, political oppression of Israel. The Gospel of Jesus Christ raises its voice and speaks against these manifestations of sin. It is a fact, then, that the Bible does not put to one side the social, political dimension of sin, as the document well affirms (Luke 4:16-20).16

But the Bible does not only speak about the oppression of sinful structures, it also speaks about the oppression of personal sin that all men experience. Romans 3:9,10 tells us:

"What then? Are we Jews any better off? No, not at all; for I have already charged that all men, both Jews and Greeks, are under the power of sin, as it is written: 'None is righteous, no, not one; no one understands, no one seeks for God. All have turned aside, together they have gone wrong; no one does good, not even one.'" (RSV)

The Bible indicates clearly and decisively that all men, rich and poor, oppressors and oppressed, have sinned and they need the salvation of God.

The document also affirms:

"...their oppression has its roots in the colonial exploitation of which they were a victim for centuries..."

The implication of this affirmation, as I pointed out before, is that the oppression of Latin America began in 1492 with the arrival of the Spaniards. Although there is a lot of truth to this, it is not the whole historical truth. The exploiters of the oppressed ones in Latin America not always were, or only were, the foreigners. We have to recognise that in certain ways, the dominators of Latin America were also part of our own people in Indo-America. Before the arrival of the Spaniards, there were empires like the Incas, the Aztecs, etc. that participated in dominating actions of conquest of other peoples that would have preferred to maintain their autonomy. Examples of this are the Chances and the Huancas in Central Peru, and many others who, after an initial resistance, had to accept the Inca domination.

We also find evidences of this resistance against Inca domination by certain sectors of our indigenous population in the Aymara and Araucana resistance. Although the Aymaras were conquered by the Incas, they developed a persistent resistance that has maintained them linguistically and culturally strong even until today. The Araucanos of Chile were never conquered by the Incas; they resisted such a conquest. Similarly, the Huancas of the central highlands of Peru, as soon as the opportunity was presented for them to enter into an alliance with the Spaniards in order to rid themselves of the Inca domination, they did it. The alliance of the Huanca people and the Spaniards became one of the factors that contributed to the defeat of the Incas (Waldemas Espinoza Zoriano 1981).

The manifestation of sin in the form of exploitation and colonization was not only limited to the arrival of the Spaniards or to our contemporary world. It has been present since the fall of man, in all times and in all places, and it has been obvious in all peoples. This is the way it is, because the basic problem of man is his disobedience and rebellion against God, and this has its manifestations in personal and structural dimensions. For this reason, all men need personal liberation from sin. Similarly, all the social structures also need to be redeemed from their sinful roots.

The manifestation of sin is not only present in the capitalist systems, but we also find it in the socialist systems as we know them today. We cannot close our eyes to the experience of Czechoslovakia, Poland or Afghanistan. In the same way, we cannot close our eyes before the dictatorial tyrancy of some of our dictators in Latin America. The monopoly of the structural manifestation of sin is not only limited to the capitalist system, but it is also present in all human systems. All social structures need liberation from sin through Jesus Christ. It is here where I notice a gap/silence in the document which we are discussing. The document only condemns capitalism but does not do the same with other systems and social structures.

I think it is time that we began to evaluate more critically the different theoretical and methodological approaches that we use in the study of social reality. The Dependency Theory is one of several approaches that help us to see the macro processes of our social context at a national level as well as an international one, but it has its limitations. The Dependency Theory is one of the windows, very important of course, that help us to have more light, but it is not the only one.

In order to illustrate what I want to say, let us take for example the categories of oppressed/oppressor. These categories do not do full justice to the complexity of social reality. One is oppressor or oppressed from a certain frame of reference. For some peasants of the Peruvian jungles, their oppressors are not only the great trans-national Companies that are exploiting their lands and their resources, but also certain other peasants from the Peruvian highlands that, because of land scarcity, have to migrate to the jungle in order to find new ways of livelihood. In this process, they are taking away the land of the jungle peasants, and they are pushing them away from land where they have lived for hundreds and thousands of years. Now, the Dependency Approach probably would put both groups under the category of oppressed and while this is true at a certain level of analysis, it does not give light on the micro-processes of the inter-personal relationships that are taking place between the peasants themselves and how they perceive each other as either oppressed or oppressors. This is only an instance of the complex processes of the social relationships and differentiations that are present within different groups, particularly within the so-called "oppressed" and "oppressors." The complexity of the social processes is not so simple as the Dependentists seem to indicate. There is much more behind the scenes.

On the other hand, all men have the potential of being oppressors. The oppressed can very easily, once they are in power, become the oppressors, not only of their ex-oppressors but also of the people that they are supposed to represent. This possibility is always present because of the fact that sin transcends social structures. It is people that build

social structures and people that sin, and therefore it is
crucial that there should be transformation not only of the
structures but also of the persons. It is here where I see
the challenge and the radicality of the Gospel of our Lord
Jesus Christ.

Although from a Christian perspective, we do not share the
historical vision of Marxism that expects the establishment
of a classless and just society by human means alone, nonthe-
less, we should be open to the contributions and critique that
Marxism makes of our contemporary world.

One of the contributions of the conflictive tradition to
development in my view is that it has sensitized and alerted
us to the fact that there are active dynamic contradictory
forces at work in the world bringing about a kind of development that is leading mankind to its final doom. For Christians, the power of sin and the activity of Satan are behind
these conflicts and are trying to lead us to a kind of development that is leading mankind to hell. This kind of development that God wants for man, for society, for creation, which
ultimately will free all those who have come to know, understand and accept the Gospel of our Lord Jesus Christ.

TOWARDS A HOLISTIC VIEW OF SOCIO-CULTURAL CHANGE

3.1 *Socio-Cultural Change*

We may define change as any modification of the ideological,
sociological,techno-economical and ecological dimensions of a
people, due to internal and/or external factors that are acting dynamically over them in time. From this we deduce that,
for example, conversion to Christianity of a person, a family
or a people would be a change that begins at the ideological
level. The introduction of new crops such as rice and rice
mechanical hullers, where they did not exist before, is change
that begins at the technological level, etc. etc. It is assumed that a change introduced in any one of the above mentioned dimensions is bound to have an effect upon the others.

I must insist that all cultures are changing, some at a
faster rate than others. There is no society that is static.
We need to be aware of this, particularly in our contemporary
world that is undergoing swift radical changes particularly
in the techno-economical, as well as at the socio-ideological,
dimensions of culture. Furthermore, we should not forget
that we live in a "Global Village" where the dealings and

interests of the super-powers oftentimes adversely affect
the lives and future of the majority of peoples of the world.
(18)

    Culture and socio-cultural phenomena need to be studied
in holistic, dynamic and historical perspectives, not only as
isolated homogeneous units that appear to be in a state of
smooth functioning equilibrium. Cultures, although they tend
to seek order, regularity and equilibrium, are also ridden
with contradictions and conflicts that need to be resolved.
Any development project must aim at the just resolution of
these conflicts and contradictions. Any Christian program of
socio-cultural change should aim not only at resolving the
symptoms of the contradictions,but must also aim at resolving
the deep causes of these conflicts and contradictions--that
is, it must seek to address itself to the integral liberation
of man, families and peoples within the unique socio-cultural
context in which they live.

    One of the problems that is often seen in development pro-
grams is Western ethnocentrism. This is usually manifested
by the tendency of many development programs to themselves
define problems and needs and to impose Western solutions.
Often this ethnocentrism is due in part to ignorance of the
culture of the people and an inability to see the potential
of autochthonous solutions, or of at least a combination of
outside techniques and local ones. It is often ignored that
non-Western societies have a long tradition of technology,
know-how and other assets that could be explored and used to
solve modern problems more adequately. As a result, ancient
agricultural techniques, medicinal traditions, building patterns, etc. are often ignored in community development projects because it is believed that modern Western techniques
are more effective--but often this is not the case.

    Although in our contemporary world there is less talk
about developmental change along the lines of the 19th Century
evolutionists, we still divide the world in terms of developed
or underdeveloped countries, using mainly the techno-economic
criteria. When we talk about the developed world, we are
talking mainly on the basis of industrial and technological
superiority or advancement, which the developed countries do
possess in contrast with the supposed lack of it in the underdeveloped world. Again, here is where a holistic and contextual cultural-social anthropology can help us to amplify
the concept of development and social change. It is not only
one aspect that should be considered when we talk about development; there are other very important aspects that are,

and need, to be considered in evaluating social change aspects
of ideology, world view, religion, social institutions, personal relationships, organizational forms, ecological, factors,
and even the historical testimony of a people. All these aspects need to be incorporated into any talk and action for
socio-cultural change. In other words, we need to see social change in its holistic dimension and not only in its
techno-economic dimension. In this sense, the rise of cultural relativism is a welcome movement in that it helps us
free Western societies from thinking that just because they
possess industrialized technology, they may be prone to think
of themselves as superior to others, as it usually happens.
But on the other hand, we have to be careful not to embrace
functionalism and cultural relativism, and on this basis
condone the status quo which often is characterized by unjust
sinful and very inhuman social conditions. We should learn
from the 19th Century view of development that we should not
impose upon other peoples our own view of what development is.
We should be open and realize that all socio-cultural change
may not take the same route as Western development. Furthermore it is preferable that the kind and direction of change
be determined by the active participation of the people affected by it, under the direction of the Holy Spirit, and the
judgment of Scripture.

The Word of God, the Person and Society

When one studies the Biblical text, one cannot help noticing
and coming to the conclusion that the Bible has an opinion, not
only about men but also about the social structures and relationships of men. As we have said before, the Bible clearly
affirms that all men, without exception, have sinned and have
rebelled against God. Everyone is guilty and is under the
judgment of God. All men need the salvation of God in Christ
Jesus. The call to repentance and to a new life, in the experience of the Kingdom of God, is clearly directed to all men.
And in the same way as sin entered through Adam, salvation is
possible through Jesus Christ. The sinful solidarity of the
human race in Adam has its counterpart in the salvation that
we find in Jesus Christ.

The consequences of sin are not only manifested and made
real at the personal level, but also at the socio-cultural
level. Man, who is a sinner, builds and creates imperfect and
sinful social structures. Even though not everything that man
creates is bad (there is a lot of beauty in it), there is much
that is imperfect and that is demonic, and this requires the
liberation and transformation that only the Gospel of the

Kingdom of God can provide (Willowbank Report 1978). Human
societies and their sinful structures are also under the judgement of God. In the words of Orlando Costas:

> "...sin is not only personal but it is structural. It is
> structural in the sense that it responds to the logic be-
> hind collective behavior (Alves). Society is not the sum
> total of its members; it constitutes a very complex net-
> work of interpersonal, cultural and institutional rela-
> tionships."   (CLADE II 1980:275)

In the same manner that the Bible integrates the personal
and the collective, it does not dicotomise the material from
the non-material supernatural. The Bible presents to us an
integrated dimension of the world and of men. This we see
clearly in the Old Testament as well as in the approach of our
Lord Jesus Christ. In the Old Testament, the liberation of
the Hebrews from Egypt was not only a socio-political liberation, but also a spiritual liberation. The Hebrews were liberated physically it is true, but they were also liberated
spiritually. The physical oppression of the Hebrews had affected their relationship with God. Perhaps many of them did
not see an end to their situation and, therefore, perhaps many
had lost their confidence and trust in God. It is a fact that
many of them were complaining and groaning for their complete
liberation.

In the ministry of our Lord Jesus, we observe that He did
not dicotomise the spiritual from the material. When our Lord
Jesus Christ brings a man to Himself, He does it through both
dimensions. For some, he cures them from their physical in-
firmity, for others he forgives their sins, and in other cases,
he does both (Luke 5:17-26). The Bible, then, presents to us
a complete and total vision of the socio-cultural reality
which integrates the physical and the spiritual dimensions of
man. In the mission of the Church, we cannot do any less. In
this sense, we agree with Costas when he affirms:

> "The basic missionological question that confronts the
> Church is not whether its mission should be perceived as
> vertical or horizontal or both, nor whether it should be
> seen as spiritual or personal or material or social...but
> whether we can recover its totality and efficacy, whether
> we can perceive it as a whole and live its global objec-
> tives."   (1979: pp xii-xiii)

Objectivity in the Study of the Socio-Cultural Phenomena.

One of the basic principles of the social sciences in the Western world is its obsession with objectivity. This is understood as an effort to understand, describe and analyse a given social phenomena or society without making value judgements, without judging whatever is studied as good or evil, superior or inferior, etc. etc. This conceptualization is closely related to the relativity of the socio-anthropological phenomena. Therefore, with this outlook, a social phenomena, a socio-cultural reality, must be understood within its own frame of reference and not judged in relation to other realities. The academic effort of the universities in the Western world and the functionalist approaches to society nourish themselves from this academic and research tradition.

This orientation of the social sciences often results,in a good number of cases, in the divorce of the researcher or scientist from his own socio-political praxis. The researcher, in his effort to be objective, does not want to commit himself to the people that he studies or the people with whom he lives. He usually adopts a position of neutrality, especially in relationship to the socio-political changes that are occurring. Fals Borda refers to this attitude in the following way:

"The objectivity of the social scientists in the developed countries consists essentially in 'not having any commitments with the social order that is being transformed. Thus it runs the risk of becoming a mere intellectual sub-product of the factors that are stopping the social historical change.' (Pinto 1963:15) This implies the belief in a dynamic and relative reality of social change, but in any event, it also recognises independent qualities from the will of the observer. Objectivity of the problems of change and development, under these conditions, is that which directs, describes and explains painful truths that may go against created interests or that reveal the ideological biases of given groups." (1968:121)

From the approach of a conflictavist dimension, objectivity is understood from a different perspective. This is an objectivity which is understood within the framework of commitment and struggle in the social transformation of society. The Peruvian ideologist, José Carlos Mariátegui refers to this commitment in a very eloquent manner in the following paragraph:

"Once again I repeat that I am not an impartial or objective critic. My judgments are nourished by my ideals, by my

feelings, by my passions. I have a very clear and energetic
ambition: that is to witness and contribute to the creation
of Peruvian socialism. I am as far away as possible from
the professorial technique and the university spirit."
(Mariátegui 1928 en *7 Ensayos de Interpretación de la Realidad Peruana* 10 ed. 1965 Biblioteca Amauta)

For Mariátegui, to make value judgements and to commit oneself in the transformation of the social order which is studied,
is very legitimate and imperative in any approach to social
reality. Value judgements about Peru are nourished by the
socialist vision that Mariategui assumes.

According to the Colombian sociologist, Fals Borda, it is
possible to be committed to social change without necessarily
losing objectivity. Fals Borda argues that particularly for
the social scientists of the Third World, it is crucial that
they be committed to the social context in which they live.
Fals Borda suggests:

"The conflictive and dramatic reality of the social problems of our world today constitute a challenge for social
scientists." (ibid p.125)

Fals Borda also concludes that:

"...the non-neutral authors can be very disciplined and very
objective. Not to be neutral does not imply to lose objectivity in the analysis." (ibid. p.124)

Christians cannot be objective either, in the neutral sense
of the word. They have a commitment which is very acute and
clear, not with the relativities of the sociological approaches,
but with our Lord Jesus Christ and with the Lord of History.
Christians cannot only describe and analyse socio-anthropologi-
cally the social phenomena before them, but they must commit
themselves, with their Lord, to the transformation of persons
as well as social structures that are unjust and anti-Christian.
I would like to paraphrase Mariategui from a Christian perspective, saying that as Christians:

"Our judgements are nourished by our commitment and loyalty
to our Lord Jesus Christ and to His Holy Word within the
context in which He has placed us. This commitment is the
engine which nourishese our ideals, our sentiments, our
passions. We have a clear and energetic ambition: that of
witnessing the expansion and establishment of the Kingdom
of God on this earth. Not by the works of men alone, but
through the decisive intervention of God." May it be so!

The above means that the Christian Church and its corresponding institutions must work and minister, having an integral
Biblical perspective of man in their actions and visions.
That is to say that human beings, the family, the community,
must be redeemed through Jesus Christ with and within the so-
cial-economic, historic and ecologic matrix of which they are
part.

Holistic development implies that one is not only content
with higher crop yields, economic growth, or changing the unjust structures of society, but one also works and ministers
with as much energy and enthusiasm for the salvation of people's lives, so that they become part of the people of God and
His Kingdom.

Within Christian circles, we like to talk about Christian
growth, about Christian maturing and discipleship. We like to
talk about becoming more and more "developing" to the image of
Christ. This view and talk about Christian growth is usually
restricted to the individual and seldom is applied to the family or to society. Here again, the Western individualistic
bias must be questioned.

The subject of culture and development forces us to think
through the meaning of growth and advancement at the group
level and not just at the individual level. What is the meaning of development within a cultural context? within a family
context? within a group context? are the questions we need to
ask.

In talking about development, we need to ask what God wants
men, society, and creation to become; we need to emphasize the
fact that God is interested in development that includes the
whole creation and that includes the hope that, although at
this point in time we may not see yet the full conclusion of
that development, we can experience today signs of the full
development that awaits us. Development should be applied not
only to our own renewal of our own individual minds, individual
behavior, or individual transformation, but it also should be
applied to the transformation, to the renewal, to the growth
of our families, of our society, to the advancement of the
world-- but not an advancement or growth that uses the criteria
of men to decide what is the right kind of development, but a
criteria that comes from God's Word which helps us to be holistic and integral in our approach to development. When we talk
about development from a Christian perspective, we need to apply the whole counsel of God to the whole of God's creation.

That is, we need to address development at an ideological level, at the world-view level, at the value-system level, at the social institutions of our societies, at the structures of our societies, at the economic and technical institutions of our societies. We need to think of development as it applies to the ecology, to the physical environment in which the world lives. This includes the exploitation of the environment. It includes the arms race. It includes the rejection of wars, the rejection of unjust relations among human beings, unjust economic and social relationships not only within a nation but among so call "developed" and "underdeveloped" nations. It includes the proclamation of God's victory over satanic forces at work against God's full development for mankind. Jesus Christ must be the paradigm of Biblical development. The Kingdom of God and the meaning of that Kingdom must also be a very intimate part of talking about development in Christian missions. We must see, and we must taste and experience the Kingdom of God, right now at this present moment. At the same time, we must be aware of the full, complete development of what God wants for His people, for this will not take place until He in His sovereign way intervenes to bring about the full consummation of His Kingdom, the full consummation of development.

In conclusion, I would like to suggest that a holistic dynamic view of God's creation and cultures, which accounts for a people's ideology, sociology, techno-economics, history and ecology, must be the framework in which a holistic development project takes place. This implies that we see God's creation, culture and development integrally related and giving its due attention to the material, spiritual, social, personal, etc. needs of man. From this perspective, we can agree with Ron Sider's definition of development as a:

"movement towards that freedom and wholeness in a just community which persons will enjoy when our Lord returns to bring the Kingdom in its fullness."   (17)

NOTES

1. *Culture: A Critical Review of Concepts and Definitions* by
   A. Kroeber and Kluckhon, New York, 1952.

2. Lausanne Occasional Papers No. 2 - The Willowbank Report
   on *Gospel and Culture*

3. *Man and His Works* by Herskovitz.
   This is a translation from the Spanish version of Herskovitz's work. (I am trying to find a copy of the English
   version.)

4. See also Ruben (Tito) Paredes: *Hacia Una Misiologiá Latin-
   americana: Modelos Socio-Antropológicos en el Estudio de
   la Realidad Socio-cultural y Misional de los Pueblos y de
   la Iglesia*; PUSEL, Lima, Peru; 1981

5. In the past, there has been a tendency, particularly within
   the functionalist approach to anthropology, to ignore or
   at least not pay enough attention to the historical past
   of peoples under study. Regarding this, Anthropologist
   E. E. Evans-Pritchard has an enlightening essay entitled
   "Anthropology and History" from which I quote his conclusion:

   "I believe an interpretation on functionalist lines (of
   present in terms of present) and on historical lines (of
   present in terms of the past) must somehow be combined..."
   Social Anthropology and Other Essays 1962:187-188

6. Durkheim, in his *Elementary Forms of the Religions Life*,
   New York, Collier Books, 1961, gives us a sociological ex-
   planation of the religious beliefs and behavior of the
   Australian aborigines.

7. I agree with anthropologist Goldschmidt when he asserts:

   "...It is necessary to appreciate the variety and character
   of the existing explanations for the divergent social systems...it is not only that each orientation should be toler-
   ant of the other or that those who seek psychological explanation should give the sociologists their due, but it
   is that each kind of explanation requires the others, that
   in order to understand a phenomenon sociologically requires
   a proper psychological orientation, and so on..." Walter
   Goldschmidt: *Man's Way: A Preface to the Understanding of
   Human Behavior*. Holt, Rinehart & Winston, New York, 1959:60

8. The publication of Darwin's *The Origin of Species* in 1959 undoubedtly represents a milestone and boost in evolutionary studies, not only for biology but for social and cultural anthropology as well. The contribution of Darwin does not lie in being the first to put forth evolutionary ideas, rather in "popularizing" them at a time when the socio-cultural climate was against evolutionism. Prior to Darwin, others in the social sciences, such as Thomas Malthies and H. Spencer, had anticipated Darwin. Darwin in turn influenced the social sciences as Herbert Spencer's later work *Principle of Sociology* (1876-1896) evidences through its many analogies of biological and social evolution. (Bee 1974:43)

9. Taylor tries to show that religion evolved out of the belief in the soul, into animism, polytheism, and finally monotheism. See E. B. Taylor's "Animism" in *Reader in Comparative Religion* by W. A. Lessa and E. Z. Vogt (Eds.), Row, Peterson & Co., New York, 1958:11-23.

10. L. H. Morgan, along with E. Taylor, are considered the classical representatives of Unilinear Evolutionism, according to which society was assumed to develop through fixed stages of development: savagery, barbarism and civilization. Under this ethnocentric conception, European and U.S.Society were at the pinnacle of progress and civilization, that societies everywhere were expected to follow in due time. See Morgan's *Ancient Society*, Meridian Books, Cleveland & N.Y., 1963.

11. Tom Sine: *Development: Its Secular and Its Uncertain Future*

12. For a discussion of these approaches that reacted against classical evolutionism and proposed alternatives, see Bee 1974:67-93 and R.H.Howie 1937:128-195.

13. This is a translation of Wagner's Spanish version *¡Cuidado! Ahi Vienen Los Pentecostales* 1973:157. Editorial Vida, Florida.

14. This section and the next one on "The Latin American Theory of Dependency" has been taken from the author's article "Different View of Socio-cultural Change...", *Missiology* Vol. IX, No. 2, April, 1981.

15. See Note 14.

16. The liberation about which this passage refers to, I un-
    derstand in its integral dimension, that is integrating
    the spiritual, economic, social and political dimensions.
    The Gospel gives us an integral liberation and does not
    divorce one from the other.

17. Regarding this, I would like to reassert what I pointed
    out in an article for *Missiology* Vol. IX, No. 2, April
    1981:190-191.

    "Dependency theory alerts us to the macrosocial pro-
    cesses affecting the international and national con-
    text. How the dominant world economic and political
    powers from West and East relate to each other and to
    the Third World is bound to have an impact upon our na-
    tions and their future. The current situation in our
    times has been shaped by the relationships of world
    powers in the past. We are part of an international
    community whose destiny is tied with ours. Missions
    cannot ignore this. How we develop mission and minis-
    try models in such a world is a challenge to our crea-
    tivity and our openness to the Spirit of God and His
    Word."

CULTURE AND PLANNED CHANGE

Purpose. The purpose of this paper is to analyze the differential value placed on change itself. Westerners give "development" high priority. If a project fails, all is lost. What are the cultural values of agencies working for socio-economic change?

Culture and Planned Change. In the U.S.,change is desirable We expect new consumer goods, new amusements, new ways to get work done better. Time is scarcer than money. With these values, we suffer from a success syndrome.

"Counting Cats in Zanzibar": Anthropological View of Culture. Anthropologists want to study culture in all its rich and confusing complexity, not just a few selected variables. And from a spectrum of different theories. they want to understand cultures in time and space, with empathy, curiosity, objectivity, and tolerance for ambiguity. They evaluate their theories based on their simplicity, their elegance, their comprehensiveness, and how well they generate significant questions and hypotheses.

"Every Man Is an Exception"; Theological Views of Culture. One possibility is that culture is in "the binding clutches of Satan" and Christ condemns culture.

Others would suggest that culture is a treasure chest of symbols, and Christ generates culture.

Then there are the creative deviants who believe Christ is in the business of transforming culture.

Culture--man's creativity within divinely-ordained structures--is blessed by God. But since culture is also involved in man's rebellion against God, we do not idolize it. Rather we balance affirmation with judgment.

How to Help a Culture Change: Culturally-Sensitive Transformation. Here are some questions we need to ask:

(1) Does the project fit with local worldview, concepts and values?
(2) Does the project fit with local social structures?
(3) Does the project fit with local economic resources?

Was Noah Literate?:   *Concluding Unscientific Postscript.*
All peoples dream. Most welcome some change. Nevertheless,
not all suffer planned social change gladly. Here are three
concerns that are common to the ethos, the world view and
the culture of people in many developing nations:

(1) Those of us involved in development need to look at
"the beam in our own eye" and the ways in which we operate
in the larger global economic/political system before we try
to change others.

(2) People resist approaches that categorize them solely
as problems.

(3) Rather than expecting success, rather than smothering
the poor with cheap cheerfulness, we may at times need to
sit in silence with them, to empathize, to share our mutual
lack of answers.

God is going to establish His sovereign rule on this
earth in His own time. He can do it without our efforts.
Yet God wills our vigorous creativity to be among His instruments for subduing the earth and manifesting His Kingdom.

MIRIAM ADENEY is a cultural anthropologist lecturing at
Seattle Pacific University and at Regent College, Vancouver,
Canada.

CULTURE AND PLANNED CHANGE

Miriam Adeney

DO WESTERNERS ONLY SUPPORT SUCCESSES?:
CULTURAL VALUES OF DEVELOPMENT AGENCIES

"Have you noticed that Westerners only support successes?"

Two Asians stood admiring a lake at an international
Christian conference. One has supervised a highly touted
indigenous socioeconomic program. Western Christian leaders
have lionized him. Publications have described his work
glowingly. But, as he looked over the lake, he mused to his
friend--who reported it to me--"Have you noticed that Westerners only support successes? I wonder, would they be interested in me if I were to fail?"

This points up one of the main issues of the interface
between culture and attempts at socioeconomic improvement--
the differential value placed on change itself. Westerners
give "development" high priority. If a project fails, all
is lost. Other peoples value change, too. Yet they balance
this with other priorities. Some value roots. Some value
the old and their heritage, as much as youth and newness.
Not all people are as eager to change at any price.

As we discuss culture and planned social change, then,
we do well to consider the cultural values of change agencies, including missions. These are the avenues through
which most people motivated by this conference will respond
to economic need in poor countries. For better or for
worse, these are the institutions purportedly organized to
channel help to such needs.

What, then, are the values represented by these agencies? Certainly their workers and project directors do not arrive on the scene value-free. This is true equally whether the workers move internationally or within their own nation. National social workers ministering to a different ethnic group--or even to a different social class--in their own country can be as imperialistic, as contemptuous of local values, and as rigid about the rightness of modernization as any Westerner. Nevertheless, because the U.S. is the place I know best and also the base for many relief and change agencies, let us consider relevant U.S. values as they affect change efforts. People from other backgrounds will do well to examine their own experiences for parallel values.

In the U.S., change is desirable. We expect new consumer goods, new amusements, new ways to get work done better. Aiming to be self-reliant, we Americans leave our birth families behind. Without extended families, we become a nation of joiners. Voluntary associations flourish. Amid this flux, our social security numbers are more important than our names.[1] Since we are inter-changeable, we think people in other cultures are. We miss precious nuances that still distinguish one role from another. Since we lack roots, we often cannot take others' roots seriously.

We admire active, assertive, ambitious achievers, self-starters.[2] We admire pragmatic problem-solving. We do not admire contemplation of the eternal mysteries. We view life in measurable terms. Intelligence can be measured. Compatability or adjustment can be measured. A girl's attractiveness can be measured on a scale of one to ten. Money is valuable not only for its intrinsic usefulness, but also because it serves to measure intangibles. Can your organization afford a word processor? Or a video cassette system? Or glossy paper in your promo magazine? If so, you must be doing something right.

From our rich and driven perspective, time is scarcer than money.[3]

So "efficiency" requires the maximum use of advanced technical devices--all aimed at saving time. And this begins to affect our attitude towards all reality. Is the task evangelism? We immediately think of money for travel, honoraria, media, printing bills, rental of facilities. Is it healing bodies? This requires money for hospitals, x-ray machines and surgical theatres,

doctors and nurses. Is the task education? We visualize
expensive buildings, equipment, and professional staff.
We quite literally lack the capacity to imagine doing
things other than this capital-intensive, technology-
intensive way.

And we bring these ideas along wherever we do the Lord's
work. Even where technology is inordinately expensive.
Even where believers are all but destitute. And even where
the most abundant resource is willing minds, willing hands.
Soon, however, it becomes apparent that local Christians
can't pick up the tab. And because they also lack the
know-how to operate the system, we end up taking over.

With these values, we suffer from a "success syndrome."
Advancement matters. Writing our annual raports, we struggle
with "gross national product neuroses."[4] Projects easily become more important than people. Should we support failures?
Of course not! What is that Asian Christian leader by the
lake thinking of?

This is not to say that other peoples don't want change.
Most people want to live beyond the age of forty-five. They
want more than half of their babies to survive. They even
want refrigerators. C.P.Snow has observed,[5]

It is all very well for us, sitting pretty, to think
that material standards of living don't matter all that
much. It is all very well for one, as a personal choice,
to reject industrialization--do a modern Walden, if you
like...But I don't respect you in the slightest if, even
passively, you try to impose the same choice on others
who are not free to choose. In fact, we know what their
choice would be. For, with singular unanimity, in any
country where they have had the chance, the poor have
walked off the land into the factories as fast as the
factories could take them.

I remember talking to my grandfather when I was a
child. He was a good specimen of a nineteenth-century
artisan. He was highly intelligent, and he had a great
deal of character. He had left school at the age of
ten, and had educated himself intensely...Yet...in fact,
he never went further than maintenance foreman in a
tramway depot. His life would seem to his grandchildren
laborious and unrewarding almost beyond belief...He was
disappointed that he had not done more--and yet, compared with *his* grandfather, he felt he had done a lot.

His grandfather must have been an agricultural labourer.
I don't so much as know his Christian name. He was one
of the "dark people,"...completely lost in the great
anonymous sludge of history...It was no fun being an
agricultural labourer in the mid-to-late eighteenth
century, in the time that we, snobs that we are, think
of only as the time of the Enlightenment and Jane
Austen.

The industrial revolution looked very different according to whether one saw it from above or below. It
looks very different today according to whether one
sees it from Chelsea or from a village in Asia. To
people like my grandfather, there was no question that
the industrial revolution was less bad than what had
gone before. The only question was how to make it
better.

Most peoples dream. Nevertheless, change may fit into
their scale of priorities somewhat differently than it does
in the scheme of a worker from an industrialized country.

"COUNTING CATS IN ZANZIBAR":
ANTHROPOLOGICAL VIEWS OF CULTURE

If we assert that change is to some extent a culturally-
specific value, what do we mean by the term "culture"?

The Blind Men and the Elephant: Description of Anthropological Theories:

In this paper we explore both anthropological and theological views of culture. We begin with anthropology. The
acolytes of culture, anthropologists, turn out to be like
the fabled blind men describing an elephant. Crudely differentiated, some emphasize the material aspects of man's
experience, while others focus on intangible mental and social patterns. "Culture," then, includes a number of variables. Depending on the theoretical framework one advocates,
certain variables will be seen to be more crucial than
others. The variables one believes to be foundational will
affect the choice of the social change approach he comes to
support.

What are the theoretical alternatives?

Evolutionists have asked: What forces of natural selection--
what variables in the struggle for survival won by those who

most effectively adapt to their environment--are operating
to develop this culture? *Ecological anthropologists* have
considered culture "an adaptive mechanism for maintaining
material relations with the other parts of man's ecosystem."[6] *Marxist anthropologists* understand social phenomena
in terms of the dialectical relations that are believed to
determine everything else. Beginning with private ownership
of the means of production, moving to class struggle, cul-.
minating in the classless society, the dialectic is seen as
materially based, directional and inevitable. Events either
serve or hinder the revolution: that is the basis for analysis. Any attempt to study them "objectively" is misguided.

Anthropology, then, must cease being a tool of the status
quo, and must start cooperating with the dialectic movement
of history. How? By selecting problems which are significant from a Marxist perspective. By researching data that
Marxist groups need. By abdicating the attempt to study man
per se, and embracing the study of men as they are molded by
their several socioeconomic contexts. By exposing our field
ties with administrators who serve the imperialistic expansion of the West. Finally, by combining theory with praxis,
by serving the revolution actively ourselves.

Against these materially-focused theories stand many
others. For *structural-functionalism,* the mainstream of
American and British anthropology, ideas, customs, and material artifacts are mutually interdependent parts of a whole
integrated system, like an organism or a machine. Social
structure is central. The question is not how a variable
adapts to the external environment so much as how it fits
and functions in the overall cultural pattern.

The *structuralism* of Claude Levi-Strauss propounds that
cultures are systems imposed on the random natural world by
the structure of the human mind. That structure is a pattern of opposed binary contrasts. *Cognitive anthropologists*
believe that systematic syntactic and semantic analysis will
give clues to what a people hold to be the constituent enti-
ties and taxonomies of the universe. Many other anthropologists assert that *idea systems* exert powerful influence.
Among them, Clifford Geertz has defined culture as a historically transmitted pattern of meanings embodied in a system of symbols which grids action.[7] He also has referred
to culture as "webs of significance" which we spin and in
which we hang suspended.

Between the naturists and the nurturists, between those
who emphasize the independent variable of the external environment and those who emphasize our response, are the
psychological anthropologists. They focus on child-raising
patterns, the cultural conditioning of the personality, and
on various areas in which the unconscious breaks through in
culturally-patterned channels, such as art or mental illness.

Emic anthropologists hold that interpretations or explanations must come from the natives themselves, in their terms.
They follow in the tradition of nineteenth century German
scholars who distinguished *Geisteswissenshaften,* sciences of
the human spirit, from *Natureswissenschaften*, sciences of
nature. Freedom is opposed to necessity. The method appropriate to *Geisteswissenschaften* is *Verstehen,* empathetic understanding, which is an aspect of anthropology's preferred
method of participant observation. Critics of the emicists
argue that we are moved by many aspects of culture of which
we are not conscious. In his research on the Tewa, for example, Ortiz found that none of his Tewa informants was
aware of the whole system of beliefs that he pieced together.[8]
However much we empathize with an informant, then, that person may not be able to articulate his culture as comprehen-
sively as we can after a systematic and somewhat more objective study.

Does Price Equal Value? Critique of Anthropological Theories.

Anthropologists who are concerned for social change argue
over these theories. In particular, which is more determinative: material environment or intangible worldview and interaction patterns? Is a local approach to community development, sensitive to values and concerned about value change,
effective? Or does this assume an unwarranted power of ideas,
rigidity of culture, and isolation of communities? Is a restructuring of national/international political and economic
structures the more effective route to community development
and culture change?

There is no one "right" theory. Different theories are
appropriate for different research questions. Different degrees of reliability are acceptable, also, depending on the
number and complexity of the variables and the amount of
philosophy as opposed to empirical data. A study on nutrition *should* be more verifiable than one on religion. Ironically, the verifiability of a study often correlates inversely
with its significance. As Thoreau noted long ago, "It is not
worthwhile to go round the world to count the cats in Zanzibar." On the other hand, some of the most worthwhile questions perennially resist easy answers.

Because nature is the independent variable, the material environment *must* be included in an explanation of culture. Idea systems may indeed be powerful: but what shapes idea systems? For example, the "meek, docile, and peaceful 'hunting and gathering' Shoshone" changed "into the horse-riding, 'fierce, warlike' Comanche"[9] almost overnight, not because of any new idea, but because of a new resource in their material environment: horses.

To date, when missionary anthropologists have given attention to material factors, we have done so in terms of a hypothetically integrated, semi-isolated, semi-static people group. We have not developed theory to encompass adequately the true range of variables in space, variables in time, and unequal power relations impinging so strongly on a people's way of life that, for example, the hiring policies of Exxon may affect their culture more than their beliefs about ancestors. For anthropoligists sensitive to these variables, the theoretical alternative employed has been Marxist. Certainly Marx is our forerunner in conflict theory. After Marx, no thinking person can look at the world in the same way. In particular, Marx formulated keen insights into the *origins* of conflict in a capitalist society. In the *development* of conflict, however, several of Marx's propositions appear to be false descriptions of what happens in the real world. (For interested readers, we elaborate this more fully in the accompanying footnote.)[10]

While material factors are necessary in an explanation of culture, they do not appear to be sufficient. Studies in ethnicity suggest that, when people share a distinctive history, even when there is no material advantage to be gained, they often will continue to affirm a distinct ethnic label for themselves because it undergirds code coherence, satisfying social structures, and a sense of primordial identity. Certainly, as some cultural materialists have pointed out, peoples are not imprisoned by their worldviews; they are well able to juggle alternatives. On the other hand, as the cultural materialists neglect to mention, there is a dearness to traditions. The ability to choose does not mean that the materially advantageous always will be chosen. Price does not always equal value.

Given all these contrasting approaches to culture, is there any underlying common ground? Between themselves, anthropologists may fight tooth and nail for their favorite theories. But they will unite around a number of common values which change agents, too, will do well to cultivate. Anthropoligists

want to be holistic. They want to study real behavior, not
just ideals. Corporate groups, not just individuals. Culture in all its rich and confusing complexity, not just a few
selected variables. And cultures throughout space and time.
Empathy, curiosity, objectivity, and tolerance for ambiguity
are some of the attitudes anthropologists cultivate. Within
this context, they evaluate theories for their simplicity,
their elegance, their comprehensiveness, and for how well
they generate significant questions and hypotheses.

"EVERY MAN IS AN EXCEPTION":
THEOLOGICAL VIEWS OF CULTURE

"The Binding Clutches of Satan": Christ Condemns Culture

Like anthropologists, theologians, too,have viewed culture
variously. "India is the tragic story of a vast nation left
for centuries to the binding clutches of Satan..." So begins
an article in a current magazine. Some Christians throughout
history have taken the position that Christ is at odds with
culture. God may well have ordained culture. But customs
that glorify God are not the reality that we observe around
us. Instead of loveliness, harmonious creativity, and admir-
able authority, we see fragmentation, generation gaps, alienation, lust, hate, corruption, selfishness, injustice, laziness, disorder, and violence cultivated by our culture. No
part remains pure. Science tends to serve militarism or he-
donism, ignoring morals. Modern art often becomes worship
without God. Mass media is full of verbal prostitutes. Ad-
vertisers exploit sex. Businessmen pull shady deals whenever they can. Politicians fill their own pockets with the
people's money. Teachers don't bother about scholarship after a few years in the profession. Workers do shoddy work.
Husbands deceive their wives. Wives tell their husbands
just what they think will promote their own interests. Parents dominate their children. Children ignore their parents
as persons.

Because man has rebelled against God, because he has cut
himself off from relationship with God, the culture he produces reeks with evil. As a rebel, man rejects the grace of
God which empowers him to live within the structures God has
set up for beautiful living. Then, because he cannot fit
into God's structures without God's grace, man rejects God's
structures and laws too. He fills this vacuum with an idol
of his own choosing. He worships close family ties, or gross
national product, or pleasure, or tradition, or proletarian
rule, or some other ideal. The rest of his culture is

integrated around such inadequate goals. As a result, every
culture is off-kilter, and the whole world lies in wickedness.

The biblical picture is not the noble proletarian enslaved
by evil macrostructural forces. We may indeed be captives.
But we love our captors if they allow us to ally with them.
We may be deprived. But how quick we are to deprive others,
given the chance. This is a classic Christian position. In
affirming it, we need not deny that institutionalized oppression and inequality of opportunity spiral effects far beyond
conscious, malicious planning. We need not deny that such
inequities must be fought at the structural, rather than personal level. On the other hand, when the young intelligent-
sia in developing nations increasingly are believing that
evil stems from environments and structures, we do well to
spell out the implications of this classic Christian doctrine of man: namely, that power encounters are needed all
up and down the continuum, not only in structures but also
in individuals. In fact, since Freud, the secular world,
too, has become more open about acknowledging the aggressive,
destructive drive within individuals.

At the cultural level, then, sin permeates all activities
to some extent. Therefore the Lord tells us not to love the
world. It is too easy for the cares of this world, and the
deceitfulness of riches, and the lusts for various things to
choke the Word in our lives and make us unfruitful. We need,
consequently, to take heed to ourselves lest at any time we
be overcharged with the concerns of this life. We dare not
think that if we are rich and have lots of goods, we don't
need anything--when spiritually we are wretched and miserable
and poor and naked. What profit is it if we gain the world
and lose our souls? The Lord advises us to set our affec-
tions on things above, not on the things of this world. Denying worldly lusts, we are to live soberly, righteously, and
godly in this present world.

We can stand against the world because Jesus Christ has
freed us from slavery to it. Once we were dead in sin,
trapped in personal selfishness and the corporate sins of
our culture. But when Jesus went to the cross, He conquered
and judged the prince of this world, the demonic power affecting us. He freed us, and raised us to a new life. Now the
world is crucified to us, and we to the world. We have received the Spirit of God in place of the spirit of the world.
Our new position is supernatural. So we are called to be
different. We are not to be conformed to this world any
longer, but rather to be transformed through the renewing of

our minds. In fact, our Christian life should be a continual,
hourly conflict with our old selves and our environment. The
fight never ends, because when we win on one level there are
more subtle enemies to fight--pride, laziness, unwillingness
to be involved, fear, worry, selfishness. Therefore, as
God's soldiers, we should not get entangled with the things
of this life, but should enter the battle ready to endure
the tribulations to be heaped on us by the world, and eager
to overcome the world.

The elements of our culture don't come from our Father,
but from man. They are going to disintegrate and pass away.
So we are not to pin our hopes and joys to them. We are to
keep ourselves from idols of any kind. For example,[11]

> "Christian women should not get too caught up in the
> latest fashions, but instead should cultivate the adorn-
> ment of a meek and quiet spirit, which is very precious
> to God. We are not to agitate for a utopian national
> democracy, but to nurture one another for life together
> in the Kingdom of Christ. We are not to become enamoured
> with worldy philosophy, since a foolish man in Christ
> is, in an important sense, wiser than a genious without
> Him. We are not to love money. We are not to worry
> about how we're going to meet our expenses. We are
> not to become slaves to industrious activity. We are
> not to worship aesthetic experiences, but should be
> able to stand spiritually with Paul on the Areopagus,
> looking out over one of the greatest artistic achieve-
> ments of all human culture--the Acropolis, the Parthe-
> non, the 'Elgin Marbles,' the temple of the Wingless
> Victory, the Propylaea, the Erectheum, and the huge
> statue of Athena Promachos--and shout that what is
> really worth knowing is Jesus Christ."

Sin permeates culture. This is a basic Christian belief.
On these grounds, some have withdrawn from established cultural institutions. Early Jewish and Roman Christians were
persecuted. For them, the affirmation of Sojourners' Jim
Wallis rang true: "When the church dares to be the church,
it becomes self-consciously marginal to the mainstream culture."[12] By the second century, Tertullian was thundering,
"What has Jerusalem to do with Athens?" and encouraging
Christians to withdraw from public life where possible, because it[13]

...required a mode of life contrary to the spirit and the
law of Christ..."We have no pressing inducement to take

part in your public meetings; nor is there aught more
entirely foreign to us than affairs of state"...Trade
...is scarcely "adapted for a servant of God," for
apart from covetousness, which is a species of idolatry,
there is no real motive for acquiring...It is impossible
to be a professor of literature without commending and
affirming "the praises of idols interspersed therein."

Since the second century, there has been a conviction that
Christians constitute a "third race," beside Jews and Gentiles. Some regularly have dropped out to form model communities. Monasteries are one example. Among their many
contributions, "the Benedictine rule...probably helped to
give dignity to labour, including manual labour in the
fields...In the midst of barbarism, the monasteries were
examples of the skillful management of the soil."[14] Some
renewed groups stayed within established churches, like
Nicholas Ferrar's "Little Gidding," which served as a disciplined house of prayer, school, dispensary, and infirmary
during the 1600's. Other groups, like the Waldenses (1160?-),
the Hussites (1418-), the Unity of Brethren (1467-), the
Swiss Brethren (1525-), the Hutterites (1418-), and the Men-
nonites (1539-), established autonomous church/communities.
In the 1800's--the "great century" for foreign mission society brotherhoods--more than 200 utopian communities sprouted
in the U.S. Some were Christian. And what more shall we
say of Christian *ashrams* and *sashrams* and *comunidades*?[15]

"In history these Christian withdrawals from and rejec-
tions of the institutions of society have been of very
great importance to both church and culture. They have
maintained the distinction between Christ and Caesar,
between revelation and reason, between God's will and
man's. They have led to reformations in both church
and world, though this was never their intention. Hence
men and movements of this sort are often celebrated for
their heroic roles in the history of a culture which
they rejected."

Treasure Chests of Symbols: Christ Generates Culture.

On the other hand, still other Christians would argue that,
far from being demonic, culture is God's gift. God has endowed people everywhere with his image, the image of a Creator, with the creativity that develops cultures. He has commissioned us with the cultural mandate (Gen.1:28). Cultures
are not, then, amoral rules holding Hobbesian man in check,

but rather they are treasure chests of symbols for exuberant
expression of the image of God.

In the beginning God affirmed that it was not good for man
to be alone. Man was made to live in communities of meaning.
So God established the family, the state, work, worship, arts,
education, and even festivals. He spelled out laws which
preserved a balanced ecology, ordered social relations, provided for sanitation, protected the rights of the weak, blind,
deaf, widows, orphans, strangers, poor, and debtors, and gave
a motivation for duty by relating it to Himself.

God affirmed the physical world, out of which material
culture is developed. He delighted in the very soil and
rivers that He gave His people. It was "a land which the
Lord your God cares for. The eyes of the Lord your God are
always upon it from the beginning of the year even unto the
end of the year." Knowing the material cravings of His people,
He put them in "a good land, a land of brooks of water, of
fountains and depths that spring out of valleys and hills.
A land of wheat, and barley, and vines, and fig trees, and
pomegranates. A land of oil olive, and honey. A land, "He
told them, "where you will eat bread without scarceness, you
will not lack anything in it. A land whose stones are iron,
and out of whose hills you may dig brass (Deut.8)." God
gave man oil to make his face shine, wine to make his heart
glad, friends like iron to sharpen him, a wife like a fruitful vine, and children like arrows shot out of his bow."[16]

God taught the Hebrews, and later the Christians, that
life is abundant. "We are not to live in quiet resignation
but to press toward the goal ahead. We are to do everything
heartily, as to the Lord. Whatever our hand finds to do, we
should do it with our might."[17] God blesses wholehearted
activity.

And we are made "in God's image." What does this mean?
Theologians have suggested that it means rationality, personality, moral sensitivity, love, freedom, dominion, or
capacity for relationships. Certainly it means that we are
more than chemicals. We are more than the sum of our environmental influences. Christian theology asserts, in Kierke-
gaard's words, that "every man is an exception." Surely,
then, being in God's image also means creativity. As God is
a creator, we are made creative. When we create, we exercise
a characteristic that particularly represents God.[18]

When God made the earth, He could have finished it, but
He didn't. He left it as a raw material--to tease us,
to tantalize us, to set us thinking, and experimenting,
and risking, and adventuring. And therein we find our
supreme interest in living.

...He gave us the challenge of raw materials, not the
satisfaction of perfect, finished things.

He left the music un-sung and the dramas un-played.

He left the poetry undreamed, in order that men and
women might not become bored, but engaged in stimu-
lating, exciting, creative activities that keep them
thinking, working, experimenting, and experiencing
all the joys and durable satisfactions of achievement.

Human culture,therefore, is not wholly alien from God, but
rather is "the result of man's creative activity within Godgiven structures."[19] Many institutions,corresponding to
man's needs for work, worship, play, and love, have been
blessed explicitly by God. Indeed, God's early words to
Adam[20]

...call man to progressive growth in culture. Far from
being something in conflict with God, cultural achievements are an essential attribute of the nobility of
man as he possessed it in Paradise. Inventions and
discoveries, the sciences, and the arts, refinement
and ennobling, in short, the advance of the human mind,
are throughout the will of God. They are the taking
possession of the earth by the royal human race, the
performance of a commission.

Man has a position of authority, under God and over
the rest of creation...He is expected to find out the
potentialities of earth, air, and sea, to use nature
and its resources...In this we can see the scientific
quest fore-shadowed, whose aim is to understand and
classify the natural world. Here is the divine charter for the immense variety of human activity: agriculture, technology, industry, craft and art. These,
according to Christianity, are God's gifts for the
enrichment of man's life.

Because human culture stems from God's gifts of creativity
and common grace, peoples with little personal knowledge of
Christ may show lovely traits.[21]

...When I looked around at my neighbors in a Philippine community where I lived for several years, for example, I saw strong families. Warm hospitality. Lots of time lavished on children. Enduring loyalties. The ability to live graciously on little money. A heritage of economic freedom for women. Creativity in music. Sauces that deliciously extended a little meat to many people. A delight in sharing. Skill in the art of relaxation. Lithe, limber bodies. The ability to enjoy being with a large number of people continuously.

Since every good gift is from above and since all wisdom and knowledge come from Jesus Christ, these beautiful qualities of Philippine culture must be gifts of God. It seems that, just as our Creator delights in a vast variety of colors and smells, just as he has brought millions of unique personalities into being, so he has ordained an amazingly wide spectrum of cultures. He has programmed into man a capacity for cultural variation that enables us to explore our potential in all its complexity, to increase the richness of His world.

The early Christians accepted different cultures. When they preached to Jews, their framework was the law of Moses and the prophets. But when their audience was pagan, they dropped that emphasis and talked instead about how God provides for our physical and spiritual needs, and how God is stronger than idols. Peter learned to accept all peoples, including their food that was repulsive to him. Paul learned to be "all things to all men." Timothy was circumcised; Titus wasn't. Both were Paul's key men. The Epistles show that churches from different cultural backgrounds had different kinds of problems. So when the mother church in Jerusalem set standards, she decided not to ask new Christians in other cultures to conform to her ways, since there was no difference "between us and them" (Acts 15:9).

Because of God's gifts of His image, the cultural mandate, and common grace, there is much in the "secular" order of every culture, in traditional institutions, structures, ideologies, and world powers for which we can thank God and on which we can build. When we probe cultural patterns, then, we do so humbly, because, as some of the early physical scientists expressed it, we are "thinking God's thoughts after him."

A specific application of this positive view is in our attitude to law. Whereas some Christians have emphasized *Lex semper accusat,* the law always accuses, others have viewed the law more positively. Calvin, for example, admitted that the law accuses: it will "render us inexcusable and drive us to despair, moving us to seek grace."[22] But, he continued, the law also restrains evil. More positively, the law gives guidelines for righteous living. Even sinners may discern the utility and appropriateness of God's laws and to some degree adapt to them, though truly to keep God's laws we need the power of God's grace mediated through relationship with Jesus Christ.

In this vein, Triton comments,[23]

> We believe that Christian morals are for all men because God is the Creator and His law is given to everyone. It is not just the rule for the church. To break God's law is always injurious and God cares about the state of society even in non-Christian cultures. You do not have to be a Christian before you are told that you ought to keep the Ten Commandments. We want to say to the whole of mankind that God is the Creator; that He has graciously told us the basic moral principles; that they are always for man's good in the long run and that they should be obeyed both for that reason and also because God says so and we are His creatures. We ought to do them merely because God says so. But if not, we should do them because they are for the best for other people and for ourselves and this we can to some extent at least discern by common observation and thought.

Because Christ has created and maintains the world, including its social structures, because man, though corrupted, is not intrinsically bad, and because history is God's drama, some Christians plead that we view culture not as demonic but as God's gift.

Creative Deviants: Christ Transforms Culture

On one hand, we see that God blesses man's involvement with this world. On the other hand, He commands man to keep separate from it. How can these positions be reconciled?

Because of man's paradoxical nature, we must hold disparate perspectives in tension, recognizing that[24]

...this world is broken. Not absurd, not suspended between two vacuums, but something extremely precious and
yet totally broken. The whole creation, which God proclaimed to be good, reflecting His glory, this world is
broken. The more it is perfect, the more we can understand the tragedy, the tremendous sadness, of that brokenness. It is only when something precious is broken
that we are sad. If something has no goodness in it,
why cry about it? That something which is the image of
the ineffable glory is wounded, bleeding, ugly--this is
the biblical intuition of evil. No, evil is not some
mysterious "it." Evil is not the ontological foundation
of the world. Evil is not the absence of good. Evil is
the presence of brokenness, the free choice of man not
to be in that wholeness and beauty.

Yet, amid this brokenness,[25]

Although sin is spread through the world, God has not
relinquished control. He still owns the cattle on a
thousand hills. He still sends rain on the just and
the unjust. He still ordains the government of every
country. The very structures of nature and society are
held together in Christ. He is moving in history toward
His own goal.

This is still God's world. So, in spite of its perversity and brokenness, we affirm it. But we appreciate
the world not only because of the beauty God programmed
into it in the past. We rejoice in it also because of
the magnificence with which God is going to rejuvenate
the world in the future. God is committed to this world.
He made that irrevocably clear when He Himself became
human so as to reconcile the world to Himself. Jesus
Christ, Son of God and Son of Man, is the first of
God's "new men." He is redeeming the world of humanity--
those who fill follow Him. In time, even the world of
nature is going to be delivered from the bondage of corruption into the glorious liberty of the children of God.
And our flabby, smelly, but precious bodies will not be
left out. They will not be obliterated, but will be
glorified. There is going to be a new heaven and a
new earth, and the kingdoms of this world are going to
become the kingdom of our Lord.

God is going to wipe out the sin of this world permanently.
And in that day--and here we see again how God understands
and blesses our love for simple, material things (even if we

interpret this spiritually)--in that day every man will call
his neighbors to come sit with him under his vine and under
his fig tree. Every man will have a home and a garden to
which to invite his neighbors.

God loves the world, right down to the smells and colors
that He has created. He doesn't want us to go out of the
world. Instead, He wants us to keep separate from the evil--
and go into all the world to reconcile it to Himself. Marriage, food, politics, and all other aspects of culture are
acceptable to God if they are experienced within the context
of His authority, love, and holiness--if they are related to
Him as He really is. Unlike Buddhism, Christianity does not
approve passivity. Christianity teaches whole-hearted involvement in the life around us, not for selfish goals but
for the glory of God. Whether we eat or drink or agitate
for political change, we should do it well to the glory of
God.

   In all our affirmation, however, we must continually remind ourselves that Christ rivals all systems--even our religious ones. This is not to say that systems, or powers,
are evil in themselves. In fact, "Col.1:16 tells us the
powers were created by Christ, and are held together in
Christ. But powerful systems become evil when they usurp
the central place in ordering our values and beliefs. Given
our tendency to idolatry, this happens frequently. Whether
Marxism or sex, Islam or money, some power constantly appears
on the horizon to nudge Christ out."26 We worship the creature rather than the Creator. We pray, "*My* will be done."

   Dutch theologian Hendrik Berkhof describes the pull of
the powers.27

   When Hitler took the helm in Germany in 1933, the Powers
   of Volk, race, and state took a new grip on men. Thousands were grateful, after the confusion of the preceding years, to find their lives again protected from chaos,
   order and security restored. No one could withhold himself, without utmost effort, from the grasp these Powers
   had...I myself experienced almost literally how such
   Powers may be "in the air"...

   The state, politics, class, social struggle, national
   interest, public opinion, accepted morality, the ideas
   of decency, humanity, democracy--these give unity and
   direction to thousands of lives. Yet precisely by giving unity and direction they separate these many lives

from the true God: they let us believe that we have
found the meaning of existence, whereas they really
estrange us from true meaning.

Human systems tend to take over. Because of this, it was
necessary that Christ's death, according to I Corinthians 15,
should dethrone all powers. It did not necessarily destroy
them, as some translations suggest, but it dethroned them.
We follow Christ in this. As Christ is not only the answer
to our questions, but also the question to our answers, so
our Christian presence too is an interrogation--a continuing
questioning of the legitimacy of the powers. Following Christ
who dethroned the powers, we must see them in proportion, as
merely one segment of creation, existing because of the Creator, and limited by other creatures. Beyond that, while we
stand questioning the powers, we ourselves need to ask God
for liberation every day from the powers that inhibit us
personally.

We who stress "power encounter" in regeneration need also
to apply it at more general levels. Anthony Campolo does this
when, "view(ing) capitalistic institutions as principalities and powers," he argues, "I believe Romans eight tells us
these institutions are 'groaning and in travail waiting for
the sons of God' to help them serve the purposes for which
they were created.[28] As a small shareholder, Campolo has
influenced the transnational conglomerate, Gulf and Western,
to contribute significantly to the economic betterment of the
Dominican Republic--up to $100 million, according to Campolo.

The danger in affirmation is that it may lead insidiously
to triumphalism. Law is a gift of God. Therefore our laws
are God's laws. Therefore our established lifestyle is good.

Even evangelical Anglicans associated with the Clapham
Sect, that small group of influential Christians in early
nineteenth century England who accomplished so much in eliminating the slave trade, nepotism in civil service, child labor, unsafe factory conditions, prison squalor, harsh punish-
ments, et cetera--even some of these dedicated evangelicals,
blinded by triumphalism, viewed Indians and Africans ambiva-
lently, almost, in Kipling's famous phrase, "half-devil and
half-child." According to Samuel Wilberforce, it was "the
vocation of the British people to leave as the impress of
their intercourse with inferior nations marks of moral teaching and religious training, to have made a nation of children
see what it was to be men." Charles Grant, "taking as his
starting point the utter depravity and corruption of the

Hindu race," argued that Britain must assume "the task of
instructing the Indian population in Christian civilization
which providence had so clearly ordained for it, by putting
the country under British control," and further that "there
was no foreseeable future 'in which we may not govern our
Asiatic subjects more happily for them than they can for themselves.'" After all, as John Lawrence explained, "In doing
the best we can for the people, we are bound by our conscience
and not theirs."[29]

If triumphalism threatens those who affirm culture, other
dangers lie in wait for those who hurl judgement down on it.
Culture is, in fact, inescapable. Though the world may lie
in wickedness, distinctions still must be made between relative rights and wrongs. Tertullian's counsel to his wife is
just such a gem. He once wrote her a letter on the subject
of his death: he advised her to remain single. Some time
later, however, a second letter included some afterthoughts:
if she couldn't bear to remain unmarried, she should at least
marry another believer. On this, Niebuhr comments,[30]

> In the end one can find in Tertullian a whole scale of
> relative goods and evils in his estimation of orders in
> man's sex-life in the interval before the resurrection.
> Compared with virginity, marriage is relatively evil; a
> single marriage in a lifetime, however, is relatively
> good as compared with second marriage; yet if the evil
> of second marriage does take place, marriage with a be-
> liever is relatively good. If Tertullian were pressed,
> he might concede that if there were to be marriage with
> an unbeliever, a monogamous marriage would still be a
> better wickedness than polygamy; and even that in a dis-
> ordered world polygamy might be relatively good compared
> to wholly irresponsible sex relations.

Because culture is inescapable, though we may withdraw
from culture, we will do so only to recreate new subcultures.
Some have advocated this, and, as we have seen, Christian
communities from the Benedictines to Sojourners community
have salted the earth. Yet they have drawn criticism.

"I don't think the young evangelicals are ever going to be
substantive because they're utopian," said Bill Bentley, president of the National Black Evangelical Association in an inter-
view with editor John Alexander a few years ago. "They don't
see the need to go back and be prophets in their own community
come hell or high water. Until they do that, they're always
going to be chasing rainbows. I regard the retreat into

communes as just that. They've got to close their eyes, hold
their nose, and jump back into their communities, taking
whatever comes."[31]

God has planted us at one spot in time and space and history. Shall we cut off our roots? Deny our opportunities?
Skip out of stewardship of the cultural resources over which
God has made us managers? Build more enclaves in segmented
society, instead of building bridges with people of all social
labels? Link up with likeminded peers in the prime of life,
rather than with our natural parents who need human warmth?
Drop out to love, rather than learning to love the neighbor
God has put next to us? Thunder that Christ's people must
love each other, and then forget about most of Christ's people
except those who think like us? Support ourselves by scavag-
ing at the edge of society rather than honing our creativity
in a salaried skill?

In the final analysis, culture is necessary for the exclusive Christian[32]

...because he is a Christian and a man. If he is to confess Jesus before men, he must do so by means of words and
ideas derived from culture, though a change of meaning is
also necessary. He must use such words as "Christ" or
"Messiah" or "kyrios" or "Son of God" or "Logos"...These
things he must do, not only that he may communicate, but
also that he may himself know whom and what he believes...
How shall demons be cast out where they are not believed
to exist?...The command to love the neighbor cannot be
obeyed except in specific terms that involve cultural
understanding of the neighbor's nature, and except in
specific acts directed toward him as a being who has a
place in culture...In his effort to be obedient to Christ,
the radical Christian therefore reintroduces ideas and
rules from non-Christian culture in two areas: in the
government of the withdrawn Christian community, and in
the regulation of Christian conduct toward the world outside...

The world (kosmos) of First John ("Love not the world...")
is the same world as the world (kosmos) of John 3:16 ("God so
loved the world..."). One passage must balance another--a
basic principle of hermeneutics. In the end, are we called
to a counter culture? Or are we not rather called to God in
the middle of every culture and institution in which we find
ourselves? Niebuhr observes, "(After recognizing) the importance of the role played by anticultural Christians in the

reform of culture, we must immediately point out that they
never achieved these results alone or directly but only
through the mediation of believers who gave a different
answer to the fundamental question...The movement of withdrawal and renunciation is a necessary element in every
Christian life, even though it be followed by an equally
necessary movement of responsible engagement in cultural
tasis."33

Culture--man's creativity within divinely-ordained struc-
tures--is blessed by God. Relating it to Him, we rejoice in
it. But since culture is also involved in man's rebellion
against God, we do not idolize it. Rather we balance affirmation with judgment. Expecting a struggle with sin in every
area--education, art, recreation, politics, or personal rela-
tions--we want to be a fellowship of creative deviants. Although we know we are lazy, self-centered, ignorant, and
afraid of getting involved, we want to be strong enough to
sweat and suffer as a saving remnant in our societies. We
want to be men of God in the middle of the mass--salt of the
earth.

HOW TO HELP A CULTURE CHANGE:
CULTURALLY-SENSITIVE TRANSFORMATION

A review of anthropological theories has reminded us to
admit a range of variables as partially determinative, spanning from macroeconomics to local values. To keep this range
in mind when embarked on a project, a checklist may be useful
such as: Does the project fit with local concepts, with traditional knowledge? With local religion, or contemporary
secular ideology? With local social structure (including law
and politics, as well as informal groupings)? With local
economic resources, infrastructure, and technologies? With
local family and child-training patterns? With local communication styles and media? With local aesthetics? With
local recreations and celebrations? With the specific pressures for culture change that this society is experiencing?
Naturally, a culture will include multiple, sometimes contradictory formulations. Nevertheless, our humble attempt to
adapt to its major themes remains important both pragmatically
and theologically.

Some may object that this is an unduly positive approach
to cultures. Confrontation, not appreciation, is what is
needed, they may contend. Indubitably, confrontation *is*
needed. As indicated in our section on "The Binding Clutches

156

THE CHURCH IN RESPONSE TO HUMAN NEED

of Satan," confrontation is imperative all up and down the
continuum, against multinational forces, against unjust national and local structures, against culturally-sanctioned
habits, against individual sins. Nevertheless, successful
confrontation cannot occur until there is understanding of
the context. Cultural integration is pervasive. It cannot
be ignored or shrugged off while we get on with our confrontations. Superficial confrontations often do more harm than
good. Furthermore, understanding the context means appreci-
ating the good gifts of God's common grace that are present
there, the dearnesses of behaviors, things, and beliefs within a people's gestalt. A review of theological approaches to
culture has cautioned us to be neither naively optimistic
nor overly judgemental, whether about the culture of the poor
or of the social workers. This is vital equally whether the
workers move internationally or within their own nation, from
an educated background to a slum, or from an urban to a rural
context. Local people are just as likely to develop through
an admiration of their strengths as through a thundering con-
demnation of deficiencies. Judgement must be present. But
appreciation also must be present. Without it, we are insecure pragmatically and offbase theologically. By far the
most effective judgement will occur when it is spearheaded by
local leaders who have immersed themselves in the Word and
the Spirit, as well as in an appreciation of their culture.

With this as background, let us consider several illustrative areas of culture where we must adapt if we are to facilitate successful change.

*Does the Project Fit with Local Worldview, Concepts, and
Values?*

Consider our approach to a polluted water supply, for
example. In village after village around the world, this is
a major source of sickness and death. Some experts estimate
that 60 percent of the diseases in some areas could be eradi-
cated if the water was cleaned up.

In many cases the solution is simple: cover the pool and
install a pump. Yet, surprisingly, often local people resist this public health measure.

Why?

In one Middle Eastern community described by Afif Tannous
of the Department of State, the villagers explained:[34]

"Our fathers, grandfathers, and great grandfathers drank from this water as it is, and I don't see why we should make a change now."

"You say that you want to install a pump at the spring; but I for one have never seen a pump, nor do I know what might happen if it should be put there."

"I tell you what will happen. The water will flow out so fast that the spring will dry up in no time."

"Not only that, but the iron pipe will spoil the taste of the water for us and for our animals."

"You So and So," put in one of Jibrail's elders, who are much more advanced than the people of (the village in question), "do you like the taste of dung in your water better?"

"Well, I admit it is bad; but we and our animals are at least used to it."

"You have told us that the water is the cause of our illness and of our children's death. I do not believe that, and I can't see how it could be. To tell you the truth, I believe that the matter if life and death is in Allah's hands, and we cannot do much about it."

"One more thing. We don't understand why you should go to all this trouble. Why are you so concerned about us?"

"You say that the pump will save our women much effort and time. If that happens, what are they going to do with themselves all day long?"

This story points up values and concepts that contrast with those of a social worker. Although many human needs and hopes are similar, values do differ from culture to culture. Some people value clean water supremely. Others value stability. Still others may value outlets for expression. Some value individual success. Others value family pride. Others may not care about advancement so long as they have an enjoyable life with their kin now. Some, immersed in ideas about imperialism, the bourgeoise, and the people's struggle will sacrifice everything else as they pour themselves into efforts for a social revolution.

In socioeconomic projects, common value conflicts may occur
between the social workers' emphasis on progress, modernity,
and youth versus others' emphasis on age and tradition; the
social workers' emphasis on efficiency; different amount of
time expected for negotiations; different work rhythms; different socialization patterns expected; indirect communication versus Western frankness; use of intermediaries in disputes; and need for multiple repetitions and much longer time
for successful communication in some cultures.

Culturally-sensitive development begins with what people
value and know, and expands this. It proceeds from the known
to the unknown. A Zaire health project did this.[35] The local people believed that disease was spread through sorcery.
Sometimes this happened unconsciously. Either human beings
or spirits were the agents of sickness.

How could you construct anything positive on such beliefs?
The health team said, "Yes, disease passes from person to
person. Yes, you can transmit it unwittingly. But you can
also transmit it willfully. If you know that you should be
vaccinated but you wriggle out, if you know you should use a
toilet but you use a field, then you purposely expose your
neighbors to danger."

"Yes, God created the world. But He is not distant, as
you have been taught. Instead he is very curious about what
we do. In fact, he holds us responsible for the condition of
our neighborhood. God is concerned for the health of his
people."

This public health program was administered by village
church leaders. Because of its obvious benefits, churches
grew greatly in numbers, influence, and respect. Within four
years, 80 villages were practicing markedly new health behaviors.

Does the Project Fit with Local Social Structure?

Bruce Olson, who has lived with the Motilones of Venezuela
and Colombia for nearly 20 years, confesses that he could do
nothing to improve the people's health care system until he
worked through and with local leaders.[36]

When Bruce began offering a few simple medicines--after
he had slept in a hammock in the local longhouse for several
years, had learned the Motilones' language, and had run barefoot with them down thorny jungle trails--the Motilones

rejected his cures. "Those medicines are fine for you," they said, "but we have our own herbs and treatments."

So, helpless, Burce saw the people fall prey to one illness after another.

One day an epidemic of pinkeye surged through the camp. Soon nearly everybody's eyes oozed and burned. Bruce stood by, frustrated. In his case was an ointment that would eradicate the conjunctivitis immediately.

Finally, desperate, Bruce stepped over to a friend and poked his finger into the corner of the man's eye. Then he wiped the goo in his own eyes--and developed pinkeye himself.

To the local healer he sped.

"Ma'am, could you please give me something for my eyes? They're burning," he pled.

"Bruce, I wish I could help you," she answered. "But I've tried every herb and chant I know. Nothing works. I'm worn out."

Then Bruce pulled out his ointment. "Maybe this would help. Would you put it in my eyes?"

She did.

When Bruce's conjunctivitis cleared up, and when he gave the healer all the credit, she became willing to try the medication on others. In three days the whole longhouse was cured. As a result, she began to listen to Bruce's health suggestions. She was willing to look through his primitive microscope, and marvel at the wiggling demons that she had always known were responsible for disease. When they beat the longhouse for spirits periodically, she was willing now to add disinfectants to the beating. Within a few years, the Stone Age Motilones were running eight clinics. Motilones were doing the diagnoses and the treatments. Motilones were giving the injections. Spanish-speaking settlers were streaming to their clinics by the thousands.

This shows the importance of working through a local leader.

Questions that will help us adjust our program to local social structures include: Who are the community opinion leaders? These may include media and national as well as

local figures. What is the community decision-making process? How do they settle quarrels? What are the natural
lines of affiliation? These may tie individuals to several
networks. In their most common groups, what are: the rights
and obligations of members; any distinctive roles; special
rituals or celebrations; myths or special reputation of the
group; models; villains; other techniques of boundary maintenance; any distinctions between formal and informal behavior?

Frequently we may anticipate tension between emphasis on
the group versus any plan that rewards individual incentive.
Farmers around the world argue, "Why should I grow a bigger
crop? It will just mean more relatives descending on me at
harvest time."

Cooperatives may mitigate the tension between individualism and groupness. Basing these on indigenous credit association patterns will increase their chances of succeeding.
One way or another, proceeding from the known to the unknown,
we must use the group wherever it is significant. Individuals are not as rootless as we may assume.

As an alternative to cooperatives, when capitalizing small
shopowners in New Guinea, missionary Don Richardson coun-
selled each one, "Go to the oldest man in your group and make
a deal. Explain why you cannot give away your goods--the
village soon would not have a store. Then ask him if you can
refer to him all the relatives and friends who come asking
for free goods. He can explain the situation to them. The
refusal will be firm but indirect. Then you tell the old
man that at the end of the year, as a token of gratitude, you
will give him a shiny new ax."

This plan has worked.

In other countries, similarly, businesses have reduced
absenteeism by visiting the employees' home provinces and
explaining to family elders why regularity is essential.

Does the Project Fit with Local Economic Resources?

Juan Flavier, director of the International Institute of
Rural Reconstruction, recalls how he learned to adjust to
local economic realities.[37] He began his medical career in
the rural Philippines. One of his first patients was an
infant with pneumonia. Standing in the simple bamboo hut
above the convulsing infant, Dr. Flavier reached automatically for his prescription pad.

"Penicillin," he began to write.

The baby's relatives looked at each other.

"Doctor," the father interrupted, "the nearest drugstore is 13 kilometers away. And it will never open at night, for fear of thieves."

Suddenly the child convulsed.

"At least let's get some ice. We have to get this fever down," Flavier said.

Again eyebrows rose.

"Doctor, we have ice here only once a year. During fiesta time."

Flavier's training had not prepared him for this. He was mentally wringing his hands when a wizened old woman tottered up. "Excuse me, Doctor. This is what we use here," she said.

She placed a bundle on the child's forehead. Shortly the fever declined and the convulsions subsided.

Later, when Flavier had the bundle's contents analyzed, he discovered that it was the trunk of a banana tree chopped fine and soaked in water. Because this substance is extremely porous, it has a cooling effect when placed on the body.

That night when Flavier walked home, he cried--and he determined that he would learn to work within the limits of the economic resources of the people.

Economic questions include: How convenient is transportation? How regular is the power supply? How dependable is the communication infrastructure? How available is water? Does the equipment have parts which are replaceable in the country at low cost? Is simplified accounting needed? How many trained personnel are available--or should an elementary skills training course be developed?

Less job-specific questions that will help make the development worker more sensitive to the economic milieu include: What is the average daily diet? Do the people consider themselves impoverished, or not? What kinds of expenditure do they delight in (clothes, fiestas, insurance policies, investments, labor-saving gadgets...)? What kinds of expenditures do they consider extravagant? What do economists think are the country's chief economic problems? Its assets? Its economic opportunities? What do your neighbors think the country's chief economic problems are? How do they experience these? Is there a Marxist movement among university students? What are their specific complaints? Is there economic tension between ethnic groups?

In our priorities, we favor producing cheap food, low cost housing, or intermediate technology, rather than luxury goods for wealthier people. We favor marketing to the poor. We favor locally made equipment, labor intensive methods, entrepreneurs with a simple lifestyle, and some degree of profit sharing and progressive opportunities among workers. We favor ways of capitalizing the poor that do not increase dependency, such as the use of revolving funds, multilateral funds, food for work, et cetera.

Professional pride may balk at the rough technology poor people can afford. We can learn from Dr. Tom Dooley, who ran a simple clinic in Laos before he died of leukemia.

"People accuse me of practicing nineteenth century medicine," he said. "They are correct. I did practice nineteenth century medicine, and this was just fine. Upon my departure, our indigenous personnel would practice eighteenth-century medicine. Good, this is progress, since most of the villagers live in the fifteenth century."[38]

At the same time, we must be aware that some poor farmers and businessmen have objected, "Don't feed us any more 'appropriate technology'! We want standard imports!"

Why is this? Even though an imported tractor-drawn weeder may cost 60 times more than its animal-drawn alternative technology equivalent, the former may be desired because it carries more status. Often, too, the standard import is part of a more attractive retail package. The sales information about it may be more colorful. Importers may offer generous credit. Installment assistance, and service and parts for repairs, may be part of the deal. We who promote alternative technology, then, need to become cannier businessmen.

As we adapt to the local economic situation, we may come to empathize with a strong felt need for political change. Such change we may be able to facilitate.

Take the Bangladesh Rural Advancement Committee, as described by the Institute for Food and Development Policy.[39] This group is supported by Oxfam-America.

In one village where BRAC has been working, 40% of the 2000 people were landless. Two per cent of the population were rich landowners.

But fallow, vacant land lay all around. This was the abandoned property of those who had fled to India during the 1971 war of liberation. Now it was government land. Rich landowners used it for illegal grazing or cultivation.

BRAC taught the people to read. It did so through discussions of real problems facing village Bengalis. Armed with a new skill and with better articulated ideas about their situation, the poor people of this village formed the Rajhason Landless Cooperative Society. They started petitioning the government to grant them title to some of the abandoned land.

Two years later, after unrelenting corporate pressure from the Cooperative, the government ceded them 60 acres. This amounted to one and one half acres per family.

Then the local hassles began. The rich landowners were alarmed. They were losing illegal use of the abandoned land. And they were losing their stranglehold on the poor laborers.

They incited other villagers to break the irrigation canal on which the cooperative's land depended. They tried to block the cooperative from using the river. But they didn't try too hard, because they suspected that starting from scratch would prove too difficult for tiny farmers with no tools or capital.

"They'll be mortgaging their farms right back to us. Give them one season," they laughed to each other.

Instead, the new farmers got a loan for equipment from BRAC at twelve per cent interest instead of the 50% to 200% rate available from local moneylenders.

At the end of the first season, in spite of bad harvest weather, the new farmers paid back the loan, plus interest. Now the cooperative wants to extend their joint activities to fishing. And they are feeling adventuresome enough to take the initiative in seeking better health care and child care. Rather than being passive recipients, they are even going out of their way to seek out family planning information.

Adapting economically may mean identifying with people's felt need for political change. In specific ways we can support their struggle for increasing control of the political processes that dominate them. The BRAC case illustrates this on the local level.

Beyond this are national and international political-economic structures. To affect international structures, Christians have bought a few shares in various transnational corporations, attended stockholders' meetings, and lobbied for specific changes in company policies. In 1979, 111 such resolutions were presented. By 1980, 25 had been negotiated successfully with management. Many more were under consideration.[40] Other Christians in "primary donor" nations have joined forces to lobby their governments for justice and mercy in regard to specific bills.

As for affecting national structures, foreign social workers often have argued that they dare not speak up for political change because they are "guests" of the government. On this, Overseas Missionary Fellowship missionary Dick Dowsett has commented,[41]

> Missionaries normally keep quiet, concentrating on a pietistic type of salvation, quietening their conscience by saying, "We are guests here, we have no business to criticize." But when we behave like this we are *not* neutral, we are simply supporting the status quo. That is often a terrible thing to do, for Christianity is not the same as middle-class conservatism. Oh for a return of the spirit of prophecy to our ministries. Amos was told to go home to Judah or shut up. But he did not use the "guest" excuse.

Adapting to local economic resources is one way to develop empathy. That is not unachievable. It is just costly. E. Thomas and Elizabeth Brewster recently have developed the concept of "bonding" with a culture, analogous to mother-infant bonding. They suggest four strategies essential to achieving such bonding:[42]

(1) Be willing to live with a local family.
(2) Limit personal belongings to 20 kilos.
(3) Use only local public transportation.

(4) Expect to carry out language learning in the context of relationships that the learner himself is responsible to develop and maintain.

These strategies apply equally to singles, couples, and families. They are fully as necessary for those crossing ethnic boundaries within a nation as for those crossing oceans. The Brewsters rightly comment, "A willingness to accept these conditions tells a lot about an individual's attitude and flexibility"--and, we might add, a lot about an agency's priorities.

WAS NOAH LITERATE?: CONCLUDING UNSCIENTIFIC POSTSCRIPT

All peoples dream. Most welcome some change. Nevertheless, not all suffer planned social change gladly. Among the many considerations that give people pause before they rush headlong into a socioeconomic project, here are three concerns that are common to the ethos, the worldview, the culture of people in many developing nations.

The Beam in Our Eye

"In many instances, demonic influence has wreaked havoc in (American Indian) communities with alcoholism, drugs, despair, and suicide a tragic part of Indian life today..." So runs a story in a current missions newsletter, typical of many reports. Is this a balanced view? What--or who--has precipitated the unleashing of this demonic chaos? Do immigrated Americans share any blame for the sense of loss among Indians today? If so, why blame the devil?

In fact, the exploitative, aggressive practices of industrialized countries are part of the reason why populations of poor countries look at their "developers" with a jaded eye. "Development is now used in a pejorative sense...in Latin America...One...reason...is that development...has been frequently promoted by international organizations closely linked to groups and governments which control the world economy[43] in such a way that the rich get richer while the poor get proportionately poorer:[44]

Transnational corporations are so enormous that they can keep a stranglehold on small nations. Unfortunately, they tend to emphasize cheap profits and united military defenses rather than good water, safe working conditions, profit sharing, increasing ownership of land for the landless, and pressure for fair and speedy trials for those arrested for civil protest. Corporations based in "developed" countries tend to press for unequal trade treaties;

squeeze out local entrepreneurs, patent-holders, trade
unions, and even attempts at food self-sufficiency; and
dump unsafe products on foreign markets. They have little
motivation to market simple products to the poor; rather
they market internationally to global islands of the com-
fortable.

Private business is not alone. Powerful governments behave similarly. "The United States does not have friends;
she just has interests," John Foster Dulles once said. At
best, in such a milieu, government and private development
schemes have been seen as aseptic. "Developmentalism came to
be synonymous with reformism and modernization, that is to
say, synonymous with timid measures, really ineffective in
the long run and counterproductive to achieving a real transformation."[45]

An agency may well argue,[46]

"We sould immediately antagonize and alienate a significant part of our constituency if we came out asserting
that the First World enriches itself at the expense of
the Third World. Many people would simply stop supporting us financially. What is the use of having morally
clean but financially empty hands? The important thing
is to raise funds, so that we can support worthwhile
activities in the Third World; others who do not risk
being put out of business will have to tell the unplea-
sant truths."

However, when, for example, private voluntary aid from
the U.S. totals about $1 billion, and missions giving per-
haps another $1 billion, while trade between developing and
industrialized nations amounts to $200 billion annually,
peoples justly may be skeptical about our goodwill if we
speak only about the ethics of spending, never about the
ethics of earning.[47] In general, they wish we would get
the beam out of our own eye, so that we would be a less unbalanced partner.

People Are Not Problems

People resist approaches that categorize them solely as
problems. "Why do magazines always write about us like we're
drunks?" American Indians exploded in a recent survey of
articles about them. "Why do they always say we're poor?"[48]
People may well have economic needs, which social workers
must tackle. But let us not see certain groups only as objects needing help. Let us not see only their poverty. Even

amid squalor and disorganized families and periodic drunkenness and stabbings, there is family warmth and children's
games and gaiety and dancing and loving sacrifice. The needy
still have some pride.

"There is absolutely no community spirit here," reported
an article in a recent development agency magazine. "The
houses are scattered all over. Very few of the children attend school. There is no sanitary water supply and there are
no toilets. There is no one to give health care and the
people just don't seem to want to try to follow directions.
We try to teach just simple things like hygiene...but often
we are unsuccessful because of their tribal beliefs. They
drink very little water because of the old belief that it
would slow down a warrior chasing his enemy. Their lives are
often ruled by spirits and there are many things that are ta-
boo. Sometimes if someone dies or is sick during a harvest
time, they will completely abandon the crop because they
think they may have offended the spirits. But we have been
patient and have started construction on the 'bridge.' The
love of Christ and modern medicine have teamed up to span
the river, but much more time and effort will be needed."

No doubt every fact in this article is true. But do the
people described see themselves this way? The report was
written about the broad-shouldered, self-assured Ifugao, who
have molded the Philippine rice terraces for centuries, managing a breath-takingly complex irrigation system without the
need for any central government. Where in this assessment is
there an appreciation of Ifugao culture? At the pragmatic
level, how are Ifugao college graduates likely to react,
should they read such an article?

People are not necessarily "culturally deprived" because
they are economically poor. Rather, they suffer cultural
deprivation when the symbols associated with their culture
begin to connote shame. When this happens, apathy, and a
resulting greater chaos in social patterns, and a resulting
reduction of trust, may develop. This *may* be based on relative economic standing. When there is restriction of economic
opportunities in the face of an ideology which claims equal
opportunity for all (such as mass advertising nurtures), this
probably will lead to shame in the symbols which are associated with the restriction. But, in the absence of symbols
connoting shame, economic differences need not mean cultural
impoverishment. For example, a member of a well-integrated
mountain tribe with a life expectancy of 45 may be in no significant way poorer than a fragmented urban slum garbage-
gatherer with a life expectancy of 50.

In our urgency to solve "problems of poverty," do we keep
in mind the crucial nature of pride in cultural traditions?
Do we remember that anomie, associated with culture loss, has
had tragic results, sometimes leading to the extinction of
whole peoples? Or do we replace time honored traditions with
dehumanizing, robot-like work procedures? Do we trivialize
art, fostering sham U.S. designed assembly-line trinkets, a
muzak of handicrafts?

Why is it so easy to reduce people to problems? Social
workers adjusting to people who are different suffer culture
shock,"the hostility (that) grows out of the genuine difficulty which the visitor experiences in the process of adjustment. There is maid trouble, shopping trouble, and the fact
that the people in the host country are largely indifferent
to all these troubles. They help, but they just don't understand your great concern over these difficulties. Therefore,
they must be insensible and unsympathetic..."[49] If, added
to this, the worker's theology emphasizes man's depravity
without emphasizing God's common grace in cultures, he may
well tend to view people as problems to be solved. Beyond
this, it has been argued that developed countries need poorer
nations, to serve as producers in jobs nobody wants, as consumers of junk nobody wants, as the source of jobs for all
sorts of service professions, and as scapegoats that reinforce
our belief in the Protestant Ethic. The latter two considerations might reinforce some workers' view of poor people as
problems.

How rarely do we train cross-cultural workers to discipline
themselves to ask affirmative questions about the culture,
questions which will dig out treasures that will enrich them.
How rarely do we make "bonding" with the local culture a top
priority. Let's remember that[50]

> ...every culture is the lifeway of people made in the
> image of God, regardless of their standard of living.
> Most people with whom God has communicated throughout
> history have lived in cultures far different from the
> industrialized nations. Was Noah literate? Did David
> believe in democracy? Did Mary have family planning?
> Yet their lives were as valid as ours. They dominated
> nature less. Fewer alternative products, customs, and
> ideas were available to them. But they experienced
> friendship, love, parenthood, creativity, learning,
> responsibility, choice, dignity, adventure, and rela-
> tionship to God. They had as many significant experi-
> ences as any modern industrialized man.

As the Christian historian Herbert Butterfield has observed,51

Each generation is...an end in itself, a world of people
existing in their own right...Every generation is equi-
distant from eternity. So the purpose of life is not in
the far future, nor, as we so often imagine, around the
next corner, but the whole of it is here and now, as fully
as ever it will be on this planet...(I do not know of)
any mundane fulness of life which we could pretend to
possess and which was not open to people in the age of
Isaiah or Plato, Dante or Shakespeare..Each generation--
indeed each individual--exists for the glory of God...

He goes on to this metaphor:

If a lamb should die in May, before it had reproduced
itself, or contributed to the development of the species,
or provided a fleece for the market, still the fact that
it frisked and frolicked in the spring is in one sense
an end in itself, and in another sense a thing that
tends to the glory of God.

Contemplative Confronters

"Oh, for Pete's sake, let's just get some ozone and send
it back up there!" An *American Scientist Magazine* cartoon
pictures an executive of Aerosol Products, Inc.,exploding in
exasperation to an underling.52

We Americans have believed that progress, not frustration,
is the last word. Any problem can be solved if we put enough
effort into it. Yet people in poorer countries find us amazingly ignorant of the rest of the world, and correlate our
optimism with our naiveté.

Americans, and to a lesser extent social workers from
other industrialized countries, are ignorant in two ways.
First, we tend to ignore the complexity of variables present
in a situation of potential change. We make decisions quickly. We consult largely in Western languages. We allow a
significant percentage of the decision-making to occur in
home offices in Western countries. And we forget that our
own motivations and assumptions add greatly to the complexity
of unexamined, enigmatic variables.

We favor a systems approach. We are goal oriented. Goals
must be measureable. Imponderables do not fit our planning

procedures. Hence, uncertainty, ambiguity, and paradoxes
get screened out.

Such ignorance can be dangerous. A Japanese nuclear
specialist argues that U.S. reluctance to admit uncertainty
as a significant variable has reduced our ability to guard
against nuclear war realistically. In the area of development, as an Overseas Development Council publication observes,[53]

Many Americans are so locked into certain assumptions
about charity that they fail to perceive that their
very humanitarianism may have inhumane effects. A pre-
mium is still placed on good intentions, and the historical American can-do mentality takes over from there. As
one observer has commented, "American optimism spurs an
impatience to confront the issues, to get on with the job,
to do something, to set things right. In sum, it is the
positive and direct action approach. It leads, however,
to the uneasy feeling among less activistically-oriented
allies that precipitate action may compound the problem
rather than solve it."

A. W. Tozer's comments on evangelism have parallels for
social workers. He wrote:[54]

I fear that thousands of young persons enter Christian
service from no higher motive than to help deliver God
from the embarrassing situation His love has gotten Him
into and His limited abilities seem unable to get Him out
of...How much eager beaver religious work is done out of
a carnal desire to make good...The popular notion that
the first obligation of the church is to spread the
gospel to the uttermost parts of the earth is false.
Her first obligation is to be spiritually worthy to
spread it. Our Lord said, "Go ye," but He also said,
"Tarry ye," and the tarrying had to come before the going. Had the disciples gone forth as missionaries before the day of Pentecost it would have been an overwhelming spiritual disaster, for they could have done
no more than make converts after their own likeness. To
spread an effete, degenerate brand of Christianity to
pagan lands is not to fulfill the commandment of Christ
or discharge our obligation to the heathen. Increased
numbers of demi-Christians is not enough...We are called
to an everlasting preoccupation with God...to be worshippers first and workers only second...The work of a
worshipper will have eternity in it.

Confronters must also be contemplatives--humbly sensitive to the transcendence that largely eludes us, and to the para- doxes that so pervade our world. And we must weep with those who weep. This introduces the second area in which workers from industrialized countries are ignorant, namely, we are ignorant of the ubiquitousness of recurring disasters.

"People with more means," says a character is Oscar Lewis's *Children of Sanchez,* "can afford the luxury of allowing their sons to live in a world of fantasy, of only seeing the good side of life, of protecting them from bad companions and ob- scene language, of not hurting their sensibilities by wit- nessing scenes of brutality, of having all their expenses paid for them. But they live with their eyes closed and are naive in every sense of the word."[55]

Rather than expecting success, rather than smothering the poor with cheap cheerfulness, we may at times need to sit in silence with them, to empathize, to share our mutual lack of answers. And then we may discover that sometimes a crisis is not a crisis, and a failure is not a failure. Speaking of "ethncentricity in one's definition of a crisis," Sommer says,[56]

> Studies have shown that in parts of the world where
> weather patterns are uncertain, social systems tend to
> respond to crop fluctuations with various mechanisms to
> insure against the consequences of that uncertainty.
> Consumption patterns may not fluctuate to the same ex-
> tent as production. In good crop years, considerable
> compensatory saving may occur, whether in the form of
> grain, gold bracelets, or other objects of wealth; this
> serves as a safety valve for the bad years. Thus what
> might be seen by some outsiders as a disaster requiring
> external assistance may not be seen as a crisis at all
> by the local people. Furthermore, there is no world-
> wide consensus on what constitutes adequate caloric in-
> take for people of varying genetic compositions...The
> result, though still little researched, may be that
> relief programs respond too quickly and excessively
> for the good of the particular society over the long
> run.

At another level, what constitutes failure? For people for whom doing is part of success, missing a final goal is not necessarily failure. As C. S. Lewis once observed, "Joy cares only for temples building, not at all for temples built." When people compartmentalize less between process

and achievement, meaningful process may be its own reward.
If aid agencies were not always thinking about justifying
themselves to their Western supporters, if workers were suf-
ficiently bonded with the receiving culture, we might be more
open to partial successes, slow successes, and successes in
terms which are not easily quantifiable.

Realizing how common disaster is may enable us to respond
more wisely. We must respond, however. Certainly God is
sovereign. He is going to re-establish His rule on this
earth in His own time. He can do it without our efforts.
Yet God wills our vigorous creativity to be among His instruments for subduing the earth. Every day that He keeps us
alive is an opportunity to give Him delight or disappointment.
So let us glorify Him by our stewardship of this perverse and
broken world. By affirmation and judgment, by skillfully
balancing our priorities, let us serve as the salt of the
earth, as creative deviants in the tradition of Isaiah, the
American and British abolitionists, Bartolome de las Casas,
Pandita Ramabai, and a great company of others, who accomplished far more for this world than any conformist or drop-
out could have.

"Men of spiritual resources may not only redeem catastrophe,
but turn it into a grand creative moment...The rarest creative
achievements of the mind must come from great internal pressure, and are born of a high degree of distress. In other
words, the world is not merely to be enjoyed but is an arena
for moral striving...History is in the business of making
personalities"[57] conformed to the image of God. Let us fulfill the cultural mandate to this end, empowered by God's
Spirit.

FOOTNOTES

1. Nida, Eugene. "Why Are Foreigners So Queer?: A Socio-Cultural Approach to Cultural Pluralism," *International Bulletin of Missionary Research,* July 1981, pp. 102-106.
2. Gillin, John. "National and Cultural Values in the United States," *Social Forces* 34 (1955-56), pp. 107-13.

3. Taber, Charles. "The Missionary Gap," *The Other Side,* August, 1979.

4. Nida, *op. cit.*

5. Snow, C.P. *The Two Cultures.* Cambridge: Cambridge University Press, 1964, p. 26.

6. Rappaport, Roy. *Pigs for the Ancestors.* New Haven: Yale University Press, 1967, p.6.

7. Goertz, Clifford. "Thick Description: Toward an Interpretive Theory of Culture," *The Interpretation of Cultures.* New York: Basic Books, 1973, pp. 4-5.

8. Ortiz, Alfonso. *The Tewa World.* Chicago: University of Chicago Press, 1969, p.xvi.

9. Kaplan, David and Robert Manners. *Culture Theory.* Englewood Cliffs, N.J.: Prentice-Hall, Inc., 1972, p.159.

10. An abyss yawns between those who find conflict a catalyst for cataclysmic change, as do Marxist anthropologists, versus those who see conflict as an escape valve which enables the system to let off steam without exploding. Does conflict contribute to change? Or to stability? Are systems in conflict moving directionally? Or are they in equilibrium? These are the questions over which such anthropologists do battle.

   In the final analysis, these alternative perspectives may be complementary. Marx zeroed in on the origins of conflict. Several factors exacerbate social tensions, he found. For example, if the distribution of scarce resources is increasingly unequal, conflict will mount. If workers become aware of their joint interests, conflict will mount. Such awareness in turn springs from certain conditions. The owners may instigate disruptive social changes. They may alienate the workers. Especially if the workers are spatially concentrated and if they have access to media, they may develop systems by which to communicate their grievances to each other. Awareness will be enhanced if the workers develop their own unifying set of beliefs. To do this, they must produce articulate ideological spokesmen and must evade the owners' propaganda. When they are aware of their joint interests, when they have organized leadership, when the owners' propaganda is not convincing, and when they view their deprivation as relative to the owners' standard of living, then workers will organize and initiate conflict.

Many of these factors have enriched anthropological studies. When Marx proceeds to the development of conflict, rather than its origins, however, his propositions ring less true. For example, Marx contends that the most highly organized workers will engage in the most violent conflicts. But the history of union disputes shows that well-organized workers are often most amenable to negotiation. It is the overwhelmingly but inarticulately frustrated who run amuck.

In explaining the development of social conflict, rather than its origins, the finds of George Simml, who connects conflict with equilibrium, generate more significant questions. For example, Simml argues that the more conflict is a means to an end, the less likely it is to be violent. As well, frequent, low-intensity conflicts in a highly interdependent society will contribute to social integration in that they allow people to vent hostilities, they give people a sense of control over their destinies, and they point the direction of needed incremental change through compromise. (See Karl Marx, Das Capital. (New York: Modern Library, 1946); and "The Communist Manifesto," in Selected Writings in Sociology and Social Philosophy, ed. by T.B.Bottomore and Maximilien Rubel (New York: McGraw-Hill Book Co., 1964); George Simml, Conflict and the Web of Group Affiliations (Glencoe, Ill.: The Free Press, 1955); and Jonathan Turner, "The Conflict Heritage," in The Structure of Sociological Theory (Homewood, Ill.: The Dorsey Press, 1978).

11. Adeney, Miriam. Book in press (Grand Rapids, Michigan: Eerdmans Publishing Co., 1983).

12. Wallis, Jim. The Call to Conversion. (San Francisco: Harper and Row, Pubs., 1981).

13. Tertullian, quoted in Niebuhr, H. Richard, Christ and Culture (New York: Harper and Row, Pubs., 1951), p.54.

14. Latourette, Kenneth Scott. *A History of the Expansion of Christianity*. (Grand Rapids, Michigan: Zondervan, 1970), pp.379-380.

15. Niebuhr, *op. cit.* p.66.

16. Adeney, *op.cit.*

17. *Ibid.*

18. Stockdale, A.A.   "God Left the Challenge in the Earth"

19. Rookmaaker, Hans. *Modern Art and the Death of Culture.* (London: Inter Varsity Press, 1970), p.36.

20. Sauer, Erich. *The King of the Earth*   (Grand Rapids, Michigan: Eerdmans Publishing Co., 1962), p.81.

21. Adeney, Miriam.   "Do Your Own Thing (As Long As You Do It Our Way"),   *Christianity Today,* July 4, 1975, p.12.

22. Calvin, John. *Institutes of the Christian Religion,* ed. J.T.McNeill, Vol. 1 (Philadelphia: Westminster, 1960), p. 351.

23. Triton, A.N. *Whose World?* (London: Inter Varsity Press, 1970), pp. 86, 43.

24. Schmemann, Alexander, "Solzhenitsyn," *Radix,* March 1974, p. 11.

25. Adeney, *op. cit.* 1983.

26. *Ibid.*

27. Berkhof, Hendrik, *Christ and the Powers* (Scottsdale, PA: Herald Press 1962), p. 32.

28. Campolo, Anthony, "The Greening of Gulf and Western," *Eternity* January 1981, p.32.

29. Bradley, Ian. *The Call to Seriousness: The Evangelical Impact on the Victorians* (New York: Macmillan, 1975), pp. 89, 81, 87, 93.

30. Tertullian quoted in Niebuhr, *op. cit.,* p.74.

176 THE CHURCH IN RESPONSE TO HUMAN NEED

31. Bill Bentley interviewed by John Alexander in "Growing Together: A Conversation with Seven Black Evangelicals," *The Other Side,* July-August 1975, p.45.
32. Niebuhr, *op. cit.* pp. 70-71.

33. *Ibid.*, pp. 67, 68.

34. Tannous, Afif, *Extension Work Among the Arab Fellahin* (Foreign Service Institute, Department of State, 1951).

35. Fountain, Daniel, "The Church and Cross-Cultural Communication in Public Health: A Project in Zaire," *Missiology,* Jan. 1975, pp. 103-112.

36. Olson, Bruce, *For This Cross I'll Kill You* (Carol Stream, Ill: Creation House, 1973), pp. 136-150.

37. Flavier, Juan, *Doctor in the Barrios* (Quezon City, Philippines: New Day Publishers, 1970), pp. 142-145.

38. Dooley, Thomas, *The Edge of Tomorrow*(New York: Farrar, Straus, and Cudahy, 1958), p. 54.

39. Lappe, Frances Moore; Joseph Collins; and David Kinley, *Aid as Obstacle: Twenty Questions about our Foreign Aid and the Hungry* (Institute for Food and Development Policy, San Francisco, 1980), pp. 143-146.

40. Fuller, George, "Making Business Behave," *Eternity* May 1980, pp. 17-21.

41. Dowsett, Dick, quoted in Michael Griffiths, *The Church and World Mission* (Grand Rapids, Michigan: Zondervan, 1980) p.101.

42. Brewster, E. Thomas and Elizabeth Brewster, *Bonding, and the Missionary Task* (Pasadena, CA: Lingua House, 1982), p.14.

43. Gutierrez, Gustavo, *A Theology of Liberation* (Maryknoll, New York: Orbis Books, 1973), p.26.

44. Adeney, *op. cit.,* 1983.

45. Gutierrez, *op. cit.*

46. Lissner, Jorgen, *The Politics of Altruism: A Study of the Political Behavior of Voluntary Development Agencies* (Geneva, Switzerland: Lutheran World Federation Department of Studies, 1977), p. 187.

47. Beckmann, David. *Where Faith and Economics Meet: A Christian Critique* (Minneapolis: Augsburg Publishing House, 1981), p.99.

48. Adeney, Miriam, "Magazine Coverage of American Indians," Unpublished Manuscript, 1968.

49. Oberg, Kalervo, "Culture Shock: Adjustment to New Cultural Environments," *Practical Anthropology*, July-August 1960, pp.177-182.

50. Adeney, *op. cit.*, 1983.

51. Butterfield, Herbert, *Christianity and History* (London: Fontana Books, 1957), pp. 89, 91.

52. Cartoon reprinted in Wilkinson, Loren, ed. *Earthkeeping: Christian Stewardship of Natural Resources* (Grand Rapids, Michigan: Eerdmans Publishing Co., 1980), p. 151, from *American Scientist Magazine*, Copyright 1976 by Sidney Harris.

53. Sommer, John, *Beyond Charity: U.S. Voluntary Aid for a Changing Third World* (Overseas Development Council, 1977), p. 146.

54. Tozer, A.W. *Gems from Tozer* (Bromley, Kent, England: Send the Light Trust, 1969), pp. 72, 73, 74, 13, 15.

55. Lewis, Oscar. *Children of Sanchez* (New York: Random House, 1961), pp. 38-39.

56. Sommer, *op. cit.*, p.44.

57. Butterfield, *op. cit.*, pp. 101-102.

GOD'S INTENTION FOR THE WORLD: TENSIONS BETWEEN ESCHATOLOGY AND HISTORY

Purpose. The question for our study is how God's ultimate intention for the world, expressed in the consummated Kingdom, relates to His intentions for the world next week, for the church, for human society, and for the historical process before the final consummation.

God's Action in History. God's activity is part of human history and calls for a response from those in the historical process itself. In prophetic eschatology, God was seen as active in the present. When the voice of prophecy was stilled, apocalyptical literature arose to take up the same issues and affirm God's activity in history. In Jesus Christ God demonstrated His activity in history and manifested His Kingdom by driving out demons, healing the sick, and reconciling relationships. It was already a leaven in society, a mustard seed growing, and an opponent and aggressor against evil in this world.

The triumph of the Kingdom at the end, validated by the resurrection of Jesus, is the basis for the New Testament Christian's faith that what can be tasted now of the Kingdom is a part of the final victory.

When the Kingdom is fulfilled, history finds its unity where people from all races, with their histories, find their fulfillment in the Kingdom.

How Far Is the Kingdom Continuous in History? The Christian faith stimulates us to look for the actualization in history of the Kingdom in terms of justice, access for all men to the creation which God has given to all, freedom to create a human community through work, love, worship and play. In light of the present and coming Kingdom, Christians can invest their lives in the building of a historical order in the certainty that neither they nor their efforts will be maningless or lost. The confession of the resurrection is the triumph of God's love, the fulfillment of man's stewardship and the vindication of all struggles against evil.

Implications for Development. How then can we measure the
activity of God in history? One clear guideline is the values of the Kingdom replacing the alien values of human
society. Human dignity is being affirmed and people are
discovering their innate self worth. People have the freedom to act according to their conscience without threat from
others. People are participants in decisions that affect
their lives. People develop a sense of hope for their common future. People share with one another. People struggle
for equity and justice. There is a sense of God's presence.
Development must focus as much on the transformation of
structures as the transformation of individuals and communities if it is to reflect God's intentions for the human future.

     VINAY SAMUEL is a theologian and pastor of St. John's
Church, Bangalore, India, Honorary Co-ordinator of Training
for EFICOR and Executive Secretary for Partnership in Mis-
sion--Asia.

     CHRIS SUGDEN is a well trained British theologian work-
ing as a presbyter at St. John's Church and Honorary Assis-
tant Co-ordinator of Training for EFICOR.

GOD'S INTENTION FOR THE WORLD: TENSIONS BETWEEN ESCHATOLOGY AND HISTORY

Vinay Samuel and Chris Sugden

Introduction

The theme of God's intention for the world focuses on the ultimate consummation of God's purpose in creation when Jesus returns. It focuses on Christ and the future he will bring to the world. The theme which relates God's intention for the world in its creation with its consummation is the kingdom of God. The image of the fulfilled kingdom is the millenial vision of a new heaven and a new earth where the righteousness of God is perfectly fulfilled under the Lordship of Christ over the whole cosmos.

The question for our study is how God's ultimate intention for the world, expressed in the consummated kingdom, relates to his intention for the world next week, for the church, for human society and for the historical process before the final consummation.

We will first examine the Biblical material on this question. How does the Bible relate God's work in bringing the final consummation with his work in human history?

God's Action in History

The whole Biblical revelation focuses on and interprets God's activity in history. God's call to Abraham, the exodus, and the settlement of Canaan were historical events in God's historical project, to reveal himself to a people. Through his people and their society, their laws and the experiences

of blessing on obedience and punishment for disobedience
he would reveal himself, his character and his purpose to
the world. Israel, her laws and her history were God's
light to the nations (Gen.17:6, Isa.42:6, 49:6).

The Old Testament made no separation between religious
history and the rest of history, between peoples' relationship with God and their participation in the history of human society, or between God's work among his own people and
his work among other peoples. The Bible credits God with
initiating the history of the Israelites, but also with initiating the histories of the Assyrians and the Philistines
(Amos 9:7). God's control over the history of Israel is not
fundamentally different from his control over the history
of other nations. Even though the nature of his Lordship
over Israel can be distinguished from the nature of his Lor-
ship over the nations, God is still Lord of all the nations.
God's work among his own people and his work among other
peoples, while distinct and not to be confused, are integrally related in the purpose and activity of God for the world.

How does the Bible perceive the relation between God's
intention for the world and his intention for his people?
The Old Testament evidence is as follows.

First a word study of the words used to describe God's
people shows that the term is not exclusively limited to Israel. In the Psalms the word "am" is used to refer to the
people of Israel but not exclusively so. Other nations may
be called "am" as in Ps. 18:43, "Thou didst deliver me from
strife with the peoples; thou didst make me the head of the
nations; people whom I had not known served me."

The usual term for nations is "goyyim" and Israel thought
of herself as among the "goyyim" (nations) (Gen. 10:11).
These nations are not estranged from God. Ps. 82:8 declares
"To thee belong all the nations" (Lagoyyim) and in Ps. 87
where the Lord calls the register of the peoples "ammim"
they include Egypt, Babylon, Philistia, Tyre and Sidon. In
Psalm 102:15, 21 and 22 the term nations and peoples are
synonymous. Thus in a detailed study of these terms Kenneth
Cracknell concludes that the English translations of the Bible are "misleading" in drawing a distinction between Israel
as people and others as nations (1). While the focus is on
Israel as God's people, the terms people and nations are used
interchangeably.

Secondly an examination of the covenants in the Old Testament shows that the covenant with Abraham (Gen.15:1-6, 17:1-21) did not abrogate the covenants with Adam (Gen.1:26-31) and Noah (Gen.6:18, 9:11, 9:16) which were general covenants with all nations. The covenant with Noah was moreover a covenant of both preservation and redemption (2). The Abrahamic covenant listed Israel with these covenants with the nations. The prophets insisted that any covenant with Israel was only for universal benefit and significance, not for exclusive blessing (Is. 42:6, Jer.4:2, Ps.67). For the prophets the particularism of God's covenant did not equal exclusivism.

Thirdly the eschatological vision in the Old Testament looks forward to Egypt and Assyria being God's people along with Israel (Isaiah 19:25). "In that day Israel will be the third with Egypt and Assyria, a blessing in the midst of the earth, whom the Lord of hosts has blessed, saying, "Blessed be Egypt my people, and Assyria the work of my hands, and Israel my heritage." Egypt will not have to join Israel to become "my people." Egypt will attain the status of God's people and at the same time retain her identity. The people of other nations will be gathered to God not as subsidiaries of Israel, but as themselves under the Lordship of the Messiah.

Thus the Old Testament shows that while Israel is distinct from other nations, and is already God's people, others will be his people. This work is not contingent on Israel alone.

The millenial vision in Scripture: the prophetic and apocalyptic traditions.

God's activity is part of human history and calls for a response from those in the historical process itself. In the prophets we see a very sharp focus on God and history. Their preoccupation was to announce and interpret the relationship between God and history, to call for obedience in present history, to interpret past history, and to announce the hope that lay in future history and call for obedient response. They made no separation between religious history and political history, nor between the brute facts of history and their prophetic interpretation. Their prophetic message was an act in itself, not only to explain, but to call, invite and condemn. (3)

The prophets were convinced that God was not only in charge of the history of God's people, but was Lord of all history.

God was ordering the history of his people and of the rest of the world to fulfill his purpose. When this did not seem obvious to the naked eye, questions were raised about the justice of God, in, for example, the book of Job. But they were raised only to be answered with the renewed assertion that God was in control despite appearances.

In the prophetic eschatology, God was seen as active in the present. The present events were decisive and bore an image of the actual end-event. The prophets related the fact of the end to the present and saw the present in terms of the end. The essence of their teaching was to motivate obedience in the present.

When the voice of prophecy was stilled, apocalyptic literature arose to take up the same issues of God's action in history. For after the fall of Jerusalem and the exile, Israel experienced a series of defeats in her attempts to rebuild her nation in obedience to what she saw as God's will. The heavens answered their prayers with a deafening and unending silence. Prophecy faded away.

Had God abandoned history? Apocalyptic literature arose to answer this question, including Daniel and Zechariah in the Old Testament and the books of Enoch and the Maccabees outside the canon. The answer of apocalyptic was that God had acted in the past, and that gave the assurance that he would act in the future; but he had abandoned the present. (4)

In apocalyptic eschatology, the end was thought to be imminent. Events were "foretold" by heroes of the past so that the readers would conclude that since all that was "foretold" had come to pass, then the next event, the end would come as "foretold." The essence of the teaching was vindication for God's people and judgement on his enemies and theirs. As for the present, God had abandoned it. His only action was to bring the end. All his people could do was wait.

Thus apocalyptic sought the meaning of history not in God's present activity in history, but in his activity behind and beyond history. God was no longer an actor on stage; he was behind the scenes where the real decisions that mattered took place.

The meaning of the process of world history was found not in historical events themselves. No longer should the Israelites plead with God to vindicate them in battle by defeating their enemies, and thus prove that He was Lord. No longer did he have to answer Elijah's prayers with flames of fire to consume the Baalites' offerings. Present events did not bear the image of the end-events. Instead, the meaning of the present was only to be found in the final conclusion, God's victory over all evil people and powers, and the establishment of his reign of peace with justice. The only relation that this end even had to present events was that it brought present events to a conclusion, but was entirely discontinuous with them.

This was a great foundation for faith. The pagan empires could win all the battles they wanted to, but they would not conquer in the end. Evil could take over the whole world, but it would finally be defeated. There was no need to despair or for fatalism. God would win. Meanwhile his people must remain faithful and loyal to him; they must patiently endure.

A widely held view is that apocalyptic represented a retreat from history and a very negative view of the whole of history. This has been challenged by Richard Bauckham and his challenge has found favour with others. (5) Bauckham suggests that apocalyptic did not begin as a dogma about the nature of history, that God cannot act in the history of the world, but with an empirical observation of God's relative absence from history since the fall of Jerusalem. The apocalyptists were negative not about history in general, but only about this specific period of history. (6) Their longing that God would intervene on behalf of the faithful was an expectation that he would vindicate his people and his justice on the stage of history, though in such a way as to transcend historical possibility. Thus they use language of a "new creation." Thus the apocalyptists must be seen as affirming the prophetic faith. God had acted in the past, so he would act in the future. Their present experience of his absence from history made hope for a total transformation the only appropriate expression of faith in God who ruled history.

This answer solved one problem; Israel should no longer be looking for visible evidence every day that God was in control, that virtue was rewarded and vice punished. But the answer caused another problem. As things seemed to get

so bad and evidence the absence of God, the question became
more acute; how would or could God win?

The pressure of this question tended to give prominence
and emphasis to the pessimistic and dualistic tendencies in
the apocalyptic tradition. One aspect of apocalyptic is its
concern for judgement: God will overthrow evil. The pressure
of the question how could God overthrow evil when it seems to
be so all-powerful, tended to emphasize that evil itself was
God's judgement on the world. The present age sees the activity of God in allowing evil to be so pervasive and the judgement of God in allowing evil to destroy everything. Evil is
God's activity of judgement in the world.

Thus there has always been a tendency in interpreting the
apocalyptic tradition among those who have made much of apocalyptic thinking in their theologies in the present day such
as Hal Lindsey, to focus on the pessimistic aspect of evil in
the present world as the only evidence of God's activity, an
activity of judgment.

The New Testament Perspective

The New Testament does not share the negative evaluation
of history because in Jesus Christ the expectation of the
apocalyptic tradition had begun to be fulfilled. In his mission, ministry and message, Jesus asserted and showed that
God was active in the world now, not to judge the world only,
but also to save; that God was now active to establish the
reality of his victory, to bring the firstfruits of the final
overthrow of evil, to introduce the kingdom of God to bind
the strong man and set his captives free. The kingdom was no
longer to be conceived of as a final bombshell that would
suddenly come and overthrow evil when God cried "Enough."
The kingdom was also to be conceived as a present reality,
driving out demons, healing the sick and forging new relationships of trust between alienated groups. It was already a
leaven in society, a mustard seed growing, and an opponent
and aggressor against evil in this world.

But Jesus drew on and affirmed the tradition of apocalyptic eschatology in referring to the future consummation of
the kingdom, the vindication of his mission, and judgement
of those who rejected him and his kingdom. The kingdom
would know no final consummation in this world as it stood,
for so pervasive was the disease of sin that the total coming of the kingdom could mean nothing less than a new heaven
and a new earth. The kingdom does not arise out of this

world, it does not take its roots and origins from it (7),
nor is it limited by this world's ideas of what is possible.

But the New Testament goes beyond both prophetic and apocalyptic eschatology. The triumph of the kingdom at the
end, validated by the resurrection of Jesus, is the basis for
the New Testament Christian's faith that what can be tasted
now of the kingdom is part of the final victory, and a real
firstfruits of the final harvest. In the struggle of the
kingdom against the dominion of evil, in the fruits of judgement and redemption, they were convinced that they experienced
the true shalom, the true peace that would one day finally
prevail everywhere. They were certain not just that the end
would come; nor that the present events imaged the end event.
They were certain that they tasted a firstfruit of that end
event in Christ.

The New Testament gives further definition to the relation
between Israel and the nations. Paul's letters stress that
in Christ the dividing wall between Jews and Gentiles is broken down and "in Christ" the one new humanity is already
formed   (Eph.2:11-22, Gal.3:23-29, Rom.15:7). The Pentecost
experience was of the Holy Spirit being poured out on all
nations   (Acts 2:7, 8, 17; 10:47). Paul had to resist attempts
to assert that this was because the Gentiles had (or should)
join Israel   (Gal.3:1-9). Finally the great vision of the end
sees the nations bringing them glory and honour into the new
Jerusalem   (Rev. 21:24-27). While the Gentiles are indeed in-
serted in the olive tree of Israel, that insertion is through
Christ the Messiah   (Rom. 11:17-27, Eph. 2:11-13). For Israel
had refused God's purpose for her, and so God fulfilled his
purpose in history through other means related to Israel but
not exclusively dependent on her   (Rom. 11:25-27).

What then is the relationship between the presence of the
kingdom in the world and its triumph at the return of Christ
with the history of the Old Testament, and with present history? Does it cancel out the history of the Old Testament
and obliterate the significance of present history? Two basic biblical themes are critically important for assessing
this issue.

The first theme is the relationship between the history of
God's people and the history of other nations in the Old Testament. The history of Israel in the Old Testament was demonstrably and indubitably God's history. God and human activity were integrally related as God exercised his theocratic
rule over his people. The history of the nations was not the

history of God's theocratic rule. There is thus a distinction between theocratic history, the history of God and his people, and the rest of history, that is the history of God and those who do not call themselves his people. There is a distinction between God and his historical activity among his people, and God and his historical activity among the nations. The prophetic challenge was that there was no separation between the two. God was just as concerned for the other nations as for his own people, his people were to be a blessing to other nations, and God could use other nations in his purpose and had a purpose for them. This concern and purpose was affirmed as the Gentiles entered the new Israel proclaimed by Jesus.

The second biblical theme is that this ingrafting of the Gentiles took place apart from their histories. The Bible considered that the history of the Gentiles did not make them God's people; they were "aliens from the commonwealth of Israel." Membership of God's people was not a logical outcome of their own history. But while the entrance of the Gentiles into the people of God was not a logical outcome of their history, they came into the people of God with their histories as nations. For the Gentiles are not considered as discrete individuals, but, as some recent evangelical studies suggest, as representatives of nations, ethne, who will lay the tribute of the nations at the feet of Jesus, while the Jews also retain their national identity within the new Israel.

Some argue that because the Gentiles came into the church and the people of God were no longer a historical nation, the New Testament differed from the Old Testament in that God was only concerned with the spiritual history of individuals separate from the rest of human history in society. It is in addressing this perception, which we believe is less than biblical, that the place of Jewish and Gentile Christians in the church and the relation between Gentiles, Jewish Christians and the Old Testament is critical for our understanding of God's action in history. We must talk about a new Israel which affirms the ethnic identity of the Gentile Christians and yet does not dispense with the Old Israel. The Old Israel is retained, and the hope is given that the Old Israel will one day enter into the full inheritance of God's promises to them. Any enjoyment that the Gentiles have of those promises is based on their being grafted into the activity of God in the history of the Old Israel, and sharing together the final fulfillment with the remnant of the Old Israel as they also bring their histories, the wealth of the nations, as tribute to the feet of Jesus.

The New Testament did not spiritualize or individualize history. When the Gentiles were converted, they were incorporated into the people of God and took the history of Israel and of the Messiah as their history also, in addition to their own natural history. (8) So the New Testament brought to the fore a theme implicit in the Old Testament--that the history of Israel was the history of God's promise to the nations. For the promise to Abraham was the promise for blessing to the nations. David Bosch writes:

"The history of Israel is a continuation of God's dealings with the nations. Precisely as the elect, the patriarch, and with him Israel, is called into the world of the nations." (9)

Now in Christ all nations have to relate their histories to the history of Israel, and incorporate the history of Israel into their history. (10) All nations have to be grafted into the olive tree of Israel if they would participate in the blessings of redemption which are vouchsafed to her and through her. Thus for Paul, the faithfulness of God in keeping his promises to Israel is the key issue on which the certainty of everyone's faith depends. If God does not keep his promises to Israel, then can he be trusted to keep his promises to anyone? Romans 9-11 is coming to be recognized as central to the argument of Paul's letter to the Romans. The final salvation of Israel is an indispensable part of Paul's eschatological scheme. J. Christiaan Beker writes:

"Israel's continuing function for the Gentile believer is grounded in both her salvation-historical priority as the people of the promise and her eschatological destiny. The consummation cannot come unless Israel is saved." (11)

This is so because God's faithfulness depends on the fulfillment of his promises to Israel, and by implication, to the nations as well.

The double historical reference into which all Gentile Christians are called to enter is of crucial significance. The temptation is to neglect the double historical reference and opt for a mono-historical approach. For example some Indian Christians who are engaging in the important process of seeking an authentic Indian Christian identity and Christian interpretation of Indian history, tend to absolutise their Indian history and regard the Old Testament and the Jewish and Christian heritage as merely paradigmatic for

their understanding of God's activity in their Indian history
and for their own involvement in it, rather than as a constitutive of their own historical existence as Indian Christians.
(12) Both histories of the Jewish Christian tradition in the
Bible and of Indian history must be constitutive of Indian
Christian identity and existence. This means that participation in the heritage of the Jewish Christian tradition of all
Gentile Christians on an equal basis is a crucial dimension
of the nature of the church. For that Jewish Christian history is a history for all nations, the bearer of God's promise to the world. If we absolutise Indian history and only
regard the Jewish Christian history as a paradigm for Indian
Christian existence rather than constitutive of it, we lock
ourselves into the ghetto of an ethnocentric church which has
no necessary theological, ecclesiological or existential relationships with other "churches" as part of its existence or
as part of its claim to be part of the body of Christ. It
would be an ethnocentric body of Christ sufficient unto itself in terms of its own historical identity and self-understanding. The same ethnocentric tendency can also be discerned in some understandings of civil religion, and in some
ways of linking Christianity and Christian mission with national destiny. But we are prevented from taking an ethnocentric view of history and of the church because we participate in two histories, in two ethnicities.

Many evangelicals go to the other extreme. They either
so identify with the new Israel that they forget about their
own national history as North Americans or Indians, or they
combine the history of the new Israel with their own history
and produce national religion.

Both the tendency to ignore the Jewish Christian history
and the tendency to allow it to obliterate all other history
is mono-historical. If we take Jesus Christ seriously, we
have to recognise that there is another history to our own
ethnic history and yet that other history affirms the true
nature of our own ethnic history and enables it to take its
appropriate place in the history of God's activity in his
world. We can then appreciate our own ethnic history without absolutising it.

The duality of history is thus united under the umbrella
of the kingdom of God. When the kingdom is fulfilled, history finds its unity where people from all races with their
histories find their fulfillment in the kingdom which ful-
fills God's promise to the nations mediated through the history of his people, when the wealth of the nations is brought
into the new Jerusalem.

Because the western church has had 1500 years of Christian history it has tended to neglect the task of relating the activity of God in the church and in the history of his people with his activity in human society as a whole. The western church has elided Christian history with human history, and often elided Christian religion with non-Christian civil religion. It is impossible to do this in the Two Thirds World, just as it was impossible to do it in Europe before the process of Christianisation of history overtook Europe. Thus at this stage in history, answers about the relation of God's activity among his people with his activity throughout human history which emanate from the west cannot be accepted without question in the completely different historical context of the Two Thirds World, even if they are valid within the western context, which may be itself open to doubt.

For example, traditionally in Protestant missionary thought, the history of mission in Africa, Asia and Latin America has been essentially written as the history of the expansion of the Protestant Churches of Europe and America. Thus African churches have to perceive their histories as part of the history of western Christianity. Their relationship to their own African histories is submerged. This biblical perspective would encourage us to relate the history of Africa to the history of Israel, and draw the continuity between God's action in Israelite history and African history. This process is crucial for the discovery of African or Asian or Latin American Christian identity as the recent conference of Evangelical Mission Theologians from the Two Thirds World affirmed. (13) It is also crucial, as we shall note later, for taking into account the difference which our contexts make to the way we perceive God at work in history.

The Messiah and History

The fulcrum on which the continuity and discontinuity between the Old Testament and the New Testament turns is the Messiah, Jesus. David Bosch writes:

"'Geographically' Jesus journeys to the temple, to Jerusalem and his death; 'theologically' he is bound for the nations. In the final analysis he himself would take the place of Jerusalem and the temple (John 2:19-21). As the 'New Jerusalem' he himself becomes the place of encounter with the nations. 'The Old Testament Scriptures locate the meeting of the nations in Zion, since, in the age of promise, God appointed Jerusalem to be the scene of His

revelation. The Gospel teaches us that God calls us to
meet him in Jesus Christ. Messiah has taken the place of
his city' (R.Martin Achard, *A Light to the Nations*, Oli-
ver and Boyd, London 1962, p.78). (14)

Jesus the Messiah is not just the Messiah of Israel or of
the new Israel. His kingdom is not just to be identified
with the church. His kingdom is the establishment of God's
eschatological rule over the cosmos, the whole creation
(Eph.1:21-22). Therefore the theocratic rule of God in the
Old Testament is not fulfilled in the church alone. It is
universalised in its fulfillment as his rule over all creation, which includes the nations. In view of the present
activity of God in the world, we therefore have a warrant to
discern that activity of the kingdom in the history of the
nations, of human society.

It was this sense that history was now the scene of the
activity of God that impelled the New Testament Christians
for mission and marked them off from other groups of their
time. David Bosch writes:

> "If the present is empty, as the Pharisees, Essenes, and
> Zealots believed, then you can only flee into the memory
> of a glorious past recorded in codes (Pharisees), or you
> can with folded arms sit and wait for God's vengeance up-
> on your enemies (Essenes) or you can play God yourself by
> violently liquidating the empty present, thus trying to
> make the utopian future a present reality (Zealots) or
> you can enter into an uncomfortable compromise with the
> status quo (Sadducees). But if the present is filled;...
> if 'the kingdom of God has already come upon you' (Luke
> 11:20)...those who partake of this new history...can only
> let themselves be taken along by Christ into the future,
> not as soldiers fighting in the vanguard, but as 'cap-
> tives in Christ's triumphal procession' (2 Cor.2:14)."
> (15)

Some views of the relation between the kingdom and history
do not accept that the Messianic concept is the fulcrum between eschatology and history. They make a sharp distinction
between the mission of Jesus and the mission of his church.
One proponent of this view was Johannes Weiss, who stressed
Jesus' role as an announcer of an impending apocalypse. When
the apocalypse did not come, the church found itself with a
task that Jesus had not foreseen. Arthur Johnston reflects
the same position when he writes that there is:

"a basic discontinuity between the Old and New Testaments,
and the kingdom mission of Jesus is largely unrelated to
the visible church which possesses an interim mission until the restoration of the historical Israel by the second
coming of Jesus." (16)

For Johnston, "the kingdom of God was present in a unique
way in the history by the incarnation," and this is not continued in the mission of the church and present historical
experience. (17)

If Johnston's view of the discontinuity between the kingdom mission of Jesus and the mission of the church is correct,
then it would be true that history would once again be empty;
it would certainly not be filled in the way the gospels record it full of the presence of the eschatological kingdom
as Bosch states. Bosch notes that the early Christians were
prevented from retreating into a gold past of the unrepeatable
experience of Jesus' ministry, or escaping into another world
with eyes only on the parousia, by the pivotal events of the
Resurrection and the Coming of the Spirit, which gave them
the consciousness that the present was still filled, that
they were irrevocably involved with the world and therefore
with mission...that it already made sense to live according
to the standards of the "coming age." (18)

Does the denial of a separation between God's work among
his own people and his work among other peoples, between "sacred history" and "secular history," mean that we are denying
any difference between special revelation and general revelation?

The distinction between special revelation and other history is the different way in which God works in all histories.
But the goal of God's work in all histories is the same. If
we used a distinction between sacred history and secular history to define the difference between special revelation and
general revelation, we would be assuming that God's special
revelation is confined to his activities with his people,
either Israel or the church. Such an assumption is not biblical. In the Bible God uses the historical events of Sodom
and Gomorrah, Nineveh, Babylon, Assyria and Rome to reveal
himself. God's special revelation does not create a sacred
history of God's own history. God identifies certain normal
human histories as revelatory of himself in a special, privileged and authoritative way. That revelation is the canon.

Our review of the biblical evidence of Israel and the nations has shown that while the destiny of the nations in God's purpose is linked with the destiny of Israel (Rom.9-11) that destiny is not mediated through Israel. It is mediated through the Messiah, who is Lord of Israel and the nations. The history of the nations does not belong only under the rubric of the providence of God. And the history of Israel is a stewardship of God's blessing for the nations. We cannot describe God's activity with Israel under the rubric of revelation and his activity with other nations under the rubric of providence. There is no such distinction between revelation history and the rest of history, because God was involved with Israel, Assyria and Philistia in both the political and religious histories and would rule them through his Messiah.

Thus we cannot divide up God's activity in history on the grounds of a distinction between Israel and the nations. His activity in history is focused on the Messiah to whom Israel and the nations owe allegiance. This activity is also contingent on the response of people. While God is sovereign to achieve his purposes, he set before Israel his blessings and his curses in Deuteronomy 28. If Israel walked in obedience to him, they would experience God's activity in blessing. But if they disobeyed, God would act in judgement within history. God announces similar activity in judgment on the disobedience of the nations in Amos. This shows that God's activity in history is not totally transcendant as a deistic suzerainty, nor totally immanent as a way of describing the historical process. It is in a process of involvement with his creatures and contingent on their response.

If we used a distinction between sacred history and secular history to define the difference between special and general revelation, we would be clubbing together the history of the church with the revelatory events of the Bible and calling them sacred history. That would be to raise the history of the church to the status of special authoritative revelation.

God's revelatory acts in scripture explain all history. All histories reveal God. Some histories are identified by God as bearing distinct, clear and authoritative witness to him, which is a basis for discerning his activity throughout history. Thus the denial of a distinction between sacred church history and secular human history does not undermine the biblical concept of God's special, unique, privileged and authoritative revelation in the Bible in any way.

The Millenial Vision in Relation to Creation and Fall.

The New Testament affirms that God is back on the stage of history in Jesus Christ, in the Holy Spirit and in the Church. God's people still look for his final victory. But in Jesus Christ that victory has already begun, and God is active in the world to establish beachheads of his kingdom, in the process of judgement and redemption.

How does God's activity in the world relate to the fall and the power of evil? Can God be at work in man's history in the light of the fall of man? For man is the crown of God's creation, and God's intention for the world is man's stewardship of creation. History is the tale of man's exercise of that stewardship. What difference has the fall made to man's exercise of that stewardship?

Any understanding of complete discontinuity between the kingdom mission of Jesus and all other history would seem to suggest that the fall has so corrupted human history that human history is devoid of God's activity unless it is demonstrably and undeniably God's activity. Such activity may be the judgement of God in allowing evil to flourish or the redemptive activity of God in such indubitably divine events as the ministry of Jesus. But human activity in and of itself is such that God cannot participate in it. It would seem that man's stewardship has been suspended, or at least that it cannot fulfil God's purpose for it. Instead of being a steward, man becomes a destroyer. We will argue later that such a view may presume that God's activity can only be involved with whatever is perfect. We are unsure whether such a concept is adequate to the biblical concept of God's grace, or to the biblical promise of the millenial vision of a new heavens and a new earth which fulfils rather than replaces man's work in stewardship.

As God is active in the world, the Scriptures tell us that the forces of antiChrist and of evil become more virulent in opposition as they see the notice of their defeat written and as they see the hour of their banishment approach. There is the telling picture of "the prince of the power of the air, the spirit who is at work in the sons of disobedience." (Eph. 2:2) The devil roams around like a roaring lion looking for someone to devour (I Pet.5:8). How do we reconcile this with Paul's affirmation in the same Ephesian letter that Christ now rules above all heavenly rulers, authorities, powers and lords? (Eph.1:21) We suggest that the centre of the stage is occupied by Christ while the roaring lion is offstage

trying to get on. Christ holds the centre of the stage of
history, and the devil has been thrown away from that centre.
Normal human perceptions do not see Christ at the centre of
the stage. It is the scriptures which tell us Christ is at
the centre of the stage. The New Testament confirms that
Jesus is Lord, that Jesus and not Caesar is centre of history.
This was a confession made possible only by the Holy Spirit
(I Cor.12:3). If we therefore only allow that Christ is de
jure ruler at the present and not de facto ruler, it may be
that we are looking too much at the problems of the context
and taking the roar of the lion for substance. Those problems are only evidence of the lion's roar and not of his
rule.

Is this presentation called into question by the exchange
between Jesus and the disciples in Acts 1:6-7 when the disciples ask Jesus whether he will "at this time give the kingdom back to Israel?" Jesus replies, "The times and occasions
are set by my Father's own authority, and it is not for you
to know when they will be. But you will be filled with power
when the Holy Spirit comes on you, and you will be witnesses
for me in Jerusalem, in all of Judea and Samaria and to the
ends of the earth." Jesus is not denying that the kingdom
has invaded the world. He was denying the ethnic implications
and limitations of its invasion. His answer is that it is
not a matter of the Davidic kingdom being restored to Israel,
but of the Holy Spirit coming so that the disciples would
witness to that kingdom and its presence in Judea, Samaria,
and the ends of the earth.

The above description of the biblical material would probably command a fair measure of agreement as far as a description goes. It is in the interpretation of this material and
its significance for the Christian understanding of history
that substantial debate arises. But we can discern in this
description tensions in the eschatological traditions of the
Bible which are mirrored in the tensions in views of eschatology held by Christians throughout history.

There is a tension between the interpretations of the prophetic and apocalyptic themes in the Bible. Some stress prophetic themes and emphasize God at work within history leading to a final consummation which gives significance to the
whole historical process. This theme does not limit the work
of God to historical processes, but views his work within
history as charging it with significance. Others stress
apocalyptic themes and emphasize God at work behind history
in another realm. What we experience in this realm are the
consequences of decisions and activity that takes place elsewhere.

The tension between these interpretations can be seen in many Christian interpretations of eschatology. The prophetic tradition can be interpreted in an extreme form as an optimistic view of history where God is reduced to total immanence within the historical process. The apocalyptic tradition in its extreme form can be interpreted to so stress pessimism about the future of this world under God's judgement, and the sole reality of a higher realm, that this world is reduced to a mere waiting room for the end to happen. Our task in theologising about eschatology is to be aware of this tension, and to interpret what both traditions at their best are trying to affirm.

The Prevailing Evangelical View on the Millenial Vision.

How is the relation between the consummation, creation and the historical process seen in present day evangelical thought? In general terms, one major evangelical view is pessimistic about the historical process which will get worse and worse. This view emphasises the transcendance of God who will intervene to bring a dramatic irreversible change. It stresses a qualitative difference between the consummated kingdom and any experience which we may have of it in the present. Reality is located in a transcendant kingdom which is a new heaven with largely undefined content. What matters is the arrival of this kingdom at the parousia, not what follows. The paramount concern is to preserve God's transcendance and initiative. What we experience here is the lesser kingdom in the hearts of people, that is in the church. This is a major evangelical view in the sense that the burden of proof tends to lie with those evangelicals who think otherwise, to show that they are not unbiblical.

The roots of this view lie in the strong pre-millenial tradition that arose among evangelicals in the late nineteenth century. To appreciate the way in which Christian views on eschatology are to some extent historically conditioned, we will briefly examine the view on the millenial vision in Christian history where the different social contexts in which people gave content to that vision and interpreted its meaning for present history were significant factors in the way Christians understood God's intention for the world.

The Millenial Vision in Christian History.

A strong tradition in the early church associated with Montanus, Tertullian and Irenaeus stressed that the millenial prophecies would come to pass on this earth. But from

the accession of Constantine to the period of Augustine the
millenial vision was progressively spiritualised. The trend
was set for the kingdom of God to be identified with the
church and related to a history of faith separate from the
history of society. God's activity and kingdom were locked
in the church, and history became void of God's present
activity.

This development was closely linked with the change in the
sociological status of the church when it began to find acceptance in the current social order at the time of Constantine. The millenium was identified with the church, and the
church became the bearer of the propaganda of a culture which
was identified as Christian and therefore superior to all
other cultures and religions. This brought a decisive change
in the mission of the church, which in previous centuries had
worked among people who had no place in the dominant society,
had been culturally despised herself, and had taken other
religions seriously. (17) Still a stubborn millenarianism
persisted among the obscure underworld of popular religion.

The Protestant Reformation was a protest against the equa-
tion of the kingdom of God with the divinised authoritarian
institution of the Church. The Protestant view of history
was to see God at work beyond ecclesiastical structures. The
Anabaptists saw God's work as primarily one of judgement on
both the world and the institutional church. The Lutheran
tradition viewed God's work outside the church as separate
from his work in the church, though parallel to it. While
Christians might participate in that realm, they might only
do so as citizens, not as church members.

Calvin focuses on the reign of the ascended Christ active
in the present age over the whole of human history. The work
of secular bodies was not adverse to the spiritual kingdom,
nor separate from it, but complementary "that a public form
of religion might exist among Christians and humanity among
men." The kingdom of God was to be seen at work penetrating
and transforming the political realm, and involvement in that
realm belonged to the witness and mission of the church.

In the European Enlightenment tradition of theology, the
understanding of God's work in the world, and the coming of
the millenial kingdom were secularised. It was a profound attempt to make the millenial vision worth something for the
whole of human history in the present and break out of the
narrowing of the concern and work of God to the church. It
was an attempt to rescue the millenial vision of God from

being domesticated in the already fulfilled epoch of the
church, and the hope of fulfillment from being deferred to a
transhistorical future which had no connection with present
history. The new age of mankind was more exciting and radical than the present ecclesiastical institutions which should
not be viewed as God's last word. In this tradition Kant
sought a basis for continuity between the kingdom of God and
human history in human reason and ethical capacity. It was
on this rock that this tradition was to founder, for it
proved too optimistic about the goodness of human reason and
the altruism of human moral choice.

The child of this Enlightenment tradition was the social
gospel movement in the United States of America. This saw
the work of God in bringing the kingdom as the work of an immanent spirit in history directing it towards its final goal.
This view coincided well with the evolutionary optimism of
many in the societies of the day. But it must not be supposed that all representatives of the tradition saw the coming of the kingdom as uninterrupted human progress. Some
attempted to preserve the divine initiative in bringing the
kingdom, and an awareness of the power of evil over humanity.
A major question to be addressed to the social gospel tradition is whether it reduced transcendence to divine initiative
in directing history.

Similar optimism had permeated the first expression of
the millenial vision in the United States, and up to the time
of the Civil War, post-millenialism was the prevalent view.
The great outburst of revival and mission, the sense of destiny and optimism about the growth of the United States, and
the apocalyptic terrors of the French Revolution and the Na-
poleonic Wars were all taken as signs of the approaching end.
In Britain, the French Revolution was construed by upper
class Christians who feared the loss of their privileges by
revolts among the lower orders, as signs of approaching catastrophe in the pessimistic framework of pre-millenialism.
In the United States it was construed in the optimistic framework of post-millenialism because of the social and cultural
optimism of the context. The United States was the land of
opportunities and hope for the world.

But as the nineteenth century progressed, premillenial
views came to dominate more and more in evangelical circles,
asserting that Christ would return before the millenium that
only He could usher in. Slowly, what Timothy Smith and David
Moberg have described as The Great Reversal took place, whereby the social concern expressed by evangelicals in the

nineteenth century was replaced by a distinct antipathy to
Christian social involvement by evangelicals in the twentieth. Moberg identifies among the reasons for this change a
hermeneutic of scripture which prevented its holders from
finding guidance for social concern, a concern for the supernatural facets of the Christian faith, which along with a
premillenial eschatology, separated this world from the
other world, and a sociological basis for the evangelical
community that was moving away from the inner cities into
suburban areas with cultural values that had proved their
worth on the frontier, but had been shown to be inadequate
in the inner city. (20)

Peter Kuzmic identifies some of the sociological factors
that surround the rise of premillenialism:

"Following the Civil War in America, things instead of
getting better were continually getting worse. This
brought about increasing disillusionment and pessimism,
which seriously undermined the credibility of post-millenialism with its optimistic outlook for spiritual and
cultural progress of society. Such disappointing developments, preceded by the cataclysmic events at the turn of
the nineteenth century and followed by two world wars in
the twentieth, provide the framework for at least a partial understanding of the reasons for the rapid spread
and popularity of premillenial views in modern times.
It is a historically observable fact that premillenialism
with its apocalyptic assumptions has a special appeal and
tends to flourish in times of great crisis and distress."
(I.J.Rennie, "Nineteenth Century Roots" in *Handbook of
Biblical Prophecy,* p.44) (21)

From this historical survey (22) we may note a number of
significant points. First we note that tension between prophetic and apocalyptic traditions in eschatology runs throughout Christian history. We also note a tension between the
concern to make the millenial vision relevant to the whole of
history, and the concern to root it specifically in the experience of the church.

Secondly, we note that the various millenarian viewpoints
which people adopted were related to the cultural values of
the time, or to their position outside the cultural mainstream.
When the church became settled in society at the time of Constantine, it embraced a spiritualised eschatology. Revolutionary apocalypticism found adherents among the socially
marginalised. While the French Revolution was interpreted as

a sign of the end in a post-millenial framework amidst the
social and cultural optimism of America, it was interpreted
in a premillenial framework among the upper classes in Britain who would be threatened by it. (23)

Thus, we note that while premillenarianism expects the
world to get worse and worse, and thus gives very little
hope for reforming it by human effort, those who hold premillenarian views often (but by no means always) strongly
support existing structures and patterns of life. The reason
for such conservatism is that the present is radically separated from the future hope. The more that this is done, the
more the existing order is without any realistic reference
point for criticism. Any social or political option is equally good or bad. But cast loose in this fashion from any
realistic critique, Christian views merely reproduce the dominant cultural values of the society of which the church is
part. Thus some Christians in the Third Reich supported Hitler and some Christians in today's world are seen supporting
oppressive regimes.

We also note that in the nineteenth century the hope of
the kingdom was identified and conflated with evolutionary
optimism by those whose experience of the world was of situations that were getting better and better.

All these views claimed to be interpreting the Bible literally. Their diversity shows that they did not have an adequate hermeneutic. The additional fact that premillenial
views do not always entail social pessimism (in, for example,
the case of Lord Shaftesbury) shows that when premillenial
views are linked with social pessimism, this may well be for
reasons other than hermeneutics or theology.

We note today that many who hold premillenarian views are
socially concerned and involved. But prima facie they seem
to be not obviously theologically integrated. If we take
premillenialism on its own, its internal logic gives no adequate theological undergirding for critiqueing or directing
Christian social responsibility. This is not in any way to
deny the committed social concern of people with premillenialist views who we would suggest are also directed by other
scriptural themes than premillenialism for their social involvement. It is not clear that it is their premillenialism
which is their theological motivation for social involvement.

The socially concerned premillenialist is motivated by a
desire to demonstrate his or her Christian faith in a socially

responsible way today, mainly in obedience to the love commandment. But in order that social involvement may make the
kind of impact that the kingdom demands, it must first be
motivated by a millenial vision of God's intention for society, history and the world, and not merely by the desire
to express the fruits of one's spirituality. For there are
two poles to Christian social involvement. One is the pole
of personal obedience to God, and the second is the activity
of God and his purpose for the whole of history. The socially concerned premillenialist tends to take the first pole
alone, so that his social engagement is not historically
oriented and therefore does not give due consideration to
the context of his action. It is an ahistorical engagement,
in that while it may address the needs of communities and
even the problems of structures, it does not take seriously
the historical context, because it is not motivated by the
God of history and by a millenial vision. We must heed the
warning of Christian leaders in Marxist countries who point
out that Christian social activity without a Christian millenial vision will give place in the end to the Marxist alternative which is rooted in a vision of history and which
will supply the missing dimension for the vacuum which such
ahistorical Christian activity will create. On the contrary
the practice of the socially concerned premillenialist may
be restricted by a millenial vision which sees the present
only in negative terms.

The close links between context and views on eschatology
does not mean that we should divorce ourselves totally from
our context in order to arrive at an objective, neutral view
on biblical eschatology. It does not mean that we should
regard most eschatology since the New Testament times as de-
clensions from an obvious and clear biblical position on the
matter. Each was a pilgrimage to discover the meaning of
the biblical material in the readers' own context. Each has
a claim to be rooted in at least some aspect of the biblical
tension between prophetic and apocalyptic hopes, the present
and the future, the immanent and the transcendant, the continuous and the discontinuous. This does not mean that each
view is as valid as any other. It means that we cannot divorce ourselves from our own historical context, assume that
we now enjoy the correct perspective and proceed to judge
every other attempt from that privileged viewpoint.

What Is Present of the Future the World is Moving Towards?

Evangelical orthodoxy which has its roots in the premillenial tradition of the nineteenth century stresses the

qualitative difference between the consummated kingdom and any experience which we may have of it in the present. Thus any possible experience of the kingdom in the present is fundamentally discontinuous with and qualitatively completely different from the consummated kingdom in every respect. Anything which we apprehend of the future in the present is only spiritual and is limited to the church. Any material dimension of the kingdom that seems to be present in the biblical records is therefore to be isolated to the mission of Jesus, which was unique, or to be located in the millenial future. This view takes a particular stand on certain important theological questions which we will now examine.

The Activity of God in History.

First it has a specific view of the sovereignty, grace and perfection of God in any activity connected with humanity. God's activity is posited in human history when his sovereignty, grace and perfection can be clearly affirmed without any further ambiguities. This limits his activity to the born-again experience, and to experiences of deliverance and guidance which are self-evidently the acts of God. This view seems to assume that when these activities of God were active in the incarnation, the incarnation was perfect. The incarnation was when God took on human flesh without sin and thus any divine human activity must be perfect.

However, if we examine the incarnation further, we see that in scripture the emphasis of the incarnation in relationship to us is not on the divine-human mingling that took place there. We are not asked to model ourselves on the nature of Jesus' divine-humanness in the incarnation. Rather the focus is on the mission of the incarnation. In this mission there were many ambiguities, misunderstandings, and apparent imperfections. For example, the group of disciples that Jesus chose contained a traitor and a leader who would deny Jesus. Yet, the New Testament affirms that in these imperfections, the sovereignty, grace and perfection of God were preserved.

We are not called to reproduce the nature of the incarnation. That nature was perfect, and in the light of it we are far from incarnate people. We are children of Adam by nature. It is by adoption as sons, by our union with the New Adam, that we are called to participate in the mission of the incarnate one. The New Testament affirms that that mission with all its imperfections, quarrels, disagreements and backslidings is by the work of the Spirit the continuance of the mission of Jesus in history through his body the church. In that mission the sovereignty, grace and perfection of God take and use the imperfections and ambiguities of man to fulfil his purpose.

The Perfect and Imperfect.

Secondly, this view which limits our experience of the present kingdom to the spiritual dimension assumes that everything that is "spiritual" in this life is perfect, and that therefore any experience we have of redemption cannot be mingled with imperfection. This assumption would seem to be questionable for the following reasons:

First, God will judge everything including our own personal response to him. Not only will the quality of that response be judged as to whether we have built gold, silver, wood, grass or straw on the foundation of Christ (I Cor.3: 10-15), but the New Testament records warnings that Christians should not presumptively take salvation for granted and do nothing in response. The parables of the talents, the judgement of the sheep and the goats, and the teaching of Romans 5-7 on grace, sin, and righteousness all presume that our response to God's gift will be subject to his judgement. Redemption is thus not a hermetically sealed isolated mystical experience that is perfect and cannot be removed. It is a relationship of forgiveness, love and obedience to God which is subject to his judgement.

Secondly the Bible does not know of a mystical experience or a relationship with God which exists separately from human relationships. The individual receives his call from God in the context of God's formation of a community and a people (24). A relationship with God of forgiveness is dependent on forgiving others in turn (Matt.18:35). If we do not love our brother, we cannot love God (I John 4:12,20). Love of God and love for the neighbour are mutually interpreting commands which together interpret the law of God. (25) There are also no laws about a relationship with God which are independent of a relationship with other people. (26) Life is union with Christ, is life in union with others in Christ (Gal.3:26-28).

Thirdly, life in union with Christ is an experience of relationships in union with others in Christ in the Church. These relationships are characterised by love, forgiveness, compassion, forgiveness, generosity and patience. Paul describes these values as "heavenly" in contrast to "earthly" values, because they will last (Col.3:1-17). These redeemed relationships between members of the church will last and be

transformed in the consummated kingdom when the bride is
united with the bridegroom. Thus we experience here on earth
relationships which are a real experience of the future kingdom. Redemption is mediated through human relationships. The
church will be judged (I Cor.3:9-15). This means that while
these relationships are a real experience of God's kingdom,
they are also less than perfect.

Therefore God's gift of redemption is not a spiritual,
perfect, mystical substance, to be received by the individual
in isolation from the rest of life. God's grace in redemption
is God at work, taking imperfect human relationships, redeeming them and using them in the context of his care and love.
The heavenly values of the kingdom are to be expressed in the
early structures of husband, wife; parent, child; and master,
slave (Col.3:18-22), the last of which certainly we can say
will not be reproduced in the consummated kingdom. God's redemptive grace is the new relationship with God experienced
in a human context and transforming all other relationships.

If the man's participation in God's grace in the church
involves a real experience of the kingdom, despite the imperfections in thoserelationships, then even though other experiences in human society outside the church are mingled with
imperfection, those experiences are not thereby debarred from
participation in the present experience of the kingdom of God.
For all redemptive experience is both ambivalent, ambiguous,
imperfect and at the same time participates in the finality
of the kingdom. (27)

Heaven and Earth

Thirdly, this view makes a radical disjunction between
heaven and earth. In the biblical material they are closely
bound together in one unified creation.

G.E.Ladd writes:

"If the kingdom is limited to the spiritual relation of
men to God, the consummation of the kingdom would be
achieved by the final inclusion of all men in the kingdom
when every last individual on earth has accepted God's
rule." (26)

The key issue here is to determine the exegetical value of
the concept of heaven in the Bible. Andrew Lincoln in his
Cambridge doctoral study *Paradise Now and Not Yet* (Cambridge
1981) suggests that the concept of the heaven lies in Paul's

letters as a way of expressing an experience of a transcendent relationship with God in cosmological language.

Lincoln points out that heaven and earth are one structure
in God's creation in the biblical cosmology. Not only were
both created by the same God, but both were affected by humanity's fall. Thus Col.1:20 presupposes that heaven is affected by the fall: "God made peace through his son's death
on the cross, and so brought back to himself all things,
both on earth and in heaven."

The heavenly world is populated now by spiritual forces
of wickedness that believers are to fight against (Eph.3:10,
6:10, 6:12). Thus heaven is still involved in the present
age with the consequence that war in heaven will continue
until the consummatory victory brings in the fulness of the
new age with its reconciled cosmos. Lincoln writes:

"Above all heaven and earth are shown to be inseparably
connected by the redemption which God has accomplished
in Christ" (cf. Col.1:20; Eph.1:10,22f; 4:10). (27)

The important point is that in Paul's cosmology heaven is
not the place of perfection that will one day replace earth.
Heaven is not set over against earth. Both form one structure of created reality, both partake in the consequences of
human sin, and both will experience the redemption of Christ.

Man's response to God's one structure of created reality
can however take two possible directions. Lincoln writes:

"The sinful response brought about disunity in the cosmos
and this direction of disobedience can be called "earthly."
In Philippians 2:19 and Colossians 3:2,5, "earthly" is
contrasted to heavenly and takes on the connotation of
sinful, with the earth being viewed as the primary setting
of fallen creation." (28)

In Colossians, the things of earth include the practices
of the old man (3:5-9), the sphere of the flesh (2:18,23),
and life in the world with its bondage to elemental spirits
(2:20). The direction of obedience, exemplified by the obedience of the second man (Rom.5:19) is associated with the
heavenly (I Cor.15:47). Insofar as believers continue in
response to God's salvation in Christ they are now seated
with him in heavenly places (Eph.1:3), they can be called
"heavenly" (I Cor.15:48) and be encouraged to be "heavenly-
minded" (Col.3:1).

Thus believers now experience the substantial restoration of the unity of the cosmos, which expresses the restoration of all things under the rule of God. What is in view here is not so much the cosmological geography, as the unity and wholeness of all creation which those in union with Christ now experience. Thus Lincoln writes:

"This stress of believers' association with heaven through union with Christ does not close the earth or this world to believers but opens them. Because they belong to Christ, all things belong to believers, including the world (cf. I Cor.3:22...) Colossians demonstrates that it is because believers participate in the triumph of the exalted Christ over the powers that they have been set free to use this world and its structures. Indeed believers are to bring the life of heaven to earth as they reflect and live out that life. The force of Philippians 3:20 is not that heaven as such is the homeland of Christians to which they, as perpetual foreigners on earth, must strive to return, but rather that since their Lord is in heaven their life is to be governed by the heavenly commonwealth and that this realm is to be determinative for all aspects of their life. Colossians 3 again shows that Paul does not believe that real life is in this other world and that as a consequence life on earth has relatively little significance, but that heavenly life is to take form within the structures of human existence, in the husband-wife, parent-child, master-slave relationships...The apostle can insist both on the necessity of heavenly-mindedness and on the fulness he expects to see in the personal, domestic, communal and social aspects of Christian living. The quality of the concentration on the things above where Christ is will ensure that the present sphere of his rule will not remain simply in heaven but will be demonstrated in the lives of his people on earth." (31)

Thus Paul in his language of the heavenlies is expressing in cosmological language man's restored relationship of obedience to and union with the Creator, which is part of the total reconciliation of the whole creation. Without focussing on the cosmology as such, Paul is describing in cosmological language that relationship with God which embraces and affects life in this world but is not limited to it. He is not speaking of a sphere of existence in the future which will invade this world, but a present restored relationship with God which is possible now and which

will last forever. That relationship is expressed in a lifestyle which gives precedence to those values which characterised the life of Jesus and found expression in the sermon on
the mount. These are the ethics of the kingdom, which John
Yoder in his book *The Politics of Jesus* (32) suggested were
the real root of Paul's ethics, in contrast to the suggestion
that devoid of any ethical resources from Jesus, the New Testament Christians cast about for current codes of ethics.
This is the lifestyle, and these are the values that Christ
lived, that God vindicated in the resurrection, and that will
last forever.

In conclusion, such a view is imprisoned by a concept of
the transcendent which can only be related to the spiritual
and individual inner experience, and by the understanding
that what will be continuous in the future kingdom will be
our spiritual life. But such reasoning fails, as it means
at the same time asserting that we experience a lesser Christ
than the one who will reign in glory. This "two kingdom's
view" in fact is deficient in its Christology and thus in
its doctrine of God, by suggesting that what we experience
here of the kingdom and the king is secondary, a pale imita-
tion of the real thing which will be experienced in the future.

What Is the Future of God's Work Outside the Church?

Is the continuity between the kingdom and this world
only continuity between the kingdom and the church, or is it
continuity between the kingdom and the whole of human history?
The question becomes the question of the future of God's work
outside the church. Some describe this as the work of God's
left hand. If there is no continuity between this work and
his work in the Church, the only continuity which is possible
between the kingdom and history is between the kingdom and
the Church in the spiritual realm. This makes certain un-
tenable theological assumptions. Therefore, we must examine
the possibility and the nature of the work of God outside the
Church, and its relationship with the presence and consummation of the kingdom.

The question is whether we can use the term redemption
for God's activity outside the church. We would like to define redemption as the activity of God in fulfilling his intention for the world. Therefore the focal points of redemption would be the Lordship of Christ in the present working
towards the consummation of his purpose. Within this over-
arching understanding of redemption, one may speak of the

experience of regeneration, forgiveness and new life. But the experience of regeneration itself cannot be the defining category for redemption. The defining category can only be Jesus' Lordship, not the individual experience of that.

The Biblical evidence that God's redemptive activity is not confined to the church is as follows.

The Experience of Redemption Cannot Be Limited to the Church.

While the church is where the activity of God in redemption is mainly focussed, we cannot limit experiences of redemption solely to those in the church. That does not mean that those outside the church are regenerate; it does mean that they can be objects of God's redeeming activity.

First the church's own experience of redemption is based on the Lordship of Christ over creation. Jesus as resurrected, ascended Lord is exalted now as Lord over all creation. His Lordship over the church is derived from that (Eph.1: 20-23). Paul writes "God put all things under Christ's feet and gave him to the church as supreme Lord over all things." Full authority in heaven and earth, that is throughout the unified creation, has been given to him (Matt.28:18). Therefore we may boldly pray "Thy kingdom come, thy will be done on earth as in heaven"--and not just "in the church." David Bosch writes:

> "The Kingdom comes wherever Jesus overcomes the evil one. This happens (or ought to happen) in fullest measure in the church. But it also happens in society." (33)

The rediscovery of an eschatology which affirmed Christ's present Lordship in the world as had been maintained by Calvin came, according to Alfred Krass, in the struggle of the German churches with Hitler. Nazism challenged all that the Reformed tradition had stood for. The issue was joined according to W.A.Visser't'Hooft with the Barmen Declaration of 1933:

> "In the light of the Kingship of Christ, it is a priori to be explained that the state stands under the Lordship of Christ, all power has been given to him." (34)

Krass continues:

> "Reformed theologians had been tempted to operate with a 'history of salvation' separate from the natural order,

but they discovered under pressure that 'the New Testament does not know a general providence apart from the history of salvation...'

"When Hitler sought to turn the course of world history against what the church knew was God's plan, the church was pushed to exercise its proper, positive prophetic vocation, to speak out on behalf of all efforts contributing to the intra-historical realisation of God's promises." (35)

Following this experience, the Netherlands Reformed Church published Foundation and perspectives of Confession in 1950 and 1954. It stated:

"We can take our place in history without fear. History is the total event, directed from Christ's first coming toward his second coming...History manifests itself in a series of crises. There is no evolution, but a continuing advance of Christ's work and consequently an increasing raging of anti-Christian forces." (36)

One of the authors of this document was Hendrik Berkhof. He maintained the tension between the transcendence and immanence of this work of the kingdom. He writes:

"The kingdom of God is the work of God himself. This is the truth of the orthodox position. The error is to believe that it must therefore be   sudden,even entirely from without. God is active in the world. The Kingdom of God grows. This is the truth of the liberal position. The error is to believe that it is therefore man's labour, and that it is identical with moral and social progress...

"In the struggle for a genuine human existence, for the deliverance of the suffering, for the elevation of the underdeveloped, for the redemption of the captives, for the settlement of race and class differences, for opposition to chaos, crime, suffering, sickness and ignorance...an activity is taking place throughout the world to the honour of Christ. It is sometimes performed by people who know and desire it; it is more often performed by those who have no concern for it, but whose labour proves that Christ truly received--in full objectivity--all power on earth...

"The new world does not fall into the old like a bomb,
nor does it take the place of the old which is destroyed,
but is born through the old in which it had been active."
(37)

The second reason why we cannot limit the experience of
redemption to the church is that the church is part of history. The church often fails in its task and shares many of
the features of secular history, which it is affected by.
(38)

The church is affected by secular history. Some of the
more tragic aspects of church history show this, such as
the "Crusades" as well as some of the more creditable aspects, such as the vast expansion of the church in parallel
with the growth of mercantile colonialism. The church also
has an effect on secular history, even "unintentionally,"
when converted individuals change society.

Therefore the kingdom activity is not the only influence on the history of the church. The church is influenced
by secular history and also influences secular history.
Therefore, it cannot be maintained that the kingdom finds
its expression in this world only in the church. The church
is both faithless to its inheritance and also spreads its
inheritance wider than its own boundaries. Thus this argument from observation also adds to our conclusion that the
experience of redemption cannot be limited to the church.

The Conscious Confession of Christ

The "limited" view suggests that, in the New Testament,
kingdom and salvation language are only used to refer to
what happens when people enter into a conscious and personal
relationship with Christ and the new body of believers, and
also that kingdom language is only used when Christ himself
is present in his earthly ministry or when people now in the
age of the church consciously acknowledge him as Lord and
Saviour.

But there is a distinction between submission to the
Lordship of Christ and experience of the Lordship of Christ.
To experience the kingdom does not mean people submit to
Christ as Lord. Jesus himself said that many would claim
to have spoken God's message, driven out demons and performed miracles in his name. While he said he never knew
them, he did not equate their activity with demonic or
devilish activity. This experience of the kingdom is

sometimes referred to under the concept of providence. We do not want to style it like that lest it split the activity of God into unrelated parts.

Instead we suggest that there are activities, structures and movements in the world that participate in God's salvation activity. God's salvation activity has redeemed the human race, broken the power of evil, and created a new humanity. The world is substantially different because of the victory of Christ on the cross and in his resurrection, through which Christ is exalted as Lord of all. Many individuals may benefit from this experience but refuse to submit to Christ as Lord. They may experience the kingdom which is moving human history forward to its consummation at Jesus' return in a new heaven and new earth.

For example, many women may experience the fruit of the kingdom in the transformation of their status in society and yet not consciously acknowledge Christ. Is transformation of the status of women only to be seen as the providential activity of God? Is it not part of God's work of breaking down the dividing wall of hostility between separated groups that he might create in himself one new man where there is neither male nor female? We must recognise as a fact of history that in many situations the church in its witness to the Lord Jesus has been the instrument of changing the status of women through pioneering literacy and education for women. Those women who benefit from this changed status to a certain extent live transformed lives; they are no longer the same people they would have been. They participate in the transformation which the kingdom brings. They do not consciously acknowledge Christ, they are not members of the kingdom nor have they entered it. But they have participated in the transformation which the kingdom is bringing about in the world. There is no biblical condition that participation in the transformation of the kingdom is limited only to its members. But such an experience is not to be equated with a saving faith in Christ. Obedience to the king is salvific, but experiencing the reign of Christ in the kingdom of Christ in a more general sense is not.

Thus we cannot define the presence of the kingdom by the scope of salvation language. We must define the scope of the kingdom by the fact that Christ the king of the kingdom is God's agent in creation, that the kingdom will consummate God's purpose in the whole creation, and that in Christ's ministry many experienced the kingdom's reality without entering it. For example only one of the ten lepers whom Christ

healed returned to give thanks to him. This man experienced
salvation in Christ.

   While redemption is experienced outside the church, there
is a qualitative difference between the experience of redemption which results in the confession of Jesus as Lord, and
the experience of redemption where such confession is not
immediately evident. In the confession of Jesus as Lord,
which is the heart of the kingdom experience inspired by the
Holy Spirit, there is freedom for Christ's Lordship to operate, to be expressed and to be experienced in its fulness.

   On the other hand, Christ's Lordship may be evident in
an area like economic justice, but cannot be confined there.
The Holy Spirit's activity of applying the Lordship of
Christ may begin with economic justice but breaks through to
all areas, with the goal of people owning the name of Christ
and bowing to him as Lord of all.

   We therefore have to seek a statement of the relation
of the kingdom to history which does not spiritualize history or relegate it to insignificance.

The Spiritualizaion of History

   The spiritualisation of history is a fundamentally Hindu
concept. It is based on a monistic view of religion, where
the only reality is God. Everything else is non-reality, il-
lusion. God (reality) cannot be experienced in history (non-
reality). Therefore any history that God is said to be encountered in must be spiritualised and put on the plane of
the truly real, of God. Thus it becomes fundamentally a-
historical and mythological. Mythology is thus the product
of a concept which fundamentally separates God and human
history.

   By the same token, any attempt to spiritualise the history of Jesus, isolating it from Old Testament history,
secular society or the church, by creating a "sacred" history or isolating the kingdom from our history, devalues
human history in comparison with what is regarded as the
truly real. This mythologises Jesus and the kingdom in Hindu fashion. It was quite logical for those who could not fit
a supernatural Jesus into a scientific world view to speak
of "The Myth of God Incarnate." But the people responsible
for mythologising Jesus are precisely those who affirm that
only Jesus and his kingdom are really real and are by that
token removed from ordinary history. The Bible states that

the "Word became flesh" and "in him dwelt the fulness of
God bodily." Many Christians affirm that of Jesus in theory,
but have a docetic soteriology. They forget that docetic
Christology was always fundamentally an argument about soteriology. Their soteriology which is an a-historical salvation
from the world shows that they are fundamentally docetic in
Christology in spite of their affirmation that Jesus was
God become man. The process of removing Jesus in practice
to a special realm, and "elevating" the king to the spiritual realm removed from our human history is strikingly similar to the Hindu process of mythologisation.

Thus those who would isolate Jesus and his kingdom to a
special realm that has no real connection with our history,
which is by contrast due to be scrapped, and who do not
therefore believe that God can be seen to be active in any
imperfect historical event, are mythologising God. For they
in fact believe with the Hindu that God's perfection cannot
be grasped in the world. Professor David Jenkins writes:

"If worshippers of God do not really believe that he is
to be encountered in and through the actualities of daily
living and contemporary history, then he is indeed merely
a cultic object sustained by a 'myth' which works effectively only as long as the myth dominates culture, but
which is simply a mere story maintained by 'believers'
against the realities of the world, once culture changes.'"
(39)

It is interesting to note that when this "mythologized"
God is the subject of evangelical preaching in India, he
elicits little response except to place him alongside all the
other 33 million Hindu gods. He is no different from them.
It is only when Jesus and his kingdom are seen as operative
in history now through healing miracles, social change such
as the end of casteism in the mass-movements, or social development in projects such as the Rural Health Project at
Jamkhed, that there is significant lasting response. (40)

This response is significant, because it recognizes that
God is in fact operative at all three levels that have been
discerned in a people's world view. Anthropologist Paul
Hiebert suggests that the three levels of a people's world
view are first, the level of cosmic gods and forces which relate to the origin of the universe, the large questions of
life, death, fate and destiny. The third level is the level
of human interaction between persons and between persons and
nature on the level of science. In between these two levels

is a level which the Enlightenment tradition of the West has
argued is illusory and therefore to be discounted: the level
of spirits, angels, demons,witchcraft, and saints.

This second level is a very potent force, especially in
the life of poor communities whose life is dominated by religion. (41) No area of life is secular in the strictest
sense. But the spiritual forces which dominate their life
are found in the second level. Their life is lived in constant interaction with the second level, which has spiritual
forces of both good and evil. In many cultures the second
level is dominated by evil forces. So day to day life is
lived in fear of these negative forces. Sin, as a rebellion
against the cosmic god, has little significance. (42)

The propitiation of a local deity or demon to heal a sick
child goes side by side with adherence to a cosmic god of one
of the major world faiths. This process takes place even
among poor Christian communities, because the tradition of
mission has affirmed a cosmic god, practiced medical science
for healing, and failed to address this level of the principalities and powers adequately. Thus the process of demyth-
ologization advocated by some Christians, and the spirituali-
zation of history practiced by others both demonstrate the
effects of the Enlightenment on Christian mission worldwide.
This description of a people's world view which Hiebert suggests, further shows the perils of spiritualizing God's involvement with history. It opens the way to a secularism
that either rejects the reality of God or removes him to a
place beyond history.

This process of pushing God out of our human history is a
process of paganisation and totalitarianism. It also turns
realism about human sin into pessimism about the human condition. Jenkins writes:

"A properly Christian doctrine of sin must be placed firmly within a Christian understanding of creation and redemption. We are to perceive what sin is in relation to
the Glory of God, His commitment to the fulfillment of
creation and his saving work in Christ to redeem, restore
and sum up all things. Realism concerning evil distortion and failure is demanded but pessimism is exorcised.
Pessimism arises out of the basic theological mistake of
pushing God out of history and out of the mistake in discipleship which will not share in God's risk of getting
close to men and women in their actual struggles, sufferings and hopes." (43)

How Far Is the Kingdom Continuous with History?

The biblical understanding of the new earth would seem
to suggest that consummated history will be part of the new
reality of the new order. The work of God in creation, and
the work of man as his steward, in history, will be taken
up in the new earth. The Old Testament clearly thinks that
history will be consummated on this earth and not elsewhere.
If the Old Testament hope of this transformed earth plays no
part in our eschatology, we have to ask how far we have effectively deleted the Old Testament from our canon.

We have suggested that the New Testament is continuous
with the Old Testament view of one history by universalising
the history of Israel and making it the olive tree into which
all Gentile nations are grafted in order to participate in
redemption.

But what continuity is there in the New Testament between
present history and the kingdom? We have seen the dangers
of asserting that there is no continuity. Do historical hap-
penings have any value in terms of the Kingdom which God pre-
pares and will establish in the Parousia of the Lord? In discussing this question, Jose Miguez Bonino argues that we must
seek an answer that states something in terms of causality.
He fears that too often the desire to protect God's initiative reduces historical action to merely producing images
that may remind us of the kingdom, but which have no actual
significance for the coming of the kingdom among us. He also suggests that fear of absolutising any human action as an
activity of the kingdom means that historical action of both
the right and the left are equally valuable or invaluable.
There is nothing to choose between them. Can a relationship
between the kingdom and history be mapped out which is biblical, and which is sufficient to enable us to commit ourselves
to a present historical project as a project of the kingdom?
(44)

What are the biblical components of an answer? The resurrection of the body is a key concept. The *body* is resurrected
so that who we are in our present historical life will be
recognisable and yet totally transformed. This transformation will not disfigure or weaken our bodily life but fulfil
and perfect it by eliminating all corruptibility and weakness.
The *resurrection* of the body is not the rescue of a spiritual
element in human life to cleanse it from the bodily experience
and identity obtained throughout life; it is the total redemption of man, the fulfilment of bodily life cleansed from

self-deception and self-seeking   (Rev.7:13-17, I Jn.3:2,
Matt. 22:29-32, Phil.3:20-21).

Thus what we do in our bodies in everyday life has a future, according to Paul, to the extent that our deeds belong
to the new order of the world of the resurrection, the order
of love (Phil.1:9-11, 2 Thess.5:4-8, Col. 3). At the same
time we perform these deeds within the structures of history,
as masters, slaves, wives, husbands, parents, and children.
Because Christ has risen and brought in a new realm of love,
deeds of love bear the marks of the new age and will find
lasting fulfilment when the new age is fully with us at the
return of Christ. This new age does not deny history but
eliminates its corruption, frustration and sin, to bring to
fulfilment the communal life of people. Whatever we do in
every sphere of life, be it social, political, economic or
religious, which is marked by the love of the new order,
will remain (I Cor.5:10-15, Matt.10:40-42). But this fulfilment is not a matter of gradual evolution. Suffering, conflict, judgement and total transformation at the return of
Christ is the pathway by which history finds its consummation
in the kingdom. The kingdom redeems and transforms the deeds
of love done in history. Thus these deeds of love are not
mere reflections or foreshadowings of the kingdom within history, but the actual presence and operation of the Kingdom,
however imperfect and partial.

Protests against expressions such as "building the Kingdom" are valid protests against a naive optimism and are a
justified protection of the divine initiative. But they are
usually cast in an unbiblical view of God as a pre-programmed
force who produces certain events like the incarnation and
the return of Christ without reference to what is going on in
human history. We must remember that God is also active within human history and prompts human action, calling for our
participation with him. Thus the metaphors and pictures of
growth, as for example in the parables of the sower, the
mustard seed and the leaven, have biblical and theological
warrant.

If we adopt this perspective, the main question is not
where is the kingdom present or visible in today's history,
but "How can I take part in, express and produce the quality
of personal and corporate life which will be fulfilled in
God's kingdom?" Such action will involve both proclamation
and deeds. Both the announcement of the kingdom and action
which corresponds to its quality are eschatologically significant, and neither can be reduced to the other. The tension

between them cannot be reduced this side of the full realization of God's kingdom between what names this future and what
corresponds to its reality. To avoid absolutising any of our
human action in the name of the kingdom, we must have re-
course not to idealism nor to divine politics, but to the
best human politics possible, and that will always be a matter open to debate.

Thus the Christian faith stimulates us to look for the
actualisation in history of the kingdom in terms of justice,
access for all men to the creation which God has given to
all, freedom to create a human community through work and
love, worship and play. In the light of the present and
coming kingdom, Christians can invest their lives in the
building of a historical order, in the certainty that neither
they nor their effort is meaningless or lost. Thus the confession of the resurrection is not a selfish desire for immortality, a recompense for sufferings, or a wish-fulfillment,
but the affirmation of the triumph of God's love, the fulfilment of man's stewardship of creation and the vindication
of all struggles against evil. (45)

The Fear of Absolutisation

There is fear among some of identifying any historical
project with the kingdom of God. They prefer to see history
as merely an image, a foreshadowing or reflection of the kingdom to prevent us absolutising a particular project as a project of the kingdom.

European theologians are especially alive to what they
perceive as tendencies to absolutise history in liberation
theologians. Liberation theologians are in dialogue with
Marxism, which represents an absolutist tradition.

We perceive that both the absolutisation and the spiritualisation of history stem from the Enlightenment tradition.
The Enlightenment began the process of reducing the transcendant in religion to immanence in individual experience and
reason. Some reacted to this by spiritualising religion and
history which leads to the danger of paganisation. The Marxist tradition was the second stage of the Enlightenment. It
further reduced individual reason and experience to being
functions of the collective life of classes and the means of
production. We may illustrate the process like this:

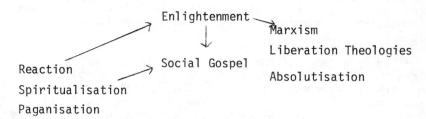

We must be aware of the spiritualisation and absolutisation of history and the fear of them as we seek an open space
for other options for Christian historical engagement.

Western theologians are particularly sensitive to anything that seems to absolutise history. We suggest that this
comes out of the Western experience set in the context and
against the background of movements and institutions which
absolutised history, or their own historical moment. The
Western experience has been that freedom and the growth of
human rights came through a process of desacralising those
institutions that wanted to absolutise history.

For example the early church desacralised political rule
when it condemned the emperor cult and replaced it with prayer
on the emperor's behalf, thus setting a limit to his power.
The Reformation identified the political orders as orders
which can and should serve the welfare of the people but cannot dispense salvation. This distinction between salvation
and welfare secularised political rule. In the English-
speaking world, Puritanism replaced the divine right of kings
with the political contract, the covenant or constitution of
free citizens. Demands for freedom of religion and conscience
were followed by demands for free assembly, freedom of the
press and civil liberties. Moltmann concludes that Christianity must stay on the path of the secularisation, desacralisation
and democratisation of political rule if it wants to remain
true to its faith and its hope. (46)

Yet those very processes where there has been some absolutisation, where God has been identified at work in historical
events, have released tremendous energy to build Christian
societies of democracy, human rights and freedom; for example
the sense of "manifest destiny" in the growth of the United
States and the British colonial empire.

Thus European theologians can now afford to be nervous
about absolutising history. Europe has suffered from

absolutisation. But it also developed by escaping from it
and benefitted to some extent by it. The nervousness of the
theologians is a product of their context and its tendency
to absolutise history.

The experience of the Two-Thirds World is somewhat different. In Asia there is little temptation to absolutise
history, because the predominant view is that history is un-
real and that God can never be experienced in it. Thus
there is hardly any expectation to see God at work in history.
So the incursion of the gospel of God's activity in history
is good news indeed. People are only too glad to see and
know of God at work in history. They are surrounded on all
sides not by Christian assumptions of justice and rights,
but by the naked exercise of power in relationships at all
levels. In this context, to see God at work for justice in
an actual situation is their great desire.

We thus see how the different contexts shape people's
responses to God's work at history. When the European
theologian hears a Two-Third World theologian speaking enthusiastically of God bringing the mighty low, he fears absolutisation. When the Two-Thirds World theologian hears
the warnings of the West about absolutisation, he fears the
same spiritualisation and paganisation of history that he
knows so well from his own context.

It is very important to maintain a partnership between
these two perspectives. The absolutisation of any categories
is the wrong road. We cannot absolutise justice or faith.
David Jenkins writes:

"Idolatry has always been a besetting sin which leads
again and again to dreadful destructions and inhumani-
ties. Idols are not always just false gods. They may
be the promotion by absolutisation of a provisional and
ambiguous good to the level of a god, and this particularly in politics...to redeem and renew the distortions
and destructions arising from false absolutisations of
valuable insights, we need a clear worship of the Presence, Power and Promise who relativises every human
activity and every created fact. We also need the hope
that comes from beyond us and makes provisional every
definition we make or every expectation we entertain."
(47)

No one group has the monopoly on the categories of redemption. We can neither absolutise justice nor the new birth

as the single aspect of Christian commitment. The mistake
of both absolutisation and spiritualisation is to require a
perfect new earth or a perfect new birth here. It is to require that whatever God does here must be perfect, complete
and final.

The fact that we deny absolutisation does not mean that
we deny that God is at work bringing either the new birth
or the new earth now. We should not let the fear of absolutisation blind us to seeing where God is at work in the imperfect and ambiguous. The reaction of spiritualisation and
the fear of absolutisation can totally paralyse people, so
that they do not expect to see God at work in history at all.
This becomes a self-fulfilling prophecy.

Such paralysis may be infecting many western Christians.
They have no expectation of seeing God at work in normal human history. They look for him only in the "abnormal" dimension of healings and tongues, and thus retreat to a God-of-
the-gaps. In Two Thirds World situations, people are more
ready to see him work in human history, and this may also be
a self-fulfilling prophecy.

The Option of Suffering

In seeking options for historical engagement, the clear
Christian option set forth in the Scriptures is the option
of suffering. In his life, cross and resurrection, Jesus'
suffering was God's means of bringing change. Jesus' suffering is God's instrument of redemption. We may participate
in Christ's sufferings and so take part in God's redemptive
process.

Nothing could indicate more clearly the imperfection and
corruption of human society than the sufferings we experience
as its members and the persecution we endure as the church.
But the New Testament does not regard these sufferings as
apocalyptic messianic woes which have to be endured before
the end comes, though this tends to be the perspective in
which some premillenialists view suffering.

Rather, in the New Testament, the presence of the kingdom
in history impels Christians to address the injustice of men
and the causes of sufferings and as far as possible remove
the suffering of the sick and the poverty of the poor.
Views which see sufferings as yet another confirmation that
this world is bound for destruction tend to cut the nerve of
addressing personal and social evil. By no means all suffering is to be endured as we await the final consummation.

Some suffering will be irremovable, such as deformities, psychological hurts and incurable diseases. But we can only identify the irremovable ones in the process of trying to remove them.

Most remarkably, far from being an experience of imperfection which cuts us off from the love of God (Romans 8), suffering is experienced with Christ (Phil.3:10-11), is a channel of his resurrection life (2 Cor. 4), and is the means of overcoming the powers of evil (Rev. 12:11). Sufferings in union with Christ are both a real *experience* of redemption and a *means* of redemption.

Suffering was the means Jesus used to change history. He resisted the temptation to use miracles as his instruments of change. His instrument was "Take up your cross and follow me." Thus the church's witness to redemption is not experienced in escape from the world, nor in an isolated mystical experience which the world and suffering cannot cloy, but is at its peak in sufferings when engaged in the process of living out redemption. Not only does this show that redemption can be mingled with imperfection and can be experienced in the imperfection of suffering relationships, it shows that suffering can even mediate redemption to others.

The experience of suffering also reminds us that the kingdom cannot be consummated in this world as it stands, nor even in the perfection of the "spiritual." For the consummation promises a world where all suffering is removed (Rev.21), not one where suffering is no longer felt. The experience of suffering prevents us from the triumphalism both of "super-spirituality" and of "utopian expectations."

Suffering implies and presupposes conflict. It is the suffering brought on ourselves as we challenge situations of injustice and so unearth hidden conflict. Yet such sufferings are "in Christ." God is at work in them bringing his change, in the midst of their imperfection. Thus we are not engaged in putting together building blocks of the kingdom of God by seeking to create perfect structures or model situations which can be proclaimed "foretastes of heaven." The sign of development and social change is not the New Jerusalem but the cross.

The resurrection also is a sign of the kingdom. But it is not a sign of miraculous deliverance from some suffering, promising that like Peter we will have angels come to open our prison gates. It is a sign that all suffering is to be borne in hope of ultimate vindication and triumph. Deliverance may come. But we may not sit looking up to heaven for it. We plan for suffering, not for miracles. If miracles come, they come as his gift.

So, the suffering of the cross is not defeat. Resurrection is experienced in this suffering, as from it flows life for others (2 Cor.4). Such experiences of suffering and resurrection in the conflict involved in social change are in their ambiguities and imperfections true experiences of the kingdom of God at work in human history.

The option for suffering and conflict is not easy. It is easier to project all change into the future as the work of God, wait passively for it, and rejoice in the "spiritual" aspect of "heaven" here. It is easier to posit blessings and success as signs of belonging to that final kingdom. It is easier to seek for demonstrations of the kingdom's presence in miracles and other events beyond our control that do not require our participation. It is easier to opt for a situation in which right is identified entirely with our cause and go forward in a righteous crusade with no compromise. It is harder to opt for involvement in a situation which is ambiguous and provisional because we are involved in it, and yet which is final because God is involved. For if God is involved, it will involve conflict and suffering, because that is his method of change. Yet we have the hope that precisely because God is involved, this work is not finally futile. Even though our perception of God's work cannot be absolutised, the work is final, because God is involved in it; it is his work.

Conclusion

From our biblical, historical and theological survey of the relationship between eschatology and history we draw the following conclusions:

One, our vision of the future (our eschatology) moulds and determines the future and the content of our mission in this world.

Two, the same biblical material on eschatology is given different emphases and meanings because of our different contexts and our commitments within them.

Three, the Scylla and Charybdis of our views of history in the light of eschatology are on the one hand a spiritualisation of history, locating God's activity principally in a

spiritual plane above history, or on the other the absolutisation of history where the kingdom is expressed only in certain historical actions.

Four, another area for caution is our understanding of
the transcendence and immanence of God. Those who are eager
to preserve the transcendence of God believe it can only be
achieved by elevating the spiritual above the historical.
Those eager to preserve the historical often seem to others
to abrogate the spiritual.

Our understanding of the transcendence and immanence of
God would affirm that transcendence is experienced within
the imperfections of the historical order. The ambiguities
and proviosionalities of history do not prevent God acting
through them. On the other hand, the very sufferings, pro-
visionalities and ambiguities of history prevent us from
absolutising history.

The antidote to the absolutising of history is the
transcendent dimension of the kingdom of God which gives
meaning and hope to the provisionality of history without
having to absolutise it. The transcendent aspect of the
kingdom affirms the reality of our personal relationship
with God, our presence in the heavenlies, our future glorious inheritance and the consummation in the future. It reminds us of the personal dimension of history and of the
provisionality of the historical experience.

Five, we have seen that the future kingdom is active in
the present. This activity is not confined to the church
but is beyond it as well. This activity is in the historical process and is based on the redemption brought about by
the life, death and resurrection of Christ.

Six, we have seen that history is ambiguous and provisional. Yet God commits himself to work through that to
bring change, which shall be a part of his future kingdom.

Seven, the option for involvement in society with the
assurance that God is part of that process is chiefly the
option of suffering to bring change.

Eight, our reading of the signs of the times is not a
matter of following a predetermined countdown to a final
destruction. However pessimistic some of the signs may appear, they are not signs of judgement and destruction only,
but of judgment on the old age and the incursion of the new

age into the old. The provisional and imperfect nature of
our work in the world is not a sign of the corruption of a
world which will be destroyed, but must be seen in the
light of the new earth that is already at work and will one
day come, as the activity of God within imperfect human
history.

We have noted that in reading history we are in danger
of either unrelieved pessimism or unalloyed optimism. Our
understanding of eschatology prevents us from reading the
signs of the times as only omens of an impending final cataclysmic destruction or as signs that the kingdom is slowly
but surely being built in history, block by block. History
is provisional. Our works will be judged. But, having gone
through the sieve of his judgement and grace, they will
participate in his final kingdom. Thus any Christian activity in society is neither an utopian dream nor a mere holding operation, waiting for the king to come. It is a matter
of going about on the King's business in his world, stewarding his property, with the aid and guidance of his counsel-
lor, preparing for his arrival when he will evaluate and
perfect everything.

Implications for Development

How then will we be able to measure where God is active
and involved in the ambiguities of human history?

One clear guideline is where we see the values of the
kingdom replacing values not-of-God in persons, movements
and structures which give concrete expression to values.
Thus where we see *human dignity* being affirmed and people
discovering a sense of self-worth, self-acceptance and a
sense of having something to contribute to the world and
others, we can see God at work.

Where we see people *free* to be able to act according to
their conscience without threat from others who control
their actions and thus their attitudes, we can see God at
work.

We can see God at work as people are able to make their
own contribution to the life of the community, especially as
participants in decisions which affect them in the family,
the community, in religious matters and the political structure.

We can see God at work as people develop *hope*, a sense that it is possible and worthwhile to plan for the future; as people develop *self-respect* and a sense of the worth that they believe the community sets on them; as people *share* in such a way that it enhances the humanity of those they share with rather than reduces it; as people are committed to *struggle against evil* and injustice and as people have a sense of equity and justice.

We can see God at work when women, the weak and the handicapped have a role which accords them dignity and equality, and when their needs receive a priority. We can see God at work when power is shared in such a way that all benefit from its exercise and none are dehumanized.

We can see God at work when there is a *sense of God's presence*, a *sense of the presence of evil* without and within and a *sense of humility* about the limitations of our knowledge in the face of God's wisdom.

We will particularly look for God's work in *actions* such as decision-making, information sharing, emergency assistance, jobs, social functions, family decisions, actions in relation to the under-privileged and marginalized, actions which involve the interaction of the individual and the community, actions which relate to the use of human and material resources and to the worship of God.

We will also look for signs of God's activity expressed in *the structures* of the family, the ethnic group, structures of political decision making, and structures of religious, social and economic organization.

The temptation is to see God at work only in values. But he is to be seen at work also when structures are transformed to promote the values of the kingdom. It is possible to be content with the expression of these values in the lives of individuals or in a small group of people. But values which do not find structural expression do not bring lasting change. So development work must focus just as much on the transformation of structures or emergency of structures which reflect the values of the kingdom.

FOOTNOTES

1. See Kenneth Cracknell "God and the Nations" in *Dialogue in Community*, edited by C.D.Jathanna (Karnataka Theological Research Institute, Mangalore, 1982) p.2-3

2. See Karl Barth, *Church Dogmatics* (E.T.), Vol. 4/1, Edinburgh, T. and T. Clark, 1956. pp.26ff.

3. Thus argues Jose Miguez Bonino in *Revolutionary Theology Comes of Age*, London, S.P.C.K., 1975. p.134-5.

4. This view is a contemporary modification of the widely held view on apocalyptic. See Stephen Travis *Christian Hope and the Future of Man*. InterVarsity Press 1980.

5. Richard Bauckham *Themelios* 3.2 pp. 19-23, quoted by Travis, op cit, p. 37-40. On apocalyptic see K. Koch *The Rediscovery of Apocalyptic*, Allenson, London, 1970 p.28-33.

6. Bauckham argues that the period after the fall of Jerusalem is the period embraced by Daniel's four world empires--not the whole of history; and that the fact that temporal dualism of the two ages did not arise until the first century A.D. shows that apocalyptic did not begin from a dualistic dogma but from an experience of history. See Travis, p. 37-38.

7. For discussion of the important text John 18:36 which impinges on this, see Vinay Samuel and Chris Sugden *The Relationship Between Evangelism and Social Responsibility*. CRESR paper Eeerdmans/Paternoster forthcoming.

8. Jose Miguez Bonino. op.cit, p-135-6.

9. David Bosch, *Witness to the World*, MMS 1980, p. 61-62.

10. Professor Andrew Walls of Aberdeen University has repeatedly emphasised this important point.

11. J. Christiaan Beker, *Paul the Apostle*, T. and T. Clark/Fortress 1980 p.337.

12. The tendency here to absolutise Indian history arises out of an evolutionary understanding of history and a tendency to reject the authority of the biblical revelation.

13. Bangkok March 1982. Papers published in *Sharing Jesus in the Two Thirds World,* Partnership in Mission Asia, 1983.

14. Bosch, op.cit. p.63.

15. Bosch, op.cit. p.64-65.

16. Arthur Johnston, *The Kingdom in Relation to the Church and the World,* paper prepared for the Consultation on the Relationship between Evangelism and Social Responsibility, p.17.

17. Johnston, op.cit., p.18.

18. Bosch, op.cit. p.65-6.

19. Bosch, op.cit. p. 105-6.

20. David Moberg *The Great Reversal* Scripture Union 1973, p.33.

21. Peter Kuzmic *History and Eschatology Evangelical Views* CRESR Paper p.4.

22. The conclusions reached in this historical survey are discussed in full detail with supporting evidence in an expanded version of this paper presented at the Wheaton '83 Review Conference, Holland, Michigan, June 1982.

23. The conclusion about the situation in England is the finding of D.N.Hempton *Evangelicalism and Eschatology* unpublished paper, University of St. Andrews, Scotland, 1977, p.15,16.

24. G.E.Wright *The Biblical Doctrine of Man in Society* SCM 1954 p.18-19.

25. Victor Paul Furnish *The Love Command in the New Testament.* SCM 1973, Ch.I.

26. See Vinay Samuel and Chris Sugden *The Relationship Between Evangelism and Social Responsibility* CRESR Paper 1982, p.39-41.

27. See further J.Moltmann *The Church in the Power of the Spirit* SCM 1977, p.196.

28. G.E.Ladd *Jesus and the Kingdom* SPCK 1966, p.179.

29. Andrew Lincoln *Paradise Now and Not Yet* Cambridge 1981 p.192.

30. Lincoln, op.cit. p.192

31. Lincoln, op.cit. p.193

32. John Yoder *The Politics of Jesus* Eerdmans 1972.

33. Bosch, op.cit. p.209.

34. W.A.Visser't Hooft *The Kingship of Christ* New York 1948 p.136.

35. Krass, op.cit. p.140.

36. Quoted Krass op.cit. p.142-143.

37. Hendrikus Berkhof *Christ the Meaning of History* Richmond 1966, p.169, 173.

38. cf Jose Miguez Bonino - op.cit. p.137.

39. David Jenkins "Doctrines which Drive One to Politics" in Wilm Ed. *Christian Faith and Political Hopes* Epworth 1979 p.145.

40. For case studies which demonstrate this consult for Bombay and Madras, Graham Houghton and Ezra Sargunam "The Role of Theological Education in Church Planting among the Urban Poor" in *TRACI Journal* No. 19 April 1981; for Jamkhed consult Vinay Samuel and Chris Sugden "Dialogue with Other Religions: an Evangelical View," paper presented at Conference of Evangelical Mission Theologians from the Two-Thirds World, published in *Sharing Jesus in the Two Thirds World,* Partnership in Mission Asia, 1983, and for case studies from Bangalore consult Vinay Samuel and Christ Sugden *Evangelism and the Poor--a Third World Study Guide,* Partnership in Mission Asia 1983.

41. Paul Hiebert, "Folk Religion in Andhra Pradesh: Some Missiological implications" in *Evangelism and the Poor--a Third World Study Guide* (Revised edition 1983) edited by Vinay Samuel and Chris Sugden (Partnership-in-Mission Asia, P.O. Box 544, Bangalore-5).

42. It is our contention that the effects of the fall are predominantly seen at the second level which controls and deforms human-kind. The effects of the atonement and resurrection of Christ also have their most significant impact at this level leading captivity captive.

43. David Jenkins, op.cit. p.149.

44. Jose Miguez Bonino, op.cit. p.139-140.

45. Jose Miguez Bonino, op.cit. p.140-142, 152.

46. Moltman, op.cit. p.179.

47. Jenkins in Willmer, op.cit. p.153.

DEVELOPMENT AND ESCHATOLOGY

Purpose. The purpose of this paper is to contribute to the task of bringing development and eschatology together into a biblical wholeness, while avoiding a false separation between the secular and the sacred.

Development and Eschatology Within a Historical Context. In the last two decades, modernization has been called into question by Western man. At the same time indigenous communities left outside of various national plans for modernization often have fared better in times of crisis than those who were included.

As the dreams for westernization and modernization are increasingly called into question, let's look at God's intentions for His people. Through the prophets he reveals the prospect for a new king, a new law, a new land, a new community, and a new creation. In Jesus Christ, God's new Kingdom invaded our world.

Man's self-sufficiency and rebelling against God underlines the one persistently negative historical trend as His Kingdom seeks to advance in human society. And God's redemptive purpose underlines the one positive movement in history. God's purpose is progressive and assured. Both salvation and judgment appear closer than when we first believed.

Development and Eschatology: Directed by a Divine Wisdom. With a cosmic and eschatological storm brewing, this is no time to leave the ship's rudder idly swinging; we must set a wise course. We need to seek biblical wisdom in doing as well as reflecting. Pessimistic premillenialism appears to under-estimate the good things God is prepared to do in the present age. We need to derive our intentions in development and social transformation from God's Kingdom intentions to bring into being a new age of wisdom, righteousness, justice, peace and compassion.

Development and Eschatology: Expanded by Substantial Hope. Biblical hope refuses to be extinguished, and it is essential for biblical development. In the resurrection, not only is our hope secured, but Jesus promised that His followers would manifest the signs of hope in healings, miracles and deliverance. Can't this type of transformation, as well as reclamation of the desert and the renewal of the city manifest, in some approximate way, the Kingdom of God?

Development and Eschatology: Applied through a Vigorous Mission. What is needed then by a people who wish to put hope into action is a high view of mission, a passionate commitment to its advancement, and a restructuring which unites rather than divides temporal and eternal goals.

To talk in ambitious terms about what the church might do, or even must do, smacks at once of triumphalism. We need to keep returning to the gradualism of the "building," the "sowing" and the "fighting." But humble steps do not preclude a giant stride. The powerful Spirit of God may yet provoke that burst of creativity and release of compassion which could bring temporal as well as eternal hope to the world.

MAURICE SINCLAIR is Overseas Secretary for the South American Missionary Society in Kent, England.

DEVELOPMENT AND ESCHATOLOGY

Maurice Sinclair

1. INTRODUCTION: TOWARDS A BIBLICAL WHOLENESS

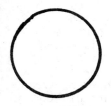 That development and eschatology should have been so rarely considered together reveals a weakness in western culture and western theology: impressively specialised as they are, yet fragmented and compartmentalised. Those of us who are western Christians share the fault of so many of our contemporaries. For us, as for them, development is a key word, representing something of vital and central concern. Especially when challenged by the poverty in the world around us, we try to respond to development imperatives concerning the rights and opportunities of the deprived. However, what is assumed in these terms to be our future and their future is not so often checked against God's future. And that this should be so would appear particularly strange, since eschatology is currently as much a key word in theological circles as development is more generally. Even so, a Christian development worker is less likely to have his mind upon the imminent return of his Lord than his evangelist colleague proclaiming the urgency of repentance. The great issues of the last things, of the divine kingdom, of time and of eternity, are less frequently considered in the health centre, the community farm or the literacy class than they are in the evangelist's tent or the discipleship meeting.

To such a separation of interests one might be tempted to respond: So what? As long as some Christians are concerned about some of these matters at least some of the time, isn't that enough? Development and Eschatology may be key topics, but are we expected to be like jailors, constantly carrying a complete set of heavy keys in our belts? It seems, however, that God will not allow us to remain too complacently in our specializations. Both evangelism and development in their current practice meet some apparently intractible difficulties and impenetrable barriers. I would argue that the imponderables in both cases are double locked and that both "keys" must be simultaneously applied.

My purpose then is to contribute to the task of bringing development and eschatology together into a biblical whole. Like a tail and batsman in cricket, I am going to take a swipe at this elusive ball. I can't manage the technical orthodoxy of the theological strokemakers, but I take courage from one of them who says, "Every believer is a theologian." Certainly the Chaco Indian believers, with whom I am privileged to work, held a unified view of things, wonderfully held together by the Father God in whom they focus such a robust and practical faith. It was in spite of, rather than because of, us western missionaries they had grasped the Old Testament insight that the life we live on earth is meaningful and coherent in itself. The fact that they came to terms so well with the here and now made it easier rather than harder for them to anticipate the hereafter. However, even within a temporal compass, they very naturally and biblically recognised the Lordship of Christ over the affairs of the church and the village alike.

Whether or not "our village" is built of adobe bricks, we should seek to learn from the biblical insights and the coherent understanding of our Mataco brothers. Following their road, we should seek to avoid a false separation between the secular and the sacred, and incidentally in so doing remove one of the obstacles towards relating development to eschatology. For the Mataco believer there is only one universe of experience, and God is at the centre of it.

Nor would it occur to him to divide the scriptural revelation. The Bible is one, and so, although we may detect differences or tensions between prophecy and apocalyptic, between Proverbs and Ecclesiastes, or between New Testament passages that speak of the Kingdom yet to come and the Kingdom here already, we must creatively and coherently hold them all together. I want to try to understand different parts of

Scripture in their historical context and in the light of the cultural milieu surrounding them, but I see no reason to try to drive a wedge between one passage and another. The biblical understanding of truth, founded as it is on the faithfulness and consistency of God, gives me every encouragement to hold on to the basic consistency of His written and normative revelation.

Furthermore, I would hope that the kind of coherence we are struggling to express might be intelligible to all our fellow Christians. If it really is biblical, they should be able to see how it affects them and how they relate to it. Our biblical message should give direction and provide a wholesome corrective, but it should also create expectancy and be full of promise. It should be something the Holy Spirit can take, in order to spur people into action. In His hands it should be dynamite.

Our consultation on a Christian Response to Human Need reflects a theological tendency: a kind of evangelical radicalism. We agree about the need for "contextualisation." We want our evangelism to be "holistic" and we are anxious that our theological reflection should stem from and lead back into a genuine "praxis." For our specialist "in group" this is wholly excellent, but for those outside, it is wholly obscure. Our words do not communicate. Who would write "evangelical radical" across his tee shirt? Who could fit "contextualisation" into a chorus beat? Would anyone say to himself, "I am going to evangelise this inner city area "holistically." And for those who are getting on with the job, would it ever occur to them that their engagement is "praxis"? Our language betrays us; we have allowed a distance to grow between the theologian and the believer. There remains the vital task of translating our theological tendency into a lay movement. Once we have worked out between us how eschatology relates to development, then we need God's grace to say how it does with words of simplicity and power.

By such standards as these, this essay obviously has a severely limited scope. It is intended to be complementary to the excellent review by Vinay Samuel and Chris Sugden on literature relating to the millenial hope. In beginning my search and in expressing my longing for biblical wholeness, which I symbolise by a circle, I can so easily fail to grasp it and remain adrift in generalities. It is all very well to say that I want to bridge the temporal and the eternal, the theological and the lay, the individual and the societal, but where is all this rooted and related?

The second section, therefore, attempts to state where we in our generation stand in relation to development and eschatology. The circle includes a point of reference. The "we" is intended to represent the present generation of believers. Clearly those in the two thirds world have a very different experience from those in the materially privilege "west." In spite of vastly different conditions, I dare to believe, though, that in Christ there is still a real community of understanding. Section 2 tries to identify where we are; it attempts a rough sketch of the historical context of our understanding of development and eschatology. Is there a pattern in the wide sweep of events and the major crises? What in outline is the prophetic word that applies to them?

We need to know where we stand, but we also need to know in which direction we should face. My third section adds a directional arrow to the point of reference. It adds a corrective to the context. By focusing on biblical wisdom, the attempt will be made to discern the true values of development.

This part of the exercise will underline the difference between our present possibilities and our promised inheritance. The closed circle must be opened to make way for a future which transcends our actual experience. It follows that the concern of section 4 will be the hope relating to development and eschatology.

It will be this hope which will provide the motivation for commitment and action. The fifth symbol, indicating the course of my argument, will suggest vibrancy, activity and life. The final section will deal with development, eschatology and mission. The basic question with which we shall conclude will not be "What shall we ultimately enjoy?" but rather "What shall we more immediately do in obedience to the God of Hope?"

2. DEVELOPMENT AND ESCHATOLOGY WITHIN A HISTORICAL CONTEXT

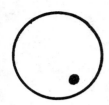

When I was studying Agriculture at university in the late fifties I remember being deeply impressed when told that, with the technology already perfected, it would have been possible to provide abundant food supplies for the existing world population, and, by bringing all available agricultural land into production, it would have proved possible to feed a population many times larger still. With such a prospect in mind, development was conceived as the widespread application of such a productive technology. Modern science had given the western nations this technology. Their prosperity relative to the rest of the world was interpreted as ample proof of the vastly greater productive potential created by that technology. Through development the great blessing could be multiplied and shared.

Since it would appear in this way to be able to make "all the difference" at any level, including the international one, it is scarcely surprising that development has become a key word and a priority concern. However, even in the optimistic fifties and sixties, it was evident that world-wide prosperity did not depend on technological development alone. Obviously choices needed to be made regarding the distribution of resources within and between nations. All that has happened in the subsequent years suggests that these choices have mostly reflected a less than enlightened self interest. Social ethics has not matched scientific technology. But there is even cause for a weakening of confidence in the technology itself. Many of its modern applications are being seen as wasteful of limited resources, environmentally harmful and even de-humanising. Modern communities are being compared critically and unfavourably with primitive or traditional communities. Western man is beginning to wonder whether his development, and even survival, is as secure as that of his more primitive or traditional ancestors.

An exactly corresponding local example of these global development issues has been impressed upon my own experience by the situation of the indigenous communities in the Argentine Chaco. Before the penetration of their area by European and mestizo colonists, they lived by hunting and fishing and forest gathering. Population levels were effectively controlled in relation to food resources through inter-tribal fighting and infanticide. Their environment remained stable and there was no appreciable deterioration of animal life or

plant cover. With the arrival, however, of the criollo settlers and their grazing animals, the natural balance in the
region has been seriously affected, and there has been serious soil erosion. In spite of this measure of damage, the
very extensive Chaco area retained a very high potential for
further development. Argentine experts were becoming increasingly aware of this fact, linked as it was with the
availability of water for irrigation, the long growing season and the remaining soil fertility. Their formula was
simple: attract immigrant farmers with technological compe-
tence and entrepreneurial spirit; use their productive potential to repay the major capital investment required to establish the necessary infrastructure of roads, irrigation canals,
power lines and essential services. The bulldozers duly arrived and this expansion of agri-business began apace. However, with the present economic dislocation in Argentina,
there has been a serious loss of development momentum. The
indigenous communities, whose interests were never seriously
considered in relation to these national plans, have survived,
in some cases though traditional subsistence, and in other
cases through agricultural development promoted in their
church programme. Their development dilemma, though, remains
acute. The traditional economic base has been fatally weak-
ened and the modern economic alternative, even assuming that
the Indians can participate in it, offers no certain future.
The picture that comes to mind is of a leaking steamship and
a small rowing boat. The wash from the large vessel is sufficient to capsize the small one, but since the liner's hold
is rapidly filling with water, there will be no safety on her
decks for those in the water clinging to their oars.

If it is true that both locally and globally the development certainties of the earlier post war years are being shaken, what can be said of the certainties of previous ages?
Wasn't fertility the central concern of people in the fertile
crescent B.C.? Their religion was geared to the multiplication of their crops, their livestock and their descendants.
Who among the dwellers in Mesopotamia or Canaan would have
questioned that fertility was what life was all about? This
all important factor determined survival and prosperity; it
made all the difference between life and death, misery and
enjoyment.

The fertility and prosperity of the Greco-Roman civilisation gave its more privileged sons more time to sit and think.
In what higher activity could they have possibly engaged?
Surely reason, not fertility, must be the golden thread giving meaning to life. Pure abstract reason must lie at the

heart of reality. Who could question such a premise; reason
can scarcely deny itself.

Reason didn't, but violence did, and so the dark ages
intervened. To grow crops for your feudal lord must have
seemed a tolerable price to pay for his protection against
marauding bands. It's hard to believe that there were de-
bates on the merits of feudalism in the baronial halls. The
important thing was to submit to the system, not to question
it. There were rivals to be subdued and battles to be won.

In the end the battles concentrated power in fewer hands.
Under these king barons a new power group arose and with it
a new preoccupation and certainty. The merchant class flou-
rished, not only through the protection of the mediaeval
kings, but more still through the scientific revolution.

So our sketch has taken us full circle; we are returning
to the certainties of our own day. If we are westerners,
our grandfathers will have talked about progress and civilisation, but behind these ideals has been the march of capitalistic and technological development. This surely is irresistible. Oh yes, we may question it, but can we effectively
distance ourselves from it? Why, even the men in the Kremlin
are trapped in the dependency it brings!

My conviction is that Scripture, not Marxist analysis, provides the profoundest commentary and most searching criticism
of the particular kind of development which, complete with
its morbid tendencies, dominates our modern world. Scripture
speaks of creativity, vice-regency and stewardship, rather
than development, and tells that God made Adam to be a gar-
dener-prince. His attempt with Eve to usurp God's throne
upset the man's gardening as well as his government.

Having placed before us God's original intention for man,
freely submissive and cooperative partnership in the ongoing
creation, Scripture then traces the successive and drastic
consequences of man's failure in cooperation and his mistaken
bid for independence. Adam must now toil away without respite. His mastery over the natural world is broken. Eve
must bear pain. Their children commit and suffer violence.
Scarcity and anxiety enter the common experience. In the
striving for scarce resources some snatch more, others secure
much less. Injustice breeds envy and vanity, while it destroys community. The ruthless who "gain the whole world"
discover that their glittering prize lacks solid worth. They
live in the shadow of death.

The Old and New Testament dispassionately record this
catalogue of errors and sorrows and thus expose every false
hope of fallen man. If the root of his problem is disobedience and alienation from his Creator, how can man imagine
that some manipulation of the sources of fertility can secure his welfare? Such a cult can only lead into frustration and perversity. Independent man-centered reason rates
no higher in the biblical estimate. "God made foolish the
wisdom of the world." The Greeks may seek wisdom and pride
themselves on their powers of reason, but the apostle offers
them no solace apart from Christ crucified. Nor would Paul
have encouraged mediaeval men to seek protection only in
their feudal lords. His criticism of our modern assumptions
would have been equally severe, and one can imagine Paul being less than impressed by our scientific technologies and
our capitalist economies, upon which so many build their
hopes. For, unless mankind reckons with his greatest ill,
he cannot realise his greatest good. Without a renewed opportunity of stewardship in a redeemed creation, man's development must remain fatally flawed. Whether or not a
particular age chooses to question its basic values, ideology
and ambitions, Scripture most certainly does and in the process leaves no illusions undisturbed.

To give the impression, however, that God's biblical
revelation is just a profound and critical commentary on human society would be thoroughly misleading. It is that, but
it is so much more. There is a passionate struggle as well
as deep criticism. Not only are false hopes exposed but
true hope breaks in.

Abraham hopes against hope. His own infertility mocks
him, but in response to the stirring of God's Spirit, he
reaches out to a hope beyond fertility, to a blessing in
which every family of the earth will share. The fascination
of idolatrous fertility must also be the fascination of power
and even violence. Abraham is taught a contrasting way of
secure relationship. He becomes God's friend.

The free trusting relationship remains very vulnerable in
a fallen world. The chosen tribe,which expresses this new
quality only in part,finds itself engulfed in Egypt by oppressive forces. These powers are challenged through Moses,
whom God inspires to inspire hope among the despairing slaves.
God's chosen leader forges a national community and points
its members to the Lord who had acted in grace towards them,
requires of them obedience to a law of liberty and who offers
them a homeland and a better country.

Once the nation is formed and the promised land is occupied, a new dimension to the struggle emerges. As well as being threatened by violent external forces, God's community becomes subject to destructive influences from within. In the face of this internal threat, the historic task of the prophets is to resist the reassertion of the fertility cult and preserve the way of responsive relationship with God and among the people. The struggle between the ideal relationship and actual compromise is unrelenting. On balance the nation disobeys the message of the prophets and, consequently suffers division, conquest, deportation and dispersion. A remnant is gathered and returns from exile, but its enclave around Jerusalem is darkly overshadowed by pagan super-powers. Once more God's people find themselves to be a conquered people. Threatened once again by despair and extinction, the prophets unveil a brilliant prospect: a new king, a new law, a new land, a new community and a new creation. The new day when this era of peace and righteousness is inaugurated will be a day of judgment for those who persist in rebellion against God and persecution of his people. Meanwhile, these faithful must endure the fiery ordeal, whether or not God should choose to intervene in their moment of trial.

When the time had fully come and God's moment of intervention had arrived, the faithful successors of Abraham, Moses and the prophets were few in number and small in influence. True, a young north country girl was willing to bear the baby king, but his appearing and his method of establishing his kingdom was a source of stumbling to his Jewish people and foolishness to the civilisation which surrounded them. By this stage the cult of reason overlay the cult of fertility but the new fascination brought no respite from violently imposed power. Roman values remained incompatible with the divine power which was being released through a man's humble service, sacrificial suffering and shameful death. What a strange intervention this was! Could the rise and fall of a messianic pretender from Nazareth herald the transcendent and decisive Day of the Lord? Could God be using a Roman gallows to stake his claim to a rebellious province of his creation? In fact Christ did not rise to fall, but fell to rise. God's servant was vindicated. God's invading kingdom was already here.

God's invasion was thus secured through a bridgehead, quite unpredictable to human intelligence. The subsequent advance of his kingdom has been characterised by a baffling mixture of human weakness and divine power. Because of human participation it has been an erratic advance. The church has

at different times misunderstood, perverted, forgotten, remembered and heroically obeyed her great commission. In
spite of the outpouring of God's Spirit in a new manner and
measure, the pattern of the partial obedience typical in Old
Testament times has been reproduced. As before, the dangers
of compromise from within have been greater even than pressures from without. If the great temptation after the settlement in Canaan was for God's people to use the manipulative
powers of the fertility religion, a new temptation to syncre-
tism followed the Constantine settlement. With the sudden
relaxation of external pressure, the western church had at
its disposal unprecedented political power and prestige. Not
surprisingly it fell into the trap of trying to manipulate and
in turn being manipulated by non-Christian forces and ideologies. Such a pattern has been repeated down the centuries.
Consciously or unconsciously the church has had to incarnate
the Gospel, but in so doing it has often compromised or even
betrayed the Gospel. Feudal tribalism re-erected barriers between Christian groups which should have been enjoying and expressing their oneness in Christ. The treasury of merit mo-
delled on commercial dealing obscured the doctrine of grace.
Enlightenment reason ultimately made no more sense of the
cross than Greek reason had before. Scientific humanism appeared to banish God, even from the perimeter of the universe.
Violence, the very antithesis of the creative relationship to
which Abraham had first been called, and the wider reconciliation made possible through Jesus, has fluctuated at scandalous-
ly high levels throughout the Gospel age. Sometimes it has
been used against the church, but worst of all, it has been
inflicted by those who claim Christian allegiance. Now nuclear
violence threatens to engulf Christians and non-Christians
alike.

If the Old Testament saints were tempted to despair on account of corruption within Israel and destruction from without
and needed the apocalyptic message for their moment of extrem-
ity, the same has been true for the Christians. The erratic
advance of the Gospel has been carried out with the prospect
of an impending crisis. On the one hand Scripture speaks of
mounting opposition to the church, natural and political trau-
mas and widespread apostasy. On the other hand there is promised the evangelisation of the nations.

Indeed, against a background of external opposition and
internal failure, God's initiative in his mission has never
been totally frustrated. What the Holy Spirit began to do in
Jerusalem, Samaria, Antioch, Asia Minor and Macedonia has been

continued. Christians of almost every tradition have been
stirred to make some significant contribution to mission
during at least one period in the church's history. Both
the frontiers and the centres of missionary advance have
constantly shifted but the momentum has never been completely
lost. In spite of lethargy, cultural insensitivity, paro-
chialism, doctrinal impurity, scandalous moral failure and
sheer incompetence, solid gains have accumulated, and mission
spans the continents and penetrates the nations as never before. The appalling weight of spiritual and physical distress in the world today must remove any trace of complacency
from the missionary church, but it can still look forward to
new gains: old Israel's recognition of her Messiah and further miraculous signs of his kingdom of healing and peace.
The ultimate crisis will be heralded by heavenly portents and
then shall appear the Son of Man upon the clouds of glory.

At this point history flows into eternity. If history is
compared with a river, the writing of history may be likened
to mapping the river, an activity which requires attention to
scale and careful choice of detail. On this analogy our present discussion would be the crudest sketch. Whether, however, the map is intricate or crude, it is legitimate to ask
what its features correspond to and what they really mean.
George Knight in *A Christian Theology of the Old Testament*
comments on the way Israel was unique in looking both back to
the past and forward into the future. He continues:

> It was natural for them to do so, because they alone be-
> lieved in the 'living'God. Before Israel was, God is.
> Thus after Israel is, God will be. Again, since Israel
> as a people was created by God for his own ends, and
> Israel's history has a purpose running through it, then
> Israel's history must have an End to which it is moving,
> as well as a point from which it began. Moreover, since
> God had set Israel within a universe which he had created
> in the beginning, then that universe too must have an
> End. On the other hand, the End to which the whole OT
> is looking forward, emphasis upon which is such a dominant
> note within it, is not merely and only the historical last
> moment in a series of historical moments; it is also and
> primarily the *meaning* of the whole.

So Israel in this way discovered meaning in history and
from the evidence of their canonical writings did not isolate
their history from that of any other people. God is the Gua-
rantor of significance. We may sell a sparrow for less than

a farthing, but we know on the authority of Jesus that not
one little bird is forgotten before God. Levels of significance and value are set as high as that, but there is a differentiation in importance between events. There is a pattern of significance and the pattern of significance for the
whole of history is given its essential outline and shape in
the unfolding scriptural revelation. With this meaningful
coherent biblical framework, there is no question of dividing
history or marginalising vast tracts of it.

My impression and understanding of that outline I have
already attempted to describe. Man's self sufficiency and
rebellion against God underline the one persistently negative
historical trend. It finds expression in different power
structures in different ages, whether based on crude violence,
accumulated wealth, scientific technology, sympathetic magic,
satanic invocation, proud reason or any combination of some
or all of these. Not all the alternative expressions of society organised from God are equally malignant. It is also
true that the good creation is the canvas on which in dark
strokes the bad rebellion is painted; beautiful colours remain. Whatever the mixture though, the result tends rapidly
and imperceptibly towards loss of community, manipulation rather than relationship, and ultimate destruction and death.
God's redemptive purpose underlines the one positive movement
in history. God's purpose is progressive and assured. At
the pivotal moment when Christ became man, history featured
perfect redemptive obedience. Human participation before and
since his earthly ministry has meant that the redemptive movement has been liberally mixed with sin. Even so, to the degree that there has been submission and response to the Redeemer, there has been enrichment of relationships, growth of
community and a different handling of the other sources of
power. At many points in history the negative has threatened
to destroy the positive and chaos has threatened to engulf
community.

It is at one such moment in history, when this threat is
again gathering strength, that we happen to be living our
lives. As Christians we find ourselves sharply under judgment
for our compromise with the power systems which are hostile to
God. More generally, God's judgment extends over the whole
world in basic disagreement with him. The way of reconciliation through the cross remains open, but time seems even
shorter now. Both salvation and judgment appear closer than
when we first believed.

3. DEVELOPMENT AND ESCHATOLOGY: DIRECTED BY A DIVINE WISDOM

Living as we do at a time of deepening crisis, there is a special urgency that we should be able to summons adequate resources of wisdom. With a cosmic and eschatological storm brewing, this is no time to leave the ship's rudder idly swinging; we must set a wise course. But just when accurate steering is most crucially important, it is also most exceptionally difficult. Turbulence increases confusion. Even so we were right to read our biblical historical map and attempt to plot our position on it. In our study the sharp lines of good and evil are obscured on the one hand by repeated compromise with sin on the part of God's people, and on the other by the creation virtues retained by those who profess no allegiance to the Creator. All the more reason then to ask for wisdom to discern the good and perfect way of God. Those upon whom "the ends of the age have come" pray more earnestly, "Teach us so to number our days that we may apply our hearts unto wisdom."

Wisdom is precious; wisdom is vital; but what is wisdom? Biblical wisdom is not like Greek wisdom: abstract, academic, dualistic, elitist. Biblical wisdom is concerned with daily living and is learnt in the experiences of daily life. It is not the preserve of a privileged elite. Neither is it divorced from morality and diligence. It informs and guides the making of workable plans and even inspires appropriate technology (Isaiah 28:23-29). In this sense wisdom is expressed in doing, as well as in reflecting. It is competent to deal with the immediate things and the ultimate things as well. The key to its versatility and authority is that it is centered upon the Creator who is at work redemptively in his creation.

God revealed in Christ is the source of wisdom. Wisdom is one of his attributes. Christ is our Wisdom. Acknowledgment and respect for God are the beginning of wisdom for his creatures. Wisdom cannot be separated from dependence upon God, otherwise it becomes foolishness. In the complex secular world of today, wisdom is something for which to pray. It is a divine gift and the fruit of God's Spirit operating in our lives. Discernment made possible by such wisdom is very different from a more typical human response reaction.

As pressures increase upon human society, so human reaction becomes more pronounced. But with the help of God's

wisdom we are not condemned to pessimism in a darkened period
of history. Regrettably, eschatological theories seem to
have been influenced by reaction to world trends as much as
by discernment of the Spirit of wisdom. Pessimistic premillenialism appears to underestimate the good things that
God is prepared to do in the present age. A biblically balanced wisdom positively increases our anticipation of what
God will do; it also nerves us to endure what Satan will do.
This wisdom encompasses vision and realism. It guides a widespread transformation of society radiating from a revived and
vigorous church. In a different historical setting it equally
applies in the last ditch stand of a Christian remnant facing
totally hostile powers.

In observing the scope of biblical wisdom, we have already
noted that it includes very practical things within its area
of concern. Nothing would appear too big or too small to be
shaped and directed by wisdom. There would be no reason to
make development an exception to this rule. Wisdom is needed
in order to discern the true qualities of a developed society.
For social transformation wisdom is required to define the
desirable state into which society should be transformed. The
Old Testament prophets looked forward to the government of
the "Wonderful Counselor" upon whom would rest "the Spirit of
wisdom and understanding, the spirit of counsel and might,
the spirit of knowledge and the fear of the Lord." This Messianic Governor would establish a kingdom and a community,
the characteristics of which would be wholly good. Wholly
good development or social transformation should therefore
reflect the characteristics of the Messianic kingdom of wisdom and peace. Notice that these familiar characteristics
interact in a dynamic way, because they are energised by
God's Spirit: "The Spirit is poured upon us from on high and
the wilderness becomes a fruitful field, and the fruitful
field is deemed a forest. Then justice will dwell in the
wilderness, and righteousness abide in the fruitful field.
And the effect of righteousness will be peace; and the result
of righteousness quietness and trust for ever. My people will
abide in a peaceful habitation, in secure dwellings and in
quiet resting places " (Isaiah 32:15-18). We should therefore
look for spiritual renewal, social justice, material productivity, and peaceful settlement together and not separately.
If we add to our vision the prophecies of swords beaten into
ploughshares and the leopard lying down with the kid, then we
can include disarmament and ecological harmony in our list of
inter-acting features of the transformed earth. Even such a
far reaching transformation, though, is not an end in itself.
The hills will break forth into singing, the trees will clap

their hands, thanksgiving and the voice of song will be heard
in the reclaimed desert. According to the prophecy therefore,
the desirable features of society are interlocking and are
not only generated by renewal in the Spirit but also evoke
worship in the Spirit.

How can we wisely apply this sunlit vision to the kind of
urban decay, rural poverty and international tension of the
world we live in? We obviously need to interiorise and appropriate for ourselves the values of the Messianic society.
We then need to distinguish these values from any conflicting
vision of prosperity. For instance, the modest extent of
property holding suggested by "every man under his vine and
under his fig tree" is very different both from unbridled
capitalism and totalitarian communism. How do you, though
bridle capitalism, especially in relation to land tenure,
something that has a particularly important bearing on development? In his study entitled *Land and Power in South America* Sven Lindquist points out that the owner of the large estates is often in effect shop keeper, policeman, member of
parliament and judge, as well as employer and landlord to his
workers. Such a concentration of power can so easily be
abused, and a biblical wisdom would seek a more equal sharing
of power, as well as a fairer distribution of wealth. At the
other political extreme, peasants are recruited to the revolutionary army through promises of land following victory. After
the successful campaign, the party proves no more willing to
relinquish land, and therefore power, than the capitalists
had been before them. The difficulty of distributing power,
land or wealth by whatever means highlights another distinction. The Messianic society is not the utopian society. The
biblical vision can neither be dismissed as unworkable, nor
can it be implemented mechanically or ideologically. Messianic society is compassionate. A political system and a framework of laws can help or hinder compassion. They cannot of
themselves generate it. Even so, the political and legal options cannot be a matter of indifference. The better option
needs to be identified through consecrated and rigorous examination. In commenting on her failure here, Jurgen Moltman observes that "the church is in many countries linked with a
social system which spreads discord and injustice in the
world."

The failure of the church in relation to the world raises
an issue that cannot be postponed further. If we are concerned to find God's wisdom in order to face today's troubles,
who is the "we"? Is the "we" limited to the church society,
or coextensive with the world society? Is God's wise purpose

for the church the same as his purpose for the world, or indeed the whole creation? Does God have a plan for the secular world which is wider than, different from, or even unrelated to his plan for the church? Without rehearsing the arguments which appear in the companion paper, I will add three comments. First, a recurring summary of God's purpose presented in Scripture is: "I will be their God and they shall be my people." The fact that this declaration stands alone does not of course preclude any other purpose that God may have towards his creation. It is, however, a prominent and even central biblical statement. Secondly, the Epistle to the Ephesians speaks of God's purpose in universal and cosmic terms: "a plan for the fulness of time, to unite all things in Christ, things in heaven and things on earth." It is "according to the eternal purpose," Paul affirms, "that *through the church* the manifold wisdom of God might now be made known to the principalities and powers in the heavenly places." More remarkable still, the apostle declares "God has put all things under Christ's feet and has made him head over all things *for the church.*" Thirdly, if God's purpose has to do with unity and community, then both relate essentially and necessarily with Himself. He is the Father, "from whom every family in heaven and earth is named." Community which is cut off from the Father of Community must wither. I conclude therefore that God's redemptive purpose for secular society must at its heart involve a restoration of sonship. He wants those who did not know their Father to cry "Abba!" Restoration of community without renewal of this fundamental relationship would seem in the final analysis impossible. God sets before his small but faithful Philadelphian church an open door. His purpose for the vast world outside that open door is not unrelated to his little church. It is a creative purpose and an evangelical purpose. A biblical balance and wisdom avoid on the one hand restricting God's generous purpose to the confines of an institutional church and a manipulative discipling, and on the other hand avoid wrongly separating that purpose from the community of the redeemed, both actual and potential. God intends that society on the outside of his embrace should be enveloped within it.

God-informed wisdom is not reactionary. It is not displaced by the shock waves of historic events. Positively it defines the good into which society should be transformed. It correctly relates God's wide purpose to his concentrated purpose in the community actually redeemed. Wisdom has many more tasks besides. It must evaluate different expressions of human culture and in so doing separate their creative and

destructive elements. There would sometimes appear to be a
serious lack of wisdom in the way Christians of different
traditions make their estimates. Radicals recognise the evil
powers in Latin American culture only in relation to its oppressive capitalism. Conservatives only recognise Satan in
the oppressive spiritism. Has the Devil outwitted both
Christian types? Conservatives dwell in the past; radicals
dream of the future. But, as John Macquarrie observes,
"There is something pathological both in being fixated in the
past and in being obsessed with the future." A biblical wisdom and hope holds past, present and future in a single span.

Finally, wisdom must relate the temporal with the eternal.
The 19th Century Christian may have been acutely aware of the
eternal plight of man, but much less sensitive to his temporal
condition. The burden of Christian conscience in our own time
is likely to have an exactly opposite bias. The correction of
these imbalances surely involves sympathy towards the anguish,
both of the materially deprived and the spiritually alienated.
Wisdom requires this double sympathy but must also attempt
some differentiation of values. Paul does not hesitate to ad-
vise the Colossians: "Set your minds on things that are above,
not on things that are on earth." Similarly he testifies to
the Corinthians: "We look not to the things that are seen but
to the things that are unseen; for the things that are seen
are transient, but the things that are unseen are eternal."
These Scriptures must not of course be mis-used to justify an
unscriptural dualism. They do, however, relate to the Christian response to endemic suffering and evil in the present
world. Paul's faith here is a pilgrim faith; his roots and
his ambitions are transferred to the new creation (as yet invisible) and rest more lightly (though still responsibly) in
the old. There must be for the Christian a certain economy of
the last days. As the crises which surround us intensify,
so more wisdom is required in applying scarce resources to the
most urgent goals.

4. DEVELOPMENT AND ESCHATOLOGY: EXPANDED BY SUBSTANTIAL HOPE

Jeremiah, the Prophet of Doom, learned to call God "Thou Hope of Israel." He had been taught, through the loneliness of his ministry, how precious a thing it is to enjoy personal communion with his Lord. Even more remarkably, in the midst of apostasy, judgment and disaster, he gained a vision of hope. On the human side Jeremiah's remarkable response to calamity appears brilliantly intuitive and nobly obstinate. The divine side of the same paradox is very helpfully and suggestively traced by John Macquarrie in *Christian Hope* . He refers more directly to the prophecy of Isaiah and with his distinction between hope and optimism he shows instead how hope is linked with judgment: "The day on which righteousness would be established would ipso facto be the day on which all unrighteousness would be judged. 'For the Lord of Hosts has a day against all that is proud and lofty, against all that is lifted up and high.' This note of judgment is nothing different from the vision of Hope. It is simply the other side of a single reality."

This conclusion brings us back to the identification we made of our own position in history. We live at a time of impending judgment and brightening hope. In our moment of crisis we hardly need reminding how near the human family has come to total despair, breakdown and hopelessness. In the post-war world with its hydrogen bomb and its iron curtain, the aged Winston Churchill confessed, "I am bewildered by the world; the confusion is terrible." Even the writer of Revelation had wept in despair over the incomprehensible succession of calamities contained in the scroll: war, genocide, scarcity, natural disaster, persecution and death. These recur in history to such a degree as to threaten its meaning. It is only 'the Lamb who was slain' who can break open the seals of significance. As Michael Wilcock says, in commenting on chapters 5 and 6 of Revelation, "Only in Christ crucified is to be found the answer to the riddle of life."

Even these first considerations of biblical hope emphasise its distance from other optimistic philosophies and ideologies. In contrast to these it is a substantial hope. I quote Professor Macquarrie again. "The Messianic kingdom is not guaranteed by a doctrine of progress or a theory of evolution." If therefore we leave our theory and practice of development with their underlying assumptions of progress or evolution unchallenged, then we are indulging in false hope. Development must

be chastened and corrected by God's judgment if it is to
relate positively to the coming kingdom.

It is not enough, however, to mark the distinctiveness of
biblical hope: we must celebrate its greatness. Hope from
God bursts wide open our circle of experience and promises
"what eye has not seen" and "that has not entered the heart
of man." Hope is fulfilled in the new perfectly integrated
creation. Man's sphere, earth, loses its distance from the
angelic sphere, heaven. All God's reconciled and obedient
creatures enjoy his immediate presence and are bathed in the
light of His glory. The environment is warmly hospitable
and sublimely beautiful. All the delights of the garden
feature in the restored Eden, and chief among them is the
privilege of walking with the King. There is rich and satisfying community here. The New Jerusalem, longed for city of
peace, welcomes the people of peace. The pilgrims have arrived; they are home at last. These are the beautiful people. Unrestricted now by weakness of body or mind, they express their increased powers through glorified bodies. The
abundant vitality strikes up a symphony. The new song of
worship is also a wedding march for the Lamb and His bride.

I write this not on a day when the trumpets are sounding
or when Christ is coming publicly to announce the new age,
but on a day when the newspapers feature the corpses of
Palestinians massacred in West Beirut. How then can we focus at the same time on the horrors of the immediate present
and on the glories of the ultimate future? The long thread
joining such a present and such a future must surely snap.
Against all appearance, though, present hope is securely
anchored in eternity.(Hebrews 6:19) It is of course a resurrection hope. Because of this, death is not a full stop but
a semi-colon; what comes after, amplifies and explains what
has gone before. There is a transformation but also a continuity. The individual who has been raised is not some
other person but the same person. Resurrection, however, is
more than an individual affair. The extent of resurrection
is boldly stated by George Knight: "The hope which Israel
entertained was the hope of a resurrection not merely of some
in Israel, or even of all mankind, but the hope of a final
consummation of a resurrection of all creation." This being
so, there will be a continuity of existence on a scale perhaps rarely considered. We are so conditioned by transience
that we may be surprised by what turns out to have permanence.
It is a natural thing for a man or woman to want to be remembered. Elaborate attempts are made to perpetuate a name.

Even so, human memory fades. God's memory, on the other
hand, is perfectly retentive. It may be helpful to think
of continuity and even discontinuity in terms of God's memory. What the eternal God remembers must have a place in
eternity. He graciously chooses to forget the sins of the
redeemed, but every good, or even every apparently neutral,
detail in his creation is remembered   (Matt.10:30). God's
creation will most assuredly be renewed. I would conclude
that the things a man creates in agreement with God's creativity will also be renewed and will also gain an eternal
significance. "The kings of the earth shall bring their
glory" (Revelation 21:24), "preserving in the new order,"
as Bruce Milne says, "all that has been true and righteous
and God honouring in the old." Hope that this should be so
greatly increases the value and meaning of all that man can
do in harmony with his Creator. This truth enhances
development also.

If the scale of the future resurrection widens our hope,
then the fact of achieved resurrection intensifies our hope.
Christ's resurrection anticipates the general resurrection
and is of a piece with it. Christ's miracles are signs of
the resurrection kingdom, and as such, signs of hope. When
Jesus promised that his followers would do "greater works,"
He was surely asserting that these signs of hope would continue and even increase. To be effective signs, their character must reflect the qualities of the eternal kingdom.
Healings will signify the perfect health enjoyed in the kingdom; exorcism will demonstrate the banishment of evil from
the kingdom. Can the cultivation of a garden or the reclamation of a desert say anything about the restored Eden? Can
urban renewal serve to point forward to the New Jerusalem?
I personally believe such social transformation can carry
this greater significance. Development which even imperfectly
represents the qualities of the kingdom of peace serves to announce that kingdom and, though fractionally, usher it in.

How remarkably resilient is biblical hope? It refuses to
be extinguished, either by the most heinous crimes or by the
most overwhelming disasters. It goes on hoping when signs of
hope are scarce. The connection of present hope with ultimate hope is never lost. Christ's resurrection provides the
essential linkage. Resurrection hope brings enhanced significance, not only to the individual, but to the society in
which the Gospel is preached. It undergirds and directs social transformation. Hope beyond history is boundless and
exulting; it surveys a glorious prospect. Hope within history can hold the line in the most desperate battle, but it

is always ready to advance. This positive hopeful hope was expressed by the Puritans, whose vision was enlarged by the promises of Scripture. Richard Sibbes learned to expect "lesser days before that great day." In particular the Puritans were looking for the conversion of the Jews and the widespread acceptance of the Gospel among all nations. They also believed that spiritual renewal would penetrate society, that the salt would preserve the perishable and that the leaven would raise the lump.

Hope needs to work its good work in the modern church. One positive step would be the recovery of the robustly biblical character of the Puritan hope. Summing up the outstanding task of re-defining hope, Stephen Travis draws attention to the vital matter of the implications of eschatology for present experience and action in the world. He refers to the "theology of hope" and "political theology" and "liberation theology" and continues "a major task is the creation of a synthesis between these 'worldly hopes' and a theology of human immortality in fellowship with God." Meanwhile advice given by John Calvin to a different generation speaks to us still: "Let us hope boldly, then, more than we can understand; Our Lord will still surpass our opinion and our hope."

5. DEVELOPMENT AND ESCHATOLOGY: APPLIED THROUGH A VIGOROUS MISSION

All things biblical have a dynamic quality. The Bible views history as neither circular nor academic; it generates meaning into events and evokes a response to the outstanding historical challenges. Biblical wisdom does even more than identify good and worthwhile goals, it interests itself in ways and means of achieving them. This wisdom is inspirational and so is biblical hope. Indeed it has been hard to talk about any of these subjects in the preceding sections without, as it were, getting catapulted into the action. In the words of Andrew Fuller, "Hope is one of the principal springs that keeps mankind in motion. It is vigorous, bold and enterprising. It causes men to encounter dangers, endure hardships and surmount difficulties innumerable, in order to accomplish the desired end." With his experience of hope, it is no surprise that Fuller became first secretary of a great missionary society. He was part of a generation who awakened faith,and hope was spilling over into unprecedented action.

Let's go further and say that biblical renewal ignites an explosion of creativity. The new experience of God's power makes the impossible seem possible. The healing of the cross cuts people free from the old morbidity. Sharpened faculties excitedly explore a world newly transparent to the glories of its Creator. The little time before His majestic appearing must be spent in the most intense and concentrated preparations for that great event.

Perhaps, though, "explosion" in this context could be a misleading word. It rightly gives the impression of a great release of power but also suggests its rapid dissipation. Christian action in the world could more normally be described as a slow burning. In Scripture,hope is suggestively linked with patience and significantly associated with love. The Thessalonians are, for instance, commended at the same time both for their "steadfastness of hope" and their "labour of love." Hope perceives the good thing that God promises, and love works to the end that the loved ones may receive that benefit. Love is not easily discouraged; "it hopes all things, endures all things."

With this in mind, it is clear that one form that Christian action must take in the world is patient building--an unspectacular brick by brick, inch by inch process. One more pastoral visit, one more mother and baby clinic, one more cooperative decision hammered out, one more sack of potatoes sold, one more broken pane of glass repaired. One more can appear less than a fraction more. Daily tasks may seem dwarfed into insignificance by the vast scale of what needs to be achieved. These small actions can be none the less the building bricks of God's dwelling.

Patient building is adaptive and ingenious. It takes notice of the cultural and political contours of the terrain. It doesn't bring in an ideological bulldozer to lay it all flat. Foundations are laboriously dug out on the hillside. Bricks are pared down to fit the awkard gaps.

Consciously or unconsciously we were searching after this kind of adaptability and relatedness in the Iniciative Cristiana programme, described in "Green Finger of God." It was obvious that in the Chaco situation many things didn't relate by a mile. The now pacific but still largely primitive Indian culture was badly threatened and marginalised by the aggressive capitalistic western culture surrounding it. In the church programme the farm betterment and the community farms represented an attempt at creative bridge building. A lot of hope has been and is being invested in this operation. Some no doubt has been ill founded but, please God, not all. The good bricks may after all turn up in some side street of the New Jerusalem!

It may be worth adding the point that patient building isn't just an approach to Christian action at a local level. The tackling of global issues requires the same undespairing patience. A letter to a member of parliament, or a signature on a petition may seem tiny drops in the ocean of influence, but Christian hope is not paralysed by these comparisons either.

This constructive drudgery of biblical action in the world I have referred to as patient building. Building is a necessary contribution but, by itself, not a sufficient one. Something is needed with multiple, not just additional powers of growth. I find in the letter of James an arresting statement which indicates what this fruitful kind of action may be. "The harvest of righteousness is sown in peace by those who make peace." I personally find it very helpful to think of biblically informed and Spirit inspired action in the world as the sowing of peace. This activity relates especially to evangelism and community education. What is sown might be a spoken word, a written word or an incarnate word. If, in

whatever way, it mediates the life-giving Word, then its potential is vastly greater than its initial size or importance
may suggest. The harvest of righteousness which results from
this sowing should normally include both personal righteousness and societal righteousness. Currently great emphasis is
placed on political and economic structures in the quest for
social transformation. According to this thinking, bad structures are closely identified with oppression and good structures promise liberation. Granted that structures are by no
means neutral in their effect, doesn't this approach attribute
to them a dynamism which they do not possess? Shouldn't it be
recognized that the dynamic for development is located elsewhere. When it comes to sowing, both capitalistic and so-
cialistic systems may prove stony soil, but the life is in
the seed.

Sowing is in fact used in the Bible as a metaphor not
only to suggest multiplication but also new life growing out
of burial and death. The seed that falls into the ground and
dies speaks primarily of Christ and His cross. In the second
place, though, it can also give meaning to suffering and apparent failure of those who act in Christ's name. Certainly
the most significant developments in the Iniciative Cristiana
programme have coincided with the set-backs and emergencies
of the last three years. A bad harvest, the liquidation of a
company launched to channel the commercial production, the
economic crisis gripping Argentina, the evacuation of British
missionary personnel at the time of the South Atlantic conflict, each shock in turn removed something which had to die
or be replaced. Each crisis has brought to life new qualities
in local leadership, greater freedom from dependency and a
more culturally acceptable and church related style of operation.

We are familiar in the Bible not only with the seed
which dies and bears fruit, but also with the seed which is
never buried; instead it falls on the hard pathway and is de-
voured by voracious birds. The reference here, according to
the gospel interpretation, is to satanic interference. Both
sowing and building are peaceful occupations, but it is scarcely possible to make peace with Satan, the enemy of all good.
The Old Testament picture of building, sword in hand (Nehemiah
4:14) may help here. Peaceful building and sowing must be accompanied with dogged fighting.

The controversy about violence and the weapons which are
legitimate in this warfare is well rehearsed. Could I, though,
plead for recognition that evil powers posess individual people

as well as political systems. Exorcism, prevailing prayer, testimony prompted by the Holy Spirit, identification with the defenceless, these are all the normal ingredients of the Christian struggle. True it is that the struggle often appears to be at "the last ditch." In the Chaco every aspect of the church's social commitment had a critical aspect: education was being carried out among those suffering serious disorientation from a dominant culture; community development struggled with the threat of dispersion of communities; economic development attempted to re-build their threatened economic base; medicine countered health standards which were dangerously low.

Whether, though, the struggle is at the last ditch or on the point of some great victory, it must be consistently pursued alongside "building" and "sowing," as part of human action, responding to God's redemptive purpose. It is an inclusive action and it is important to review its inclusiveness. First, though, how inclusive is the company of actors? This question resembles a previous one about God's plan for the church and for the world. Repentance, faith and sonship are written across all God's plans for the restoration of all his creatures. They must be necessary aspects of all human action which is responsive to His saving grace. The actors with a positive role in the redemptive transformation of society are those who are Christian believers and those who are in the process of coming to faith.

This last statement may appear restrictive, but if the first inclusiveness is pitched too wide, the second may not be set wide enough. Human action, responding to the eschatological vision, I would want to identify with holistic evangelism. By definition this kind of gospeling brings together the spoken message of hope, the compassionate actions of hope, the selfless service of the needy and the Christian nurturing of the re-born. If Christian participation in development does not adequately relate to the Messianic kingdom, it will share the frustration and failure of all development apart from Christ. Approaches, such as "peoples participation," though excellent in themselves, will not compensate on their own for any basic lack of reconciliation with Christ the Redeemer. Development is not advanced by the abbreviation of the Gospel and its limiting to a this-worldly dimension. Neither, though, is discipling advanced by a different abbreviation: evangelism which is careless of social misery and relies too much on the word pronounced from afar and too little on the word which lives and suffers alongside those who need both to hear and see it.

Now if holistic evangelism really is holistic, then it can
be identified with Christian mission. Mission also needs to
be rescued from its abbreviations. The sending of the Son by
the Father is self evidently of central importance to those
to whom He was sent. If the Son sends His followers, as He
himself was sent, then mission in these terms must be the
most important enterprise to which we can be committed.

So it is this all important enterprise of mission which is
so often fragmented and trivialised. As a staff member of
one, I have to say that our missionary organizations share
blame in reducing mission. Half are dedicated to discipling,
with a nodding assent to social action; half are committed to
relief and development, with an anxious thought spared for the
issues of eternity. It is often economic pressures that force
us into these divergent groupings, but the net result is that
none of us bears witness as we should to the totality of mission.

Our action in mission should bear this witness, and we
ought at least to question the extent to which discipling and
social concern have been organizationally divided.

What is needed then is a high view of mission, a passionate commitment to its advance and a structuring which unites
rather than divides its temporal and eternal goals. In a
world in which three thousand million people make no Christian
profession, the size and urgency of the eternal issue may
daunt believers, but they must realise that no other human
agency except His church will bring good news of eternal life
in Christ to these masses. In the face of the corresponding
weight of temporal need and physical distress, the church must
be careful not to underestimate its responsibility. Governments and government agencies are effectively ignoring some
of the most serious global issues. Their bland response to
the Brandt Commission betrays their refusal to commit themselves to any larger undertaking which they deem politically
inexpedient and costly. Take one example: Production based
on high technology is marginalising ever increasing proportions
of the world population from participation in productive work.
What government body is tackling this issue with any commen-
surate degree of seriousness? Those marginalised need their
own technology and economy, enabling them to live in a mutual
and just relationship with the modern sector. Who might give
thought to such complementary development? Who would research
techniques for modern subsistence? Who would invest resources
on an adequate scale? The church which pioneered hospitals

and schools may have to take entirely new and major social
initiatives. Who else will care even for the minimal needs
of the millions on the margin of society? Secular education
has other priorities. Why not then found open universities
of Christian Education to begin to equip people to tackle
global issues such as these?

   To talk in ambitious terms about what the church might
do, or even must do, smacks at once of triumphalism. We need
to keep returning to the gradualism of the "building," the
"sowing"and the "fighting." But humble steps do not preclude
a giant stride. The powerful Spirit of God may yet provoke
that burst of creativity and release of compassion which could
bring temporal as well as eternal hope to the world.

RELATED READING

George A. F. Knight   *A Christian Theology of the Old Testament*

John Macquarrie   *Christian Hope*

Michael Wilcock   *I Saw Heaven Opened*

Iain Murray   *The Puritan Hope*

Stephen H. Travis   *Christian Hope and the Future of Man*

                         I Believe in the Second Coming of Jesus

Jürgen Moltmann   *The Future of Creation*

Bruce Milne   *The End of the World*

Sven Lindquist   *Land and Power in South America*

Maurice Sinclair   *Green Finger of God*

EVANGELISM AND SOCIAL TRANSFORMATION

Purpose. The purpose of this paper is to concisely and directly seek to answer four questions:

(1) What are the social implications of evangelization?
(2) What is the relationship between forgivenesss and personal and social sins?
(3) What is the historical relevance of the proclamation of the gospel?
(4) What are the social effects of the proclamation of the gospel?

The Lausanne Covenant and the *CRESR Report* are accepted as givens, and I hope to take the discussion a little further.

(1) What are the Social Implications of Evangelization? In a way, the results of evangelization can only be ascertained by its social manifestations. John and Jesus both made the same basic point: Repentance is made real by the fruit that it bears. Throughout the New Testament, evangelism aims for total transformation, personal and social.

(2) What Is the Relationship Between Forgiveness and Personal and Social Sins? Forgiveness has social as well as personal implications. To be sure, a person who turns to the living God is not instantaneously aware of *all* his personal and social sins. It is often more difficult for Christians to face up to their participation in global and social sins. However, in Christ's death and resurrection, both our personal and social sins are forgiven.

(3) What Is the Historical Relevance for the Proclamation of the Gospel? At the very heart of social transformation is the conviction that the proclamation of the Gospel is socially relevant. Reconciliation with the God of Justice should normally result in a dissatisfaction with the *status quo*. For we know that even though full justice and redemption are not possible in this world, our reconciliation with God should cause us to promote the good of neighbor, nation, and world.

(4) What are the Social Effects of the Proclamation of the Gospel? The very presence of the church in a given society is already the beginning of social transformation. It is a

sign of the righteous Kingdom of God in a world of unrighteousness.

Evangelism and social transformation are actually two
sides of the same coin.   I have attempted to show that
social transformation is a visible demonstration of evangelization.   If we really mean business, let us begin "bringing
forth fruits worthy of repentance" and let us work for justice in the land!

TITE TIENOU is a theologian from Upper Volta, West Africa,
presently lecturing at Fuller Theological Seminary in Pasadena, California.

EVANGELISM AND SOCIAL TRANSFORMATION

Tite Tienou

Introduction.

It is necessary, at the very beginning of this paper, to set forth as clearly as possible the purpose and the limits of the task before us. We live in a time of inflation. Besides the obvious monetary inflation, there is (as of late) an inflation of words and meetings. One gets the feeling that everything worth saying or writing has been said or written. If only we would be more attentive to our immediate and distant past!

At any rate, there are countless meetings, seminars and conferences devoted to specific and general themes. The temptation is great for some of us to call for a moratorium on words and meetings. Let us stop talking and let us start doing! This is particularly true for the topic of Evangelism and Social Concerns. In one form or another, it has been present in most conferences of the past decade. Has not the issue been clarified enough? So much for the expression of personal frustration!

For the reasons just mentioned and keeping in mind the target audience and the overall purpose of Wheaton '83, I have deliberately chosen to undertake a straightforward presentation rather than the usual academic verbiage. I have also restricted myself to the questions raised in the outline of the various topics for the plenary papers.

The basic given, that is the starting point, of the present paper is the Lausanne Covenant (paragraph 4). This is the background against which the questions were asked in conjunction with Evangelism and Social Transformation. I should also add that the report of CRESR '82 represents, in my mind, another given. In other words, I will consciously attempt here to avoid unnecessary repetition of either Lausanne '74 or CRESR '82. In a limited way, I hope to take the discussion a little further.

I will therefore briefly summarize the relevant data of the Lausanne Covenant and the Grand Rapids Report before addressing myself to the following questions: What are the social implications of evangelization? What is the relationship between forgiveness and personal and social sins? What is the historical relevance of the proclamation of the Gospel? and What are its social effects? I have opted for conciseness, although each one of these questions could be treated at greater length.

Background: The Lausanne Covenant and The Grand Rapids Report.

The Lausanne Covenant.

For Evangelicals, generally speaking, the matter of Evangelism and Social Concern was honestly discussed, at least globally, at the International Congress on World Evangelization held in Lausanne in 1974. Since then, Evangelicals worldwide have been called to reflect on the issue and act appropriately. It is therefore good for us to set our thoughts in the context of this widely circulated and accepted document.

Paragraphs 4 and 5 deal very directly with "the nature of Evangelism" and "Christian Social Responsibility." Let us quote from them:

Paragraph 4:

"To evangelize is to spread the good news that Jesus Christ died for our sins and was raised from the dead according to the Scriptures, and that as the reigning Lord He now offers the forgiveness of sins and the liberating gift of the Spirit to all who repent and believe...The results of evangelism include obedience to Christ, incorporation into His church, and responsible service in the world."

Paragraph 5.

"Although reconciliation with man is not reconciliation with God, nor is social action evangelism, nor is political liberation salvation, nevertheless we affirm that evangelism and socio-political involvement are both part of our Christian duty...When people receive Christ they are born again into His kingdom and must seek not only to exhibit, but also to spread, righteousness in the midst of an unrighteous world. The salvation we claim should be transforming us in the totality of our personal and social responsibilities."

I will omit comment on the quotations from the *Lausanne Covenant* except to say that, as it is readily apparent, it advocates the case for a link between evangelism and social transformation, following in this the general belief of Christians throughout the ages, according to which the results of evangelism should be "translated" into society. The *Covenant*, however, does not clarify the nature of the link or relationship.

The Grand Rapids Report

The Consultation on the Relationship between Evangelism and Social Responsibility (CRESR) held in Grand Rapids in June 1982 sought to go beyond Lausanne and provide some clarification. The document which came out of CRESR, known as the *Grand Rapids Report,* is doubly significant: 1) It is a joint publication of L.C.W.E. and W.E.F.; 2) It represents contemporary Evangelical attempts to understand the link between evangelism and social responsibility. Let us again quote from a well known document.

The matter of the relationship between evangelism and social responsibility is treated in Section 4 of the *Grand Rapids Report*. That section begins with a sketch of the historical understanding of the relationship (Section 4, Para. (a)). It then presents three kinds of relationship: 1) "Social activity is a *consequence* of evangelism. That is, evangelism is the means by which God brings people to new birth, and their new life manifests itself in the service of others" (para.c); 2) Social action is "a *bridge* to evangelism. It can break down prejudice and suspicion, open closed doors, and gain a hearing for the Gospel" (para. c.); 3) Social action and evangelism are sometimes undistinguishable; they are partners (para.c).

This brief background, by way of reminder of the present discussion, was necessary to situate ourselves and provide the needed perspective. For we should never act as if we were the

first ones to discover evangelism and social transformation.
Rather, we participate in a long history, Biblical and church
history.

Evangelism and Social Transformation in Four Questions.

1. *What are the social implications of evangelization?*

    Let us first note that this question assumes that evangeliza-
tion *has* social implications. And so it is. In a way, the results of evangelization can only be ascertained by its social
manifestations, whether negatively or positively.

    It is not without interest that the first evangelist (i.e.
proclaimer of the good news), known as John the Baptist,
preached the gospel in terms of social implications (Luke 3).
I will briefly note the salient features of his message. John
came with the expressed purpose of "preaching a baptism of repentance for the forgiveness of sins"   (v.3). I do not wish to
discuss "baptism of repentance;" I would rather point to
John's chief goal: the forgiveness of sins. So, his was a
spiritual ministry. And yet it is in social terms that the
salvation of God will be manifested to society at large. This
seems to be the intention of the Isaiah quotation. Straight
paths, filled ravines, levelled mountains, crooked roads made
straight and rough roads made smooth all "speak" of the restoration of justice in the land and that is the salvation of God
(vv.4-6).

    In his dialogue with the multitudes who came to hear him,
John emphasized the same basic point: repentance is made real
by the fruits it bears. Forgiveness is not just "escaping the
wrath to come." Every forgiven person has the responsibility
of "bringing forth fruits in keeping with repentance" (v.8) and
all barren trees will be burned (v.9).

    Seeing the implications of repentance, the people ask: "What
shall we do then?" (v.10) Note John's reply. It is both
general and specific but always cast in terms of "fruits" or
signs of transformation. In general terms, the repentant and
saved person should be merciful and kind to those in need round
and about him (v.11). All people, when they respond to the
message of evangelization, should manifest the transformation
wrought in them by "righting" the specific wrong which they
were accustomed to doing. That is the sense of the replies
given to the tax-collectors and the soldiers (vv.12-14).

The same kind of social implications of evangelism and salvation runs throughout the New Testament. Whether people are intuitively aware of it (for instance Zaccheus in Luke 19) or have to be exhorted to achieve it (for instance Paul's admonitions in Phil. 4:8 and II Thes. 3:10-13), the New Testament teaching is clear: evangelism aims for total transformation, personal and social.

This, I think, is how far we can go to answer the question: What are the social implications of evangelization? It is not advisable, or possible, to establish a list of the social implications of evangelism. Justice in society and the land which results from spiritual transformation is the aim of evangelization.

2. *What is the relationship between forgiveness and personal and social sins?*

It is difficult, if not impossible, to separate personal and social sins, just as it is a fallacy to discriminate between the so-called private and public life of a person. Everything we do has social implications. There are biblical reasons for making such a statement: Sin takes root in the inside of a person and reveals itself outwardly. When Jesus says that a tree is recognized by its fruit, or that a person speaks from the fullness of his heart, and when James describes the process of our sinfulness (James 1:14-15), the message is the same: Sin germinates inside, infects the person, and spills over to others.

I will further substantiate my point with two Biblical examples, one from the Old Testament and the other from the New Testament. Nowhere is sin shown as personal and corporate as in the story of Achan in Joshua 7. Achan's hidden disobedience is called Israel's unfaithfulness and is reason for God's anger to reach *all* Israel. Peace and harmony are established in Israel and between God and Israel only after the removal of the evil one from their midst. Let us note that this was entirely in keeping with the refrain found in Deuteronomy 22, 23, and 24 to "purge the evil from among you."

The well-known New Testament example is that of Ananias and Sapphira found in Acts 5. Here again Ananias and Sapphira die as a "purge of evil" from among the disciples. That the Bible has no category for just personal sin with no social dimension is again seen in Paul's amazement with tolerance of immorality in the Corinthian Church (I Cor. 5:2): they should have removed the evil doer from their midst.

It is quite clear then that forgiveness has personal as well as social dimensions. To be sure, a person who turns to the living God is not instantaneously aware of *all* his personal and social sins. As that person progresses in the Christian way, *normally* sins in his life are brought to his attention and he should repent, be forgiven, and sin no more.

I know that it is nearly impossible for all Christians to agree on the nature of the "social sins" of their immediate contexts. The difficulty is even greater when we think of global social sins. Nevertheless I think that the Biblical data warrant this definition of social sin: any action or thought which violates another's right to the good to which we think we are entitled. I have deliberately worded this definition this way so as to point to the implications. In other words, social sin is that which, on my part, reduces a person's dignity before God. (It is evident that indifference as well as some social programs are social sins by that definition.) Therefore, if I say that I am personally transformed through an encounter with God and forgiven of my sins, my highest priority should henceforth be to restore people to their full dignity through proclaiming the Gospel *and* promoting justice in society.

So far I have argued that forgiveness is not something which can be privatized and interiorized without visible and social effects. Christ's death and resurrection bring us forgiveness of personal as well as social sins, but, in both cases, we have to show evidence of salvation and forgiveness.

3. *What is the historical relevance of the proclamation of the Gospel?*

This question is rather of an ambiguous nature. As far as I understand it, it asks whether the proclamation of the Gospel has historically been relevant to social transformation. As I have tried to show above, the proclamation of the Gospel is, I believe, at the very heart of social transformation.

We are heirs of a tradition which, broadly speaking, has always recognized the centrality of the proclamation of the Gospel. The proclamation is, of course, in *word* and *deed*. The messengers of the Good News from God have almost always been concerned with bringing justice in the land, precisely because they believed the Gospel to be relevant. Obviously this is not the place for a full historical survey of the matter. Moreover, I do not consider myself qualified to do that. I just wanted to point out this aspect of the Christian faith.

It is indeed a sign of our times that we should ask if proclaiming the Gospel is relevant! For most Christians throughout
history, the answer is self evident. And for most of us in the
so-called Third World, this is largely the case: Gospel proclamation (repeat in *word and deed*) is as relevant today as it has
ever been! Let us never forget that the aim of our proclamation
of the Good News is to call people to reconciliation with God
through Christ. And what can be of higher value than to be
reconciled with the living God?

Reconciliation with the God of justice should normally result
in a dissatisfaction with the *status quo* of our present situation. For we know that full justice and redemption are not
possible in this world. And yet our reconciliation with God is
sufficient ground for promoting the good of neighbor, nation,
and world. Herein lies the historical relevance of the proclamation of the Gospel. Far from being a promise of "pie in the
sky by and by" only, it is the recognition of the fact that, as
long as we live in this world, it is impossible that we not concern ourselves with the affairs of society.

4. *What are the social effects of the proclamation of the Gospel?*

The proclamation of the Gospel results in the creation of the
Church, the community of Christ. I think that we should understand the social effects of the proclamation of the Gospel in
relation to that essential purpose of evangelism.

The very presence of the Church in a given society is already
the beginning of social transformation, if social transformation
is understood as a move toward justice. For the Church as a community of disciples of Christ is the light of the world and the
salt of the earth. It is a sign of the righteous kingdom of God
in a world of unrighteousness. The establishment of the Church,
then, is one of the social effects of the proclamation of the
Gospel.

Obviously we should not be so naive as to think that the
Church is always an agent of social transformation. On the contrary, in many places of the world churches are agents of repression, and many Christians are just as immoral as non-Christians. In such situations churches fail to be signs of social
transformation, as indeed they should be.

But when a church is truly light and salt, the social effects of its Gospel proclamation do not depend on its numerical
strength. Rather the quality of its life, its refusal to be
monopolized by any segment of society, prove to all that it is

a community of the Ruler of the Universe, albeit not a perfect community. The impossibility of creating a perfect community should not mean, however, a resignation to see evil triumph and, worse yet, Christians promote evil. How is it that, in some countries with heavy concentrations of Evangelical Christians, corruption and all forms of wickedness are rampant? Let us not be blind to think that our proclamation of the Gospel will bring transformation in society if the people fail to see such transformation in the community of faith! (cf. Phil.4:8 and I Tim.3)

Conclusion.

Evangelism and Social Transformation are actually two sides of the same coin. Of course there can be social transformation apart from evangelism, but normally there should not be evangelism which does not result in social transformation. I have attempted to show that social transformation cannot take place, through evangelism, without a visible demonstration of it by the lifestyle of Christians and Churches. If we really mean business, let us begin "bringing forth fruits worthy of repentance" and let us work for justice in the land!

EVANGELISM AND SOCIAL TRANSFORMATION

Purpose. The purpose of this paper is to examine the relationship between evangelism and social transformation, particularly as it relates to salvation, the church, and disciplemaking.

The Early Church: Evangelism from the Periphery. Christian communities emerged as something entirely new. As a peripheral movement, they really didn't consciously initiate a program to work for the social transformation of the Roman Empire.

Contemporary Parallels: The Church without Privileges. There are churches today which are still an almost silent anti-body, unobtrusively undermining the *status quo,* keeping the smoldering wick of hope alive. The real challenge is to continue operating silently and consistently as an antibody, refusing to subscribe to the values of the world. Therefore we will take the church in the catacombs as the truer church rather than the church in the palaces and Houses of Parliament. This church is our reference point.

Our Eschatologies. The real theological issue among evangelicals is not the primacy of evangelism, but our view of eschatology. Those who expect their salvation only from the future are pre-Christian. As a result of the resurrection and the coming of the Spirit, the early Christians believed the future had invaded the present, and so should we.

Our Understanding of Salvation. According to the Scriptures, salvation was never the saving of individual disembodied souls. The Bible always sees a human person as a living body-soul. Salvation is the re-creation that overcomes sin and regains control of God's great plan. Not only are individuals offered new life now and for eternity, there is also the assurance salvation will culminate in the fulness of the Kingdom, in a new order of life, characterized by love, freedom, justice and peace.

The Church. To offer assurance of personal salvation in Christ is therefore only *part* of the gospel. The church is called to incarnate a gospel that results in a drastic "conversion" of lifestyles and value systems.

Current Conceptions of Evangelism. Evangelism and prophetic ministries are not the same. Authentic evangelism should have a profound significance for development, liberation, justice and peace, but they aren't categories of evangelism.

Contextual Evangelism: Making Disciples. Authentic evangelism is disciple-making. In Matthew's gospel, disciple-making means commitment to both the King and His Kingdom, to both righteousness and justice.

Expectant Evangelism. Salvation in Christ has to be realized in the world *now* already--this is a logical consequence of the incarnation. We evangelize with a sense of expectation.

We thus affirm the Kingdom as the only absolute in history. And as we witness to the gospel of present salvation and future hope, we "identify with the awesome birthpangs of God's new creation."

DAVID BOSCH is a Professor of Theology at the University of South Africa, Pretoria, South Africa.

EVANGELISM AND SOCIAL TRANSFORMATION

David J. Bosch

"To transform," the dictionaries tell us, is "to change in character or condition, to alter in function or nature." The noun, "transformation," would then refer to the action of bringing about such a change. The Greek-derived synonym of this Latin-based word is "metamorphosis." It clearly refers to more than an outward or superficial change; transformation affects the very nature and character of that which is transformed.

In the title above, "transformation" is characterized as "social" and is linked with "evangelism." The suggestion appears to be that there is--or may be--an intimate relationship between evangelism and the transformation of the fabric of society.

THE EARLY CHURCH: EVANGELISM FROM THE PERIPHERY

The history of the Christian Church seems to bear this out. The first Christians were a tiny minority in the populous and far-flung pagan Roman Empire. In a society described as "macabre, lost in despair, perversion and superstition" (Rosenkranz 1977: 71), Christian communities emerged as something entirely new, as communities of "faultless children of God in a warped and crooked generation, in which you shine like stars in a dark world (Phil.2:15). Their contribution, in those early years of non-recognition and persecution, was particularly in the area of preaching and practising what Adolf von

Harnack describes as the "gospel of love and charity." This
was a witness that included alms, care of widows, orphans,
the sick, prisoners, mine-workers, the poor, slaves, and
travellers (Harnack 1961:147-98). It is necessary to draw
attention to the fact that this practical witness of charity
would gradually, in the cause of centuries, lead to the universal health services and education we today take for granted.

The early church was, however, very much a minority
institution. It existed, to a large extent, on the periphery
of society, among slaves, women and strangers--in other words,
among people who had no particular influence on the shape of
society. It was held in contempt by both Greek philosophy
and Greek pagan religion. (cf. Celsus) It was struggling
against overwhelming odds and frequently persecuted. So
Christians did not really imagine that they would be able to
initiate any "social transformation" in the fabric of the
powerful Roman Empire.

In spite of this, the Christian faith became a leaven in
society. Gradually the position of women changed. The evil
institution of slavery would also gradually succumb. Indeed,
it managed to stay alive and well for almost nineteen centuries in the "Christian" west. This has to be attributed,
however, not to the fact that the intention of the Gospel was
unclear, but to Christians' hardness of heart and self-in-
flicted blindness.

CONTEMPORARY PARALLELS : THE CHURCH WITHOUT PRIVILEGES

In the early church the socially transforming dimension of
the Church's evangelistic outreach was, as indicated above,
most probably unintentional, or at least indirect. This, I
suggest, had to do with the nature of the society in which
those early Christians lived. It would have been totally impossible to confront the structures of society head-on, as it
were, because these early Christians realised full well that
those who shaped society did not share their (the Christians')
presuppositions. Modern parallels to the situation faced by
the early Christians can be found in countries such as China,[1]
some other Communist countries, and in some Muslim States. In
situations such as these the Church can only operate as an
almost-silent anti-body, unobtrusively undermining the *status
quo*, keeping the smoldering wick of hope alive, and in this
way preparing for a possible new role in a changed future society.

In such circumstances the type of evangelism that has developed in the Western world during the past two centuries is totally unthinkable. Some years ago I read a moving report by a Roman Catholic missionary, Fr. Jean Kermarrec, in Vietnam (Kermarrec 1976:45-48). He describes how he has prepared his congregation to live and witness as Christians after the take-over of South Vietnam by the Vietcong. He anticipated that the Vietcong would destroy all visible vestiges of the church: chapels, church buildings, crucifixes, etc. He therefore, with his parishioners, deliberately destroyed all these, until there was no list of names left, no prayer book, no cross, no church bell, no rosary, no picture, no altar, no cassock. All these things, he taught them, were to survive invisibly where the believers live, work, weep, and are bleeding. All peripheral, exterior and incidental things were to fall away. He even taught them an invisible way of crossing themselves: A drop of Christ's blood drops on my forehead. It enlightens my thoughts, and I say: "In the Name of the Father...." That drop of blood trickles down to my heart to enkindle love, also for my enemy; I continue: "... and in the Name of the Son." It goes from my heart to both my shoulders, to give them strength to carry their cross. I conclude: "...and in the Name of the Holy Spirit."

In this way Fr. Kermarrec prepared his flock for life in the desert, where they would only have an invisible Shepherd to guide them.

It would be wrong to suggest that in situations such as these evangelism has ceased. Indeed, it differs radically from the evangelism many of us have become accustomed to in the West--radio and television evangelism, evangelistic crusades, etc.--but it is genuinely *evangelism* none the less. A silent witness may, in certain circumstances, be more eloquent than amplified rhetoric.

Whenever a church which used to be a privileged sector of public life (and in most parts of the world this is a situation that obtained until well into the twentieth century) loses its props and through circumstances beyond its control becomes a church without privileges, it faces one of two temptations: either to withdraw into the ghetto, preoccupied with self-preservation, or to attempt to become the religious arm of the new regime, thus regaining a position of semi-establishment. Recent history provides us with examples of both.

It is difficult to remain a church without privileges for a long period. It is easier to fall prey to either of these

two temptations, which, each in its own way, is nothing but
an adaptation to the world. The real challenge is, however,
to continue operating silently and consistently as an anti-
body, refusing to subscribe to the values of the world, silently challenging society, becoming a sign of hope not only
to the Christians, but also to those outside the Church. Martyrdom has always been one of the lesser threats to the
Church's survival. As long ago as the third century A.D.
Tertullian of North Africa wrote to the persecutors of the
Christians: "You achieve nothing by your ever more refined
techniques of cruelty; they become simply the bait that en-
tices people to the church. *As often as you mow us down, we
multiply; the blood of the martyrs is the seed of the church.*"

OUR POINT OF REFERENCE

Now, the overwhelming majority of those invited to participate in "Wheaton '83" do not come from countries and situations such as the one Fr. Kermarrec faced. They may therefore
legitimately ask: What has the excursion above to do with the
Wheaton theme, and, more specifically, with the theme of this
paper?

I suggest that it is of extreme relevance. In the first
place, it may be necessary to remind ourselves that we do not
know how the situation of the church in the world may change
in coming decades; it may very well be that one of our major
tasks in some parts of the world will not be to teach our
Christian communities how to speak, but rather how to be silent effectively.

In the second place it needs to be pointed out that, in the
history of the church, it has always been in the periods of
persecution and suffering that the real issues become crystal
clear. Whenever the church is a privileged partner in society,
having a say in public life, the real issues become blurred
and the essence of the gospel watered down. This means that
the church in the catacombs is church in a truer sense of the
word than the church in the palaces and the houses of parliament. Not that we, in a masochistic manner, should desire or
perhaps even work for a situation where the church is persecuted. Far from it! But we should take the church-without-
privileges as our *point of reference,* to help us *define* what
the real issues are. The New Testament church was such a
church without privileges and unless we recognise this fact--
not only intellectually but existentially--we may fall into
the trap of reading it through the eyes and from the perspective of a society where the church is a tolerated, perhaps
even valued, even if somewhat boring, aspect of public life.

OUR ESCHATOLOGIES

In the paper I prepared last year for the Consultation on
the Relationship between Evangelism and Social Responsibility
(CRESR), which met in Grand Rapids, I pointed out that the
main area of difference among evangelicals is not that some
espouse the primacy of evangelism whereas others do not. That
difference is only a symptom of a much deeper divide within
the evangelical camp. The real difference lies in the area
of *eschatology* and unless we address ourselves to *that*, there
is little point in trying to sort out matters in our definitions of evangelism.

There are Christians who hold that the Kingdom of God is
an entirely future reality and that the supreme task of any
Christian is to do his share so that others may be saved
eternally. Such a saved person may indeed have some responsibilities in the world, also in the area of justice, but these
responsibilities are merely a *result* of the fact that he or
she is now saved eternally. Some would even hesitate to put
too much emphasis on such "results," since they may detract
attention from heaven and cause Christians to forget that the
most important result of being saved is not to change the
structures of society and practise justice, but rather to persuade others to become followers of Jesus so that they, too,
may be saved eternally. Naturally, in circles where such a
view is held, the subject of this paper would hardly be mooted
as something worth considering.

I suggest that this understanding of eschatology is closer
to Jewish apocalyptic than to the New Testament. A pessimistic view of history is essential to this kind of thinking.
The world is evil. The present is empty. The past is a Golden Era for which people yearn nostalgically and which will
be superseded in a future which bears no relationship to the
dreary present. Corruption, evil and injustice can (or *must*?)
be tolerated now, since they are signs of Christ's imminent
return, as they show us the lateness of the hour.

Church history provides us with examples of countless variations of extreme forms of such Christian apocalypticism, from
the Montanists of the second century up to the Millerite movement and some Mennonite colonies in Russia in the nineteenth
century and various groups in our own time.

However, Christians who expect their salvation only from
the future are essentially maintaining a pre-Christian position. For Christ has cleft that future in two and part of it

is already present. "If the present is empty, as the Pharisees, Essenes and Zealots believed, then you can only flee
into the memory of a glorious past recorded in codes (Pharisees), or you can, with folded arms, sit and wait for God's
vengeance on your enemies (Essenes), or you can play God yourself by violently liquidating the empty present,thus trying
to make the utopian future a present reality (Zealots), or
you can enter into an uncomfortable compromise with the status quo (Sadducees). But if the present is filled; if Isa.
61:1-2 has come true, 'today, in your very hearing' (Luke
4:21); if 'the Kingdom of God has already come upon you' (Luke
11:20); if it is no longer necessary to call out that God's
Kingdom is 'here' or 'there,' because in the person of Jesus
it is already 'among you' (Luke 17:21); if many prophets and
kings have longed to see and hear what you now see and hear
(Luke 10:24); if the 'strong man,' the devil, is bound and
his house ransacked (Matt.12:28; Luke 11:21-22); if Satan
falls out of the sky like lightning and the demons submit to
the disciples (Luke 10:17-18); if the Son of Man has authority to do what even the Messiah according to Jewish expectations could not do, namely, to forgive sins on earth (Mark
2:10); if even 'the least' in the newly inaugurated Kingdom
is greater than John (Matt.11:11); if the One in our midst is
greater than Jonah or Solomon (Matt.12:41-42) (Bosch 1980:
64-5), then surely the presence of that Kingdom has significance also for our ministry of evangelism. We cannot possibly, in the face of the fact that in Christ the forces of the
coming age have flowed into the present, proclaim an only
future salvation. We live on the basis of the "already" en
route to the "not yet."

The belief of the early Christians that the future has invaded the present was based on two events: the resurrection
of Christ, and the coming of the Spirit. The New Testament
witness is unanimous on this point; these two events were experienced as *aparchē*--first-fruits of the harvest--and *arrabōn*
--pledge of what is to come, first instalment of the expected
full settlement (cf. I Cor. 15:20,23; 2 Cor. 1:22;5:5; Eph.
1:14). The old order has passed, the new has already begun
(2 Cor.5:17). Christ's resurrection and the presence of the
Spirit were to the early Christians clear signs that it made
sense already to live according to the standards of the "coming age." The new creation, says Newbigin, is "promised in
Christ, pledged in his resurrection, present in foretaste
through the Spirit..." (Newbigin 1982:149).

OUR UNDERSTANDING OF SALVATION

Of course, many would go along with what I have just said--
our salvation is indeed a reality now; we are already saved
and experiencing the first-fruits of the coming age--*but,*
they would define all this in exclusively *spiritual* and
individualist categories. Salvation is indeed a present reality, but it is something exclusively *personal* and *religious*.
Individual souls are saved--saved *from* the world in which they
live, like survivors from the sea after a shipwreck. These
survivors now cling to one another inside an uncomfortable
little life-boat, and have no relationship to the sea around
them other than going round and round and trying to save
others from the perils of the sea.

This interpretation falls short, I believe, in its understanding both of sin and of salvation. It is closer to Greek
and Hindu thinking than to the Bible. For the Greeks *sōtēria*
meant being saved *from* physical life, salvation from the bur-
dens of material existence. In the Hindu scriptures, says
Newbigin, "the real human person (*purusha*) is found by strip-
ping away all the 'sheaths' (*upadhis*) that constitute one's
visible, contingent, historical being as part of the ever-
circling wheel of nature (*samsara*). In...contrast to this,
the Bible always sees the human person..as a living body-
soul...; continued existence as a disembodied soul is something not to be desired but to be feared with loathing. The
New Testament is true to its Old Testament basis when it
speaks of salvation not in terms of disembodied survival, but
in terms of the resurrection of the body, a new creation and
a heavenly city" (Newbigin 1982:149).

In the biblical understanding, sin--personal *and* societal--
is the great disorder that tries to frustrate the work of God;
salvation is the re-creation that overcomes sin and regains
control of God's great plan (Costas 1982:27). Salvation is
therefore intimately related to creation, which means that
the history of salvation cannot be isolated from "secular"
history. Referring to the events in the Nazareth synagogue
described in Luke 4, E. Stanley Jones said that Jesus, in declaring that the prophecy of Isa. 61:1-2 had been fulfilled
in his coming, was giving us the agenda for evangelism: "...
good news to the poor (that is, the economically disinherited)
...release to the captives (the socially and politically disinherited)...recovering of sight to the blind (the physically
disinherited)...to set a liberty those who are oppressed (the
morally and spiritually disinherited)...to proclaim the acceptable year of the Lord (a new beginning on a world scale)"

(Jones quoted by Mollenkott 1983:34). Sin and the presence
of evil manifested itself, according to the teaching of the
Old and New Testament, in sickness of body or mind, in demon-
possession, in lack of love for God, in words and deeds and
in the absence of both, in the loveless self-righteousness of
the godly, in the hypocrisy of ecclesiastics, in the maintaining of special class privileges, in the abuse of authority, in the unjust distribution of the burden of taxation, in
the exploitation of the masses, in selfishness and self-
destruction.

In the Old Testament the reversal of these and similar
personal and societal maladies is summed up in the pregnant
concept of *shalom*, peace. In the New Testament the corresponding concept is the *basileia*, the Kingdom of God. Not only
are individuals offered new life, now and for eternity; there
is also the assurance that salvation will culminate in the
fullness of the Kingdom, in a new order of life, characterized
by love, freedom, justice and peace.

THE CHURCH

In the light of this it is not strange that the community
that began to grow around Jesus of Nazareth gradually became
known as an *ekklēsia*. This was basically a *civil* concept,
not a *religious* one. The Greek language had several words for
specifically *religious* groups. One of these was *thiasos*, a
concept frequently used in connection with the mystery religions which were, indeed, exclusively religious. The word
ekklēsia indicated, however, that the Christian church was at
the same time a sociological and a theological reality. It
was involved in and distinguished from society. Had this not
been the case, had the small group around Jesus been a *thiasos*,
it would have been inconceivable for the Roman authorities to
have regarded Jesus as an enemy of the state. Similarly, had
the early church been a *thiasos*, its confession that Jesus was
Kyrios (Lord) would not have placed it on a collision course
with the rulers of the time. Those early Christians kept on
calling him *Kyrios*, however--a title the Roman emporors had
usually arrogated to themselves--and for three centuries, until
Constantine, they paid the price for this stupendous claim.
Had they been members of a *thiasos*, they would at most have
confessed that Jesus was *sōtēr* (Redeemer; Saviour) and they
would have been saved any serious confrontation with the powers-
that-be. However, to proclaim Jesus as Lord of all is no less
the *evangel* than to proclaim him as Saviour from sins and from
eternal perdition.

To offer the assurance of personal salvation in Christ is therefore only *part* of the gospel. If this *part* is regarded as the whole of the gospel, the gospel is dissociated from the world and the incarnational essence of the Christian faith is denied. The content of the gospel we proclaim then is--in the words of Orlando Costas--"an other-worldly kingdom, a private, inwardly limited spirit, a pocket God, a spiritualized Bible, and an escapist church...Such a gospel makes possible the 'conversion' of men and women without having to make any drastic changes in their life-style and value-systems " (Costas 1982:80).

I am, of course, addressing myself to *evangelicals* in this paper. I know that, on the whole, it is unnecessary to remind you that only he or she who has been inwardly renewed and reborn can be an evangelist. Neither is it necessary to remind you that all good structural changes taken together still fall short of the Kingdom. Therefore, even if the vision of the heavenly *polis* forbids us to exclude politics and societal structures from our understanding of salvation, we know that those structures are doomed to decay and dissolution. For this reason we will show no *ultimate* concern for them, perishable as they are (Newbigin 1982:149). We know that the new order announced by the gospel will not be exhausted by historical structures, that the hope of a new creation is not to be replaced by the hope of an earthly utopia, and we know that it is impossible to speak exclusively of social salvation, since that would leave untouched the personal root of sin (Costas 1982:26).

We will therefore reject a gospel that is ultimately spiritualized to such an extent that it does not touch reality, but also a gospel that has been secularized to the point where there is no call to repentance and no relation to transcendence.

CURRENT CONCEPTIONS OF EVANGELISM

Against the background of what has been said so far, we may now venture some remarks on the nature and purpose of evangelism, particularly as this pertains to our specific subject: Evangelism and social transformation.

The way I intend doing it is to discuss, briefly, some current understandings of evangelism, indicating, in doing so, why I find them wanting.

First: In some circles the goal of evangelism is, for all practical purposes,understood as the *expansion of one's own church*. Particularly in well-churched societies there is sometimes an increasing preoccupation with ecclesiastical in-gathering at the expense of other churches. The church is here--consciously or unconsciously--regarded as a divine institution, franchised by God, to whom "customers" are sup-posed to come.

David Watson correctly argues that--particularly in a well-churched society such as the U.S.A.--evangelism and the re-cruitment of church members are by no means the same thing. This is not to say that the two are disconnected: they are distinct but also inseparable. If once we understand this, we will be saved from false triumphalisms (believing that the numerical growth of our church is a direct result of our "effective" evangelism) and from defeatisms (believing that absence of numerical growth proves the absence of genuine evangelism)   (Watson 1983a:71-73).

Secondly: It is not very helpful to use the term "pro-phetic evangelism"--a term introduced by David Watson and others (cf. Watson 1983b:7)--particularly if it is argued that it is the task of such evangelism to unmask the princi-palities and powers, stand up to them, outlast them, and care for their victims (G.W.Webber, quoted by Mollenkott 1983:40). That this kind of ministry is legitimate is uncontestable, but it is not *evangelism*. Neither is it evangelism to "call ...societies and nations to repentance and conversion" (Wat-son 1983b:7). Principalities and powers, societies and na-tions can be challenged through the church's prophetic mini-stry, but they cannot, *as* principalities, powers and societies, repent and come to faith. It confuses the issue if this kind of ministry is called evangelism, whether we specify it as "prophetic" or as "holistic" evangelism. (cf. also Newbigin 1982:149) This is what nowadays frequently happens in ecu-menical and Roman Catholic circles, where "evangelism" tends to become an umbrella concept covering the entire Christian ministry, for instance when John Walsh says, "The church is in the process of reaffirming this most important scriptural insight when it states that human development, liberation, justice, and peace are *integral* parts of the ministry of evangelization" (Walsh 1982:92). It is one thing to say (as I also do--see below) that authentic evangelism indeed has profound significance for development, liberation, justice and peace; it is something else to claim that these are (on-ly?) parts of the comprehensive concept evangelism. We then have a confusion of categories.

Thirdly: In many Western churches the understanding of
what evangelism is has been deeply influenced by the cultural
context. David Watson (1983a) reminds us that evangelism, as
practised in many parts of the American church, has a long
pedigree in the Augustinian piety that has motivated Protestant missions since the eighteenth century. It has had some
outstanding paradigms: the direct and succinct articulation
of the gospel (Jonathan Edwards), its persuasive communication (George Whitefield), the effective nurture of incipient
discipleship (John Wesley), and the evocation of personal
response with immediacy (Charles Finney). These paradigms
were, however, frequently transplanted to our own time without appropriate historical and theological judgment. This
resulted in an understanding of evangelism which was, in
many respects, culturally determined.

Watson mentions some of the features of this kind of
evangelism: It leads to an alienation from the world, it
preaches an over-personalized gospel wedded to the idol of
success, it imposes a psycho-spiritual crisis which does
little to address the more basic challenge of discipleship;
under the pressure of the consumer culture it offers the
gospel as an inducement and packages salvation as a market-
able asset. In summary, our evangelism reflects the church
as it functions in the culture--"a place where fellowship can
be sought and found, where emotional and spiritual needs can
be met, where moral standards can be affirmed, and where God
can be worshipped" (Watson 1983a:72).

All three understandings of evangelism discussed above
(and it should be remembered that there are vast differences
between the proponents of the extreme forms of numbers 1 and
3 on the one hand and of number 2 on the other), are, in fact,
examples of evangelism made subservient to culture. We are,
however, gradually beginning to understand that the church,
if it is true to its being, will counteract the values of the
culture. Authentic contextualization does not mean that the
church becomes subordinate to the context, but that its message becomes relevant *in* the context. Part of that relevancy
is that a contextualized gospel would *judge* the context in
which it operates, pointing it beyond itself. There is--
alas!--always the danger of *over*-contextualization, and perhaps this is what happened in the three understandings of
evangelism referred to above.

CONTEXTUAL EVANGELISM : ITS PURPOSE

What, then, would be the features of an authentically contextualized evangelism, particularly as it pertains to the
subject of this paper? Let me attempt a few remarks.

First, much current evangelism in effect fosters pious ego-
centrism. On the one hand it operates within the orbit of
the narcissistic pursuit of a fulfilled personhood; thus the
church to which the new convert comes is expected to fulfil
the role of a social agency for the relief of painful disap-
pointments; it is to be the place where uncomprehended fears
can be suppressed and uncomfortable memories as well as awkward expectations can be covered up. On the other hand evangelism operates as an insurance policy: it offers a safe
passage to the next life with a minimum of hazards en route.

In both definitions of evangelism--whether it offers a
psychological panacea or a seat on the train to the hereaf-
ter--it fosters a self-centred and self-serving mindset among
church members. Pastors "find themselves trapped in the role
of personal priest to people who feel they are paying for a
service and are entitled to it"   (Watson 1983a:73).

Now, undoubtedly Christ gives peace of mind and eternal
life to all who come to him. That is part of the very bed-
rock on which the gospel stands. Christ saves us, yes, but
what is it that he saves us *for*? What is the *purpose* of evangelising people, of calling them to repentance and faith?

Karl Barth, in a penetrating excursion in Vol. IV/3 of his
Church Dogmatics, addresses himself to this topic (Barth
1962:561-614). Christian teaching, he says, has tended to regard the church as a kind of institute of salvation and
Christians as enjoying an indescribably magnificent private
good fortune (p.567). The terrible danger in this view,
Barth says, is that eventually Christ may be downgraded to
little more than the Dispenser and Distributor of special
blessings (pp.595-6). People's chief concern is then with
the saving of their souls, or their experiences of grace and
salvation, in short, with establishing their personal relationship with God (p.572). Barth regards this whole understanding of becoming and being a Christian as thoroughly unbiblical and ego-centric. The personal enjoyment of salvation nowhere becomes the theme of biblical conversion stories,
not in the case of those who listened to John the Baptist
preaching (Luke 3:10-14), nor of Zacchaeus or the Philippian
jailer (p.572). Not that enjoying salvation is wrong, unimportant or unbiblical (cf. Col.3:15; I Tim.6:12; Heb.9:15;

I Pet. 5:10; Rev.19:9), but this is incidental and secondary (p.593; cf. p.572)--people receive it, as it were, without expecting or seeking it. What makes someone a Christian is *not* primarily his or her personal experience of grace and redemption, but his or her *ministry*. Indeed, the new Christian receives forgiveness, justification and sanctification *in order to* become a servant (p.593). Being called by God to faith in Christ means being simultaneously commissioned by God to perform a task in the world. If this dimension is played down in our evangelistic outreach, we are offering people nothing but cheap grace.

CONTEXTUAL EVANGELISM : MAKING DISCIPLES

In the light of the above we may, *secondly*, describe authentic evangelism as *disciple-making*. With this, few evangelicals would disagree. If, however, we endeavor to explicate what "discipling" or "disciple-making" entails, we part company. With reference to the imperative "make disciples!" in Matt. 28:19 (one of only four instances in the New Testament where this verb occurs), Donald McGavran argues that "to disciple" means to lead non-Christians to a first commitment to Christ. This first commitment has to be followed by a second, on-going and more comprehensive stage, which McGavran calls "perfecting" and which he clearly distinguishes from "discipling." "Discipling" is, for McGavran, a synonym for "evangelising," "perfecting" is a *sequel* to "discipling" and, in the Great Commission, finds expression in the words "teaching them to observe everything I have commanded you."

In some evangelical circles the distinction between "discipling" and "perfecting" has been described in another way: we have to distinguish, some say, between the "*evangelistic* mandate" and the "*cultural* mandate" (cf. Wagner 1981:12-14, 190-93). In a recent response to an article by Lesslie Newbigin, Peter Wagner explains the difference as follows: "The goal of evangelism is the conversion of sinners, saving souls, making disciples. ...The goal of social ministry is to make people healthier, wealthier, less oppressed and less oppressing, more peaceful, fairer, more just, liberated, enjoying shalom, more secure" (Wagner 1982:153).

I fear, however, that the distinction between the "evangelistic" and the "cultural" mandate--in spite of any help it may give us in the area of *conceptualizing*--is putting asunder what God has joined together. In spite of all talk to the contrary, in *practice* the isolating of the "evangelistic" mandate as primary and as something separate, tends to make the so-called "cultural mandate" optional.

The problem is, however, not only that the "evangelistic mandate" does not always lead to the "cultural mandate," but, rather, that it is wrong to define "discipling" or the "evangelistic mandate" as narrowly as McGavran and Wagner do. I have argued elsewhere (Bosch 1983) that, in the Great Commission, the participle "teaching them (to observe everything I have commanded you)" is to be understood as *explicating* the imperative "making disciples!" People are made disciples by being taught to follow Jesus, to do what he has commanded.

The Jewish rabbis also had disciples. But Jesus' disciples differed from them in several crucial aspects. They had their legitimation not from the *Torah* but from Jesus himself; he expected his disciples to renounce everything for his sake alone; he took the place of the *Torah*. Moreover, for Jesus' followers, discipleship was never the beginning of a promising career but in *itself* the fulfilment of life's destiny; the disciple of Jesus never graduated into a rabbi, like the Jewish disciples did. Thirdly, Jesus disciples were also his servants; they did not merely listen to him, they obeyed him. And since they are called to *follow* him, they will--unlike the rabbinic disciples--share his destiny. "If anyone would come after me, he must deny himself and take up his cross and follow me" (Matt.16:24 par.). To follow Jesus did not merely mean passing on his teachings, or becoming faithful trustees of his insights, but to be his obedient witnesses, his "martyrs."

It is in this demanding sense that we must understand the verb "make disciples!" in Matt. 28:19. People become disciples by being incorporated into the church ("baptizing them..") and by obeying Jesus ("observe...what I have commanded you"). If we read Matthew's gospel carefully in order to establish what this latter phrase refers to, we will discover that Jesus' "commandments" can be summed up in the twin expression *justice-love*. *Love* is the key word in the six powerful antitheses of the Sermon on the Mount (5:21-47) and in the twin commandments of Matt. 22:34-40. But love manifests itself in *justice*. The justice of the disciples ought to surpass that of the Pharisees (5:20) who did not follow "the way of justice" shown by the Baptists (21:31-2). Those who hunger and thirst to see that justice is done will be satisfied (5:6), and those who suffer persecution for the sake of justice will be blessed (5:10). Only when our minds are set on God's Kingdom and his justice, will all the rest be given to us as well (6:33).

Of course, most of our English Bibles do not translate the Greek word *dikaiosynē* in the references above with "justice." They usually prefer "righteousness," which is a moral or spiritual quality we receive from God and which is, on the whole, a religious or spiritual concept. Justice, however, is the form in which we conduct ourselves in relation to our fellow human beings and seek for them that to which they have a right. So we have usually understood all the references above only in a *moral* and *religious* sense. But gradually our eyes are being opened! Waldron Scott rightly says that disciple-making involves more than was commonly assumed in evangelical circles. He adds: "One must understand discipleship in order to make disciples, and discipleship is not fully biblical apart from a commitment to social justice...To be a disciple is to be committed to the King and his Kingdom of just relationships" (Scott 1980:xvi).

The central thrust of the Great Commission is indeed aimed at disciple-making. However, that includes more than only the first stage of a two-staged program. It includes, *simultaneously,* the challenge to practise love and uphold justice. In view of this it has to be said that Harold Lindsell is in error when he says, "The mission of the church is pre-eminently spiritual--that is, its major concern revolves around the non-material aspects of life " (Lindsell, quoted in Scott 1980:94).

This entire tendency--to see mission, indeed, the gospel itself, almost exclusively in personal, inward, spiritual and vertical categories--is nothing but a travesty. It has become almost endemic in the West and, through our far-flung missionary efforts, has been exported to all corners of the globe. Waldron Scott tells of twenty-four North American mission executives with mission work in Latin America who were questioned about the relationship between evangelism and social justice. Only two of them recognized any relationship at all. The remaining twenty-two did not. Some of their responses have been summarized as follows: "The church exists for the purpose of worship, communion, spiritual growth, and evangelistic witness...The growing churches in Latin America are those which minister most to the soul and least to the body. When the decision is left to the national brethren they stress evangelism...Preach the gospel, win the lost, and social ills will gradually vanish as the number of believers in society increases " (Scott 1980:157).

These and similar interpretations narrow the scope of God's kingdom activity to making individuals new creatures. They

falsely teach that if individuals have a personal experience
of Christ in traditional pietistic terms, they will automatically become involved in the changing of society. The evidence teaches otherwise. So does the Great Commission! It
talks about *making disciples*. And in Matthew's gospel discipleship means commitment to both the King and his Kingdom,
to both righteousness and justice. The three concepts disciple, kingdom, and righteousness-justice are like plaited
strands woven into the very fabric of the first gospel. We
cannot, on the basis of Matthew's gospel or of the Great Commission, declare the one element to be primary, the other
secondary, the one to be the root, the other the fruit.

T. K. Thomas of India cries bitterly, "We have freedom in
many Asian countries to preach the gospel, to speak in
tongues, to conduct healing ministries...as long as the gospel
we preach does not disturb, the tongues do not make sense,
(and) the healing does not extend to the diseases of the body
politic"   (Thomas, quoted by Scott 1980:156).

Is this evangelism? I submit that it is not. In fact, it
may be the very opposite. Says Newbigin, "Where...the church
invites men and women to take refuge in the name of Jesus
without this challenge to the dominion of evil, then it becomes a countersign, and the more successful it is in increasing its membership, the more it becomes a sign against the
sovereignty of God. An 'evangelism' that seeks to evade this
challenge and this conflict, which--for example--welcomes a
brutal tyranny because it allows free entry for missionaries
...becomes a sign against the gospel of the kingdom" (Newbigin 1982:148).

CONTEXTUAL EVANGELISM : THE EVANGELISTS

Thirdly, To evangelize is not only to invite people to accept Christ as Saviour, but also to tell prospective converts
what following Jesus implies. In the words of the Lausanne
Covenant, paragraph 4: "In issuing the gospel invitation we
have no liberty to conceal the cost of discipleship."

This does *not* mean that the gospel is superseded by law.
When we challenge people to take the cost of discipleship into consideration, we do it on the basis of the fact that the
Kingdom *has* come in Christ. On the basis of what God has
done and is still doing we offer them new life, we give them
an authoritative word of hope, we announce the New Age. The
response to our evangelism is an overflow from the recognition of the reality of the Kingdom.

It follows from the fore-going that it makes little sense
to try to establish whether evangelism is *only* a verbal ministry. Even the verb *euangelizomai*, to evangelize, can hardly
be understood as referring to an exclusively *verbal* activity,
as Richard B. Cook has illustrated with reference particularly to the Epistle to the Galations (Cook 1981:490-94). For
Paul, evangelism was a way of life that involved his total
being. In addition, it should be remembered that, biblically
speaking, "word" and "deed" are not opposites the way they
are in Western thinking. It is the "Word made flesh" that
is the gospel. The deed without the word is dumb, the word
without the deed empty. The words interpret the deeds, the
deeds validate the words (Newbigin 1982:146-9).

This certainly has some bearing on evangelism today. The
Greek word for witness, *martyria*, in the course of time acquired the meaning of martyrdom. In other words: the verbal
witness of the *martyr* (the witness) was frequently sealed
with his suffering for the gospel. Remember Tertullian:
"The blood of the martyrs is the seed of the church." It
will not be different with us today if our evangelism is authentic. The disciples recognized the risen Christ by the
scars on his body. The disciple, however, is not greater
than his Master. If our evangelism is to become credible,
it will be when those outside see our scars. We seem to
think our *muscles* will convince them and win them over. They
won't. The Galatians believed because they recognized the
marks of Jesus branded on Paul's body (Gal.6:17). It will
not be different with us.

"EXPECTANT EVANGELISM"

Lastly: Long ago Max Warren coined the expression "expectant evangelism" (Warren 1948:132-145). To evangelize ex-
pectantly is to prepare for the end by getting involved in
the here and now. The world may indeed be enemy-occupied
territory but the enemy has no property rights in it. He is
a thief and a liar. *Our* responsibility is to be good stewards
of the King. We may therefore not be indifferent to the way
in which the world is governed, nor to the injustices that
appear to be endemic in it. Salvation in Christ has to be
realized *in* the world *now* already--this is a logical consequence of the Incarnation. In Warren's own words: "Preparation for the 'end,' which is the triumph of God *in* history,
involves taking history seriously as the sphere within which
moral issues are real. Preparation consists in such a demonstration by the Christian Church of the rightness of the
righteousness of God that the world cannot gainsay the witness,

although it may refuse to repent because of it. The 'end'
comes when the rightness of this demonstration is vindicated
by the establishment of the reign of God"   (Warren 1948:132).
And again: "If the temporal order cannot see the vindication
of God then His experiment with time has been a failure"
(Warren 1948:135).

We thus affirm the Kingdom as the only absolute in history.
And as we witness to the gospel of present salvation and future hope, we "identify with the awesome birthpangs of God's
new creation"   (Watson 1983b:6).

N O T E S

1. For an account of the life and witness of some early Christian Communities in Red China, cf. D. Vaughan Rees, *The "Jesus Family" in Communist China*. London: Paternoster, 1959. A more recent account can be found in Raymond Fung, *Households of God on China's Soil*. Geneva: World Council of Churches, 1982.

REFERENCES CITED

1. BARTH, Karl: 1962, *Church Dogmatics IV:3*, Edinburgh: T. & T. Clark.

2. BOSCH, David J.: 1980, *Witness to the World*. The Christian Mission in Theological Perspective. London: Marshall, Morgan & Scott/Atlanta: John Knox.

3.   1983. The Structure of Mission: An Exposition of Matthew 28:16-20, in Wilbert Shenk (ed.): *Exploring Church Growth*. Grand Rapids: Eerdmans.

4. COOK, Richard B.: 1981, Paul the Organizer, *Missiology* 9:4 (Oct.) 485-98.

5. COSTAS, Orlando E.: 1982, *Christ Outside the Camp*. Mission beyond Christendom. Maryknoll: Orbis.

6. HARNACK, A. von: 1961, *The Mission and Expansion of Christianity in the First Three Centuries*. New York: Harper

7. KERMARREC, Jean: 1976, Auf dem Wege zur schweigenden Kirche, *Die Katholischen Missionen* 95:2 (March-April) pp.45-48

8. MOLLENKOTT, Virginia Ramey: 1983, New Age Evangelism, *International Review of Mission*, No. 285 (Jan.) pp. 32-40

9. NEWBIGIN, Lesslie: 1982, Cross-currents in Ecumenical and Evangelical Understandings of Mission, *International Bulletin of Missionary Research* 6:4 (Oct.) pp. 146-151

10. ROSENKRANZ, Gerhard: 1977, *Die Christliche Mission: Geschichte und Theologie*. Munich: Chr. Kaiser

11. SCOTT, Waldron: 1980, *Bring Forth Justice*. Grand Rapids, Eerdmans

12. WAGNER, C. Peter: 1981, *Church Growth and the Whole Gospel*. San Francisco: Harper & Row.

13.   1982, Response to article by Lesslie Newbigin, *International Bulletin of Missionary Research* 6:4 (Oct.), pp. 153-4

14. WALSH, John, MM: 1982, *Evangelization and Justice*. Maryknoll: Orbis

15. WARREN, Max: 1948, *The Truth of Vision*. London: The Canterbury Press

16. WATSON, David Lowes: 1983, The Church as Journalist: Evangelism in the Context of the Local Church in the United States, *International Review of Mission* No. 285 (Jan.) pp. 57-74

17.   1983, Evangelism: A Disciplinary Approach, *International Bulletin of Missionary Research* 7:1 (Jan.) pp. 6-9

CHRISTIAN COMPASSION AND SOCIAL TRANSFORMATION

Purpose. The purpose of this paper is to examine the prophetic compassion of Jesus Christ and look at three facets of His compassion that led to His death, to understand the relationship of Christian compassion to social transformation in the church today.

Service: A Sharing of the Stagnant Pool of a Selfish Society. In John chapter 5, when Jesus asked the man to take up his bed and walk on the Sabbath, He challenged an inhuman society by a deliberate act of defiance of its regulations. This act of compassion led the establishment to make an attempt on Christ's life.

Service: A Judgment of a Blind Society. In Chapter 5, Jesus asked the sick man to break the Sabbath. Now in Chapter 9, He does it Himself. This was a deliberate provocation of the establishment. He exposed by his act of opening the eyes of the blind man the blindness of a self-righteous establishment. The world was able to see the rulers didn't care for their people. Christ did. His acts of compassion judged the established order. The authorities not only excommunicated the man who was healed--Jesus became persona-non-grata. Being seen with Him could lead you into trouble.

Service: Confrontation in Chhatarpur. We have been involved in acts of compassionate service to the rural poor in the Chhatarpur District in India. Our service exposed the insensitivity of those in positions of power. As a consequence 30 of us were arrested on four different occasions. Such service hurts. You lose friends. They choose not to associate with you lest they too get into trouble. Our compassionate service must not only reach out and restore the sight of the blind man, but the sight of a blind society as well.

Service: A Source of Creating Alternative Power for Social Change. It is not enough to stir a society or to judge a blind establishment. If leadership does not repent, it becomes our responsibility to provide an alternative to meet the needs of the people. Servanthood is the biblical means of acquiring power to lead. However, when they discover the purpose of our service is to change the status quo, you are in trouble.

Jesus became an alternative centre for social power by:
(1) being a moral force in contrast to the immoral Jewish
establishment, (2) standing for the smallest men instead of
the establishment, (3) even being willing to lay down His
life for His powerless sheep. Jesus and His new community
were naturally and intentionally a threat to the establishment.

Jesus built up a mass following to give Him power which
further threatened those in power. His willingness to lay
down His life was evidence that He was a servant--not a
power seeker for His own ends.

Like a few of the early missionaries in India who threatened the established order of things by publicly opposing
the oppressive indigo system, our acts of compassionate service will threaten those in power today. Rev. James Long,
who went to prison for his opposition to the Indigo Trade,
demonstrated a "...willingness to suffer for the sake of
others in the cause of peace with justice...."

VISHAL MANGALWADI is the Director of the Association of
Comprehensive Rural Assistance (ACRA) in Chhatarpur, India.
ACRA is a Christian development project that begins in community and reaches out in relief and development activities
in twenty-five villages in their district.

CHRISTIAN COMPASSION AND SOCIAL TRANSFORMATION

Vishal Mangalwadi

Compassion for the suffering individual and concern for the glory of God were undoubtedly the prime motives of Christ's service. But if compassion or mercy had meant for Christ merely what most Christians understand by them today, then Jesus would never have been killed. He would have been a fit candidate for a Nobel prize, not for the cross.

In an earlier article, *Theology of Power in the Context of Social Involvement,** I have argued that Christ's compassion was a prophetic compassion, which went to the roots of human misery and dealt with them. In this article I want us to look at three facets of Christ's compassion and service which were crucial factors that led to His death. In an earlier age, when Protestantism still believed in social protest, such an article would have been redundant. But today? Well, we have drifted so far away from our Biblical and historical heritage that it would seem "too radical" to some of my dear friends.

SERVICE:
A STIRRING OF THE STAGNANT POOL OF A SELFISH SOCIETY

In John, Chapter 5, Jesus healed a man who had been sick for 38 years. He was lying near a pool of water. When the waters of the pool were stirred, they carried therapeutic powers. This was not a superstition but something a man had witnessed who had been lying by the side of the pool for decades. He was sick. The treatment was free and within his sight. Yet he could not get it. Why? He explained to Jesus

that his problem was that he did not have anyone who would
put him into the water when it was stirred. No one cared for
him.

Jesus asked him to pick up his mat and walk. He did. And
it was a Sabbath. In Israel you could forget whether it was
Tuesday or Thursday, but no one ever forgot that it was Sabbath. Their society was so well organized that in no time
the Jewish authorities (vs.10, TEV) knew that this little
unknown man had dared to break the Sabbath rule: he had picked
up his bed and was walking. An on-the-spot inquiry began.
How efficient! But that was precisely the problem. An establishment which didn't care for a man for 38 years was so
prompt in caring for its own stupid rules. The sick man had
complained to Jesus that his problem was not that he was sick
or that treatment was not available. His problem was that
the Jewish society had no compassion.

It was not by mistake that Jesus asked him to take up his
bed and walk on a Sabbath. Jesus asked him to challenge this
inhuman society by a deliberate act of defiance of its rule.
God had provided the stirred-up pool of water for the healing
of this man. It was the social pool of a stagnant, selfish
society that needed to be stirred up for the healing of men
like him. That was precisely what Jesus did. He not only
healed the man; he asked him to break the Sabbath rule, which
led to an attempt by the establishment at Jesus' life.
(John 5:18)

Does the healing ministry of the Church today, even its
community health work, lead to such retaliation from the society? No, because our service does not touch the real issue
at all. There are any number of sick men, women and children
in our villages and slums who die daily, not because treatment is not available or is expensive, but simply because no
one cares to take the treatment to them.

The establishment plans for the Olympic games to be held
in India; it plans for colour T.V.; it can send satellites
to the sky; but it cannot take the available treatment to the
dying destitutes in its slums. The Church says it cares, yet
it does not dare to expose the selfishness of the élite which
is the real cause of the hundreds of basic diseases which
should have been wiped out by now, only if clean water, hy-
gienic sanitation, adequate nutrition, health education and
immunization were made available to the poor masses. Christ's
mercy did not touch an individual alone. It sought to touch
the heart of a society. It sought to awaken the sleeping conscience of a society.

SERVICE:
A JUDGEMENT OF A BLIND SOCIETY

After Jesus opened the eyes of a beggar who was born blind,
in John Chapter 9, Jesus did not portray himself as a "servant." He said, "I came to this world to judge, so that the
blind should see and those who see should become blind" (v.39).

The incident in John Chapter 5 was not an isolated happening. It was part of Christ's pattern. On that occasion Jesus
had simply asked the sick man to break the Sabbath law. Now
in Chapter 9 he does it himself. In order to open the eyes of
this blind man, he did not need to spit on the ground and make
mud with the spittle, especially on a Sabbath day when he knew
that it would be seen as a deliberate defiance of the establishment's laws. Yet he did it. It does not seem to me that
one can interpret this act of Jesus as anything other than a
deliberate provocation of the establishment. Jesus also asked
the blind man to break the law--"Go and wash your face in the
Pool of Siloam   (v.7). Jesus didn't need to do this in order
to heal him. Yes, but healing him was not the only objective
of Christ's service. His objective included exposing the
blindness of the self-righteous establishment and condemning
it publicly.   Had God not commanded Israel in the Old Testament to have mercy on its poor? If Israel was righteous and
obedient, why did this man have to beg on the streets in order
to live?

The establishment was blind enough to fall into the trap
laid by Christ. Instead of containing Christ's service by
patronizing it, they condemned the healing of a blind man,
simply because it was done on a Sabbath day. They ex-communicated the man from the synagogue and thereby further exposed
their own blindness. The world was able to see that a mighty
prophet had risen amongst them who can open the eyes of a man
born blind, yet the establishment could see nothing more than
the violation of its own petty rules. Its values, its ideals,
its attitudes, its priorities--all stood exposed and condemned.
The world was able to see that its rulers did not care for
their people; Christ did. The sheep were able to perceive
that Jesus was their true shepherd, who dared to stand against
the wolves who pretended to be their custodians.

Jesus made the blind man pay a heavy price for his healing.
He was ex-communicated from the synagogue because he chose to
speak the truth. No doubt he would have been welcomed into
the community of Christ's disciples to lessen the impact of
social ostracism, yet his ex-communication must have helped

many sincere Jews to make up their minds against their own
rulers whose blindness had been exposed and judged.

Such service which judges the world is not pleasant. The
authorities not only ex-communicated the man, they made it
known publicly   that Jesus was persona-non-grata. Whoever
said that Jesus was Christ would be ex-communicated. It became harder to associate with Jesus. Being seen around him
could lead you into trouble.

The Association for Comprehensive Rural Assistance (ACRA)
is the Community with which I serve the rural poor in
Chhatarpur district of Madhya Pradesh. We have been involved
in service which stirs the social pool, which judges the
blindness of the establishment when you judge the world. The
world retaliates by judging you. In May 82, 30 of us were arrested on four different occasions because we not only served
the victims of a hailstorm, but through our service exposed
the insensitivity of the politicians towards the victims of
this natural calamity. Such service hurts. It makes you
lose friends. They choose not to associate with you, lest
they too get into trouble. Yet one has to decide whether he
wished to walk in the footsteps of his Master and serve the
oppressed or please his friends. Jesus' mercy did not touch
a blind beggar alone. How many blind could he heal anyway?
How many blind can the church heal through its hospitals and
eye camps? How many beggars can we take in our institutions?
We must have compassion for the individual. But we must understand that he is a beggar, not because he is blind, but
because the society in which he lives is blind to his needs.
A blind man can be happy and fulfilled if the society cares
for him.

Our mercy must reach out not merely to open the eyes of
the blind man but also to restore the sight of a blind society. Karl Marx rightly understood that true compassion calls
for dealing with the social context which makes men miserable.
That is a Christian understanding of compassion. Marx, however, defeated his own purpose by trying to build a case for
compassion on atheistic premises. If the individual man is
merely a product of random chance in an impersonal universe,
then there is no meaning in caring for him, especially when
he is too weak and powerless to be of any use to us. But if
man is a created being, then he is special to his Creator.
If he is created as the image bearer of the Creator Himself,
he is even more special. If each individual is to relate to
the Creator on an intimate personal relationship of sonship
and to carry out His will for him in this world, then he is

very very special indeed. That is how Jesus saw this blind beggar. "He is blind, so that God's power might be seen at work in him" (v.3). Because an unknown blind beggar is very very special to God, we must have compassion for him individually. This compassion must be visible in specific acts of mercy. But our compassion for him must go deep enough to create a society which can see that this beggar is a special person for God, who ought not to be allowed to destroy his self-respect by begging and to live a hand-to-mouth insecure existence, until one day he falls sick, becomes too weak to beg and rots by the roadside, to be eaten by beasts and birds.

If a society cannot see that a blind beggar is a special person, then it is blind to truth. And if it does not acknowledge its blindness, then it is hypocritical, self-righteous and sinful. Our compassion for the blind beggar must lead us on to expose and condemn the blindness of our society.

SERVICE:
A SOURCE OF CREATING ALTERNATE POWER FOR SOCIAL CHANGE

It is not enough to stir a society or to judge a blind establishment. If the leadership does not repent, if it does not decide to fulfill its responsibility to its people, then it becomes your responsibility to seek to provide an alternative. Servanthood is the Biblical means of acquiring power to lead. However, if it becomes known that to change the status quo is the purpose of your service, then you are in trouble. The final decision to kill Jesus was made by the Jewish authorities after He raised Lazarus from the dead in John 11.

Jesus loved Lazarus and his sisters Mary and Martha. These sisters sent word to him that Lazarus, his beloved friend, was sick. Jesus could have healed him by a word from wherever he was and saved his sisters from much agony. But no, his healing ministry had purposes other than mere healing. He waited until Lazarus died. He waited until the Jews in Jerusalem heard of his death and had assembled in his village of Bethany to comfort his sisters. Then, in front of a crowd, Jesus displayed his love for the dead man and his sisters. Jesus displayed his sorrow and anger at sickness and death which caused such anguish to his beloved. Jesus displayed his relationship with God his Father, and he displayed his authority and power to give life to the dead.

This display of love, sorrow, anger and power was not hypocritical, but a means of exhibiting who he really was, so that people could make an intelligent choice for or against him. Jesus's prayer in Vs. 41-42 makes it abundantly clear that even though Jesus could have healed Lazarus or raised him from the dead without exhibiting who he was, he felt it neces- sary at that point, to enable the world to see his heart, his being, and his power.

The miracle had the intended effect; many people believed in Jesus. Their choice of Jesus was an automatic rejection of the establishment (John 12:10). Jesus had provided an alternative to Israel, and people began to accept it. The Jewish establishment was in alliance with the exploitative Roman regime (John 19:15). It existed because it not only al- lowed but enabled Rome to continue its exploitation of the people. The chief priests knew that if Jesus was allowed to extend his influence over the people, a new centre of mass power would be created which would be in the interest of the common man. Rome obviously could not tolerate a leadership which defended the interests of the people. Therefore it would be inevitable that "the Roman authorities will take ac- tion and destroy our temple and our nation!" (John 11:48) Therefore if the nation is to be saved, Jesus has to be eliminated (John 11:49-50).

The healing ministry of Jesus was intended not merely to heal but to build up a mass following just as his preaching aimed not merely at educating but at drawing out a whole- hearted dedication to follow him. The following which Jesus thus built up made him an alternative centre of social power. It was a threat to the status quo not only naturally but also intentionally, because it was the very antithesis of all that the establishment stood for. *First* of all it was a moral force in contrast to the immoral Jewish establishment. Jesus had not only healed men but called them to "sin no more" (John 5:14).

Secondly, it was a social power that stood for the smallest of men in contrast to the establishment which protected the powerful exploiters (Mark 11:15-18). Jesus called his follow- ers to serve "one of these least important ones" (Matt.25: 31-46).

Thirdly, it was a courageous power that was determined to stand for the protection of the "harassed and helpless" sheep to the point of laying down its own life (John 10:1-21) in contrast to the Jewish establishment which was concerned pri- marily for its own safety and well-being in the face of the Roman threat (John 11:45-48).

Jesus built up his following, his church, intentionally as a power structure to withstand the mighty forces of destruction and death. He said to Peter, "You are Peter and on this rock I will build my church, and the gates of Hades will not overcome it" (Matt. 16:18). The destructive forces of death will fight against this new society but will not prevail against it. The church was meant to stand against the forces of oppression and death, because it was asked to "Feed my lambs," "Take care of my sheep." In an unjust, oppressive society, when a group stands up for the littlest of lambs, it automatically stands up against the mighty vested interests who grow fat on the flesh of the lambs.

Jesus and his new community were naturally and intentionally a threat to the then establishment. When Jesus set his face to go to Jerusalem and precipitate a face to face confrontation, the establishment had to choose between its own survival and the status quo on the one hand and a titanic socio-political change and transfer of power to another group on the other hand.

Even though it is true that the Sunday School Jesus confines himself to changing of men's hearts, the Jesus of the gospels aimed both at changing human hearts as well as human society. He prepared shepherds to replace wolves from the leadership of Israel. He verbalized his intentions explicitly a number of times; for example in the parable of Tenants in the Vineyard (Matt. 21:33-46), he concludes this parable by saying to the chief priests, "And so I tell you that the kingdom of God will be taken away from you and given to a people who will produce the proper fruits" (vs.43). Here was as explicit a statement of call for revolution, of social transformation as you can get anywhere. The Jews understood it and tried to arrest him on the spot "but they were afraid of the crowds, who considered Jesus to be a prophet" (vs.46). Jesus announced his intention of a social revolution to the establishment itself after he had carefully build up his own mass support.

Power was not an accidental by-product of service. It never is. The Church has no real competitor in the field of service in India today. But it continues to be powerless. This is because our service is very different from Christ's. He consciously cultivated a mass following.

Jesus was a man of the masses, and he built up his massive following by his service. Look at his strategy following the raising of Lazarus in John 11:53-12:33.

First, he brought a dead man back to life. He allowed the
story of this fantastic miracle to spread to the point that
it started ringing alarm bells in the ears of the establishment (11:45-53). Then he hid in a desert town, Ephraim (54).
The Passover Festival had come near. Jews poured into Jerusalem and gossiped about him (11:55-57). After he had become
the hot topic of debate, he came back to Bethany, to Lazarus'
home. The word spread in Jerusalem, crowds flocked not only
to see him but also Lazarus (12:1-11). Then when a large
enough crowd had gathered, all excited about Jesus, he asked
for a colt, allowed his disciples to organise a procession,
and march into Jerusalem, sloganeering, proclaiming him to be
the King of Israel. The whole city was stirred up, until the
authorities sat up and said to each other, "You see, we are
not succeeding at all; the whole world is following him"
(John 12:19).

The result of this strategy was of course that the Jews
decided to kill both Jesus and Lazarus (John 12:9-11). Did
the strategy backfire? No. That this would be the consequence of what he was doing was known to Christ. But he had
no choice. The establishment had refused to repent. It had
refused to believe the truth. It had decided to continue in
its evil ways. So either Jesus had to give up his call for
repentance and change, or he had to precipitate a confrontation, to give a last opportunity to the establishment, either
to repent or to kill him. Jesus was prepared to pay the price
of such a confrontation.

Jesus did not heal the blind man or raise Lazarus from the
dead merely to make them live comfortably. He was paying the
price for the world,and his followers had to pay the same
price too. But paying this price was his glory. Yes, Jesus
accepted his death as a criminal as his glory.

The purpose of cultivating a mass following was not to gain
a selfish crown. Satan had offered the kingship to Jesus at
the very beginning of his ministry (Matt. 4:8-10). But he refused to have the kingdom for himself. He wanted the kingdom
for the poor (Matt. 5:3, cf. Luke 6:20), the sorrowful (Matt.
5:4), the meek (5:5). The poorer masses saw him as their Messiah and began to follow him; that naturally threatened the
status quo. When the Greeks came looking for Jesus, he immediately perceived what the Jewish authorities had perceived.
"The whole world is following him; therefore he has to be
eliminated." That was his real glory--crucifixion.

His service gave Jesus a mass following, which gave him power, which threatened the establishment, which meant death, which was the final proof whether Jesus was really serving others or only himself. An all out love for God and for one's neighbour has to be tested. The proof of the pudding is in the eating. Jesus was prepared to be tested by fire.

When some people are so committed to change the social status quo in favour of the poor and the oppressed that they will lay down their lives for the cause, they are bound to create ripples in history that never cease.

There is no better way of concluding this Bible study on service than by quoting what Jesus said at the conclusion of the episode which began with the healing of Lazarus.

"The hour has come for the Son of man to receive great glory. I am telling you the truth: a grain of wheat remains no more than a single grain unless it is dropped into the ground and dies. If it dies, then it produces many grains. Whoever loves his own life will lose it. Whoever hates his own life in this world will keep it for life eternal. Whoever wants to serve me must follow me, so that my servant must be with me where I am. And my Father will honor anyone who serves me."

Through his service Jesus deliberately became a champion of the masses. But that is not to say that he went after cheap popularity with the masses. He demanded costly discipleship, not cheap "fannism." Only if we can create disciples who are prepared to care for the sheep at the cost of their own lives can we hope to stand up against the gates of Hades.

Our service today lacks power because it is often marked by self love, or it is produced by a compassion which does not understand the social roots of human misery and gives no answer to them. When we choose to live for others in a way that we are willing to lay down our lives for them, we will produce fruit for God, because we will have power. This will bring honor to us but through the cross.

A Story from Indian Church History.

Indian society has gone through enormous change and improvement during the last 200 years. Many are forgetting that this process of social change was initiated by Christian missionaries who understood that Christian compassion called for a crusade against those social institutions and practices which oppressed and dehumanized man.

The battles against sati, caste, child-marriage, female infanticide, bonded agricultural labour, drunkenness and opium, etc., were generally initiated and led by the missionaries. The Hindu reformers took up the battle following the missionaries. I would like us to focus our attention on the story of a missionary crusade against the exploitation of forced labourers by indigo planters in Bengal.

Indigo is a plant out of which dye is made. After indigo plantations ceased to be very profitable in West Indies and America, many European planters came to Bengal and joined the Indian zamindars in indigo plantations. They leased or bought large estates which were rented out to Indian peasants (ryots) for cultivation. Peasants were given initial loans which landed them and their children in virtual slavery. According to the terms of loan and cultivation rights, they had to grow a fixed quantity of indigo for landlords' factories, whether or not they could grow any food for themselves. For decades, when the cost of other agricultural produce doubled or tripled, the price of indigo was kept fixed. The result was that production cost was often higher than the selling price. This kept the ryots on the point of perpetual starvation. If anyone protested, he was kidnapped, locked in a factory and beaten up by the musclemen of the landlords. The police and judiciary were bought by bribes. If there were honest officers and magistrates, they could do little, because no peasant would dare to witness against a landlord or his muscleman. It was a reign of terror.

These cruel landlords were a great help to the missionaries whenever they went on their preaching excursions amongst the peasants. But when the missionaries heard their tale of woes, they realized that these men with empty bellies could not possibly pay attention to the gospel. Even if they could hear it, they couldn't accept it if the missionaries were patronized by their oppressors.

Rev. F. Schurr, a C.M.S. missionary, was amongst those who were deeply grieved by the cruelties of the indigo planters. Like Moses of old, he chose to reject the patronage of the planters in order to participate in the sufferings of the peasants. He exposed the cruelties of the indigo plantation system by reading a paper, *"On the Influence of the System of Indigo Planting on the Spread of Christianity,"* in September 1855 at the conference of Bengal missionaries held in Calcutta.

This sparked off a great controversy. Some missionaries initially opposed the idea of getting involved, but gradually

as the facts became better known most joined the battle. A
powerful appeal was made to the Government to appoint a Commission of Inquiry and change the system of forced labor.
The planters predictably fought back, blaming the missionaries
of leaving religious matters and meddling in political and
secular affairs and creating class conflict. The Government
sided with the planters and turned down the appeal for a commission of inquiry without even giving a reason.

The missionaries were infuriated and moved the matter in
the British Parliament and aroused public opinion in Britain
and in Bengal. One of the means was arts and dramas. Rev.
James Long, another C.M.S. missionary, translated, published
and distributed a Bengali drama *Mirror of Indigo*, which was a
satire on the indigo system, portraying the effects of the
system on a labourer's family. A criminal case for libel was
started against him for this, and he was finally imprisoned
for serving the oppressed.

Here was a service that stirred up a society, exposed and
condemned the cruelty of a blind establishment and brought
power and honor to Christian servants. An Australian historian, G.A.Oddie, wrote thus about the results of Long's imprisonment:

"Long's apparent willingness to suffer for the sake of
others and in the cause of peace with justice for the ryots
of lower Bengal, his lack of bitterness and self-regard and
his cheerful acceptance of what he believed was an inescapable duty made a profound impression. Indeed, his attitude
and stand on the indigo issue probably did more to commend
his faith than any amount of preaching could ever have accomplished and, at least for the time being, affected Hindu
and other non-Christian perceptions of Christianity. It
reinforced the impression created by the missionaries'
earlier participation in the indigo controversy that they
totally rejected the racial arrogance of fellow Europeans
and were not 'partakers of other men's sins.' 'The Rev. J.
Long,' wrote the editor of the Indian Mirror, 'has acted
manfully and precisely in the manner a *true* Christian missionary should have done when placed under the same circumstances.' Dr. Kay of the S.P.G. who visited Long in prison
remarked on the tone of vernacular newspapers and quoted
one as saying that, 'If this be Christianity, then we wish
Christianity would spread all over the country.' Duff,
Wylie, Stuart and others believed that Long's imprisonment
was creating 'a very favourable impression for Christian

missions,' and catechists informed Long that as a result
of his imprisonment 'people have listened...more willingly
to their preaching.'"

*(From Ch. 6, The Trial and Imprisonment of Rev. James
Long, P.192, G.A.Oddie - *Social Protest in India:* British
Protestant Missionaries and Social Reforms 1850 - 1900,
Manohar Publications, New Delhi, 1979)

MERCY AND SOCIAL TRANSFORMATION

Purpose. The purpose of this paper is to analyze Christian ministries of mercy in relationship to the task of social transformation.

Introduction. Mercy is the disposition to forgive or show kindness when severity is merited or expected. Mercy implies compassion so great as to give help and comfort even to the lowliest...Understood in this way, mercy is primarily an act of God.

Ministries of Mercy in the Early Christian Church. The earliest Christians were challenged to perform deeds of mercy as opportunities arose. The ministries of mercy were seen not primarily an individual obligation but a corporate responsibility, flowing out of communities in which resources were sold to minister to those in need. In the first two centuries, it can hardly be maintained that the Christians toiled to restructure the Empire. As a small minority their concern was to shape a new community, motivated by compassion and characterized by communal justice.

Ministries of Mercy in the Middle Ages. Among the barbaric tribes in Europe during the Middle Ages (roughly A.D. 500-1500) charitable institutions were introduced by missionaries who established convents. These were expected to exercise hospitality to strangers and give help to the poor. Little thought appears to be given to remodelling the conditions which gave rise to poverty and illness.

Ministries of Mercy After the Reformation. After the Reformation there appeared to be a decline in giving to charity. In due course Protestants developed their own agencies for the care of the destitute. The efforts to not only provide relief but to actually reform social structures reached its zenith in the Nineteenth Century.

Ministries of Mercy Today. With twenty centuries of traditions behind us, it is not surprising that conscious compassion is expressed today in a multitude of forms. Christians are reaching out individually, through local churches, denominations and para-church organizations. Let me offer some tentative conclusions. Ministries of mercy:

(1) are both an individual and corporate expression of
     the Spirit of Christ;
(2) have validity whether or not they aim at social
     transformation;
(3) can lead to radical social transformation;
(4) can, when wrongly motivated, sabotage the Kingdom;
(5) whether nationally or foreign based, are easily co-
     opted by ungodly principalities and powers;
(6) ought to be the natural expression of the Body of
     Christ in its congregational incarnations and as
     such, accountable to it.
(7) To accomplish the above ministries of mercy should
     devote a significant portion of their time, energy,
     and money to dialogue with the churches in order to
     achieve a higher level of church/parachurch inter-
     dependence.

WALDRON SCOTT is President of the American Leprosy Mission
in Bloomfield, New Jersey.

MERCY AND SOCIAL TRANSFORMATION

Waldron Scott

INTRODUCTION

Mercy is one of the great words of the Bible, extraordinarily rich in its implications. Twice our Lord challenged his critics to "go and learn what this means, 'I desire mercy and not sacrifice'" (Matthew 9:13; 12:7; cf. Hosea 6:6). Without doubt, to "learn mercy" is to intuit the very nature of God and to grasp the essence of the Gospel.

What then is mercy? It is kindness, or compassion, or pity extended by one person to another who is in his or her power, but who has no claim on that kindness, and from whom no requital can be expected. Mercy is the disposition to forgive or to show kindness when severity is merited or expected. Mercy implies compassion so great as to give help and comfort even to the lowliest or most undeserving, to enable one to forebear even when justice demands punishment. Or as James, the brother of our Lord, noted, 'mercy triumphs over justice" (James 2:13).

Understood this way, mercy is primarily an attribute of God. ("But God, who is rich in mercy..." (Ephesians 2:4). Because God is full of mercy, Jesus commands us to be merciful also (Luke 6:36). And as R.E.C.Browne points out, to be merciful is to lead a particular style of life which makes both extending mercy and receiving mercy possible.1 "Blessed are the merciful, for they shall obtain mercy" (Matthew 5:7).

We can trace the semantic core of mercy back to the Hebrew word *hesed*, which appears 250 times in the Old Testament. *Hesed* denotes God's faithfulness to His own gracious relationship with Israel despite Israel's unworthiness and defection. *Hesed* is variously translated into English as kindness, lovingkindness, steadfast love, goodness. Its range of meaning includes the concept of solidarity.[2] The Septuagint translates *hesed* into Greek as *eleos*. *Eleos* is then carried into our English New Testament where it is translated as mercy.

Another frequently used word in the Old Testament, *raham,* and its plural, conveys the idea of motherly or brotherly feelings. It is usually translated into Greek as *splangchnon* and into English as mercy, or tender mercies. The feelings referred to here point to the origin of God's gracious disposition to human beings. Karl Barth says in this connection, "The primal, basic decision of God with regard to man is His mercy, the engagement of His heart."[3] The English word that comes closest to conveying *raham* today is compassion. So in the New Testament *splangchnon's* verbal form (*splangchnidzomai*) is translated: "I have compassion on them" (Matthew 15:32).

The Old Testament meanings of *hesed* and *hen* (kindness, favor) are combined in the New Testament in the word *charis*, i.e., grace. Now grace has to do with guilt (e.g., "but where sin increased, grace abounded," Romans 5:20) whereas mercy has to do with misery. The modern notion of mercy-- compassion extended to someone in need or helpless distress, or to someone in debt without a claim to favorable treatment-- is variously rendered in the New Testament by the Greek words *eleos, splangchnon* and (rarely) *oiktirmos*.

Pity is a sister to mercy and compassion. Pity is that emotion that inclines one to spare or to succour. It has a noble history, but in modern times tends to suggest a measure of contempt for its object, on account of some supposed intellectual or moral inferiority.

Compassion, on the other hand, does not seem to harbor negative connotations. Compassion has to do with suffering together, with participation in suffering. Compassion is that feeling or emotion experienced when one is *moved* by the suffering or distress of another ("He had compassion on them, because they were harassed and helpless," Matthew 9:36) and more importantly, *by the desire to relieve it*. "And he had compassion on them, and healed their sick" (Matthew 14:14). It is a sign of weakness when compassion is merely sentimental or ostentatious.

Contrasting words for compassion are indifference, aloofness, unconcern. Contrasting words for mercy are vengeance, indifference, retribution, punishment.

With all this in mind, it would appear that when we speak of mercy and social transformation we are referring primarily to *acts* of mercy and compassion toward suffering fellow creatures who are not immediately positioned to return the favor. This, of course, is precisely what the Apostle Paul refers to in Romans 12:8, "he who gives aid, with zeal; he who does *acts of mercy,* with cheerfulness."

Such acts of mercy, especially when offered in the face of contrary social mores, are valid proof of neighbor-love, as the story of the Good Samaritan makes clear. Jesus concluded that story by asking, "Which of these three, do you think, proved neighbor to the man who fell among the robbers?" To which the lawyer replied, "The one who showed mercy on him." And Jesus replied, "Go and do likewise" (Luke 10:36-37).

When acts of mercy are rendered with some degree of organized, systematic intent, and especially when they are rendered as some sort of corporate endeavor, they are better described as *ministries* of mercy. Thus this paper might be entitled more accurately: "Ministries of Mercy and Social Transformation," or better yet, *The Contribution of Ministries of Mercy Toward Social Transformation.*

One more introductory word about our subject matter. Societies are formed as people live together in more or less organized communities. Societies are a natural, ordinary condition of human life, but they are organized in a variety of ways. Each social constitution, therefore, presents special problems dramatized by the fact that certain individuals and groupings within a given society are affected adversely. At best they may be merely disadvantaged; at worst they live in misery. This misery is caused in large measure by the unjust structure of the society.

Social transformation, consequently, works to change the form or character or condition of society, altering both its nature and function. Radical social transformation will result in a more or less complete change in the character and condition of a society. It would appear, therefore, that the following questions should be the main subjects of our inquiry:

* To what extent over the past 2000 years have Christian ministries of mercy induced social transformation radical or otherwise?

* Should Christian ministries of mercy aim directly at social transformation? Or do they indirectly, yet inevitably, transform social values and structures?

* What is the relationship in our day between modern ministries of mercy and the often desperate struggle for social justice throughout the world?

* Should the churches delegate their ministries of mercy to parachurch agencies? Or to secular governments?

What role do indigenous ministries of mercy have to play in social transformation?

I. MINISTRIES OF MERCY IN EARLY CHRISTIAN HISTORY

The earliest Christians were challenged as individuals to perform deeds of mercy as opportunities arose. "If a brother or sister is ill-clad and in lack of daily food, and one of you says to them, 'Go in peace, be warmed and filled' without giving them the things needed for the body, what does it profit?" (James 2:15-16) Again, "But if any one has the world's goods and sees his brother in need, yet closes his heart against him, how does God's love abide in him?" (I John 3:17)

Peter, who had no silver or gold on his person, gave a crippled beggar what he did have: the gift of health (Acts 3:6). Tabitha (Dorcas) is cited as an early disciple "full of good works and acts of charity" (Acts 9:36). Paul, in an illuminative situation, was deeply moved[4] at the sight of an exploited slave girl and healed her (Acts 16:16-18). This act of compassion on Paul's part brought him into direct confrontation with the girls's owners who dragged him before local authorities who proceeded, in turn, to beat him and throw him into prison.

Summing up his own ministry, Paul argued that he had labored partly in order to be in a position to help others. "I coveted no one's silver or gold or apparel. You yourselves know that these hands ministered to my necessities, and to those who are with me. In all things I have shown you that by so toiling one must help the weak, remembering the words of the Lord Jesus, how he said 'It is more blessed to give than to receive '" (Acts 20:33-35). Paul challenged new converts

to follow his example. "Let the thief no longer steal, but
rather let him labor doing honest work with his hands, so
that he may be able to give to those in need" (Ephesians
4:28).

Generally speaking, however, the New Testament sees the
ministry of mercy not only as an individual obligation, but
as a corporate endeavor of the church, to be carried out first
of all within the church itself. "So then, as we have opportunity, let us do good to all men, and especially to those who
are of the household of faith" (Galations 6:10). Thus members
of the first Christian congregation "sold their possessions
and goods and distributed them to all, as any had need"
(Acts 2:45).

Again, when it became apparent that widows were being over-
looked in the daily distribution of food and other necessities,
the church at Jerusalem acted to relieve their need and to ensure that a repetition would not occur (Acts 6:1-6). In due
course the care of certified widows was institutionalized by
the early church (I Timothy 5:3-16).

When Agabus predicted the widespread famine that in fact
occurred during the reign of Claudius, the church at Antioch
acted immediately. "And the disciples determined, every one
according to his ability, to send relief to the brethren who
lived in Judea" (Acts 11:29). As time went on, and the
faith spread, this spontaneous response evolved into something
more systematic (1 Corinthians 16:1-4). An important part of
this more systematic approach was instruction. "And let our
people learn to apply themselves to good deeds, so as to help
cases of urgent need, and not to be unfruitful" (Titus 3:14).

This same concern for the well-being of others in need is
elaborated in the letters of Clement, Bishop of Rome around
AD 95, and in the *Didache ton Dodeka Apostolon* (The Teachings
of the Twelve Apostles) which was composed sometime between
AD 70 and 200 and reflects the life of the church in the second century.

As the church spread through the Roman Empire its ministries
of mercy underwent considerable development. In Rome and
Alexandria social relief became a monopoly of the church. It
took the form of distributions to the poor, and the establishment and upkeep of hospitals, orphanages and homes for the aged
By the fourth century the church was also bringing relief to
people whom inflation had plunged into distress.

Post-Constantinian churches spent great sums (for their endowments were growing enormously) on the work of ransoming captives. St. Ambrose proposed selling the precious vessels on the altars of his church in Milan to ransom captives. He declared, "There is one incentive which must impel us all to charity; it is pity for the misery of our neighbors and the desire to alleviate it, with all the means that lie in our power, and more besides."[5]

Julian the Apostate, pagan emperor at Constantinople during the fourth century, witnessed the impact of the church's ministries of mercy and was deeply challenged. "Can we not see," he asked, "That what has contributed most to the development of atheism (Christianity to him was atheism) is its humanity towards strangers, its thoughtfulness towards everyone, even its care of the dead? These are works to which we should apply ourselves quite openly. It would be shameful if the impious Galileans, in addition to succouring their own beggars, were to feed ours too, if we stood by and watched our poor lacking the aid which we owe them."

The Apostle Paul believed the Gospel was given to the Gentiles in part to provoke the Jews to a kind of spiritual jealousy (Romans 11:11-14). In like manner we see reflected in Julian's complaint the way in which Christian ministries of mercy gradually evoked a new set of values within the Greco-Roman world and eventually, a thoroughgoing social transformation.[6]

In spite of what we have just noted, however, it can hardly be maintained that the early Christians deliberately attempted to restructure the Empire. Instead, during the first two centuries when Christians constituted a small minority, their concern was to shape a new community motivated by compassion and characterized by communal justice. This community was set apart from the world about it and ultimately became a viable alternative to the prevailing social order. Even when Christians attacked certain immoral features of the prevailing order, they believed that they were conserving, not destroying, the Empire and its civilization.

Still later, when Christians had become a majority of the population of the Empire, one might have thought that the church would undertake the systematic restructuring of society. But the emergency of monasticism precluded this. Nevertheless, a social transformation most certainly occurred over a period of five centuries, and in this transformation corporate Christian ministries of mercy, wittingly or unwittingly, played a decisive role.

II. MINISTRIES OF MERCY DURING THE MIDDLE AGES

Among the barbaric tribes in Europe during the Middle Ages (roughly AD 500-1500) charitable institutions were introduced by missionaries who established convents. These were expected to exercise hospitality to strangers and give help to the poor. Irish missionaries, for example, cared for the bodies as well as for the souls of the heathen to whom they preached the Gospel.

A synod at Aix in 815 AD ordered that an infirmary should be built near each church and in every convent. A few years earlier the Capitularies of Charlemagne had privileged charitable institutions in order that strangers, pilgrims and paupers be taken care of. The Knights of St. Lazarus were entrusted by Louis IX with the care of leprosy sufferers. Houses for those burdened with leprosy were established in England by King Stephen and others.

In the midst of all this institutional expression of Christian compassion, certain individuals stand out. St. Francis of Assisi kissed the hands of leprosy victims, and Queen Mathilda washed their feet, believing that, in so doing, she was washing the feet of Christ. This kind of intimate contact, then as now in some parts of the world, communicated God's care and compassion to a people cruelly stigmatized by society.

At the time of the Byzantine-Persian wars of the early years of the seventh century, the Catholic Patriarch of Alexandria was John the Almsgiver. A devout layman whose wife and children had died, he lived austerely in his high ecclesiastical position, devoting the revenues of his see chiefly to the poor and to refugees from the Persian conquest of Palestine. It can be said generally that throughout the Eastern part of the church during this period monasteries were associated with philanthropic enterprises and had hospices for the aged and the poor and hospitals for the care of the sick.

Toward the end of the Middle Ages, during the turbulent fourteenth century, lived Catherine of Siena, whom Latourette describes as a "practical mystic." She gave herself to the service of the poor and the sick, including a year when an epidemic of the Black Death swept across Italy. She also served prisoners and saw a notable conversion of one who was condemned to death. But she also concerned herself with politics. She endeavored to heal chronic feuds among prominent families in Siena. She urged Pope Gregory XI, then engaged in war, to make peace, even if it cost him his worldly goods. She spent much of her brief life in prayer. Yet her life was also one of intense activity in ministries of mercy and in the stormy and intricate complexities of Italian and Papal politics. She had a profound influence upon her generation.

During the fifteenth century Girolamo Savonarola became the most famous man of his time and the most influential personage in the city-state of Florence. He preached judgment and pled with the citizens of Florence to accept Christ as their king. He exhorted his hearers to give to the poor everything beyond their barest needs. Florence was transformed. According to Latourette, bankers and tradesmen restored ill-gotten gains, and alms to the poor increased. But when Savanarola began to speak against the Pope the tide turned against him. Ultimately he was arrested, condemned, hung, and his body burned.

Monasticism and the Papacy were the two decisive institutions of the Middle Ages in the West. Often, as when a leading monk became Pope, the two combined. Gregory the Great (AD 590-604) was one such person. As Pope he continued the austere simplicity of monastic life. At the same time he excelled in charity.[7] He fed the hungry from his own frugal table. He interposed continually in favor of injured widows and orphans. He redeemed slaves and captives and sanctioned the sale of consecrated vessels for objects of charity. He made efforts (though in vain) to check the slave-trade.

Gregory the Great represents the best in medieval charity. Yet he was a strong believer in the efficacy of almsgiving to gain merit. The more alms the better, both for one's own salvation and for the relief of departed relatives and friends. This idea, as the historian Schaff notes, ruled supreme in Europe during the Middle Ages. At the height of the Middle Ages many gave and ministered no longer for the sake of helping and serving the poor in Christ, but to obtain for themselves and their loved ones release from Purgatory. To a great extent poverty was therefore not contended with, but actually fostered.

With this judgement Walter Rauschenbusch, the great advocate of the so-called "social gospel," agrees.

"For sheer willingness to give, modern Christianity cannot match its beneficence with ascetic Christianity.[8] But this giving was not essentially a social conflict with the

moral evils of pauperism, but a religious conflict with
the moral evil of the love of property. The aim was not
primarily to lift the poor recipient to social health, but
to discipline the soul of the giver... The desire to discipline the soul and the desire to win merit united in making men give large amounts to charity, but they also vitiated the social effectiveness of the giving... The poor,
through whom this virtue was acquired, were 'the treasure
of the Church,' part of its equipment, a kind of gymnastic
apparatus on which the givers increased their moral mus-
cle."[9]

In contrast to this negative judgement, others assert that
during the Middle Ages the church effected a complete revolution in morals by regarding the poor as the special representatives of Jesus Christ, thus making the love of Christ, rather
than the love of man, the principle of charity. Some would
say that for the first time in the history of mankind thousands of men and women, at the sacrifice of all worldly interests, and often under circumstances of extreme discomfort
or danger, were inspired to devote their entire lives to the
single object of assuaging the sufferings of humanity, covering Europe with countless institutions of mercy, unknown to
the Pagan world.[10]

Surveying this medieval period Latourette concludes that
"little thought appears to be given to remedying the conditions which gave rise to poverty and illness. The majority
accepted as inevitable a social and economic order in which
poor existed, and attempts at public hygiene were usually rudi-
mentary or entirely absent."[11]

III. MINISTRIES OF MERCY AFTER THE REFORMATION

The German historian Uhlhorn notes that the first effect
of the Protestant Reformation on charity was a decline in giving! In large measure this was a reaction against the unbiblical motives for almsgiving that had come to dominate the late
Middle Ages. Moreover, as Latourette perceptively observes,
Protestantism, by its rejection of monasticism, deprived itself of the organizations through which ministries of mercy
had long expressed themselves.

In due course, however, Protestantism developed its own
agencies for the care of the destitute. The Pietist movement
created the famous orphanage at Halle, for example. While
Pietists, and Lutherans in general, concentrated on measures

of relief, Calvinists tended more toward the reformation of
social structures. In Scotland John Knox advocated the idea
that those unable to work should be supported out of public
funds, that all those able to work should be compelled to do
so, that every child should be given an opportunity for education, and that each promising student should have a way open
to the university.

Wesleyans did not set out to effect basic changes in society. However, John Wesley himself worked strenuously to relieve poverty and started missions to prisoners. It was one
of his warm friends, John Howard, who became an outstanding
pioneer in prison reform.[12] Wesley also was a pioneer in the
anti-slavery movement. Wesley persistently contended against
such evils as bribery and corruption in politics, smuggling,
and the plundering of wrecked ships. Wesley's followers
worked against the exploitation of one group for the benefit
of another. Quakers, meanwhile, pioneered in the advocacy of
equality of women with men, the abolition of slavery, and the
humane treatment of the insane and the criminal.

Latourette cites the work of John Oberlin (1740-1826) as
one of the more striking examples of the transforming effect
of Christianity in a particular community. As the pastor of
a poverty-stricken parish in France, Oberlin led out in building roads, founded what are said to have been the first "infant schools," pioneered the application of scientific agriculture, introduced seeds for his people from other parts of
Europe, shepherded his parish through the trying years of the
French Revolution and, in a region of intolerance, shielded
Jews from persecution.[13]

This impulse, which led Christians to respond to the plight
of sufferers first with direct measures of relief, then with
efforts to reform social structures, reached its zenith in
the nineteenth century. It is simply not possible, in the
short confines of this paper, to list, much less describe,
the multitudinous ministries of mercy that evolved into programs of social reform. From the Inner Mission in Germany
came schools for infants and cripples, rescue homes, clubs for
apprentices, and campaigns against beggary, drunkenness, and
prostitution. Kaiserswerth, an obscure village on the Rhine
that became a major training center for philanthropy, provided
the vision and example, as well as the training, for Florence
Nightingale. Out of her memorable service in the Crimean War
came schools which created the modern nursing profession. In
England the evangelical Earl of Shaftesbury was the prime mo-
ver in legislation that improved the treatment of the insane,

brought better conditions for laborers in mills and factories, barred boys under 13 and women from the mines, protected chimney sweeps, and improved housing conditions, meanwhile promoting a variety of missionary endeavors overseas.

A famous evangelical, William Wilberforce, led the successful campaign to abolish slavery throughout the Britisn Empire. In the United States revivals led by Charles Finney fed antislavery impulses which strengthened the movement for emancipation. Jonathan Blanchard, founding president of Wheaton College, was a renowned abolitionist. Another evangelical abolitionist, A. J. Gordon, founder of what developed into Gordon College and Gordon-Conwell Theological Seminary, advocated the "complete enfranchisement" of women "and their entrance into every political and social privilege enjoyed by men."[14] After the Civil War, out of a warmly pietistic background, came Walter Rauschenbusch. He was pastor to a working-class German Baptist congregation on the border of Hell's Kitchen in New York City. His pietistic inheritance broke down under the intolerable situations and questions put to him by his parishioners, many of them unemployed, without clothes, shoes, or hope. Rauschenbusch became the prophet of the emerging "social gospel," claiming that "if Jesus stood today amid our modern life, with that outlook on the condition of all humanity which observation and travel and the press would spread before him, and with the same heart of divine humanity beating in him, he would create a new apostolate to meet the new needs in a new harvestime of history."[15]

The nineteenth century, of course, was the great century of missionary advance. And it was in the mission fields that Christians, time and time again, were led from isolated acts of mercy into dramatic programs for social reform, often in confrontation with imperial authorities in their homelands as well as local authorities in the colonies.[16] Vishal Mangalwadi notes that the battles against *sati* (immolation of widows), caste, child-marriage, female infanticide, bonded agricultural labor, drunkenness, opium, etc., were generally initiated and led by missionaries "who understood that Christian compassion called for a crusade against those social institutions and practices which oppressed and dehumanized man."[17]

He refers only to missionary effort in India. In other parts of Asia, as well as in Africa and Latin America, similar crusades were carried out in the name of Christ on behalf of suffering peoples.

IV. MINISTRIES OF MERCY TODAY

With 20 centuries of tradition behind us it is not surprising that Christian compassion is expressed today in a multitude of forms. Countless individual acts of kindness are effected daily, making life more tolerable for tens of thousands. Local congregations also reach out quietly, unobtrusively in Christ's name to the sick, the homeless,the forlorn. Denominationally founded and funded institutions do their share as well.

But it is the parachurch agency, especially the newer relief and development agencies, that dominate the 20th Century scene, exemplifying all the strengths and weaknesses of modern Christian charity. Catholic Relief Agency, Church World Service, Compassion International, Mennonite Central Committee, Tear Fund, World Concern, World Vision, and many others of European and North American origins spearhead our ministries of mercy today.

Relief is big business--startlingly so. In 1979 five of the larger North American relief agencies reported a combined income approaching 125 million dollars[18] and the 1983 figure may well be 200 million, perhaps more. Such bigness represents power, often intimidating in its impact, and raises serious questions with which we must grapple. The director of EFICOR (Evangelical Fellowship of India Committee on Relief) tells this story:

"After the worst cyclone this century on India's east coast, EFICOR provided immediate relief to some villages. The state allocated us a number of villages, including one where only one house remained standing. We realized that more was needed than food and clothes. We discussed with the villagers what they needed. They wanted houses. In dialogue with us they also saw the need for employment opportunities so that they could break out of bonded labour and so that the women could supplement their income. The people suggested trades that were appropriate for the area.

"The large expenses involved meant we had to approach and consult foreign donors. They sent across representatives with experience in relief and rehabilitation in the Caribbean and the Americas. The government advised us to provide cement concrete roofs for the new houses that would be constructed, and offering matching grants if those roofs were provided...however, the foreign representatives insisted that we should provide the villagers with the sorts of houses that they had lived in before, made from wood, bamboo and palm leaves, but strengthened against future storms. We urged that the government's recommendations should be heeded. But to no avail. In the ensuing time taken over debate, the delay caused uncertainty among the villagers. In the end they sent our volunteers away as they felt that they were wasting their time...

"In another 45 villages we followed the experts' advice and provided materials and skills for building traditional houses. Inevitably we lost heart somewhat as we had this policy forced on us. Had we not followed it we would have received no money at all. We had expected that our visitors would respect the views of their hosts who worked in relief and development in their own country for a little time. After one year an assessor from the same agency who forced this policy on us came to review the programme. He discovered what we had feared. White ants and termites had eaten through the main supports of these traditional houses, and they were now useless. The funding program of a quarter million pounds immediately halted. But the villagers were obviously left with the need to repair those houses each year, a process which costs about one month's salary each year. Unfortunately this mistake cannot be corrected, as to rebuild the village from scratch as we had the opportunity to do would require another cyclone."[19]

Bigness can be a blessing. The good work being done today by parachurch agencies specializing in relief, development and health activities, is too well publicized to require documentation in this paper. But there is a darker side to our ministries of mercy. As EFOCOR's experience so clearly demonstrates, large-scale relief capability frequently promotes the *misuse of power* which is, after all, the ability to affect social life, to make things happen.

Three types of power are commonly exercised, derived from finances, expertise, and organization.[20] Parachurch agencies often are in a position to wield all three unilaterally, sometimes insensitively. Indian mission executive Theodore Williams reminds us that "It is not the fulfillment of programmes but the fulfilling of human relationships that matter. If we ride roughshod over the feelings of people and have no time for individuals, under the guise of carrying out projects and programmes for God, our mission has no credibility."[21] It was prophesied of Christ that "He will not break a bruised

reed or quench a smouldering wick." (Matthew 12:20) This
same Jesus instructed his own disciples, "You know that those
who are supposed to rule over the Gentiles lord it over them,
and their great men exercise authority over them. But it
shall not be so among you..." (Mark 10:42-43)

Alongside this impulse to ride roughshod over those to whom
we minister is an equally devastating *tendency to co-opt the
best leadership* of the national churches in order to achieve
parachurch agency objectives. The attraction of higher salaries, coupled with broader opportunities for exercising leadership abilities, can be irresistible to a younger national pastor or layperson. At the same time it demoralizes the indigenous churches that must succor their communities long after
the relief agency has come and gone. As I have noted elsewhere, this free-wheeling entrepreneurial spirit merely perpetuates the worldly values of our era. It works against the
kingdom while purporting to extend it.[22]

A third area of concern relates to *politics*. Most evangelical ministries of mercy claim to be apolitical. This of course
is an absurdity. We may not be consciously political, but in
fact our relationships with governments--or alternatively, our
identification with oppressed communities with a nation state--
are political stances. *Newsweek* magazine quotes a World Vision
staff member as saying, "We do our best not to offend the government. If we offend the government, we're gone."[23] The
problem is, the world being what it is today, many of these
governments are unabashedly right-wing, that is, committed to
the preservation of an unjust status quo. At the moment this
state of affairs is most evident in Central and South America,
but examples can be cited from Africa and Asia as well.

SUMMATION: A WAY FORWARD

Guatemala provides a provocative case study. Evangelicals
have been preaching the gospel and patiently planting churches
in Guatemala for a century. But it is generally agreed that
the current and most impressive wave of church growth has occurred during the past six or seven years. In the aftermath
of the 1976 earthquake that killed more than 20,000 people
and reduced hundreds of villages to rubble, North American
relief agencies came to the rescue. That they made mistakes
cannot be denied. Yet their overall impact was perceived by
the populace as positive. Tens of thousands embraced the gos-
pel--for evangelical relief agencies were prominent among the
plethora of agencies that had descended upon the country--and
today it is estimated that 22 per cent of the population is
identified with the evangelical movement.

Among these recent converts is General Efrain Rios Montt, Guatemala's president. The general has mounted a powerful and apparently effective counteroffensive against communist-supported insurgents and justified it on Biblical grounds. Evangelical leaders in Guatemala are reported to be support-ing the general with enthusiasm.[24] It is quite clear that Guatemala is in the process of social transformation. Whether that transformation, stimulated in part by evangelical relief agencies, will result in a better quality of life for the country's masses (as over against its middle class) is still very much open to question, however.

International evangelical relief agencies in Guatemala are not aiming directly at social transformation. In contrast, an indigenous ministry in India, the Jamkhed Comprehensive Rural Development Project, has that as its primary thrust, as can be seen in the use of the words "comprehensive" and "development." This project, encompassing about 200 villages of Maharashtra State in India, is spearheaded by two dedicated physicians, Drs. Raja and Maybelle Arole.

The Aroles are motivated by a combination of compassion and justice. Their initial thrust into the area was designed as a ministry of mercy. Their point of entry was the plight of leprosy sufferers, the living dead. Their specialized training qualified them to offer four-dimensional healing--physical, spiritual, social and vocational--to villagers bur-dened with a disease notorious for its devastating impact on individuals and communities. Had they accomplished only this they would have earned the undying gratitude of their patients.

But the Aroles' vision was much greater. They saw leprosy sufferers in the total context of rural life in India today. Consequently they developed leprosy care as an integral facet of a larger primary health care program, in line with the World Health Organization's declared objective of "health for all by the year 2000." But health, of course, is not merely a matter of medicine. The Aroles recognized from the start the relationship between primary health care and the economic realities of Indian village life. Soon they were involved in well-digging, the introduction of new crops and appropriate technology, the establishment of agricultural cooperatives and revolving loan schemes, and numerous other ventures.

Even this was seen in its larger context. The Aroles under-took an intensive long term educational, or conscientizing, effort. Women began to understand the extent to which they were dehumanized by male domination. The men began to compre-hend the measure by which they were being exploited and permanently marginalized by rapacious landlords. Entire villages were taught to insist on their rights in the face of pervasive corruption by petty government bureaucrats.

At a still deeper level, as the message of Jesus was introduced, villagers experienced victory over the fear of spirits that was, in fact the source of their lifelong bondage to disease and sickness. Little by little the Kingdom of God has invaded a portion of Maharashtra State, transforming the quality of life of the poorest of the poor for whom Christ died and rose again. The Aroles avoid the term "anonymous Christians," yet they assert that the Hindu villagers know full well it is Jesus, working through those who minister in his name, who has effected this transformation.

Two questions emerge from the Jankhed experience, however. The first has to do with relations with the national and state governments of India. Jamkhed has become a recognized model of rural development. The Aroles have been honored by the government and now serve on Prime Minister Indira Gandhi's advisory council for health. They speak favorably of the Prime Minister. Taking into consideration the skepticism with which many evangelical leaders, Indian and foreign, regard Mrs. Gandhi and her government with respect to human rights and other values, it is not unreasonable to ask whether the Aroles have been co-opted, and perhaps domesticated, by their government.

The second question that emerges relates to the church. To date the Aroles, devout Christians, have studiously avoided inviting the church--the church of North India specifically-- to be involved in the Jamkhed experiment. They are convinced that church involvement at this stage would spell disaster, since church leaders, in their judgement, lack understanding of the overall process of development. This may be true, but is it right?

We have seen how, during the European Middle Ages, ministries of mercy were divorced from local parishes and made the exclusive activity of the hierarchy. Is there not something fundamentally askew in our own day when ministries of mercy appear to be delegated either to high-powered parachurch agencies or, as in the case of Jamkhed, to independent indigenous organizations?

As a result of this study, superficial and truncated as it may be, I have reached some tentative conclusions which I offer to Wheaton '83 participants for consideration. Let me couch them in the form of theses:

* Ministries of mercy are both an individual and corporate expression of the Spirit of Christ.

* Ministries of mercy motivated by Christian compassion have their own validity whether or not they aim at social transformation, and whether or not individual conversion and/or church growth is an immediate outcome.

* Ministries of mercy, holistically understood in the context of the Biblical demand for justice, can be instruments in God's hand to directly effect radical social transformation, including spiritual conversion in line with Kingdom values.

* Ministries of mercy, wrongly motivated by the lust to exercise power, or inadequately understood in terms of their social implications, have the potential to sabotage the Kingdom of God.

* Ministries of mercy, whether national or foreign based, are easily and unwittingly co-opted by ungodly principalities and powers. This must be guarded against.

* Ministries of mercy, while necessarily functioning as specialized endeavors, ought to be the natural expression of the Body of Christ in its congregational incarnations, and as such accountable to it.

* Ministries of mercy, to accomplish the above, should devote a significant portion of their time, energy and money to dialogue with the churches in order to achieve a higher level of church/parachurch interdependence.

NOTES

1. MacQuarrie, John (editor) *Dictionary of Christian Ethics.* (Philadelphia: Westminster Press, 1967) p. 213.

2. J.D.Douglas (editor) *The Illustrated Bible Dictionary, Vol. 2* (Wheaton: Inter-Varsity Press/Tyndale House Publishers, 1980) p. 982.

3. Karl Barth, *Church Dogmatics, Vol. II,* Book 2 (Edinburgh: T. and T. Clark, 1957) p. 211.

4. This is one of those rare instances where the King James version ("grieved") more accurately expresses the original Greek than the Revised Standard version ("annoyed") does.

5. H. Daniel-Rops, *The Church of Apostles and Martyrs* (New York: E.P.Dutton & Co., 1960) p. 575. For the historical sketches that follow I draw upon Daniel-Rops, Philip Schaff's *History of the Christian Church,* and Kenneth Scott Latourette's *A History of Christianity,* and his *A History of the Expansion of Christianity,* all of whom rely in some measure on G. Uhlhorn's pioneering study, *Die christliche Liebesthaitigkeit* (Stuttgart: 3 vols., 1882-1890).

6. For a more extended discussion of these early ministries of mercy and their impact on the social structures of the Roman Empire see Volume 1 of Latourette's *Expansion,* p. 265ff.

7. From the Latin *caritas,* which originally denoted dearness or costliness, and assumed in the church in the Middle Ages the more significant meaning of benevolence, especially to the poor and suffering. It is the equivalent of our "acts of mercy."

8. His reference here is to the medieval Church.

9. Walter Rauschenbusch, *Christianity and the Social Crisis,* Robert D. Cross, editor (New York: Harper Torchbooks, 1964 pp. 168-169.

10. Cf. W.D.H.Lecky, *History of European Morals,* Vol. II (New York: D. Appleton and Co., 1884) p. 79ff.

11. Latourette, *Expansion*, Vol. 2, p. 366.

12. He lost his life while travelling in Russia, searching for ways to prevent the spread of the plague.

13. Cf. Marshall Dawson, Oberlin, *A Protestant Saint*, (Chicago: Willett, Clark and Co., 1934).

14. Donald W. Dayton, *Discovering an Evangelical Heritage* (New York: Harper & Row, Publishers, 1976) p. 93.

15. Ronald C. White, Jr. and C. Howard Hopkins, *The Social Gospel* (Philadelphia: Temple University Press, 1976) p. 43.

16. Cf. James S. Dennis, *Christian Mission and Social Progress*, 3 vols. (New York: Fleming H. Revell Co., 1897-1906).

17. Vishal Mangalwadi, "Christian Compassion and Social Transfiguration, mimeographed paper prepared for the Wheaton '83 Congress, p.8.

18. Samuel Wilson (editor) *Mission Handbook*, 12th edition (MARC, Monrovia, CA, 1979) P.56.

19. Ronald Sider, editor, *Evangelicals and Development: Towards a Theology of Change* (Exeter: UK, Paternoster Press, 1982) P. 91ff.

20. Cf. Donald B. Kraybill, *The Upside Down Kingdom* (Scottdale, PA, Herald Press, 1978) P. 262, 283ff.

21. Theodore Williams, "The Servant Image," AIM, September 1980, P. 20.

22. Waldron Scott, "The Fullness of Mission" in Gerald H. Anderson, editor, *Witnessing to the Kingdom: Melbourne and Beyond* (Maryknoll, NY: Orbis Books, 1982). p. 53.

23. *Newsweek*, November 29, 1982, p. 26.

24. Wade Coggins, "Guatemala Report," unpublished memo (Washington, D.C.: EFMA, January 3, 1983).

JUSTICE, FREEDOM AND SOCIAL TRANSFORMATION

Purpose. It is my intention in this paper to discuss from a personal perspective some of the mechanisms that perpetuate injustice and inequality in the world. I will also attempt to analyze the role of the church in the process of liberation, in the combat against poverty, and in the struggle for justice.

Introduction. There is a saying in Haiti, "that when God made the world He did a good job, but He forgot one thing-- to distribute wealth evenly."

As never before in human history, humankind today confronts the stark reality of abject poverty amidst plenty, with one-quarter of the world's population in unprecedented affluence, while the rest is condemned to absolute poverty.

Mechanism of Injustice. It is clear now that when we speak of poverty, we are not dealing with conditions of scarcity but rather the more fundamental questions of power, control, and distribution. Certain relationships in society are responsible for the continuing poverty of the poor. These are relationships of ownership, social, racial, economic, cultural and political power. Outlined below are a few of the structures that foster injustice and inequalities:

(1) Capitalism Expansion. Capitalism has used systems of private ownership of land and resources, the control of high technology and expansion across national boundaries to control human beings in ways that are often oppressive and dehumanizing.

(2) Marginalization. Another mechanism of injustice is the growing marginalization of the poor by excluding them from decision-making processes that affect their lives.

(3) Dependency/Paternalism. Often well-intended individuals, governments, and Christian agencies treat the poor as objects of their charity.

(4) Support of Dictatorial Regimes. Dictatorial regimes in Asia, Latin America and Africa tend to institutionalize systems to keep the poor down.

(5) Thought Control. Modern communication systems are increasingly being used to control and oppress the poor.

(6) Brain Drain. The rich countries drain away the most highly trained leaders from poor countries.

(7) Church. It has become common practice for the Church to identify with those who are dominant and provide some of the ideological glue to hold oppressive regimes together.

Biblical Perspectives on Freedom and Justice. Both the Old and New Testaments speak clearly on the need for social justice, freedom, and social transformation. God's intentions for His people are not just religious; they are economic and political. Jesus' deep involvement with the poor started a social revolution.

Practical Implications for the Church. As custodians of the gospel, we must identify with the poor--not the powerful. We must not only defend the poor but enable them to reach their full potential through more justly stewarding the resources within the church international in our efforts to create a just society.

CHAVANNES JEUNE is the Director of Integrated Rural Development, working through the Evangelical Baptist Church in Haiti.

JUSTICE, FREEDOM AND SOCIAL TRANSFORMATION

Chavannes Jeune

INTRODUCTION

There is a saying in Haiti, "When God made the world He did a good job but He forgot one thing--to distribute the wealth evenly."

As never before in human history, humankind today confronts the stark reality of abject poverty amidst plenty, with one quarter of the world's population in unprecedented affluence, while the rest is condemned to absolute poverty.

According to the latest estimates 800 million people in the world are destitute and live in conditions of absolute poverty. Their lives are characterized by malnutrition, disease, illiteracy, unemployment, low income, inadequate shelter and high birth rate. Some 40% of Haiti's 6 million people fall into this category, scratching out a living through subsistence farming.

On the other hand, the standard of living of the rich minority has been increasing steadily, widening the gap between the rich and the poor.

Millions of people die of starvation each year while 40% of the U.S. population is overweight and 30% of the world's population eats 3/4 of the world's protein.

Nine hundred million people subsist on less than $75 a
year, while people earning $15,000 a year in U.S. are class-
ified as on the edge of poverty. One third to half of mankind lives without access to health services of any kind.
The rich 34% claims 87% of the world's total GNP each year
while the poor two-thirds is left with 13%.

How can we understand these contradictions? How can we
overcome them?

It is my intention in this paper to discuss from a personal perspective some of the mechanisms that perpetuate
injustice and inequality in the world. I will also attempt
to analyze the fundamental questions of the role of the
church in the process of liberation, in the combat against
poverty, and in the struggle for justice.

Being a part of both the church and the third world,
the poorest country in the western hemisphere, I feel my
background qualifies me to write about the subject of justice, freedom and social transformation. Since 1977 I have
devoted my life to working very closely with grassroots people in various capacities such as community organizations,
adult education, cooperatives, leadership training, etc.

In the course of my work and dialogue with these people
I have discovered that poverty is not an accident but rather
a fundamental phenomenon of a world of abundance in which
many people are poor in order that a few others may stay rich.
The present situation of injustice, exploitation and oppression is created and sustained by the rich and the powerful.
Thus, they seem to be too large to change. But certainly
this is already part of the historical purpose of the church.
The gospel has always dealt with the social and economic
structures that oppress the people. The gospel included
preaching "release to the captives and...liberty to the oppressed."

MECHANISM OF INJUSTICE

As the Uruguayan theologian, philosopher, sociologist, Julio Santa Ana clearly puts it: "The suffering of the poor is not only limited to material needs (scarcity of goods, lack of basic health care services, lack of job opportunities, inadequate school facilities, etc.) Their life is also characterized by dependency and oppression. They have very little opportunity for their own decision-making to shape their lives. What and when they eat, where and when they work, what wages they should receive and what price they should pay, where and how they should live, how many children they should have and how to bring them up, what they say and how they should say it, even when they should laugh and when they should cry and how--all these things and many other aspects of life are determined or conditioned by the economic system, political power and religious sanctions controlled by the rich, the powerful and the influential."

It is clear now that when we speak of poverty we are not dealing with conditions of scarcity but rather with the more fundamental questions of power, control and distribution. Certain relationships in society are responsible for the continuing poverty of the poor. These are relationships of ownership, social, racial, economic, cultural and political power.

I shall not attempt to make a comprehensive analysis of all the structures that foster injustice and inequalities between the powerful and the powerless, rich and poor, those who benefit and those who are victimized. I shall merely underscore a few of them.

Capitalism Expansion

Injustice or oppression around the world has been reinforced during the last quarter of the twentieth century by the expansion of capitalism. This system of private ownership of land, resources from the land, means of production and high technology, has provided for some the necessary power to own and control even the lives of other human beings and has resulted in every conceivable kind of oppression and dehumanization (slavery, racism, economic exploitation, dependency, etc.). It has also given some nations the right to cross geographical boundaries and in the name of civilization to impose colonialism and government control on other peoples while exploiting human and natural resources.

International corporations are a typical example of the ways in which capitalistic forces in the national and international spheres join together to oppress the poor and concentrate economic and technological power in the hands of a few. All of them claim to bring capital and technology to the countries where they operate and thereby to create employment and income. But, essentially, their primary motive is to take advantage of the available cheap labor and to draw out profits from them, making use of immense control they exercise over world trade and prices.

Marginalization

A word for the poor in the Indonesian language means "They who are not," the linguistic expression of their state of exclusion.

Another mechanism of injustice is the growing marginalization of the poor in the economic, social, political and even religious life of their communities. The poorest do not count in the affairs of life and have no voice in decision making processes. They are considered ignorant and worthless and are treated as outcasts. They are excluded from whatever benefits and opportunities are available even to poor communities.

Dependency/Paternalism

It must be admitted that there are individuals, groups, governments, churches and voluntary agencies with the support of well-meaning and good intentioned people who have genuinely tried to do their best for the poor and the oppressed. But often they tend to look on the poor as objects of their charity and good efforts, the passive recipients of their good will. Their efforts have mainly been for the poor and seldom with the poor and have proved inadequate as they fail to involve the poor as agents of their own situation. They fail to realize the fact that what the poor are striving for is to be treated as subjects rather than mere objects. What the poor are fighting for is recognition of themselves as people having the potential to change their own situation and society as a whole. The last two decades of intensive development in the Third World constitute enough proof that conditions of the poor cannot and will not be solved by doing things for them or by giving handouts. The very character of structural poverty demands that its root causes be tackled by appropriate methods at the level of their causes rather than at the level of their effects.

Support of Dictatorial Regimes

The period of colonialism and imperialism is over. Yet the same process is in operation today, that is, the lust for economic gain finds expression through political power which oppresses weak nations and lets loose oppressive regimes in individual nations to preserve and perpetuate the system that works for the exclusive benefit of the few. Every effort is made by the national elite and international oppressive forces to keep the system working for their benefit, thus maintaining the poor where they are. The rise and fall of dictatorial oppressive and authoritarian regimes in countries in Asia, Latin America and Africa tend to institutionalize human rights violation as a necessary measure to maintain prevailing patterns of domination at home and abroad.

Thought Control

Thought control is a new mechanism of injustice and oppression and is intimately linked with twentieth-century developments in the technology of communications. Before the advent of modern communications, it was technologically impossible for an old-style, traditional dictatorship to compel the acceptance of an official dogma, to require the constant and enthusiastic adoration of the regime and its leader, to see that news, culture, teaching, writing, and entertainment all reinforced the dictatorship's control and to force the cult of the dictator to permeate almost every facet of existence. Through these techniques the majority of the Third World leaders maintain absolute thought control, thereby depriving their people of the chance to exercise independent choice or judgment.

Brain Drain

The rich countries deprive the Third World of its professionals. Doctors, scientists, and artists,who would have been of great help to their poor countries, take their skills acquired at the cost of their own poor people, and migrate to affluent countries to serve there at lower wages than their counterparts.

In 1970 11,236 University graduate students from the under-developed countries migrated to U.S. In Haiti there is only one doctor for ten thousand people, while over 30% of all Haitian doctors exercised their skills in Canada.

The Church

It has become common practice for the church to identify with the socio-economic-political system based on the dominance of the few over the many. This practice often degenerates into what many have called a civil religion which blesses the established status quo instead of calling it into question. Civil religion is devoid of moral content and carries with it little capacity to bring a word of judgment or correction to social order. Its function is to provide religious justification for the social order, to serve as the ideological glue which holds the society together in consensus and conformity.

BIBLICAL PERSPECTIVE ON FREEDOM AND SOCIAL JUSTICE

Both the Old and New Testaments are full of teachings concerning social justice, freedom and social transformation. For our purposes a brief review of some biblical principles may help us to understand God's desire for His people.

Principles from the Jubilee Year (Leviticus 25:10-12)

The Jewish tradition of the jubilee year was premised on the biblical principle that the earth is the Lord's, that we are only stewards of the earth and its resources. That is, God's intentions for His people were not only religious and political, but economic and social as well. The jubilee year provides for a periodic redistribution of land and wealth, which militated against the accumulation of riches. God's purpose was to create a new social and economic order by making it difficult for a few to achieve a vast accumulation of wealth at the expense of the many. As demonstrated in this passage, God's desire was that the poor were to be given a new opportunity to help themselves.

Principles from the Prophets

Questions concerning wealth, poverty and social justice take a central place in the ministry of the prophets. Isaiah tells us that the fast in which God delights involves breaking the yoke of oppression, treating fairly those who work for us and giving them what they earn, sharing our bread with the hungry, bringing the homeless poor and destitute into our houses, and clothing those who are cold (Is. 58:5-7).

Amos claims that worship and praise are not acceptable to God unless justice rolls down like waters and righteousness like an overflowing stream (Amos 5:21-24). Jeremiah, Hosea, and Micah rebuked oppressive affluence and exploitive power and demanded economic and political justice for the poor, the exploited, the oppressed, the defeated, the defenseless, the weak, the alien.

Principles from Jesus' Life (Luke 4:16-21)

Jesus begins his ministry anointed by the Spirit to preach good news to the poor...to proclaim release to the captives and recovering of sight to the blind, to set at liberty those who are oppressed, to proclaim the acceptable year of the Lord. He later tells us that our profession of love for God will be concretely tested by our actions in feeding the hungry, clothing the naked, caring for the homeless and ministering to the practical needs of the afflicted   (Matt. 25:31-46).

The parable of the good Samaritan demonstrates that our responsibility for our neighbour extends to anyone in need and leaps over the human barriers of race and class at personal cost of time, money and danger (Luke 10:30-31). Jesus' deep involvement and close identification with the poor, the sick, the outcast, the downtrodden, the ignorant and the worthless brings social revolution.

Principles from the Early Church (Acts 4:32-35; II Cor. 8:1-5)

The common life and sharing were the distinguishing marks of the early church. They realized that nothing was their private property and that resources are to be shared and freely given for the good of the body, rather than for the personal advantage of the owner. A whole new system of distribution had been created, with each person in a process of giving and receiving according to ability and need.

PRACTICAL IMPLICATIONS FOR THE CHURCH

If the church is truly to become a viable and dynamic agent in the glorious tomorrow that God has promised us, it cannot choose to play safe by adopting policies of neutrality or ally itself with the powerful when dealing with the issues of the poor. The principles from the Jubilee, the prophets, Jesus' life, and the early church really challenge the church to participate and identify with the suffering of the community of the poor, the disinherited, the victimized, the outcast and the broken-hearted. As the custodian of the message of the gospel, the church cannot remain uninvolved and indifferent.

It is impelled to side with the poor instead of the forces
of society that create oppression, dehumanization, marginalization, paternalism, dictatorship, capitalism and poverty.
To respond to these challenges for greater justice, I see
the following tasks before the church:

Prophetic Task

Taking social justice to mean the fair and equitable
distribution of services and resources, major injustices in
all sectors of life are widespread nationally and internationally. The underlying causes, as has already been pointed
out earlier, are deeply imbedded in the social, economic and
political structures of society, and attempts to root them
out often involve direct confrontation with the power centers of society. This challenge requires the church to denounce injustices, recognizing that silence in the front of
oppression speaks even louder than words. It also implies
that the church should preach a full gospel that does not
separate the spiritual and the physical needs of man. Within this perspective, the mission of the church is threefold:

1. To plead the cause of the poor, defending the weak,
   helping the helpless (Prov.22:22; Ps.12:5; 10:17-18)

2. To stand for equality and social justice (Prov.14:21;
   Ps.41:1)

3. To institute a structure that would create a more
   just and equal distribution of wealth (Lev.25:28)

Educational Task

Ignorance is considered by many experts in the field of
development as the number one strategy to maintain an existing imbalance between the church urban and rural, the rich
and the poor, the powerful and the powerless. The church
has a great deal to do in this area. Education is not only
to be promoted but also oriented in a spirit of love, service and dedication to one's neighbor. It must be concerned
about the whole person in his bio-physical and socio-economic
development. The church has an educational task to accomplish among those of its members in order to keep before
them the precepts of respect for the human person, justice
and human dignity. It should alert its members to remain
critical of any approach whereby the individual is seen as
an object, a mere case study, or experimental material.

The church should support and encourage its members to participate in government-run public services in order that they may, like Daniel and Joseph, play an active part in a process of humanization and growing justice within these services.

The church should remind its youth of the possibility of social service and humanitarian vocations which should be undertaken in a spirit of self-denial and dedication to one's neighbor. There is also a labor of justice to be accomplished to ensure that the marginalized strata of society has access to equitable distribution of resources, because this is God's will, His preference for the poor and the forsaken.

Self-Reliant Development Task

Over the last two decades a number of development projects have been initiated by Christian organizations in the Third World and have received substantial support from donor agencies in developed countries in the West. These programs were expected to become self-supporting and provide examples of self-reliance and successful participation by the people. Instead, most of them tend to become new institutions, depending largely on outside funds. They also become symbols of power and patronage or instruments for creating a new elite. That seems to be the tragedy of many countries of the Third World thus far.

Self-reliant development concentrates on people and requires a structural change in society. This would be possible if policies of social justice are followed in a society. When people receive a fair share of social production, they are motivated to contribute to social effort. Instead of the rich becoming richer and the poor poorer, there has to be a reduction of inequalities, a better sharing of economic, social, and political power between the privileged few and the majority.

Conclusion

In conclusion, the church's mission is not to be a member of the existing status quo. Rather, its mission is to be always on the move, to get people serving, to be a prophet in the midst of an unjust society. Its mission is to be always in the breach in defense of the rights of the oppressed. This is the experience of the Integrated Rural Development of the Baptist Mission in Southwest Haiti. Currently there are 270

MEBSH Churches spanning the entire southwest peninsula. Forty years of successful ministry of preaching the gospel did
not change the physical situation of the people. The churches had a paternalistic attitude toward the poor until recently, when they realized that they cannot remain passive
in facing today's challenges. A meeting was held in August
1979 in order to analyze the situation of the church in the
context of the Haitian society. This gathering was attended
by pastors, missionaries and lay people, and as a result, it
was decided to create a program of Integrated Rural Development in order to enable the churches to play a major role as
change agents, so they are involved not only in the proclamation of the gospel but also the demonstration of the gospel.

Emphasizing the need to motivate the people who are too
poor and powerless to speak up for themselves, the Integrated
Rural Development of MEBSH/Worldteam through its village motivators program seeks to bring a new awareness among the
poor of their condition and helps them struggle for a better
life through their own efforts by means of development programs, stemming from and carried out by the community, giving them a sense of dignity, a sense of achievement and a
sense of hope.

The motivators' primary aim is to be with the people,
sharing their everyday life and winning their confidence.
Their presence helps the villagers to reflect and analyze
their situation, ask questions not asked before, define their
needs, and establish a list of priorities, and thus begins
a common search for a constructive program of development by
themselves. These motivators often deal with questions of
injustice, exploitation, capitalism and oppression. As a
result of this process of interaction, development activities
are planned and carried out by the people themselves. Health
care programs are implemented with their participation at
decision-making levels; local leaders are trained; agricultural cooperatives are organized for economic production, and
most important of all, the message of the liberating gospel
of Jesus Christ has gained deeper meaning for these people.
It is no longer a manifestation of paternalism from the
church, but rather a proclamation which helps them to understand better how to reaffirm their deep convictions and
values.

For example, this past year our motivators worked with
one community in southwest Haiti and persuaded them to take
their coffee directly to market, bypassing the middlemen. As
a result of selling their coffee beans directly to buyers in

Port au Prince, they not only bypassed what has become a
very unjust economic structure, they increased their profits
two and a half times. They are now forming an economic cooperative to take greater contol of their lives and their
economic future.

Diaconal Task

   In the struggle for justice, the church is challenged to
join hands in solidarity with those who live in poverty,
hunger and oppression. It can only do so by its tradition
of service and the central theme of biblical thought, "You
shall love your neighbour as yourself." Service stimulates
reflection, draws Christians from different cultures together, and helps us to discover the Lord in each one of
our neighbors. We must also join hands north and south to
change those systems that oppress the poor and rob people
of their dignity and their freedom.

   The church's ministry of service is directed toward human
promotion, toward enabling humankind to develop its full creative potential. In choosing to serve the poorest, most
marginal sectors of society, it seeks to redeem both the
oppressed and the oppressor. This aim excludes all the
paternalistic, charitable attitudes that belittle the human
personality. This aim requires that Christian organizations
in the more affluent countries give Christians in the poorer
countries equal justice in the use of resources in their nations in true partnership.

Stewardship Task

   The church and Christian organizations are responsible
for managing the resources available for ministry according
to moral standards and ethical principles and also in such
a way as to respond to the felt needs of the most marginal
backward segment of society. In practical terms, the church
and Christian organizations need to use the times, talents,
and monies that God has placed in their care in order to
make the greatest possible kingdom impact. When people followed Jesus, their decision always altered their lifestyles
and radically changed the way they use their time and resources. Those of us working in development need to model
more responsible lifestyles, as well as challenge our constituencies to live more justly.

   Peter and Andrew left their boats to follow Jesus.
Matthew resigned his job. Zacchaeus and Nicodemus gave up

their relationships with the power structure of their society. Anyone who chooses to follow Jesus must not rationalize the radical expectations of Jesus in relation to his life of affluence by adopting a fractional view of stewardship, that is, to give to God a fraction of his money, time, and talents. Instead, he is called to follow the doctrine of "active redistribution"; that is, to actively redistribute all of our time, talents and resources to seek first the kingdom of God in our world.

This whole-life approach to stewardship would allow every single member of the church and Christian organizations to start using the global resources of God more intentionally and equitably and to examine institutions and personal lifestyles for wasted resources that could be invested in the kingdom. The church must provide leadership by example and by action in the biblical struggle for justice, freedom and social transformation.

BIBLICAL FOUNDATIONS FOR SOCIAL JUSTICE AND HUMAN LIBERATION

Purpose. This paper hopes to present a biblically anchored reconciliation within the evangelical community between those who emphasize personal piety and those who emphasize social justice.

Beginning Point: Toward a Biblical Hermeneutic. Since Christianity is uniquely a biblical religion, it is important that we identify what we believe is truly shaped by the biblical Word. The diverse character of the biblical witness suggests a dynamic rather than a static role. Scripture describes a kind of "inner-dialectic" between community and canon. As the community reads the Bible, the "prophetic" work corrects and resolves threats to its faith. A truly biblical faith must be shaped by the *whole* Scripture.

Toward a Canonical Definition of Justice. A biblical definition of justice must draw on both Old Testament prophets and sages. Even as God had compassion on an impoverished Israel in Egypt, so a liberated and redeemed Israel was to have compassion on its impoverished. Jubilary economics is rooted in grace--not greed. Because God has fulfilled His salvific promises in Christ, His church is obliged to reflect His grace rather than the world's greed. Social justice is more than "rule"; it is revelatory of God's triumph over evil by the cross.

How is wisdom theology of the sages related to a definition of social justice? The sages were men of affluence who wrote primarily for society's elite. They are concerned to maintain the status quo, respect authority, and oppose change. They see justice as: (1) living according to wisdom and receiving one's "just desserts"; (2) practicing "fair play,"not mistreating the oppressed in one's quest for the good life. This view of justice reflects a more human viewpoint and is not as radical as the prophetic idea, which is defined by grace. This wisdom theology was passed on to early Christian evangelists, who re-interpreted it in light of Jesus Christ. Christ radicalized the Old Testament notion of wisdom, and in fact collapses it with the more prophetic (i.e., jubilary) notions of life. However, the most direct application of Old Testament wisdom is seen in Paul's concerns for stability and structure.

Application to the Church's Engagement with the Developing Third World.

(1) Development contains both the notion of form and reform.

(2) The Church must be open to new reforming ideas.

(3) Development must begin with reform, which will become form.

(4) Development must reflect an interplay between the individualism of wisdom theology and the communalism of the prophetic word.

Toward a Canonical Definition of Human Liberation. Human liberation is specified by rules which insure the presence of God's mercy in history. What I am calling for is "rule agapism"; God's love and the love His people share with each other and for the world are always controlled by "rules of right conduct."

ROBERT WALL is a Professor of Theology at Seattle Pacific University, Seattle, Washington.

BIBLICAL FOUNDATIONS FOR SOCIAL JUSTICE AND HUMAN LIBERATION

Robert W. Wall

It is the positive achievement of evangelical Christianity to understand faith and discipleship in personal and spiritual categories. As evangelicals, we share a faith in the Gospel of God which proclaims good news to the individual in need and which promises life to all who live in death. We believe that human wisdom and personal, if not corporate, forms of fulfillment result from a personal relationship with God through Christ and His Spirit. This consensus must be maintained and indeed celebrated as foundational for the people of God.

However, it is also true that this distinctively evangelical point of view has led us to a religiosity excessively preoccupied with "selfhood."[1] One's relationship with God is privitized which in turn determines a religion that often dulls the social contour of the Gospel. We are shaped by the spirit of the Reformation where protest against the professional priesthood led to the recovery of the biblical idea of the "priesthood of all believers." Yet, without balance and correctives, the protest of the Reformation can become institutionalized into something dangerously close to the old heresy of gnosticism. Gnosticism was fundamentally a religion of the exalted self, who is made God-like by *gnosis*, by spiritual knowledge. Social or more public material concerns were rejected by the Gnostics as demonic and unnecessary for one's personal salvation. The central confession of the Church--Christ is Lord--repudiated such a bifurcation between one's personal and public lives; Christ is

Lord over both creation and the Church (Col.1:15-20). Thus,
God's justification of the Church was demonstrated both by
private acts of piety (Matthew 6) and by public acts of mercy (Luke 6)--acknowledging the common confession of faith
that Christ is Lord over all.[2]

Over the last decade, a prophetic voice has emerged within
evangelical Christianity to call the North American Church
back to a more balanced understanding of discipleship. Maintaining the necessity of drawing upon the resources of God's
power and grace through faith in his Gospel, persons such as
Ron Sider, Jim Wallis and ministries such as World Concern,
ESA and VOC have defined repentance in terms of a more public
and systemic perception of evil.[3] The reversal of the inroad
of demonic action in human history bids the whole Church to
engage in justifying and liberating activities humbly dependent upon the powers and instruments of God's kingdom. As a
result of their proclamation, evangelicals are found at those
discussions and demonstrations for human rights, for social
and human justice--not as secular agents but as the sacred
agents of God's Word which announces freedom for the oppressed and contentment for the impoverished. Yet, such
work must continue within the evangelical community. Not
everyone has heard this prophetic voice; others like the Israel of old have resisted the call to repent and to turn in
obedience to God's revealed Word. Like every social group
as complex and multivalent as this one, various opinions and
interpretations are sure to abound. For various reasons,
some wish to maintain battles on other fronts or wish to retain personal piety as the single content of the Gospel.

Perhaps part of the problem exists at a cultural level.
Christopher Lasch's important critique of American life, *The
Culture of Narcissism,* recovers a mythology of individualism
as the very ground of how we view national-human existence.[4]
Peter Berger and others have convincingly argued that institutional myths are dependent upon and shaped by the larger
societal-cultural myths; thus, religious institutions conform to the drama and to the will of society at large.[5]
The American Church, including the evangelical community
within it, remains controlled by the American myth of the
individual, blunting even more the prophetic voice which
calls it to overturn social evil.

We would acknowledge that the diversity within the Church
is in part due to the diversity within the Bible which the
Church reads as Scripture. To that extent, such diversity,
when fully rooted in the biblical Word, is legitimate.

However, at the same time, we must resist the rigidification of parochial interests--whether prophetic or establishment-- and begin to celebrate and to converse with those who recover different although fully biblical agendas from Scripture. We must also be willing to recognize and to critique our own societal mythologies which color everything we see out there. This paper hopes to begin the process of dismantling the secular on the one hand, while bringing about, on the other hand, a biblically anchored reconciliation within the evangelical community--between those who might emphasize different contours of the common Gospel or who might draw battle lines at different places in our common struggle against the powers and principalities of this evil age.

BEGINNING POINT: TOWARD A BIBLICAL HERMENEUTIC

Christianity is a biblical religion; no one Christian would disagree that our faith is grounded in and transmitted through a common book. Thus, what we identify as important and what we believe is true are shaped by the reading and hearing of the biblical Word. It is yet another positive contribution of the evangelical tradition to remain steadfast, even in the midst of skepticism and agnosticism, to the critical and essential role the Scripture plays in the life of God's people. Yet, the justifying reasons for such a biblical faith, or the ways in which Scripture should be used by the Church are contested.[6] The battle for the Bible is a battle for a certain kind of hermeneutics and not for its on-going function as the Church's canon.

An emerging field within biblical scholarship, called "canonical criticism," has offered an important critique of existing hermeneutical programs within the Church as well as a new approach for interpreting Scripture which seeks to take seriously the hermeneutics arising naturally from Scripture itself.[7] Indeed, the context for studying and using Scripture as the Church's canon *is Scripture* (rather than Enlightenment historiography, or literary criticism, or other modern/ancient methods of exegesis and interpretation); Scripture itself provides us with the decisive clues! While the discussion continues, two central points seem to have resulted from this promising discussion: First, the diverse character of the biblical witness suggests a *dynamic* rather than a static role in the Church's life. Whether one sees the diversity of God's revelation, the diversity of the genre which narrates it, the diversity of the perceptions which interpret it, or the diversity of problems which address it, the diversity of gospels enshrined within the Scripture call attention to a *living* God who continues to speak to a *living* people within a *living* situation. Thus, the function of the Bible is to facilitate the on-going conversation between God and his people in the light of the new concerns which any historical situation generates for both God and his Church. Critiqued by this norm is the scholastic view of the Bible as static, sacred *text* from which transhistorical codes of right conduct and right doctrine can be prescribed. Critiqued also is the critical view of Scripture which views and judges its authority as a book of past history instead of as the book for present faith. Either view locks the Bible into the past and strips it of its dynamic and canonical character.

Second, James Sanders in a series of important articles argues that Scripture describes a kind of "inner-dialectic" between community and canon.[8] The believing community has always identified a bible and has always been shaped by what it says. The good news of God for Israel and in Christ, however, has always been adapted to the new situation in relevant ways--both to preserve the story of God and to preserve his people! The diversity of "story" is the precipitate of that dialectic. Yet, Sanders goes on to suggest that the adapting of the community's Bible to its life (a process called "midrash") is not merely to inform and to transmit "Thus saith the Lord God," but to correct and resolve something which threatens the faith of God's people. Thus, the function of Scripture is "prophetic"--it calls the Church to turn to God, to repent in light of his Word, so to persevere through the threat and on to salvation (Jms.1:21-25). The community of faith continues to read its Bible, then, as the "prophetic" Word of God which corrects and resolves those theological and historical threats to its faith. The various "polarities" one finds in the Bible--prophet and king, Mosaic and Davidic, Paul and James, Synoptic and John, apocalyptic and institutional--provide the Church with the boundaries of a kind of self-correcting apparatus, which enables a continuing dialectic between community and canon. Even as the prophet of Yahweh corrected a royal theology, or Paul corrected the more Jewish interests of James, or John answered the questions the Synoptists left untouched (so Calvin), so the prophets continue to correct a theology which identifies consciously or unconsciously with royal interests, Paul continues to check and balance the potentially legalistic *ethos* of James, and John continues to provide us with a fully incarnational Christology to balance the human Jesus narrated by the synoptic evangelists. Critiques by this second norm are those confessions and theologies composed with an eye to a "canon within the Canon." A truly biblical faith must be shaped by reading and reflecting upon the *whole* Scripture. History teaches us that an *exclusive* use of Paul or of Revelation or of Wisdom results in perverted interpretations of what it means to be the Church and to do as the Church ought. Further critiqued is a kind of harmonizing hermeneutic which imposes a single and uniform theology upon the whole Scripture, and invariably does violence to the multiform and multivalent revelation of God found there. The point is that if the Church is to recover a truly biblical agenda, it must use its whole Scripture for teaching, reproof, correction, and training the Church up in the righteousness of God (2 Tim. 3:16).

TOWARD A CANONICAL DEFINITION OF JUSTICE

The purpose of this section of the paper is to establish a biblical definition of justice by drawing upon both the Old Testament prophets and sages. While articulating different perceptions of God's Word for Israel, both prophet and sage did share a common ground. Both recognized that social forms of justice were desirable for Israel's survival as the people of God. Both recognized that social justice was a reflection of divine norms. Both recognized that the lack of a social conscience not only led to societal failure (denial of history), but it also impugned the reputation of a holy God (denial of transcendence). Israel and Israel's God were preserved within human history by the maintenance of a covenant which demanded a radical concern for the poor and a rejection of those social structures which impoverish. The content of both wisdom and of the prophetic word calls attention to God's requirement that the sociology of true Israel promote just forms of life in keeping with his own definitions of justice, so that as a people they might reflect him in history.

The Prophetic Word. While there is substantial agreement in how the sage and the prophet defined and encouraged Israel's social conscience, the underlying theologies of these two trajectories are really quite different. The wisdom tradition in the history of Israel is fully grounded in its monarchy (and so in the *Davidic* conceptualization of the covenant between Yahweh and Israel),[9] while the prophetic word, beginning with Samuel, is fully grounded in Moses and is anti-royalistic (cf. 1 Sam. 8).[10] Actually, as James Barr notes, the prophets of Yahweh tended to be apolitical and were primarily interested in Israel's spiritual condition; i.e., in

Israel's obedience (or lack thereof) to Torah.[11] They did
associate, however, Israel's disobedience with the king whose
utilitarian concerns often caused the people to drift from
their dependence upon God and his Torah.

Critical for a correct understanding of the prophetic Word
is how Moses came to understand Israel and its covenant with
God. Central to the Mosaic understanding of Israel is the
recital of how God saved his people from Egypt. Israel's
life was shaped by this revelation of God's goodness in its
history so that Torah enshrined the kind of life which reflected the radical character of the God who saved his elect
people. Israel's life, whether socially or religiously construed, was very different than other nations because its God
was very different. Israel's obligation according to the
covenant Torah describes is to be the historical representative of the transcendent God; thus, the manner of its economics, its politics, its cultus, its social structures made
concrete the character of Yahweh revealed in the Exodus and
to Moses. It is clear, then, that the kind of justice encouraged by Moses and so by the prophets was grounded in the
revelation of a transcendent God; that is, it is a form of
justice which was not managed nor shaped by human conceptions.
Israel's justice was not Egypt's! Rather it is a form of justice given its content by a merciful and forgiving God--an
uncommon idea in a world whose *best* notions of justice were
construed in terms of fairness rather than grace.

One of the oft-heard slogans of those advocating a biblically based definition of justice is *jubilee*.[12] Set forth in
Leviticus 25 and in Deuteronomy 15, the principle of jubilee
orders a distinctively Mosaic understanding of social justice.
The Hebrew word *yobel* (LXX=*aphesis*) means "release;" it refers
specifically to the freeing of slaves and the restitution of
property to those bankrupt debtors turned into slaves. The
interpretations and applications of this principle within the
prophetic tradition, however, were much more general: Jubilee
became the essential sociological model for Israel.[13] The
release of enslaved debtors became a metaphor for the release
of any who were oppressed by injustice. On a more positive
level, jubilee became the model for an *egalitarian* people--
a sociology which critiqued those structures which kept peace
by keeping marginal people marginal, and a sociology of "equal
opportunity" which affirmed the endowment of each member of
the community with the necessary stamina and talent to achieve
and maintain equality with the other members of the community.

Jubilee also became the soil for prophetic critiques of Israel's economy. Wealth, under a jubilary economy, was recycled rather than hoarded, redistributed rather than retained as a way of reflecting the electing and saving mercies of Yahweh. Even as God had compassion on an impoverished Israel in Egypt, so a liberated and redeemed Israel was to have compassion on its impoverished; not to do so was an indictment and denial of God's saving grace. Jubilary economics is rooted in grace and not greed; social structures in keeping with the revelation of God's grace must advocate a form of justice which shares possessions and redistributes wealth so to liberate the poor from their material impoverishment.

We must hasten to note, however, that the social critique--a central feature of the prophetic word--was *more diagnostic than prognostic*.[14] The perception of social evil (*qua* injustice) and the prophet's protest of economic or of human inequality was the *illustration* (more than "rule") of spiritual need--of their need to repent and turn back to Torah as that which shaped their corporate and spiritual life with God and one another. The royal word could not provide the resources necessary for that renewal; the hope of restoration and of salvation lie in the revelation of God in Torah and not in the words of the kings or his court. Thus, the prophetic protest was preface to the demand of repentance. This qualification of the prophetic notions of social justice is made to remind us that their mission was primarily *theocentric and not anthropocentric;* our mission must continue to be the same. Social critique and our protests against social injustice must fit into a larger, more theocentric agenda which calls earth back to its Creator-God.

The principle of jubilee, enshrined in the prophetic word, becomes a central feature in the ministry of Jesus.[15] His compassion is directed to the outcast of his world; his message as messiah calls attention to the character of jubilee which is fulfilled in his ministry (Lk.4:18-21).[16] Especially in Luke's gospel, the conditions of discipleship (9:51-19:27) are shaped by a jubilary *ethos*: thus, to follow after the Christ of God, the disciple must be merciful even as God reveals his mercy through Jesus (Lk.6:36). The description of mercy, in turn, follows the sociological (Lk.3:7-14; 10:25-37; 11:1-13; 14:1-14) and economic (16:1-15; 18:18-30) structures of jubilee--conforming to the conceptions of the messianic age in later Judaism (cf. Acts 2:42-47; 4:32-5:12). Because God has fulfilled his salvific promises in Christ, his Church is obliged to reflect his grace rather than the

world's greed (Lk.12:13-34). Social justice is more than
"rule"; it is revelatory of God's triumph over evil by the
Cross.

The Wisdom of the Sages. When the student of the Hebrew
Scriptures enters into that biblical material which transmits
the wisdom of ancient Israel (Proverbs, Job, Ecclesiastes,
Daniel, etc.), she/he enters a different world of discourse
and theological insight. For instance, the sages taught that
the created world embodied God's Word; thus, the *norms of hu-*
man observation and experience which arise from interaction
with the natural order transmit God's truth to those wise
enough to heed it. This resource of revelation--different
from the Torah of prophetic protest--provided a different
contour for Israel's definition of social justice. Further,
since the sages were counselors on the king's court, they
were aligned with his royal interests.[17] While the king had
special responsibility to provide justice to the poor and oppressed, and the sages often reflected this as an obligation
of their readers,[18] the prophets of Yahweh, who had no status
in the monarchial hierarchy, criticized the king's neglect
and grounded their protest in a larger criticism of royal
theology--the very same theology enshrined in the sapient
writings of the Hebrew Scriptures. To the point, the agenda
of the sages, which is an interpretation of the David trajectory of Israel's covenant with Yahweh, engages in a "canonical conversation" the agenda of the prophets, which is an interpretation of the Mosaic trajectory of Israel's covenant
with Yahweh. This on-going conversation within our Scripture
in turn engages the on-going people of God in conversation
so to illumine, correct, and set forth a fuller understanding
of justice, according to the whole Scripture.

Our purpose in this part of the paper is to trace the dimensions of wisdom theology as related to a definition of
social justice. It is generally believed by biblical scholarship, for a whole host of reasons, that the sages were men of
affluence (e.g., Solomon, Lemuel, BenSira, Qoheleth), who
wrote primarily for society's elite.[19] Even during the exile,
the wisdom of Israel's sages was preserved by the wealthy as
their promise. And the attitudes reflected in the wisdom
material of the Old Testament are consistent in general with
those of any affluent class: There is a concern to maintain
the status quo, a respect for authority, an opposition to
change (Prov.14:35; 16:10). They respect the power which
money brings (Ecc.10:19; Prov.22:7; 18:23; 10:15); wealth
produces friendship (Prov.14:20; 19:4) and honor (Prov.10:30-
31). Not only societal power, but affluence also brings

personal happiness (Ecc.5:18-19). God's blessing is construed in material and worldly terms. In this sense, the
retribution view of economics rather than the redistribution
view of the prophetic literature is championed by the sages
(Prov.3:16; 10:4; 21:20).

A theology begins to emerge from these attitudes of affluence. The world of experience is interpreted in a cause-
effect way. Proverbs, which summarize and order the observa-
tions of the sages, set out a view of society based upon a
"trickle'down" theory of life. If persons are wise enough
to follow the advice (i.e., the proverbs) of the sages, an
efficient, orderly, productive, just society will result.
God has created a world with certain patterns which yield and
order the "good life." Wise persons are affluent persons because they have obeyed God's ordination transmitted through
creation and have recovered by observation and experience the
wisdom which insures the good life. The poor and the peasant
of society are encouraged to be wise instead of foolish as
the way to prosperity.

It is critical to note that the retributive view of wealth
translates the sages' concern for social justice in two ways:
First, justice is "just desserts"; a society which lives according to wisdom achieves *for themselves* the good life for
all persons.[20] Second, justice is "fair-play" (cf. Prov.1:3;
mesharim); justice to the oppressed, as a part of society's
quest for the good life, means not mistreating them as others
do (cf. Job 31:21-22). Again, this form of social justice
is construed by human notions of justice, and is not as radical as the prophetic idea which is defined by grace--a transcendent norm. For the sages, concerned with national life,
the maintenance of a stable family life, of moral business
practices, of compassionate treatment of the poor, of political alliances, of humble limitations of power--all marks of
a wise life, the State would survive and indeed prosper as
the "just desserts" of following the wise pattern of life
laid down in their proverbs.

Perhaps because the Davidic rendering of the covenant was
more individualistic (2 Sam.7), the wisdom paradigm tends to
transmit a theology concerned more with "self" than with community. Society is a community of individuals, each of whom
is responsible to be wise, each responsible to his/her own
social conscience, each left to accomplish his/her good life
which is the right of each person. It is the individual who
gets what she/he deserves; justice comes to the person who

is responsible enough to deserve it. Thus, the just society is the net result of wise individuals who live fairly and so beget just desserts.

This wisdom theology, especially as it was rehearsed by the rabbis of later Judaism, was passed on to the early Christian evangelists, who reinterpreted it in light of Jesus Christ. *Christ became the incarnation of the "wisdom from above"* (esp. in Matthew's gospel[21] 11:19; 12:42; 13:54; cf. 1 Cor.1:30). It is the obvious conclusion for Christians then, to follow after Christ as the fulfillment and embodiment of the wise (i.e., good) life. Of course, Christ radicalizes the Old Testament notion of wisdom, and in fact collapses it with the more prophetic (i.e., jubilary) notions of life (cf. the New Testament book of James for a most compelling rendering of this new form of wisdom, which reverses the old formulae of the sages in the light of the imminent Day of the Lord).

However, there is a more direct application of Old Testament wisdom found in the New Testament: the theology of wisdom is reflected in the theology of the institutionalized Church (e.g. Pastoral Letters of Paul).[22] Paul's concern for stability, for structure, and his formalizing and personalizing of the charismata (*contra* 1 Cor. 12-14) is wise advice to those pastors and their struggling churches which seek to survive and indeed grow in the world. The "sound" teaching and life which anchors such agenda is in fact rooted in Jesus, who is wisdom for the Church (1 Tim.6:3), and in the community's Scripture, which makes it wise unto salvation in Christ Jesus (2 Tim.3:15-16).

Application to the Church's Engagement with the Developing Third World. Paul Hanson suggests that the Old Testament conversation between kings and prophets describes "indispensable sides of an essential polarity."[23] Israel's kings, and the sages who spoke the royal word to Israel, were concerned with *form* in the face of military defeats and the grim memories of slavery. The purity of their charismatic confederacy needed the form of a sophisticated bureaucracy if they were to survive as Israel! Wisdom teaches us how to survive in the world; indeed, it teaches us how to succeed and prosper! The political and religious climate of Israel was established to maintain a nation. Wisdom theology, which builds upon an unchanging cosmos created by a good God, shaped a static view of reality which in turn helped preserve the national status quo. However, out on the fringes of the ordered society, a battle was being waged by the prophets of Yahweh. Hanson calls this a "battle to reform"; even as the sages were concerned with *form*, so the prophets were concerned with *re-form*. Indeed, Israel's life was to be ordered by righteousness and not wisdom, by the revelation of Torah and not by human experience. The reformers were concerned with a shalom which resulted from compassion and justice rather than by political alliance and social hierarchies, which numbed and oppressed lower classes as a means of maintaining national security and peace (cf. Rehoboam!). The forms of the monarch were necessary for Israel to survive, but the reforms of the prophets were necessary for Israel to survive *as Israel*.

This represents a pattern for the Church's involvement in Third World development.[24] *We must understand that the idea of development contains both the notion of form and reform;* the Church must act in accord with the wisdom of an institution concerned with survival and with the critical faculty of a community concerned with reversing all that is wrong in a nation's life. Even as Christ fulfilled *both* the prophetic and the royal, so must the Church! Our concern here is to trace out what this agenda might consist of in the Christian praxis of social justice.

1) Most basically, the *Church must allow for and be open to new and reforming ideas.* All too often the Church comes into a new territory with old and rigid methods; it evangelizes by unwavering confessions and formulations of theology which resist self-criticism and which refuse to be adapted to the new and living contexts. The forms of religious triumphalism, which impose a vision for which there is no revision, is the unfortunate character of many of the Church's efforts in the Third World. Just as unfortunate, however, is the reformer's reaction, which calls for a *total* change of the existing structures of the nation as the effective remedy for evil. These protests from the doom-sayers only encourage chaos as the atmosphere of development. While the first offered form *as* reform, the second offers reform *as* form; the net result of either agenda is failure. Development must flow from an on-going dialogue between those who work within institutional forms of development (i.e.,programs, services, mission agencies, Church, government) and the prophets of reform (i.e., Liberation theologians, labor leaders, missionaries).

2) Even as the reformation of Moses gave way to the formation of David's kingdom which in turn provoked the reactionary protest of Yahweh's prophets, so this same kind of historical

dialectic provides the Church with an authoritative paradigm: *Development must always begin with reform which is then institutionalized within stabilizing forms and continually nourished if not revised by the prophetic Word of God.* Let's trace this idea out a bit more. The development of any nation by the Church must always begin as a reforming movement. The proclamation of the Church and its witness within a nation must always reflect a primary concern for reform so to reverse all that is wrong with a nation. Indeed, empowered by the Spirit of God, the Church is enabled to correctly perceive what is wrong and to courageously proclaim and enact what is right according to the Scriptures. Fundamental to the Church's protest in the Third World is the jubilary notion of social justice, which is against political, social and economic oppression and encourages compassionate action on behalf of the nation's poor. We do not forsake the need for spiritual reversal either; but the prophetic pattern moves from social critique to spiritual reconciliation, systemic evil to individual and national repentance. Further, we protest always in the name of our risen Lord, in whom God announces his victory over evil and its historical manifestations. We call for justice and for justification because we are motivated, not only by compassion engendered by the Spirit, but by a God who bids us to be his instruments of righteousness in reversing all that is wrong with his creation.

Yet, prophets do not endure; they are not favored in their own country, and less so perhaps in the Third World. The reform-loving charismatics who introduced Israel to God's shalom, and the reform-loving Messiah who introduced the world to God's salvation, both yielded to institutions which enshrined and adapted their more radical words to a people which needed orderliness and stability if they were to survive and endure. The prophetic message, accommodated to national life, continues to inform the people in ways which continue to work. The Church's continued attempts to develop the Third World must finally realize that reform and the language of protest must take on concrete, institutional forms in order to continue its reforming work. Thus, we understand that social justice as called for by the reformers of Israel is also enshrined in the writings of the sages, but propped up by a theological program and a bureaucracy more suitable for a kingdom than a charismatic confederacy. The visionary language of transcendence is translated by the sages into a language of human experience and observation--concrete, realistic, workable, practical. The reformers' notion of jubilary justice, which calls for *undeserved* justice (grace!), is moderated by the proverbs which exalt fair-play and promise just desserts. Such proverbs, when taken up and lived out by the wise, lead to a just society where even the poor are cared for in a manner similar to the demands of Torah. The point is that the idealism (visions) of Torah is adapted to (revised by) the realities of trying to make it in a fallen world; obedience takes the world into account, and wisdom articulates that kind of world view. The Church's plans for developing the Third World's human and natural-societal resources must accommodate fallen reality; the norms and values of a fully biblical view of social justice must be set in the institutional forms of the Third World to safe-guard a distinctively Christian idea of justice. At the same time, the Church must be willing to hear its prophets, and to reform those forms which compromise biblical truth when influenced by the demonic.

3) Finally, there is *an important interplay between the individualism of royal (wisdom) theology and the communalism of the prophetic word*. Development according to the reformers is often too vague, too ambiguous to be effective; often this is the result of a concern with social programs, with global problems and with national "tendencies." That is, our visions of social justice are too often shaped by concerns which are hard to get a handle on. In part, this problem arises out of the West, which tends to think in abstract and spectacular ways;[25] to think "small" is condemned as "short-sighted." Similarly, the prophets saw no historical ambiguity when proclaiming the vision of Yahweh; situational complexity was easily dismantled in broad, bold sweeps. To their credit, they were concerned with a *people* of God and not with indivi-dual persons. The sages, on the other hand, were concerned with persons rather than with a people. Thus, they articu-lated specific, concrete actions (proverbs), and developed an *ethos* of individual responsibility. I would readily ad-mit to an unease with "personal ethics" when promoted to the exclusion of "social ethics" even as I would be uncomfortable with a self-centered Gospel. I would admit to the dangers of encouraging individual responsibility uncritically in this evil age of narcissism which promises the good life to the individual who minds his/her own business and who construes piety in personal ways and promises in material ways. We do need the prophetic emphasis on community to enlarge our vi-sions of social justice beyond ourselves to include all those who are mistreated.

THE CHURCH IN RESPONSE TO HUMAN NEED

However, the fact of the matter is this: Until we can
become concerned with individual persons, and until we can
feel a sense of compassion and responsibility for specific
victims of greed and violence, our visions will simply not
work well. Individual accountability produces intimacy, and
intimacy is the motivating force of all justifying action.
Intimacy is never achieved at a distance; it arises only out
of personal relationships. The Church's identification with
poverty, then, begins only when we are willing to relate
individually to poor persons.26 Concern and compassion are
intensified and made urgent when there is an experience, an
actual acquaintance with injustice. Our motive for involvement, indeed, our *authority* to be involved in developing
Third World nations as the Church, must be related in part
to human experience. The sages advised individuals to experience and so know life. Visions which work well must appeal to the motivations and insights derived from contact
and communication with the people we are called to help;
experience erects the form of reform.

TOWARD A CANONICAL DEFINITION OF HUMAN LIBERATION

Many definitions of liberation proliferate in our world--
especially in the Third World. It has come to mean freedom
to make individual choices, to do certain things; it has
come to refer to those things we are liberated from. All
these definitions refer to a liberation from limitations
placed upon human existence, whether ontological or sociological. In this age of heightened autonomy, we are perhaps
more inclined to speak about liberation as the deregulation
of law, which in turn provides the individual and society in
general with more rights and less restriction.

In the Church, liberation has become the catchword of an
influential theology--"Liberation Theology"--which attempts
to interpret God's involvement in reversing social (and less
often spiritual) evil. Actually, social justice and liberation are flip sides of a common agenda: justice is the
Church's and God's justifying action in the world. What is
not so clear, however, and what must be clear if the Church
is to use the liberation theologies in its mission to the
Third World, is how what is called "liberation" shaped by a
distinctively biblical understanding. This is made all the
more important by the Church's apparently easy appropriation
of secular models of liberation, which are then dressed up
in Christian rhetoric and promoted as "biblical" by the
Church.

In this part of the paper, I want to continue the work
done previously with social justice; jubilee, which is the
central prophetic idea for justice, means "release" or liberation. Justifying work accomplishes liberation from social and personal forms of evil which enslave. But what
form does such liberation take in the world? If the goal
of social justice is human liberation, should we not try to
mark out the specific promises (i.e., goals) of our reforms?
To the point, *a biblical definition of liberation will describe the PRODUCT of development, even as a biblical definition of social justice will describe its PROCESS.*

   Human Liberation According to Romans 5-8. In many ways,
Paul's letter to the Roman Church is, as Gunther Bornkamm
suggests, a "last will and testament," containing the preci-
pitates of all Paul's controversies, now past him.[27] One of
those controversies was about the nature of human liberation.
Indeed, it was a concern of fundamental importance for his
gentile mission, touching everything from household relationships to missionary strategies.[28] In fact, it could be
said that the question of human freedom lies behind the clos-
ing paraenesis (Romans 12-15:13) which illustrates the righteous life. For Paul, human liberation in its various contours
is the product of God's justifying action in human history;
it is the *historical demonstration of God's goodness* and it
is worked out in the life of the believing community.[29] To
be sure, Paul's concerns are religious and not social; right-
ousness is the character of life *for the believing community,*
and not for the world, which stands cursed by God (1:18-3:20).
However, there can be no question that for Paul the righteousness of the Church demonstrates God's grace before a watching
world. Further, as we read Romans as Scripture, Paul's gospel arms us with a promise for that world which extends from
spiritual to social spheres of human existence. In fact, the
Church's worship of God consists of its own life in the church
(12:3-16) and in the world (12:17-13:7). There is, then, a
politics of righteousness which bears the evidence of God's
justification and human liberation for all to see!

   It is in Romans 5-8 that Paul lays down the theological
description of human liberation; to this description we now
turn to erect a paradigm which should control how the Church
defines liberation and what it promises for development in
the Third World. Human liberation is demonstrated by *peace
with God* (Rom.5:1). In fact, this new relationship is experienced in two forms by human beings. First, our reconciliation with God reverses our interests in self and in a
world controlled by demonic powers, and causes us to "boast

in God" (5:2b, 11).[30] There are two perspectives to this
realignment: the existential perspective (*contra* Kasemann)
which breaks from more immediate forms of death (e.g., de-
pression, hopelessness, hatred, doubt-cynicism), and the
eschatological perspective which allows for a reinterpreta-
tion of reality in the sure light of God's final triumph over
evil. Paul says elsewhere (Phil. 4:4-7) that such peace results in joy. Second, peace with God allows humans to endure
life in the face of historical ambiguity and tribulation
(5:3-5)--God's justice in the face of demonic injustice.
Again, Paul is describing the product of a spiritual process;
however, fundamental to any paradigm of liberation must be
the promise of *freedom from* death (5:12-21), both now and at
the future Apocalypse.

The second demonstration of human liberation with history
is *human sinlessness* (chapter 6). The promise of *freedom
from sin* (6:1-11) interplays with the Christian duty to serve
the righteous interests of God (6:12-23) as slaves under the
aegis of God rather than the evil dominion. Social justice,
in fact all development rooted in social justice, promises a
pattern of life which rejects evil and embraces a holy life
(6:15-19).

The third demonstration of human liberation is *freedom
from legalism* (chapters 7-8). There is no question Paul
taught that an over-emphasis on *ethos* rather than *muthos*
(i.e. grace of God) promoted legalism and so prevented human
wholeness. Yet, more than any other element of his doctrine
of human liberation, this one is described in personal:inter-
nal terms (7:14-25).[31] How does the repudiation of legalism
serve the interests of a social paradigm!? The answer has
more to do with the Lordship of Christ than with the legalism
which comes by the Law (7:4-6). For Paul the antithesis between letter and Spirit is the same as between flesh and
Spirit. The reality of the risen Christ (vis. his Damascus
Road vision) takes the place of the Torah and makes righteous
the works which otherwise, even with a "holy, just and good"
Toray (7:12), would be cursed.[32] The moral frustrations
caused by legalism (7:14-25) only demonstrate God's curse
even as human sin (1:24-27) and social vice (1:28-31) do. The
real point, then, is not freedom from legalism but a human
life shaped by the Spirit (8:2), who produces spiritual fruit
(7:4; cf. Gal.5:22-23, Rom. 12:1-15:13); indeed, such *fruit
is profoundly ethical and social*. The lordship of the Spirit
manifests itself by the supernatural infusion of love and joy,
and kindness and self-control which continues to reverse evil
in human history (8:18-39).

Human Liberation According to James. Like Paul, James is concerned with how the community of faith demonstrates in history the mercies (i.e., grace) of God. Like Paul, the theology of James is profoundly eschatological, describing the dialectic of God's present and future salvation and judgment. Like Paul, James understands human liberation both in terms of the Church's response of love (2:1-11) and in terms of God's response of mercy (2:12-13). But there are differences between Paul and James even as there were between the gentile mission and Jerusalem (Gal. 2, Acts 15).

The history of interpreting James reflects its sharp disagreement with Paul.[33] Some have tried to harmonize the two, most often by imposing Pauline ideas upon James. Yet, this only does violence to James' intent and meaning. Others, like Luther, resist the authority of James because of its contradiction of Paul at critical points. Yet, this only does violence to the Church which recognizes the inspiration and authority of James as well as of Paul's letters. Perhaps again we are faced with another "essential polarity"!

James ties human liberation to the Church's obedience of Torah; it is the "law which liberates" (1:25; 2:12), and thus the believing community is to obey the whole law (2:10). James is against any notion which relates God's justifying mercy to a *sola fideism*: (2:24), which confesses orthodoxy (2:16, 19) but fails to enact orthopraxy (2:17, 20). For him, a religion based upon words is worthless (1:26; 2:14, 19a); the religion approved by God demonstrates God's mercy concretely and historically (1:27). In fact, God is unimpressed by social status (2:1); he is concerned rather with the poor who are oppressed by the wealthy (2:5-7; 1:9-11) and will judge harshly those who do not conform to his form of mercy (2:12-13; 5:1-6). It is Torah which enshrines God's mercy; thus, to obey Torah liberates people in accord with God's design for human liberation. Torah also serves God as his criterion to grant either the crown of life (1-12; cf. 2:12-13) or judgment (4:11-12; cf. Rom. 2:5-11)[34]; God's justification is for those who do the works which liberate humans in need. The difference between the demonic dominion (2:19b) and those in the kingdom of God is not orthodoxy but orthopraxy.

Thus, the idea of "faith" in the book of James comes to stand for a worthless religion of the mouth, consisting of confessions (2:19a) and good intentions (2:16), which mean well but fail to put into practice God's merciful commitment

to his creatures (3:9). His blessing will come to those who
quickly "hear" (i.e., obey) the Torah, because it liberates
those who are victims of injustice. Whereas in Paul's
thought, human liberation is the product of human faith and
God's grace, in the book of James human liberation is the
product of human obedience and God's grace; whereas in Paul,
God's justification is revealed in the life of the *believing*
community, for James, God's justification is revealed in the
life of the *obedient* community.

   Application to the Church's Engagement with the Developing
Third World. Some have tried to explain this polarity in
terms of the historical division between the Jewish and Gentile Churches; thus, James is written to correct the presence
of a gentile gospel (based upon Paul's preaching) within the
Jewish Church.[35] While I find some merit in these discussions, they tend to retain the polarity and resist any effort
to read the two together. Especially when we read both James
and the letters of Paul as *Scripture* (rather than as "books
of history"), both provide the authoritative crucible in which
Christian faith is shaped and understood. The *Sitz im Leben*
which counts most is the *canonical* one and not the historical
one.[36] In this light, it is again my suggestion that this
polarity be utilized as a self-correcting conversation through
which James corrects those tendencies in Paul while Paul
balances those tendencies in James which lead to an unproduc-
tive faith. Specifically, this is true in defining human
liberation according to the Scriptures. There are at least
two aspects of the canonical conversation between James and
Paul which are useful in building a thoroughly Christian definition of human liberation which in turn may serve the Church
as it seeks to liberate those who live in Third World nations.

   First, a biblical definition of human liberation emerges
from the *conversation between Pauline orthodoxy and Jamesian
orthopraxy.* There is a tendency for evangelicals to define
mission and development in exclusively evangelistic terms.
The statements coming out of the Lausanne Congress reflect
this bias.[37] Thus, human liberation results from faith in
Christ; development is the means to evangelize and evangelization is the means to development. Primary emphasis is placed
upon the liberation of souls more so than the liberation of
society. This emphasis is grounded in a Pauline formulation:
right faith yields good deeds; without justification there
can be no liberation. Justice, then, is understood only in
the shadow of justification. While this emphasis is thoroughly biblical, what often happens by this secondary concern for matters of social conscience and human liberation is

that such a concern is often put on the shelf as unimportant. What ultimately matters for the Church which emphasizes this agenda is whether people are being saved or how many are being baptized into Christian churches. A missiology which is concerned only with orthodoxy shapes a Church dangerously close to the one James rebukes as being worthless--a church concerned with confessions of faith rather than with actions of mercy.

James reminds us that the Church is called to be the agent of God's mercy in the world; even as Abraham was known by God for his hospitable deeds and called "his friend" (2:23) for that reason, so the Church demonstrates its relationship with our Lord by its primary concern for those who are poor and oppressed by the evil in society. For James, religious life is construed in terms of social responsibility; faith *is* deeds, evangelism *is* obedience to Torah, because God's Word is disclosed in a life which transmits his mercy to humanity concretely and historically. *The development of human resources within Third World nations requires, therefore, an orthopraxy of mercy as much as an orthodoxy of faith.* Programs for development should not consist of formulae which suggest that one results logically from the other; rather, each must be given its own integrity and importance. Likewise, missiology which consists only of an orthopraxy--a social gospel--fails in matters of faith and spiritual formation even as a missiology which consists only of an orthodoxy--a personal gospel--fails in matters of material compassion and societal formation. Both contours of the gospel are critical to fully form a human community.

Second, a definition of human liberation emerges from the *conversation between Pauline muthos and Jamesian ethos*.[38] Neither Paul nor James rejects the centrality of God's grace; their theologies reflect differing sides of the Gospel's center. For Paul, human liberation is the product of God's gracious action in Christ's atoning death; this is the *muthos*, the story of Christian faith which shapes our identity and our perceptions of reality. God is victor; Christ is Lord! Certainly James Sanders is correct when he argues that Paul's emphasis on "story" is a response to the overly legalistic status of later Judaism--a misdirected emphasis on human merit which reduced Torah to a set of regulations (oral and written). The net result of legalism is a form of agnosticism which portrays God as an absent landowner, who divides up the blessings after all the work is properly done. Of course, the potential for a Christian legalism is resident in the book

of James with its emphasis on a "works righteousness."
Paul's ethics (paraenesis) were more illustrative than
regulatory; his desire was to describe the pattern of grace
in the world in order to emphasize the good news which was
the power of God in human history.[39] Following Paul, human
liberation must be cast in the perspective of good news rather than bad news; it must be promised by words of hope and
encouraged by a theology of goodness. Indeed, the product
of social justice is thoroughly good for human life as all
products of God's grace must be. Further, Paul's attitude
toward the Law results from a religiosity and a missiology
whose concerns are theocentric rather than anthropocentric.
Human history is after all God's history, and the climax of
that history is Christ. Both story and law, haggadah and
halachah, are rooted in God's revelation in his Son and are
spiritually enforced by his Spirit (2 Cor.3:4-6).

This pneumatic dynamic which applies the norm of Christ
to the Church, however, is too easily lost to ambiguity and
individuality. Pauline ethics led the Church in a couple
of different directions--each direction judged by Paul himself to be a perversion of human liberation. In one direction, freedom was judged to be autonomous; there were no
rules and everything was permissible (1 Cor.5-10). The need
to control and limit--to define concretely and historically--
the nature of human liberation becomes Paul's concern after
his gospel is misinterpreted by the libertines in the
Church.[40] Further, his emphasis on knowing the "story" of
God's grace in Christ as the basis of Christian life was
taken up by the nascent gnostic religion and used to justify
a view of revelation which rejected the authority of the
apostolic word and its constraints on the Church. The indi-
vidualized *gnosis* became the basis for an individual's own
conceptions of faith and life.[41] In several letters (e.g.
Colossians, Pastorals), Paul takes great pains to root his
own gospel in the Lordship of Christ over *all* things (spiritual *and* material) and in a Church which shares its life
around such a gospel (Phil.1:3-11).

It is interesting to note that the New Testament canon
places a group of letters--called the "Catholic Letters"--
alongside of Paul's letters, and this group of Catholic Letters consists of the writings of those same Jerusalem "pil-
lars"-"James and Cephas and John" (Gal.2:9)--who were concerned with Paul's mission to the gentiles. It is clear from
Acts 15 that one of the concerns of the Jewish Church was
with Pauline ethics--his rejection of Mosaic regulations
(*ethos*) and his exclusive emphasis on Gospel (*muthos*). This

same conversation continues in the canon. James' emphasis is on the community's *ethos*, and there is a sense in which this emphasis balances Paul and even corrects an exclusive interest in Paul's gospel--something perhaps Paul himself would find beneficial! Human liberation needs the "form" of Torah to regulate and encourage *action* in the light of concrete needs. In this sense, the Paul and James polarity might be viewed in very much the same way the prophet and royal polarity is viewed: in terms of vision and revision, charisma and institution. Paul's charismatic vision (re: Damascus Road) too easily erodes into moral anarchy and re-ligious triumphalism; James revises Paul's vision by empha-sizing the religion's moral responsibility (Jam.1:27). Thus, human liberation is specified by rules (*ethos*) which insure the presence of God's mercy (*muthos*) in human history.

What I am calling for is what Paul Ramsey has called, "rule agapism": God's love and the love his people share with each other and for the world are always controlled by "rules of right conduct." Such rules emerge from reflection on both Scripture and the situation under scrutiny--the situ-ation of need. The Spirit works within the context of this dialectic to bring to light the "rules" (i.e., the concrete, specific actions of love) which liberate impoverished humans and which maintain their liberation. Notice my emphasis on *situation*; rules emerge only when there exists biblical *and* cultural exegesis. The Church must listen to its biblical scholars *and* its cultural anthropologists if these rules of human liberation are to be construed.[42] To the point, James' emphasis on the Church's *ethos* reminds us that human libera-tion must be specified; it cannot be left to good intentions or to confessions of trust.

A FINAL EXHORTATION

Two critical contexts exist within which the Church's self-understanding is shaped with respect to the Third World and its concerns for it. On the one hand, the community of faith is shaped by its on-going conversations with Scripture. It is there that it learns what it means to be the Church and to do as the Church ought. I trust that this paper provides some help for that conversation, fully recognizing that this is only one interpretation among many. The meditation upon Scripture must continue "day and night"! But on the other hand, the community of faith is shaped by its on-going con-versations with other professionals and agencies which are engaged in a common task--to develop the resources of the

Third World. Rather than uncritically denying the value of
what the non-Christian community is doing, we must participate with them in finding better ways to get our common task
accomplished. At the same time, however, the Church must
not be timid in recognizing and making clear its distinctive
and powerful role in reversing injustice and bringing human
liberation into history. The Spirit of God and the power of
his Kingdom is our possession! We must be convinced that
our perceptions of reality are indeed true ones because they
are from God who is truth; and we must be convinced that we
are empowered to act upon what we know is for God and for
his creation.[43]

ENDNOTES

1. Jim Wallis, *Agenda for Biblical People,* (New York: Harper and Row, 1976) pp. 47-50; I might add here two brief but important comments: First, the very nature and uniqueness of evangelicalism is contested at almost every point. While agreeing in principle, evangelical scholars often do not agree when it comes to *interpreting* those principles which determine faith. Even those fundamentals which lie at the heart of our common tradition--"saving faith," "biblical authority," "Lordship of Christ," "gospel preaching," etc.-- are given different content and importance by those different confessional and cultural heritages which comprise the evangelical Church. For this, see the forthcoming work by the British evangelical scholar, William J. Abraham, *Evangelicalism,* (London: Marshall, Morgen, & Scott, forthcoming). Second, because my own interpretation of these fundamentals of evangelical faith have been shaped with an heritage and an experience which differs from that of my readers, some may well disagree and wish to contest the conclusions this paper reaches as well as the methods this paper uses. Hopefully, such disagreements will not prevent a careful reading and honest dialogue with this contribution in the on-going discussion of what social justice and human liberation mean. Further, I would add that this contribution is limited by my own desire to say something fresh about these matters so critical to the program of the Church. I would encourage the reader to add to this paper by reading widely as she/he continues to shape his/her convictions about that it means to be a Christian and to do as a Christian ought.

2. For an interesting treatment of the interplay between Matthew's "Sermon on the Mount" (5-7) and Luke's "Sermon on the Plain" (6), see Eugene Lemcio, "The Gospels and Canonical Criticism," *BTB* XI (1981): pp. 117-119.

3. Stephen C. Mott, "Biblical Faith and the Reality of Social Evil,"*CSR* 9 (1980): 225:40 for an excellent summary of "systemic evil" from an evangelical point of view. Mott's larger work, *Biblical Ethics and Social Change* (New York: Oxford University Press, 1982), is, I think, the single most important work from an evangelical in *clarifying* both the socio-political character of evil as well as the corresponding socio-political character of redemption.

4. Christopher Lasch, *The Culture of Narcissism,* (New York: W.W.Norton, 1978).

5. Peter Berger, *The Sacred Canopy*, (New York: Doubleday, 1967).

6. See David Kelsey, *The Uses of Scripture in Recent Theology*, (Philadelphia: Fortress Press, 1975), who argues that the terms one uses in arguing for biblical authority are interrelated and attached to the way one understands revelation.

7. For an excellent introduction to this new discipline in biblical studies, see James A. Sanders, "The Bible as Canon," *CC* 98 (December 2, 1982): 1250-55.

8. Esp. "Adaptable to Life: the Nature and Function of Canon," in *Magnalia Dei: The Mighty Acts of God* (G. Ernest Wright *Festschrift*), ed. by F. M. Cross and W. E. Lembke, P. D. Miller, (Garden City, N.J.: Doubleday, 1976), pp. 531-60.

9. Walter Brueggemann, "Trajectories in OT Literature and the Sociology of Ancient Israel," *JBL* 98 (1979):161-85 for the correspondence between shifts in Israel's social structures and in its perceptions of the Covenant; see his *In Man We Trust*, (Atlanta: John Knox Press, 1972) for a rich treatment of wisdom and its relationship to the Davidic Covenant and royal theology.

10. There is a large and growing body of literature tracing this religious phenomenon in the Old Testament literature; one of the very best popular treatments of the subject is Brueggemann's, *The Prophetic Imagination*, (Philadelphia: Fortress Press, 1980). Also, R.B.Y. Scott, *Proverbs and Ecclesiastes*, AB (Garden City, N.J.: Doubleday, 1967) pp. xl-xlv.

11. James Barr, "The Bible as a Political Document," *BJRL* 62 (1980) pp. 268-89.

12. The jubilary motif is repeated and applied constantly in such journals as *Sojourners, Christianity and Crisis,* and *The Other Side;* Ronald Sider's book, *Rich Christians in an Age of Hunger,* (Downers Grove, Ill: IVP, 1977), which gained a wide hearing among evangelicals, is also responsible for introducing a wider audience to jubilary forms of socio-economic justice.

13. Robert North's monumental study, *Sociology of the Biblical Jubilee,* (Rome: Pontifical Biblical Institute, 1954), although finally prejudiced by a Roman Catholic ecclesiology, shows that elements of the Old Testament Jubilee became decisive in how later Judaism (and thus early Christianity) understood the kingdom of God and so eschatological Israel.

14. These are Claus Westermann's categories in *A Thousand Years and a Day,* (Philadelphia: Fortress Press, 1962).

15. So Robert B. Sloan, Jr., *The Favorable Year of the Lord,* (Austin, TX: Schola Press, 1977), who argues for the centrality of Jubilee in Luke's narrative of Jesus.

16. James A. Sanders, "From Isaiah 61 to Luke 4," in *Christianity, Judaism and Other Greco-Roman Cults* (Morton Smith *Festschrift*), ed. by Jacob Neusner, (Leiden: E.J.Brill, 1975), pp. 75-106.

17. This is the consensus of those scholars studying the wisdom literature during this century; so Bruce V. Malchow, "Social Justice in the Wisdom Literature," *BTB* XII (1982): 121; however, note Roland Murphy's caution, *The Forms of the Old Testament Literature: Wisdom,* (Grand Rapids: Eerdmans, 1981), p.3.

18. It should be noted here that the sages did not set forth (vis. "propaganda") an explicit pro-king agenda; rather, an elitist view of the world is reflected and applied generally to the audience; so, R. Gordis, "The Social Background of Wisdom Literature," *HebUA* 18 (1944): 77-118.

19. Malchow, 121.

20. Brueggemann, *In Man,* 14-17.

21. Perhaps the most important monograph in this regard is by Jack M. Suggs, *Wisdom, Christology, and Law in Matthew's Gospel*, (Cambridge, Mass: Harvard, 1970), who argues convincingly that the evangelist identifies Wisdom with Christ. While we do not have time to fully develop this matter, it might interest the reader to note Paul Minear's monograph, *To Heal and To Reveal: the Prophetic Vocation According to Luke,* (New York: Seabury Press, 1976), which recovers the prophetic trajectory within the synoptic tradition (esp. Luke). The sum of the matter is this: The same "essential polarity" between wisdom and prophetic found in the Hebrew Scriptures can also be recovered within the New Testament

gospels, and specifically in the revelation of God in Jesus. Jesus is the fulfillment both of wisdom and prophet, and so of this polarity. Of course, this means, then, that the Church must continue to incarnate the wisdom-prophetic conversation embodied by our Lord.

22. Bengt Holmberg has utilized (not uncritically, however) the sociology of authority developed by Max Weber in interpreting the development of Paul's view of authority from charismatic-apostolic to institutional. Without explicitly developing parallels, and without applying his conclusions to the Pastorals (which I found puzzling), Holmberg describes a theology of institution which is very much akin to the sapiential interpretation of society and authority.

23. Paul D. Hanson, *The Diversity of Scripture,* (Philadelphia: Fortress Press, 1982), pp. 18-36; the following draws heavily on Hanson's splendid work.

24. Cf. Hanson's treatment of "liberation movements" (essentially he treats only the feminist movement) for another interpretation-application of Scripture to the Third World.

25. See Henri Nouwen's critique of the American myth of "upward mobility"(including its concern for the "spectacular") in *Sojourners* 10 (June-August, 1981).

26. In Jim Wallis' new book, *The Call to Conversion,* New York: Harper and Row, 1981), the point is made that for true repentance, the Church must be converted to a *personal* identification with the poor as the way of finding a personal relationship with God.

27. Günther Bornkamm, "The Letter to the Romans as Paul's Last Will and Testament," in *The Romans Debate,* ed. by K.P. Donfried, (Minneapolis: Augsburg, 1977), pp. 17-31.

28. Note the various applications of freedom in Peter Richardson, *Paul's Ethic of Freedom,* (Philadelphia: Westminster Press, 1979).

29. Ernst Käsemann, *Commentary on Romans,* (Grand Rapids: Eerdmans, 1980), p. 131.

30. Esp. Ralph Martin, *Reconciliation: A Study of Paul's Theology,* (Atlanta: John Knox Press, 1981) for the existential-personal account of Paul's doctrine of reconciliation.

31. Cf. Robert Gundry, "The Moral Frustration of Paul Before His Conversion: Sexual Lust in Romans 7:7-25", in *Pauline Studies* (F.F.Bruce *Festschrift*), ed. by D.A.Hagner and M.J.Harris, (Grand Rapids: Eerdmans, 1980), pp. 228-45.

32. Käsemann, p. 191.

33. The literature is enormous; cf. Dibelius' important discussion in his commentary, *James*, Hermeneia, (Philadelphia: Fortress Press, 1976), pp. 174-80; also Peter David's recent commentary, *James*, NIGTC, (Grand Rapids: Eeerdmans, 1982) 127-34; and C. Burchard's individualistic, "Zu Jakobus 2:14-26", *ZNW* 71 (1980): 27-45.

34. William Dyrness, "Mercy Triumphs Over Justice: James 2:13 and the Theology of Faith and Works," *Them* 16 (1981): 11-16.

35. James Dunn, *Unity and Diversity in the New Testament,* (Philadelphia: Westminster Press, 1977), pp. 251-57, et al.

36. See Dunn's programmatic article, "Levels of Canonical Authority," *HorBT* 4 (1982): 13-60, which argues for the primacy of the *canonical* form of traditions.

37. Darrell Whiteman, "Special Report on COWE", *Catalyst* 10 (1980): 284-87 for this criticism.

38. James A. Sanders, "Torah and Paul," in *God's Christ and His People* (Nils Dahl *Festschrift*), ed. by J. Jervell and W.A.Meeks, (Oslo: Universitetsforlaget, 1977), pp. 132-40 for the ideas of *muthos* and *ethos* in Pauline literature.

39. Ernst Käsemann, "Worship in Everyday Life; a Note on Romans 12," in *NTQ*, (Philadelphia: Fortress Press, 1969), pp. 188-95.

40. For this thesis see John Drane, *Paul: Libertine or Legalist?* (London: SPCK, 1975), pp. 61-71; 95-108. I perhaps would not be so inclined to see the Corinthian opponents as nascent gnostics as Drane does; however, the general line of his argument is quite helpful.

41. For the nature of the gnostics' "revelation-tradition", see Birger Pearson's helpful summary in his monograph, *The Pneumatikos-Psychikos Terminology,* SBLDS, (Missoula, Mt: Scholars Press, 1973), pp. 2-6 (and endnotes on pp. 87-9).

42. For a missiology which marries critical anthropology
and evangelical biblical studies, see Charles Kraft's superb
article, "Can Anthropological Insight Assist Evangelical
Theology?", *CSR* VII (1977): 165-202.

43. I received Chris Sugden's most helpful response to an
earlier draft of this article too late to include in this
final form. Of many excellent and necessary suggestions,
one deserves mention here if only as a final endnote. Sugden
says, "A Christian plan for the world church to participate
as a global body to achieve justice in every place...need(s)
the insights and encouragement and even rebukes of the brothers from the Two Thirds World to address some of the injustices and brokenness in their society which they (i.e. Christians from North America and Europe) may be blind to. Those
from nations which in former decades have been overtly imperialistic, and continue to be so in more covert forms today, need to learn in partnership with people from Two Thirds
World nations how the resources of the west may be most accep-
tably received and shared by those struggling for Christ's
kingdom in the economically poorer nations of the world."

THE LOCAL
CHURCH AND
DEVELOPMENT

Purpose. The purpose of this paper is to examine what development is in the local church in relationship to the passage "And Jesus kept increasing in wisdom and stature, and in favor with God and men" (Luke 2:52).

Introduction. There is, I believe, a connection between the development of Jesus as a person and His fulfilling the purpose for which God sent Him into the world. If Jesus is our model, certainly His development sets a model for the development of men, and enables us to fulfill the purposes for which God sends us into the world.

Development Towards a Purpose. God's purpose for Jesus was related to the Kingdom. Jesus' chief message was the Kingdom of God. His life was a foretaste of the Kingdom. Jesus died and rose again that we could share in the Kingdom. Jesus is advancing His Kingdom through His church. Therefore in biblically based development we are working for the present and future purposes of God.

A Unified Definition of Development. We will define development as every biblically based activity of the Body of Christ which brings men to complete reconciliation with God, one another, and His environment.

Implications for the Local Church. Development is the mission of the local church and needs to be balanced with the other areas of mission in holistic ministry.

Steps of Application. The following steps are suggested for the local church:

(1) Develop a sound understanding of holistic ministry.

(2) Examine the assumptions and practices of the church's mission activity in holistic mission.

(3) Examine assumptions and practices in relation to balanced ministry of denominational boards, mission societies and relief and development agencies.

(4) Initiate programs to enable Christian organizations to minister more holistically where that is appropriate.

A *Global Development Strategy for the Local Church*. I am arguing for the direct involvement of laity in the mission of the church. I would like to suggest two models of direct involvement. (1) The first is a partnership model between a local church in the Third World and a local church in North America. (2) The second is a possible relationship between families in the Third World and families in North America. This reciprocal partnering is intended to help both groups complete their mission and start a development project together in the community of need. Through partnership, the church can complete both the mandate of the Great Commission and the Great Commandment.

BOB MOFFITT is founder of HARVEST, a Christian organization acting as a broker between churches in the United States and churches overseas, enabling them to partner together in Christian development.

THE LOCAL CHURCH AND DEVELOPMENT

Bob Moffitt

This paper is written to the local, evangelical church in the West. Many of the principles discussed in this paper are applicable to the local church in the Third World and local churches of non-evangelical persuasions, but the emphasis, the examples, and many of the problems for which I try to provide helpful responses are those in this, the church of my spiritual heritage. Some of what I say will sting, yet I write this paper with a sense of deep appreciation and love for a branch of the Body of Christ which I deeply desire to see reach its maximum impact for both the present and the coming Kingdom of our God.

A second note. The words "development" and "mission" are used interchangeably--especially after the first section where I try to show why I believe they are one and the same.

WHAT IS DEVELOPMENT?

Development from Dr. Luke's Perspective

A close friend recently directed me to a little noticed verse of Luke that has become full of meaning and implications as I have struggled with the meaning of development. "And Jesus kept increasing in wisdom and stature, and in favor with God and men." Luke 2:52. I think this verse is an excellent place to begin an understanding of biblical development. I think this for several reasons. First, this verse talks about the development of a model person--the person Jesus. How Jesus grew, how He developed is at the very least instructive.

Second, God had a purpose for Jesus to fulfill. There is an obvious connection between the development of Jesus as a person and his fulfilling the purpose for which God sent Him into the world. If Jesus is our model, certainly His development sets a model for the development of men if they are also to fulfill the purposes for which God put us here.

Third, as we consider the development of communities of men and then of societies, we must consider the development of their primary units--the individual persons of whom communities and societies are composed. Jesus was an individual person. He lived in a family, in a community, and in a society. God's plan for Jesus' development as an individual would not be inconsistent with His plans for the development of Jesus' family, community or society.

I don't know if Dr. Luke meant to be exhaustive in his listing of the areas in which Jesus developed. But as I study Luke's list, it appears to be inclusive. Luke mentions four areas in which Jesus developed: 1) wisdom, 2) stature, 3) favor with God and 4) favor with man. If we were to translate these four areas into contemporary equivalents, we might say the four areas of Jesus' development listed by Luke are: 1) mental development, 2) physical development, 3) spiritual development, and 4) social development.

Jesus' Development Covers Human Development

As I examine these four categories, I have difficulty thinking of any human need not covered. The need to observe, remember, integrate, analyze and make wise decisions is covered under mental development - wisdom. Physical needs like food, shelter, exercise, a healthy physical environment, etc., are covered by physical development - stature. The need to develop, nurture, and maintain a vertical relationship with our Creator is covered under spiritual development with God. And, the need to develop, nurture and maintain horizontal relationships with other individuals and groups of individuals is covered under social development - favor with man.

This list is by no means meant to be an exhaustive accounting of human need but is presented to illustrate that much, if not all, human need can be accounted for under Luke's four broad developmental categories. If, in guiding Luke's pen, the Holy Spirit meant to cover all areas of human development, as Luke described Jesus' growth, we definitely have a biblical basis for looking at development. If not, the list still appears to be a very workable outline.

Development Towards a Purpose

Just as Luke's concern was Jesus' development toward God's purpose for Him, our concern is man's development toward God's purpose for us as men.

God's purpose for Jesus was Kingdom related. Jesus' principal message was the Kingdom of God. His life was a foretaste of the Kingdom. By looking at Jesus we have a much clearer picture than we do in any other of God's interventions into human history of what the Kingdom of God is about, what it is like. Jesus died and rose so that men can share in that Kingdom. And now, through individual believers and through His church, Jesus is advancing God's Kingdom and moving it toward its fulfillment.

God's purpose for man is Kingdom related. The loved but archaic Westminster Confession helps us remember God's purpose for man is to be part of and to have a part in God's Kingdom. Scripture tells us that ultimately God's purpose is that man

> "...will be rescued from the tyranny of change and decay, and have *his* (my emphasis) share in that magnificent liberty which can only belong to the children of God!" (Rom. 8:21, Phillips)

It is ultimately that

"...God has his dwelling among men! He will dwell among them and they shall be His people, and God himself will be with them. He will wipe every tear from their eyes; there shall be an end to death, and to mourning and crying and pain; for the older order has passed away! Then He who sat on the throne said, 'Behold! I am making all things new!'" (Rev. 21:3-5, NEB)

But what about the intervening time? Scripture describes God's purpose for man by telling us that it is that he love and honor his Creator.

"And He said unto him, 'You shall love the Lord your God with all your heart, and with all your soul, and with all your mind!' This is the great and foremost commandment!" (Matt. 22:37, ASV)

God's purpose is that redeemed men demonstrate, as Jesus did, the wonderful nature of God's plans for man's future.

"By this all men will know that you are My disciples, if you have love for one another." (John 13:35, ASV) "There is neither Jew nor Greek, there is neither slave nor free man, there is neither male nor female; for you are all one in Christ Jesus." (Gal. 3:28, ASV) "This is pure and undefiled religion in the sight of our God and Father, to visit orphans and widows in their distress, and to keep oneself unstained by the world." (James 1:27, ASV)
        "Is this not the fast which I chose,
        To loosen the bonds of the wickedness,
        To undo the bands of the yoke,
        And to let the oppressed go free,
        And to break every yoke?
        Is it not to divide your bread with the hungry,
        And bring the homeless poor into the house;
        When you see the naked, to cover him;
        And not to hide yourself from your own flesh?"
                            (Is. 58:6,7, ASV)

God's purpose is that redeemed men tell unredeemed men the good news about and recruit them into the Kingdom of God.

...."And He said to them, 'Go into all the world and preach the gospel to all creation.'" (Mark 16:15, ASV)

"Go therefore and make disciples of all nations, baptizing
them in the name of the Father and the Son and the Holy
Spirit, teaching them to observe all that I commanded you,
and lo, I am with you always even to the end of the age."
(Matt. 28:19-20, ASV)

If these are the purposes of God for man, then in a broad
sense, growth into God's purpose is the highest view of human
development. If we accept this perspective, biblically based
development would be any movement of individual men or groups
of men, in the mental, physical, spiritual and social arenas,
toward God's present and future purposes for man.

The Secular View Is Limited

For those familiar with contemporary theories of development, it will be immediately recognized that this definition
goes beyond the more commonly held view in which the focus of
development is primarily of material and social concern. It
is understandable that secular development agencies such as
CARE, USAID, and OXFAM have this more limited perspective.
(See DEVELOPMENT: ITS SECULAR PAST AND ITS UNCERTAIN FUTURE
by Tom Sine. (Paper, Pub. World Evangelical Fellowship, March
1980.) (See Footnote I.)

It is natural, then, that secular development agencies would
feel that material and social development are sufficient in
and of themselves to bring mankind to the attainment of his
secular ends.

A Christian Heresy--A Dichotomized Perspective

The Church, of course, cannot stop there. In part it has
not. Yet it has been influenced by Enlightenment thinking.
Western Christians understand man's need for growth in physical, social and spiritual areas, but they have accommodated
the influence of the Enlightenment by often separating physical and social development from spiritual. Unfortunately,
this dichotomy is not limited to the church in the West. Third
World churches have been influenced by Western missions even
when a dichotomized perspective thinking is not indigenous.

This dualism is heresy. It is heresy because it creates
and supports a dichotomy which is patently not biblical. Jesus, the Prophets, the Apostles, and other writers of Scripture do not separate man's developmental needs in this dualistic sense. Jesus' answer to the question, "Teacher, which

is the great commandment in the Law?" (Matt. 22:36) tells us
that man's completeness is found in responding to spiritual,
social and physical needs--together. The prophet Isaiah ties
man's relationship to God and his response to human need
tightly together in the 58th chapter of Isaiah. The Apostle
James, probably the most pointed of biblical writers in integrating the physical and spiritual, says "Faith, if it has no
works,is dead." (James 2:17) It is safe to say that the Bible
not only integrates what the Enlightenment separates, but it
does not make room for a "Christian dualism" in which all the
elements are there but separated.

Another consequence of Christian dualism is the division
it creates in the ministry-arms of the Church. It permits
churches and missions agencies, sometimes smugly, to see their
calling as either relief and development--ministry to physical
and social need, or as evangelism and discipleship--ministry
to spiritual need. It underlies the great debate between
liberal and conservative churches over the social gospel. It
encourages the sin of pride in Christian liberals who are involved in a primary ministry to physical needs. They look
down their noses at conservative Christians who focus on
evangelism. Vice versa, Christians of a conservative persua-
sion have for decades criticized liberals who minister to
physical needs but pay little attention to evangelism. This
division leads to lack of cooperation, poor communication and
name calling. We all have witnessed those on both sides doubt-
ing the authenticity of the faith of those in the other camp.

At the very least, the consequences of a dualistic view
are not complimentary to the mission of the Church. At the
worst, men and women are turned away from God's purposes for
their development and the Kingdom of God is both diminished
and discredited.

A *Unified Definition of Development*

Our definition of development then must unite what the
Enlightenment helped and many churches continue to separate.
Therefore, we will define development as every *biblically
based activity of the Body of Christ, His Church, which assists in bringing men toward the place of complete reconciliation with God and complete reconciliation with his fellow and
his environment.*

"And we proclaim Him, admonishing every man and teaching
every man with all wisdom, that we may present every man

complete in Christ" (Col. 1:28) and "Until we all attain
to the unity of the faith, and of the knowledge of the Son
of God, to a mature man, to the measure of the stature
which belongs to the fulness of Christ." (Eph. 4:13).

Activities which produce this reconciliation include the
whole range of spiritual, social and physical ministries, including specific ministry areas like evangelism, discipleship,
literacy, medicine, community health, community development,
relief, agriculture, church planting, worship, etc.

Different Emphasis But Equal Importance

Consistent with the biblical teaching on gifts and on
different responsibilities for separate members of the body
(I Cor. 12), God does call different individuals and organizations to minister with emphasis in one or more specific
areas of development--of mission. But that emphasis is to be
seen as an essential part of--not as better or more important
than another facet of ministry. Further, one aspect of
ministry, such as evangelism, is not meant to stand alone.
Unless a given ministry emphasis fits into a plan for complete growth--unless men can be helped to develop in all
areas of God's purposes for them, growth will be lopsided,
incomplete--even abortive. (See Footnote 2)

IMPLICATIONS FOR THE LOCAL CHURCH

Development Is the Church's Mission

What are the implications of this definition of development for the local church? First: it is that development as
we have defined it, *is* the mission of the local church. It
is a biblical mandate to balanced ministry to all of man's
needs. It is nothing less than the obedient response of the
church to both the Great Commandment and the Great Commission.
Together the Great Commandment and the Great Commission present a view of individual followers of Jesus and the church
ministering to the entire spectrum--the whole range of human
need. It is a view of holistic ministry.

The second part of the Great Commandment focuses both on
a relationship to our neighbor--a relationship to our neighbor in whatever way *we* would wish to be related or ministered
to. We tend to think of this relationship to our neighbor as
focusing on physical needs. But the implication of the Great
Commandment is that we must serve all--the entire spectrum of
our neighbor's needs--including spiritual needs.

Further, we generally think of the Great Commission as instructing us to share the content of the good news of the Kingdom of God--a spiritual ministry. However, the Great Commission definitely implies a mandate of service to the social and physical needs of man. "Teaching them *all* things that I have commanded you."

Though the Great Commandment and the Great Commission have traditionally been viewed by the evangelical church as focusing on physical and spiritual ministries respectively, they both imply, if they do not speak directly to, a balanced ministry to the entire spectrum of man's needs. (See "Christian Missions in the Modern World" by John Stott, Pp. 20-30. Pub. InterVarsity Press, 1975.)

Not A Limited Calling

Why make so much of the balance in each of the biblical directives? Because individual Christians and churches often act as if they believe their calling to be either a ministry to spiritual need, *or* a ministry to social need. They see themselves as Great Commission Christians *or* Great Commandment Christians. This observation is not based so much on what Christians say their calling or mandate is, as what their *actions* demonstrate. Even if it were admissible that a calling could be to one mandate or to the other, a proper understanding of either would not permit an exclusive focus on spiritual or social ministry.

Disobedience to the Mandates Leads to Serious Consequences.

The consequences of disobedience to these mandates is frightening. Further, the consequence of disobedience to the spiritual ministry mandate and to the physical/social ministry is different. For example: when Paul was addressing the elders of the church at Ephesus, (Acts 20:24-37) he says that because he has been faithful in sharing the gospel of the grace of God (obedient to the Great Commission) he is innocent of the blood of all men.

Paul was given a commission to preach the gospel, the whole gospel. The church then and today has that same commission. If Paul had disobeyed his commission, he would have been guilty of the blood of those to whom God led him but to whom he did not share the gospel. If the church or individual Christians disobey this commission, they too will be guilty of the blood of those to and with whom they do not share. We are not responsible for the consequences of sharing the gospel, but we are responsible for sharing.

But what if we are not obedient in ministering to the social and physical needs of men? The consequences are different and at a personal level substantially more grave. James says that faith without works is dead (James 2:17). Several times in the 14th chapter of John, Jesus said that to be his disciples is to keep his commandments.

"He who believes in Me, the works that I do shall he do also." (John 14:12) "If you love Me, you will keep My commandments." (John 14:14) "He who has my commandments and keeps them, he it, is who loves me." (John 14:21)

All through the Gospels Jesus relates belonging to Him to obeying Him. Perhaps one of the most convicting passages is Jesus' message in Luke 6:20-49. Jesus goes into detail about kingdom ethics and behavior. He tells us how we are to relate to and serve our fellow man. He then concludes with an illustration of a man who hears and obeys and a man who hears but does not obey. The prognosis for the man who does not obey is disaster.

These passages deal with the disciples' responsibility in horizontal relationships--responsibilities in the social and physical arenas.

I do not think it is stretching scripture to say that lack of obedience in the area of social and physical ministry calls into question the very existence of a vertical relationship with God. Could we even say that it may be possible to be a Christian and neglect spiritual ministry (e.g. evangelism) but not possible to be a Christian and neglect social and physical ministry? I will not try to answer this question but its consideration should be sobering--especially to evangelical churches who seem to sometimes minister exclusively to spiritual needs. (See Footnote III.)

Ministry Can Be Focused But Not Exclusive.

If we agree that scripture is clear that the individual Christian does not have an option of *exclusive* ministry to a particular developmental need or ministry focus, then by implication I believe the same is true for the local church or para church agency.

The key word in this statement is "exclusive." God gives
individuals, organizations and local churches, different
gifts, different opportunities of service. This is clear from
Paul's teaching on gifts--separate ministries for different
members of the Body of Christ. (Romans 12, I Cor. 12:4-8).
Even though a local church may be called by virtue of gifts,
opportunity and/or calling to an emphasis of mission to one
or more specific categories of service, it is not exempt from
obedience, at least in the broad sense, to either area of
ministry.

For example, I believe God has gifted and called me to a
primary focus of ministry to social and physical needs. Further, I feel quite awkward in some areas of spiritual ministry.
I get tongue tied and hyperventilate when I am involved in personal evangelism. But I am not exempt from obedience to the
spiritual ministry implications of the Great Commission. Every
opportunity God gives me, through my ministry of gift and calling, to share the content of the Gospel must be bought up. And,
if I am personally unable to spiritually minister because of a
language barrier or some other obstacle, I have the obligation,
out of obedience, to do whatever is reasonable (e.g. arrange
for an interpreter) to insure that the Gospel is communicated.

The same is true in a spiritual ministry orientation. For
example, if God has called a local church, individual or organization to a primary ministry of evangelism, that church or individual or organization must buy up all the opportunities,
either directly or in collaboration with others, to minister to
the social and physical needs of those being evangelized.

A church called to evangelism is not exempt from the Great
Commandment, as is clearly implied by the story of the Good
Samaritan. (Luke 10:30-37) The priest and the Levite (church-
men) were likely busy with spiritual ministries. Jesus condemned them because they acted as though they were exempt from
ministry to physical needs.

Steps of Application

How can this balance be applied to the local church? I
suggest at least six initial steps.

1) Develop a sound *understanding* of *and* and *teaching*
about the biblical principles of a balanced ministry.

2) *Examine the assumptions and practices of the church's*
past and present missions *activity* for a balanced ministry.

3) *Examine assumptions and practices* in relation to
balanced ministry of *denominational mission boards, mission
societies or relief and development agencies* which the local
church supports or with which the local church cooperates.
For example, don't take for granted that the relief and development organization your church supports also has a passion to see its work integrally tied to evangelism and discipleship. Check it out. If it doesn't, stop supporting it
and tell why. Are the church's missionaries or evangelistic
organizations your church supports making sure that their efforts are related to mental, physical and social deveopment?
Check it out! If they are not, stop supporting them and tell
them why.

It is not good enough that the local church supports an
evangelistic mission here and a relief mission there. To be
biblically sound, specialized ministries should, whenever
possible, be directly related to services which cover *all*
basic areas of development: mental, physical, spiritual and
social.

4) If the local church's development activities and/or
relationships with missionaries, agencies, societies, etc.,
are not consistent with biblical principles of balanced ministry, *initiate a plan to correct the activities and relationships which are inconsistent with biblical teaching.* If
those individuals or agencies being supported by the local
church are not willing to change, then adjustment of the local church's support for them is in order. It is probably
unrealistic to expect that your church's admonition to change
will be heeded--especially if you are dealing with an independent agency. It is probably more efficient to withdraw support with a clear explanation of why. Also, don't take a
simple answer of "yes, we are committed to balanced ministry."
Ask for documentation. If you don't get it, balanced ministry
probably isn't happening.

5) *Make sure that your church's ministry emphasis comple-
ments and/or fits into a total development strategy.* Your
church may not be able to change outside agencies, but it
should be able to correct itself.

6) *Remember that the objective of all missions is to
minister to men in such a way that they will develop in every
area of God's purpose for them.*

A GLOBAL DEVELOPMENT (MISSIONS) STRATEGY
FOR THE LOCAL CHURCH

In the last section of this paper I have tried to demonstrate that the local church does not have the option of choosing, in an exclusive sense, which developmental area it will invest in. The church has a non-optional mandate to be involved in all mission or development areas.

We have categorized these ministry areas as mental development, physical development, spiritual development and social development. Though I will not attempt to support the proposition here, I believe there is a further but geographic implication for ministry in Jesus' statement to the apostles in Acts 1:8, "and you shall be My witnesses both in Jerusalem, and in all Judea and Samaria, and even to the remotest part of the earth." Is it not consistent that, to the degree possible, the Lord would have the local expresssion of His church demonstrate God's geographically balanced or global concern for man? If so, each local church--especially affluent Western churches --can have its "Jerusalem," and its "Judea," its "Samaria"and its "remotest part of the earth."

Of course most local churches, even the local mega-churches of our era, cannot simultaneously engage in all developmental ministries in all parts of the earth. But in some significant way, I believe that the local church, if it can, *should* be engaged in *all* major categories of mission, *and* in parts of the world that represent their respective church's Jerusalem, Judea, Samaria and remotest part of the earth. It is not consistent that any other plan would represent the heart and compassion of our Lord. It is a big order, but it is not an impossible one.

Many local churches do attempt to reflect this global and mission perspective. For example:

1) The church ministers in its home community, its "Jerusalem." Most of the church's resources are targeted here.

2) The church ministers, through missionaries or mission agencies, to people of other countries. The types of ministry usually express the orientation of the local church. This ministry represents the local church's "remotest part of the earth." The largest portion of "missions" resources is usually invested here--yet it is often a paltry sum when compared to the resources spent at home.

3) The church ministers to areas near home, like the inner city, or to the American Indians, or to migrants or refugees. This represents the local church's "Judea and Samaria." Probably the smallest amount overall of resources is invested here.

A Litany of Problems

This strategy has some positive elements. But often the manner in which it is carried out leaves much to be desired. The strategy has several and some serious problems. I see the major problems as follows:

1) There is skimpy awareness of either the biblical nature of or the mandate for balanced ministry.

2) The investment of local church resources in global missions, including "Jerusalem" but especially in "Judea, Samaria, and the remotest parts of the earth," is uninformed, haphazard and more than likely not the best investment that could be made.

3) Ministry, especially in areas away from home, is often a response to the easiest way out. Instead of getting directly involved, others--missionaries, relief and development agencies--are "hired" to do the work on behalf of the church. The ministry is vicarious. This is true even when it is possible and potentially more effective and rewarding, both for the local church and for those being ministered to, for the local church to be directly involved.

4) There is very little accountability between the church and those who represent the church in its missions programs. The local church is often so ill informed that even if it knew the facts of problems on the field, it would not know how to evaluate and/or respond to them.

5) There is very little personal contact between the local church members and the church's missions representatives (missionaries or mission agencies), let alone between the church members and the people being ministered to. In my home church, for example, there are more than twenty missionaries' names on the back of our weekly bulletin. There is no possible way that I or my family can really know or have personal relationships with all these missionaries. Yet we are supposed to be intelligently praying for our missionaries! Every year at the annual missions conference the membership gets a guilt complex because it hasn't been faithful in letter writing, intercession, support, etc! How can it! It is difficult enough to

keep up with the eleven couples in our fellowship group who get together every Friday night.

6) Support for missions programs is primarily financial. Occasionally an individual or a couple of a given local church will sense the call of God and go into full time missions. But when they do, the local church rarely underwrites the majority of their support. Further, because support is primarily financial, the membership gets the feeling that the appropriate response to the mandate of the Great Commandment and the Great Commission is to throw money at the problem.

7) Support for missions is shotgun rather than rifled. It is broadcast in insignificant amounts to many different targets rather than being focused in a few areas with enough investment to both make a difference and to encourage accountability.

8) Mission agencies, relief and development agencies, denominational mission boards, etc., often inhibit genuine accountability and meaningful personal relationship between the local church and the mission endeavor. Because they are the experts and offer their services, (and some denominational groups demand that their services be used) the local church sees little need to develop its own expertise and/or global missions strategy.

9) It is not clear that a biblical basis exists for parallel mission structures, such as mission boards and relief and development agencies, which do missions and/or development on behalf of the church. There is evidence, however, of people-to-people and church-to-church missions or development activities. II Cor. 4:18.

10) Missions in the local church is often the responsibility of a missions committee instead of the entire church. Instead of being a catalyst to involve the entire congregation in missions activity or serving as a spring of encouragement, ideas and energy, the missions committee is a bottle-neck.

11) Missions are viewed by church leadership, often including the pastor, as secondary, as a threat to meeting the need for new choir robes, the new building program, staff salaries, etc.

12) According to scripture, we are the first fruits (James 1:18) of the Kingdom of God--an inviting demonstration

of God's plan for the future. One of the most appealing
dimensions of the Kingdom in a world split by national economic and racial enmities is that in Christ we become one. There
are exciting possibilities of getting significant numbers of
members of the local church directly involved in partnership
ministries with believers of local churches in the Third World,
or in the local churches in "Judea." This direct demonstration
of oneness is both exciting and powerful as a witness to the
reality of the Kingdom. But with the one-way funnel effect
of traditional mission structures, this possibility is severely diminished.

A Problem of Delegation

One way the local church can seek for solutions to this
litany of concerns is to design structures to solve each problem. This strategy, however, tends to deal with the symptoms
rather than the root of the problem. All of the problems
listed above are related, some more closely than others, to
an overall spiritual problem that pervades, not just the local
church in the West, but the whole of our Western industrialized
societies. If we focus on correcting this root problem, many
of the problems addressed above will tend to solve themselves.

What is this spiritual problem? It is the tendency to
delegate our responsibility for ministry to others. It is the
tendency to "let George do it." It is the tendency to hire a
"professional" to take responsibility that belongs to the corporate body of individuals doing the hiring. In complex industrialized societies we have an unholy respect for the wisdom of the service professional: the preacher, the social
worker, the counselor, the probation officer, the mental health
worker, the missionary, the development worker, etc. We have
an unfounded belief, or if not belief--hope, that professionals
can solve our spiritual and social problems. Yes, professionals should and generally do have greater knowledge and technical expertise than laymen. Though knowledge and expertise
are needed to solve problems, wisdom is more important in spiritual and social problem solving than either knowledge or
technical expertise. Wisdom is not any more the birthright of
the professional than it is the birthright of the layman. (See
Footnote IV).

I believe that professionals, including pastors and missionaries and development workers, other than as an individual
part of the human community, never have been able to, nor will

they in the future be able to provide solutions to human problems--including the problem of mobilizing the local church for its mandate of world mission. (See Footnote V)

A New Role for the Professional

The primary responsibility for being the "light of the world," the "salt of the earth," "the firstfruits of the Kingdom" has been delegated to professionals rather than kept where it belongs--in the laity. The solution is not to get rid of the professional. It is to first change the role of the professional from implementor to teacher, to coach, to catalyst, to facilitator, to encourager. Second, it is to insist that the laity, as much as is possible, take responsibility for direct ministry.

The task is complex. There are many sharks in the water and they are hungry. Untrained and poorly guided laity will not only get hurt themselves, but their mistakes can and will discourage others who also would otherwise engage in the difficult task of direct ministry. It is not that professionals are not needed. They are. Far more can be accomplished, however, if professionals are primarily enablers and not doers.

This is not a new idea. Jesus spent almost three years teaching twelve men to minister. He taught by example. He taught well enough that after three years he was able to send eleven of them out into direct ministry--to carry on the work he started. (John 20:21) At first, Jesus provided the model of ministry. Then after an adequate period of training, he commissioned *them* to carry out the direct ministry. When he commissioned them, he didn't abandon them. He continued to be available for teaching, leadership, encouragement, facilitation, and comfort--through the Holy Spirit.

Paul understood this principle. He told Timothy, "And the things which you have heard from me in the presence of many witnesses, these entrust to faithful men, who will be able to teach others also." (II Tim. 2:2) Paul went from community to community, teaching, preparing, establishing and then moving on. But in the moving on he continued to encourag to teach, to facilitate--but he did *not* often get reinvolved in direct ministry in these communities. Now that he had done the spade work, he could leave it to faithful men who would carry on the task. Then he was free to move on to new areas and begin again.

Why should the pattern be any different with the local church today? If we will be satisfied with a state of static, then let's continue the way we are. But if the local church is to be dynamic in its "Jerusalem," its "Judea," and its "remotest part of the earth," then we have got to use the same pattern Jesus used to establish a beachhead for the Kingdom and the same pattern which Paul used to plant churches.

A Strategy for Direct Involvement on a Global Level

The principle I am arguing for is *the most direct involvement of laity in ministry as is possible*. It is the laity's birthright. But that birthright has been both *taken* away by the professionalism of our society and *given* away by the willingness of laity to let someone else care for the problems that are rightfully theirs.

It is easier to see how direct involvement can work for ministries in "Jerusalem" and perhaps in "Judea" and "Samaria" than it is to see how it can work in the "remotest part of the earth." Let me suggest how. The model I will develop here has a focus on world missions, but the principles can be used for developing a strategy for mobilizing the local church for other areas of mission.

Church Leadership Makes:

1) *Preliminary decision to directly involve the laity of the local church in the implementation of the church's global mission.*
   * decide from reading this paper and exposure to other similar challenges.
   * decide from confirmation by the Holy Spirit that this is a direction church leadership should explore.

2) Church selects individual(s) to lead related research/planning effort.

3) *Selected leadership engages in research/study program*
   *Conduct inductive study of the scriptures in relation to the missions mandate of the church.
   * Review and analyze relevant literature from missions agencies, boards, etc. (Most missions organizations will be biased toward more traditional missions implementation strategies, but, when requesting information, explain your interest and intentions. There are often forward thinking professionals in these organizations who can be of great help in directing you to relevant materials.)

* *Enroll in short mission training courses* such as those offered by Missionary Internship Training Program of Farmington, Michigan, or the U.S. Center for World Missions in Pasadena, California. (Focus course work on practical, hands-on, rather than theoretical curricula.)

4) *Design a study program for church membership on basis of above research/study.*
* A survey of training materials for local churches is currently being conducted in conjunction with Wheaton '83.
* On the basis of Step #3 and consultation from mission and educational consultants (get them free: they can volunteer!) put together study materials of a survey nature.
* At a minimum, try to include the following content areas:
- Inductive Bible study of the believers' global mandate for balanced missions.
- Cross cultural communication.
- Inductive Bible study of development.
- Review of biblically sound development case studies.
* Each content area should be at least 2, but no more than 4 one to two hour sessions.
* As much as possible make studies practical and relate them to the church's existing missions programs.
*As much as possible design curriculum to include all age groups.

5) *Train the leadership and the laity.*
* The leadership of Step #2 trains other sub-leadership of the church, who in turn will train the laity.
* Trainers should keep one or two sessions ahead of the people they are training, but it is essential that as much as possible, they go through all the material *and* experiences through which they take the laity *before* they teach the lay course.

6) *Have committees of the membership examine current mission strategies.* (Simultaneously with Step #5)
* On the basis of the above examination, recommend changes of existing strategy and new strategies.
* Possible recommendations:
   a - reorder financial support priorities, including the possible deletion of some projects;
   b - fewer missionaries but more support for those remaining;
   c - higher percentage of church budget going to global missions;

d - take on the majority or even full support, including the project costs of remaining missionaries;
e - divide the congregation into units - each unit being responsible for the full support of a given missions project. Each section of the congregation
should have maximum contact with the missionary and
the missionary's mission project (s);
f - examine the possibility of establishing partnerships
with churches in the Third World and sending a delegation to potential partners to explore the dimensions of that partnership;
g - pastoral exchange, student exchange, delegation exchange with a partnering church in the Third World;
h - insure that all missions efforts, wherever possible,
are part of a balanced development strategy;
i - encourage members to discover their own personal
global missions involvement and then provide them
the technical assistance they need to implement thei'
vision;
j - encouraging members, especially young people and re-
tired people to consider full time missions;
k - provide in-church discipleship and internship programs for members who feel God's call on them for
world missions;
l - make missions the central activity of the church in
both statement and practice;
m - make long term investments in partnership with
Christians in the Third World;
n - begin to prepare the hearts and minds of very small
children for a lifetime of commitment to the global
advancement of the Kingdom of God;
o - make the local church its own mission-sending agency
can of course be in cooperation with established
agencies, boards, etc., if they are willing;
p - set up programs which will allow local churches to
learn from and receive from partners in the Third
World; and
q - develop and implement accountability procedure for
each missions effort.

7) *Implement appropriate recommendations*
   * Retain professional counsel where needed--try to make
   it volunteer.
   * Allow maximum number of members to be involved in decisions in order to develop sense of ownership for decisions.
   * For each recommendation adopted, set measurable goals
   and a time frame in which those goals should be measured

8) *Evaluate and readjust to findings and new recommenda-*
tions
    * Evaluation time frames should interlock with guide-
lines specified in #7;
    * Overall evaluation should occur at least once every
six months.

MODELS

At this point I would like to suggest two models of direct
involvement. These models should be viewed as a place to begin rather than a place to end--models to work from rather
than models to work toward. The first model is of a partnership between a local church or similar group in the Third
World and a local church in North America. In the second model, I briefly describe a possible relationship between a
Christian family in the Third World and a family in North
America. The assumption here is that both families are acting
and working in the context of and in collaboration with their
local churches.

A Model of Two Churches in Partnership

The diagram below shows the key participants in the suggested partnership and the primary relationships between them.

PARTNERSHIP MINISTRY RELATIONSHIPS

Development Community

*Spiritual Need
*Physical Need
*Potential for Ownership of Problems & Solutions

Coordinating Team

* Initiating Partner Representative
* Responding Partner Representative

Harvest

Initiating Partner
(Third World Local Church,
Christian Organization)

Responding Partner
(Church, School, Group,
Family, Indiidual)

* Leadership
* Initiating Vision
*On-going Presence
*Language & Cultural
Sensitivity

* Encouragement
* Coordination
* Technical Assistance
* Training

* Financial Resources
* Technical Resources
* Personnel
* "Can Do" Mentality

*First, a denominational mission board or other agency, such
as a relief and/or development organization, subsequently referred to as Agency, contacts representatives of a Third
World country's national church leadership.

*They in turn refer the Agency to local, grassroots church,
the Initiating Partner. This church should be in or near a
community where there is spiritual and physical need. Further, this church should have a vision for ministering to
the above community of need and also be willing to be involved in a partnership with a local church from the more
developed world, the Responding Partner. Together they
should possess the necessary leadership, human and physical
resources to carry out a joint and balanced ministry to the
Initiating Partner's community.

*The Initiating Partner then introduces the Agency to the
leaders of the potential Development Community, the community
in which the Initiating Partner is ministering. Together the
Agency and Initiating Partner assess this community's appropriateness as a Development Community, the community which would
be the site of development projects conducted by the partnering churches.

*The Agency then assists the Initiating Partner and the De-
velopment Community in preparing a preliminary project proposal. This proposal describes the priority needs of the
community as defined by the Initiating Partner and the Development Community. The proposal details: 1) the resources
the Initiating Partner and the Development Community can
give to meeting the priority needs; 2) the resources they
need from the Responding Partner; and 3) a strategy for
jointly meeting the priority needs.

*The Agency then goes to the more developed world to find a
local church interested in becoming the Responding Partner
for this partnership.

*Representatives from the potential Responding Partner group
are led by the Agency on a reconnaissance visit to the Initiating Partner and Development Community. During a two to
three day visit, the members of both partners get to know
each other, worship with one another, and socialize together.
Most important, they carefully define the detail and timing
of the proposed project and the roles of each partner.

*Upon returning home, the representativesof the Responding
Partner relate their experiences to their home church or
group and make recommendation regarding the advisability of
the partnership. The project has both short- and long-
range possibilities, but the Agency will encourage all participants to commit to only one phase of the project at a
time. If the potential Responding Partner group agrees to
a partnership, they commit to a short-range immediate project
(the project to meet the priority need described above), but
remain open to the possibility of a long-term relationship
as and if the Holy Spirit blesses the relationship.

*Once the commitment is made, the Initiating Partner and
Responding Partner each select one or more project Coordinating Team Members to: 1) coordinate the partnership; 2) facilitate communication between the partners; and 3) to assist the
Development Community in long-range community development
planning. If the partners are unable to identify appropriate
individuals for this position, the Agency can supply personnel who will be supported by the partners. The Agency is
responsible for training the Coordinating Team members.

*After training by the Agency, the Coordinating Team Members
move into the Development Community to prepare for coordination of the first project, such as installing a well or building a school. The team serves under the direct supervision of
the Initiating Partner and the indirect supervision of the
Agency.

*Both partners now begin an orientation program, facilitated
by the Agency,in order to prepare them for the first project
of the partnership. During this first project stage, Volunteer Work Teams from both partners can be engaged where appropriate. This phase should be carefully designed, not only
to complete the first project, but to build understanding and
relationship between the partners.

*Upon completion of this short-term project, the Coordinating
Team settles into the target community for building relationships with the people and to develop a long-range comprehensive community development proposal. This proposal will be
an integrated community development plan based on needs, resources, national development strategies and the political
and economic realities of the area. Examples of integrated
projects include instituting basic literacy programs, developing a primary health-care center, strengthening economic

development through hand crafts, home bakeries, concrete-block manufacturing and agriculture.

*The entire process of the above physical and social development is directly linked to or under the direction of the Initiating Partner, the local church in the Third World. The Initiating Partner insures that the Development Community interprets these activities as an expression of God's love. The Initiating Partner "buys" the opportunities presented by the above social and physical ministries to evangelize and disciple the Development Community.

*As soon as feasible, the Agency withdraws from a formal relationship with both partners but remains available for consultations. The relationship between the two partnering churches continues.

The Model of Two Families in Partnership

Suppose a family in a local U.S. church would like to become Responding Partners. The Agency could link it with Third World believers who want to join with them for a ministry project in their country.

The steps you would follow are similar to those previously outlined, but are less complex.

For example, the U.S. family would be linked during its vacation with a Christian Third World family. Together they would adopt a third family--perhaps a refugee family which is homeless. The three families would build a house for the refugee family. The church of the U.S. family might cover the cost of the materials (which can be a fraction of the cost of building a home in the more industrialized world). The house would not be a gift. The mortgage would be paid back through a no- or low-interest loan. Proceeds from the loan would be used to create a revolving loan found for housing other homeless families.

There are many other possible models, but these two help to illustrate the possibilities.

Can It Work?

For more than a decade I was professionally involved as a community developer. I helped lay people catch a vision of what they could do to meet the needs of delinquent young people. I developed the support systems to train and support

lay volunteers as they took responsibility for helping young
delinquent youth, their families and their communities address the conditions which produced delinquent behavior. The
successes God allowed me to see as people got directly involved in solving their own problems were an important element in allowing me to believe that people of the local
church can become successfully and directly involved in missions.

The organization I now lead was strongly influenced by the
successful involvement of lay people in an international mission. This illustrates part of the reason I believe direct
involvement of lay people in international, cross-cultural
missions can work.

I designed and coordinated a village adoption between a
needy community of sugar cane cutters called Caballona in
the Dominican Republic and a high school in Ohio.

Anna, a young mother in Caballona, wrote a letter requesting help for her village. She wrote of no food and bad water.
In a neighboring village more than two dozen children had recently died, probably of water-born dysentary that their malnourished bodies were too weak to fight. Anna wanted to help.

I visited the village of approximately 80 families and
asked for a meeting to determine priority needs and ways to
meet those needs. The people expressed a willingness to enter into a partnership with a group of Christians from the
United States, if one could be found, who would link up with
them for helping to meet the needs of food and clean water.

In the meantime, God had touched the heart of Carl, an
administrator at M. Christian School. Carl wanted to celebrate the school's anniversary differently than the traditional self-serving fund raising event. Instead, Carl wanted
a project to demonstrate the school's thankfulness for God's
blessing over the past 20 years--a project which would do
something for someone else. When Carl called, I suggested
that his school adopt a village, Anna's village. The school
accepted the challenge, and a miracle began.

Carl and I had our initial phone conversation in January,
1981. By August an amazing and exciting string of events
had occurred:

EVENT: The students of M. Christian School set a one-day car wash world record. They washed 3,517 cars, and through one penny per car pledges they raised approximately $60,000.

EVENT: 30 students and 20 parents and faculty were screened and trained and journeyed to a 3 week work project in Caballona. Moms cooked. Dads and faculty guided. Everyone worked--hard.

EVENT: 20 Dominican young people from local churches volunteered and were trained to join the team of 50 Americans.

EVENT: 32 acres of land were found and secured for a very low cost from a sympathetic Christian. The land, only 1 klm. from the village, was to be used for food production and a community development center.

EVENT: The villagers dug a large fish pond for protein production and helped prepare the land for the arrival of the work teams.

EVENT: During the 3 week project a transformation took place on the 32 acres. A water cistern was installed. The front acreage was fenced. A road was built into the property. A house with a poured concrete roof for volunteer staff and a community center for meetings and training were both started from hand dug foundations and constructed.

EVENT: On the last day of the work project the student workers, both American and Dominican, landscaped the property with 25 coconut palm trees, donated by a Dominican Army Colonel who had become enthusiastic about the project.

EVENT: Two of the MCS teachers began to consider committing their lives to full time missions. (They are now both in training.)

EVENT: Several young Dominican students decided they wanted to commit their lives to helping their people in full time ministry.

EVENT: A visiting U.S. businessman was so touched by what he saw that he and his wife decided to sponsor a mobile medical van for medically needy villages like Caballona.

EVENT: A young Dominican volunteer gave one year of his life to serve the people of Caballona for room and board, but no salary. At this writing he is planning to give a second year.

EVENT: One of the Dominican students was invited and accepted the invitation to come to MCS as an exchange student.

EVENT: A set of parents decided that when their last boy finished high school they would consider giving their full time to this type of ministry.

EVENT: Since August the relationship between the school and the village has continued, and the school has sent other teams both to Caballona and a second needy village.

What made a Christian school in a small Ohio town which was experiencing economic recession respond with such vigor? Spiritually, of course, God's Holy Spirit led and blessed. Sociologically, the sense of project ownership and direct participation on both sides prompted all participants to make a maximum investment of creativity, time, effort and finances. It is highly unlikely that the above and other but unlisted benefits would have been realized if the school had been challenged traditionally. Normally, churches and groups like MCS raise money and give it to a missions agency which in turn helps needy people in unknown villages somewhere in the remote parts of the world.

A second example:

I recently invited a Christian brother, Scott, a member of my church, to accompany me on a reconnaisance trip as a photo-journalist. Scott had not travelled in the Third World before, except on a short trip. We visited several very needy communities in both Haiti and the Dominican Republic. Our organization could not pay Scott's fare or buy his film. He could not afford to do it either, but the Lord had made the financing available through a set of special circumstances. While on the trip, the Lord touched Scott's heart. He returned determined to share a vision for direct ministry with the people of our church.

Scott is an elder of our church, a fairly large body of believers. Two weeks after his return, the elders asked

Scott to give a report of his trip. He did! Scott's report began with a powerful 3-1/2 minute slide presentation which he had composed of 150 slides; he then made a gift of a book which encourages direct involvement that I had earlier encouraged Scott to read, *The Mustard Seed Conspiracy*. The book was given to each of our pastoral staff and each of the elders on the condition that they not keep it but read it and pass it on. Scott then handed out passport applications to each of the pastors and elders and told them that if God was going to give our people a vision for missions that it needed to start with them. Scott said that he wanted each of the men to be ready to go on an international exposure trip if the Lord would make such an opportunity available. Since no one knew when the Lord might present such an opportunity, he felt they needed to be ready to go on short notice. In order to minimize later excuses, Scott brought along his passport camera from his camera store and took passport photographs of each of the men! Finally, Scott placed a mustard seed in each of the pastor's and elder's hands and told them that he felt our church needed to be ready to die to itself, like the mustard seed, if the Lord was going to use us.

Since that time two of our pastors have approached me with an increased interest in getting themselves and our people more directly involved in missions. One of the Sunday School classes and a youth group have decided to become directly involved with a Third World orphanage. Subsequently a second elder, as a representative of the Sunday School classes, took a reconnaisance trip to investigate the possibility of the direct involvement of the people of our church in mission partnership with Christians in the Third World.

The outcome is yet to be seen, but all that has happened has developed out of the vision of a layman who had a missions project of his own--a one week trip as a lay photojournalist.

A third example:

Several years ago I had the privilege of taking my family with me to work on a community development center in a refugee community made homeless by Hurricane David. At the time my three children were 6, 8 and 10 years of age. For three weeks we worked alongside a Canadian team of Christian young people and nationals from the community. As we labored together to build a building which today is the center of a bustling witness to God's love, my children were deeply touched by the

poverty of the refugee children. When we returned home, the
object lesson of our fortune and the needs of others was not
lost. As a result, our children and my wife and I each sponsor one child in that community. Every night as a family we
pray for them--often by name. Each of their pictures is
framed in our family's gallery. Because we know something of
their circumstances, we have done more than the required $15
per month asked for by the program.

We provided money last Christmas which paid for shoes for
our children as well as many of the other children in this
village. We are paying for school fees and have purchased
the school clothes for one of the children. We've sent lots
of clothes. We have sent extra money to help two of the children's families. Recently, we told the workers in the community that, as we could, we would pay for emergency needs such as
medical care for any of "our" children.

My daughter Tasha tried to get a read-a-thon started in her
elementary school to raise money for the children in the community. It didn't happen because the principal turned her
down--but she tried. The boys went through their toy closet--
with some reluctance, I might add--and sent many of their toys
to the children there.

Why have we done this? Because we were close enough to the
need to know how great it was. Close enough to feel affinity
for those children and their families. And close enough to be
able to help.

These stories or examples are only illustrative of what can
happen when God's little people catch their *own* visions for
mission--for the development of people whom God is inviting
into His Kingdom. As Christian leaders I believe it is our
responsibility to *help* the lay people of the local church to
catch their own vision of world missions and then give them
the assistance they need to carry out that vision. As lay
people, it is our responsibility to take back our birthright
as followers of Jesus to directly minister to others.

The task before us is far too vast to be accomplished
through the professional pastor, missionary, or relief and
development agency. If the people of God's church are un-
leashed and aided in their ministry by the professionals who
would train, support, encourage, facilitate, enable, etc., I
believe what can be accomplished is beyond our dreams.

Footnote I

WHAT IS DEVELOPMENT?

As a Peace Corps Volunteer in the mid '60s, I was hurt to
see young brothers of the Third World turn away from the Kingdom of God because of well intentioned Western missionaries
who didn't separate the good news of the Kingdom of God from
the bad news of Western culture, politics, and Western Christian legalism.

If we are honest, too many Westerners, including Christians,
think that development is helping the less fortunate in the
Third World to "become like us." It is easy to see why we
should think this way. We in the West think of ourselves as
successful, as developed, as a model for those who have economic, population, political, health and other problems which we
don't have--at least to the degree they seem to exist in the
Third World.

In the first place, by whose standards are we successful?
Is God more pleased with our lifestyles, politics, and value
systems that He is with the equivalents in the Third World?
Yes, we are materially better off. Yes, most in the Third
World would gladly share our material abundance. But are we
happier? Do we have closer families, better social systems?
Do we care more for each other? Are we closer to God ? Is
our society more what God means societies to be? Do we really
believe the way we act--as if the Third World models itself
on the West that the Kingdom of God will be advanced?

Do we really want people and nations of the Third World to
"become like us" because we think in the process they will
have more of what God intended for them? Or is it because it
gratifies our egos when we are the model. Or, is it because
we are in control if we are the teachers? Or, perhaps it is
because we would feel safer in a hostile world if there were
more like us.

For too long, development in Western industrialized, cy-
bernetic thinking has meant that the less developed of the
Third World need to develop industrial, economic, educational
and political systems which, if they are not like ours, come
as close as possible. Of course, we in the West have recently learned from our own minority groups that it sounds patronizing to say that others should model themselves on the mainstream of the West. So, we don't say it--we just support
development programs that we think will lead in that direction.
And we withhold support from programs that don't.

I must be careful to point out that I am not saying all development a la the Western model has no place in a Christian perspective of development. Such models may in fact be useful. If they are to be used, however, their use must be on some other basis than wanting the people of the Third World to "become like us." (See *Thoughts on Development*, by Edgar Stoez--monograph, Pub. Mennonite Central Communite, 1977).

Footnote II

How Do People Know?

"How do the people of your community know that God loves them when they look at you?" is one of the questions I ask representatives of local churches when I travel in the Third World. The question is just as relevant to the church in the West and to individual members of either.

What is it that the church is doing which demonstrates God's intention that the people of the secular community in which the local church exists be invited into citizenship in the Kingdom of God? For too many the sad answer is that they do very little.

Some try by providing an inviting model of internal, loving relationships which are a direct result of God's love for the members--and of course for mankind. Christ loves the members and, in turn, they love each other. They care for, nourish, support, and encourage each other.

Others joyfully and corporately celebrate their faith. Through worshipful praise they demonstrate God's grace by openly thanking Him for His goodness to them and all mankind.

Still other churches show people in their community that God loves them by telling them so. They proclaim the good news of redemption and reconciliation. They develop and implement culturally relevant systems and strategies to communicate the message of salvation. Evangelism is paramount. It is of high and sometimes even consuming importance.

There are other churches that demonstrate God's love by ministering to the physical and social needs of their community. They assist the poor. They advocate for justice and fairness. They provide education, social programs, employment, and health care for those who otherwise could not access them.

All of these methods of demonstrating God's love are good and necessary. But they lack the wholeness of the biblical mandate for expressing God's love in our world. In and of themselves, these activities create an eccentric, off center, and unbalanced witness. Any church which focuses on one or several, but not all or the whole of the biblical means for witness will miss both the joy of service and the potential for impact in their community for the Kingdom of God.

They Know Best Through Balanced Witness

Fortunate is the church which has been led by the Holy Spirit into a balanced or holistic ministry and witness to its community. Fortunate are the people of a community who know that God loves them, because they see how the people of God love each other. And because they see the people of God thanking Him for His goodness. And because they hear from the people of God that God loves them and that He has prepared a way and invites them too into His love. And because the people of God show the nature of that love by caring for the poor, by standing with the powerless, and by living peaceably.

Footnote III

Two Other Reasons: Compassion and Enlightened Self Interest

I want to mention at least two other reasons besides obedience for the church to be involved in balanced ministry. The first is compassion--when Jesus approached the city of Jerusalem during the triumphal entry, He had compassion on the city and her people because of what He knew would happen to them--and He wept. (Luke 19:41) Paul had so much compassion for his people, the Jews, that he was willing to be separated from Christ for their sake. (Rom 9:3) The Psalmists remind us in several passages that God is a God of compassion and that in spite of our iniquity, He forgives us of our sins. (Ps.78:38; 6:15; 111:4; 112:4; and 145:8) In the feeding of the five thousand, Jesus looked on the multitudes, and because of His compassion for them, He healed their sick (Matt. 14:14) The writer of Hebrews commends those to whom he is writing because they showed compassion for prisoners. (Heb. 10:34) Finally, John reminds us that unless we show compassion for our brothers in need, the love of God is not within us. (I John 3:17) Our God is a compassionate God. His Son, Jesus, demonstrated that compassion time and again. The writers of the Epistles commend compassion.

God has not only placed the Western evangelical church in a unique position in history to know about the physical and spiritual needs of men around the world, but He has placed this church in a unique position in history to do something about it. No people in human history have had such easy access to resources and such an incredible opportunity for mobility.

As we allow Christ to fill our hearts with Himself, as we realize the undeserved compassion Jesus has showed us, our hearts should be a time-bomb of compassionate response to the needs of men throughout the world.

The second reason is enlightened self interest. The church cannot give without receiving more than it gave. This is a principle of the King, and it is at exact odds with the world's wisdom. As a matter of Kingdom fact, it is only as we as individuals or as the church give away what we have been given that we possess it at all. Jesus said that the one who would keep his life should give it away. (Matt. 10:39; 16:25) I think it is a safe implication that Jesus was not only talking about life proper but many of the things that make life--including possessions and talents.

The rich young ruler had to give up his possessions before he could gain eternal life. Why? They stood between him and God. (Luke 18:18-23) In the same story, but in the Matthew account, Jesus told the young man that by giving his possessions away now, he would be able to retain them in heaven. "If you wish to be complete, go and sell your possessions and give to the poor, and you shall have treasures in heaven." (Matt.19:21)

The widow who gave all that she had into the temple offering gained far more than she gave. Even though the amount she gave was much less than the amount the rich were giving, God credited the widow with more than the combined money the rich gave. (Mark 12:41-44)

When the lad in John's account of the feeding of the five thousand gave his five barley loaves and two fish, Jesus multiplied them till the boy not only had what he needed, but in Jesus' hands his gift fed the multitude. (John 6:9-13)

One of the best summaries of this principle is found in Jesus' statement in Luke,

"But love your enemies, and do good, and lend, expecting nothing in return; and your reward will be great, and you

will be the sons of the Most High; and He Himself is kind
to ungrateful and evil men. Give and it will be given to
you; good measure, pressed down, shaken together, running
over, they will pour into your lap. For whatever measure
you deal out to others, it will be dealt to you in return."
(Luke 6:35-38 ASV)

The other side of the coin? If we keep our treasures to
ourselves, we lose them. Two examples. In Luke 12:16-21
Jesus told the parable of the rich man who had prepared for
retirement and was now ready to settle down, take his ease and
be merry. He lost it all that night. In the second example,
Jesus told of the beggar Lazarus and the rich man who wouldn't
share his wealth. (Luke 16:19-31) At death the rich man lost
everything, including eternal life.

So to hold or to keep is to lose, to give is to gain. I
wonder how many churches have lost for eternity the resources
they have kept for themselves, that they have put into beautiful buildings and sophisticated programming, when they could
have invested it in the Kingdom's bank.

Will there be people in hell for eternity because the church
didn't train and support its people in sharing the good news?

Will there be people who miss eternity with Christ because
the church didn't train and support its people in ministering
to social and physical needs?

Jesus' "good measure, pressed down, shaken together, running over" is by any standard a good return on investment.

Other Thoughts

That we will be held accountable is certain. But just "giving it away" is not the only aspect of handling our gifts and
our resources for which we are accountable. We will also be
evaluated on the basis of the soundness of our investment. In
the Kingdom parable of the talents, Jesus makes it clear that
the Master's reward for good stewardship is related to the
soundness of the investment. (Matt. 25:14-30) The church has
a responsibility, like a wise financial investor, to study
Kindom investment opportunities and then to put the resources
which God has placed in its stewardship to good use.

However, the church is not excused from meeting a pressing
need which God places in its path because it desires a better
investment. The Good Samaritan may have been able to make

"better use" of his time and money. But Jesus honored him
because he responded compassionately to a pressing need
which God allowed to come into his day and to which he was
able to respond.

Jesus also told us that if asked we should lend, expecting nothing in return. (Luke 6:35)

Suppose we were not obligated to the Great Commandment
and the Great Commission, and that the compassion of Christ
did not fill our hearts. In enlightened self interest, the
church should be interested in investing *all* available resources in the development of men toward the purposes God
has for them.

The exciting thing is that the church *is* mandated to obey
the Great Commandment and the Great Commission--to be His
ambassador--His personal representative to man. Further, the
church *does* have the compassion of Jesus in the hearts of its
people. And, finally, the church's people *are* encouraged by
Jesus Himself to act in enlightened self interest. What more
reason could there be to enthusiastically engage in a spirit
of abandon to the mission of development Jesus has given us!!!

Footnote IV

Knowledge vs. Wisdom

Let me illustrate the difference between knowledge and wisdom with an example from an earlier career in community development. In an urban slum of a large city there was a serious
delinquency problem. Years before the slum had been a stable
blue collar neighborhood of single houses, detached garages
and green lawns. Garbage trucks went weekly through the alleys of the neighborhood to pick up trash. In those times
there was tangible community pride and spirit. But in later
years the alleys became clogged with trash. People could no
longer use their garages. Youth first used the empty garages
as their clubhouses and then later as their private domain for
all description of illegal and immoral activities. School at-
tendance dropped. Crime in the neighborhood became so serious
that the residents feared to leave their homes. After many
requests for help, the city council hired professional urban
planners to study the problem and make recommendations for
change. Months later the planners presented the council with
a multi-million dollar plan which included youth and recreation centers, better street lighting, rennovated school curriculum and other progressive but expensive programming. As

a final step to accepting the program, the council members took the plan to neighborhood residents to discuss it and get their response. The visit which stopped the professional plan was one at the home of an old black woman who had lived in the neighborhood for many years. After being told of the plan and asked for her evaluation, she said that she had lived there for many years. She had watched this neighborhood turn into a slum. It started turning into a slum when the alleys got potholes so big the garbage trucks wouldn't go through. When they didn't come, the trash started to pile up and people couldn't get into the alley to get their car in the garage. "We asked the city to fix the alleys, but it didn't. The kids started to use the garages for doing what they wanted. That's when the problems started. Now, if it was me, I would fix the alleys and start picking up the trash." The old woman wasn't a professional, but she had the wisdom needed to solve a serious social problem--a solution that had evaded the knowledgeable and skilled urban planners.

Footnote V

Rural Porches - Urban Boxes

I think it would be helpful at this point to review, from a secular perspective, how our society has come to the place where it now delegates to the professional responsibility for containing and solving human problems. To illustrate, I will use a conceptual model called Rural Porches and Urban Boxes. The term "rural porches" will symbolize our society in a more simple time--a time in which most of our society lived in relatively small towns or rural communities. When there was a community problem, the people in the community would often spontaneously and voluntarily respond with help. When Farmer Smith was sick and couldn't harvest his crop, Jones would get on his tractor and harvest Smith's field.

In these smaller communities, there were sharp-eyed neighbors who, when a neighbor's house was being vandalized, burglarized, or when young people fought in the streets, got off their porches. They took personal responsibility by intervening in the crisis they observed--even though the crisis did not directly affect them.

The Urban Boxes in our model relate to our current and increasingly urban living environments. We now tend to live in a series of boxes--"ticky-tacky houses all in a row." We get in a box with wheels. We get in a vertically mobile box called an elevator and walk down a rectangular box called a hallway to a cubicle box--our office. After eight hours of shuffling paper, we reverse the process. We come home to our house-box, turn on an electric box and watch the world through a glass screen. We see our communities' social problems pass in review. We may have personally passed by the problems earlier in the day in our box with wheels. As professionals, we may have dealt with them in our office-box. But there is precious little opportunity or encouragement, however, for direct lay-citizen involvement with the problems to which we have been exposed.

As a consequence, citizens in New York City, who are just like us, look out of their apartment windows and watch a girl on the street below being murdered--but don't get involved.

Analysis: The following comparative analysis of phenomena found in the Rural Porch and Urban Box model helps illustrate why the sense of volunteerism or spontaneous concern, or direct involvement for meeting our neighbor's need was much more of a reality in our society's earlier history:

In a Rural Porch environment we find:	In an Urban Box environment we find:
1. Visibility	1. Anonymity
2. Belonging	2. Alienation
3. Predictability	3. Unpredictability
4. Security	4. Fear
5. Ownership of community problems	5. Abdication of social responsibility
6. Volunteering to solve the problem	6. Hiring a professional--the hired gun--to solve the problem
7. Resulting sense of significance	7. Resulting sense of insignificance
8. Deepening involvement	8. Decreasing involvement

In the Rural Porches environment, people are visible. There is a sense of belonging. The community and its people are predictable. As a consequence, there is a sense of security. Individuals are willing to take ownership for the community problems they see. The people then have a tendency to volunteer spontaneously to meet community needs--the needs of their neighbors. As they volunteer, the people volunteering become significant. Being significant gives a feeling of importance and pride in community, and consequently the people are willing to get even more deeply involved.

In the environment of Rural Porches, we have neighbors who spontaneously accept responsibility. John Augustus of the last century is a good example of a spontaneous volunteer. He was a shoe cobbler in Boston, Massachusetts. He didn't agree with the rationale of locking debtors in prison till they could earn money to pay debts. He offered to take them out of prison and find them jobs so they could pay. (In a sense, what he started was so successful that we institutionalized his volunteer activities and created professional probation officers. Ironically, probation systems have become reluctant to let volunteers "back in.")

The opposite tends to happen in our Urban Box environment. People not only feel but *are* quasi-anonymous. As a consequence, they can easily avoid getting involved in community problems. No one will know the difference. People tend to be alienated from one another. There is a sense of unpredictability about life. People don't know what is going to happen to them or to their neighbor, and they are afraid. They don't know how to get involved--and so they don't. Because they are afraid and don't know how to get involved, people delegate responsibility for community problems to the public sector. The public sector then hires professionals. But when people delegate responsibility for social problems to others, they begin to feel insignificant--powerless. The more insignificant and powerless they feel, the less inclined they are to become spontaneously involved in solving the problems of their community. The consequences of living in the context of Urban Boxes is all too obvious.

In an Urban Boxes environment, people delegate responsibility. Then as a logical extension of delegation, institutional systems to support the professionals to whom responsibility has been delegated are created. These systems become large, costly bureaucracies which all too often do little to solve the problems they were created to address. Even more alarming, these systems stand as barriers and road blocks between the community problems and the very people in the community who should be encouraged to take responsibility for solving the problem.

Delegation Doesn't and Can't Work

Why does delegation to professionals fall so short of our expectations? There are a number of reasons.

1. Currently, our service institutions act in a manner which implies that they, rather than the community at large,

have the responsibility for solving community problems. This perception of mandate is in juxta-position to that of service as facilitators--giving citizens the coordination and guidance they need to solve their own problems.

History shows us that institutions do not solve the specific problems. The people must solve their own problems. I contend that service institutions operate more effectively when they assist the public, the people, in voluntarily acting to solve their own problems.

2. Community problems do not belong to the professionals: Community problems belong to the community, not to service professionals--except as they are citizens. Since community problems do not belong to professionals as professionals, it is unlikely that they will be able to solve community problems as professionals. Where professionals do make a difference, they tend to make those differences as caring members or citizens of their community--not as professionals.

3. Principle of Non-Involvement: Professionals tend to operate on the principle of professional non-involvement with clients, the people. For example, they say, "Schedule your problems, please. Our counseling hours are from 10:00 to 12:00 and 2:00 to 4:00." This posture is not conducive to trust or to promoting the feeling that people are significant.

4. Not enough money: Assuming the fact that professionals could make a difference as professionals and could solve community problems, there is not enough money to hire enough professionals to solve the problems. The problem is simply too big. The economic reality is that current professional levels of service delivery are being further and further eroded as human service monies are reduced.

5. Distributive vs. Re-distributive economy: Increasingly, our economy is moving from a distributive to a re-distributive model. In the past, when we had new social problems, Americans were always able to tap into new resources to meet these new problems. If we have not already reached it, we are fast approaching an end to that pattern. There are no more vast untapped, easily accessible resources. As we have new social problems or new emphases to address, we will have to take resources from one area and redistribute them to the area of increased concern.

6. Current system cheats lay people of what could be: Our current system used limited resources inefficiently. It

essentially delivers fewer services than are possible through the mobilization of volunteers. For every hour that a professional invests in a client, the client gets an hour in service. If the same professional were investing the hour in a carefully trained and managed volunteer, the hour invested in the volunteer could multiply itself many times.

7. Volunteers are trendy: It's trendy to use volunteers, but when they are available, they are often given tasks that professional staff do not have time to do or do not want to do or feel are non-essential. If a volunteer fails, it really doesn't make any difference, because essential tasks were never given or shared with volunteers. Volunteers are viewed and managed as an appendage to the "real tasks."

A more appropriate perception is to realize that the only difference between paid staff and volunteers should be the element of compensation--a pay check. Volunteers can be seen and treated as staff--non-paid staff. Yes, there are some legal and administrative limitations but from a capability viewpoint, there are, theoretically, no tasks that professional staff can do which competent and equally supervised volunteers cannot.

8. Professional resistance: Professionals think volunteers don't have enough sophistication or experience to understand, solve or address community problems. Professionals think they can do it better. Empirical evidence suggests that they often do it worse. They fear volunteers may take away their jobs. Volunteer programs almost always create jobs. Professional staff enjoy the psychological rewards of direct service to the client. They are afraid that if they work with volunteers instead of clients, they would not have the direct contact with clients which gives them gratification. Professionals can be lazy. Working with volunteers *is* harder. Professionals think that token volunteerism equals volunteer programs. It doesn't.

9. Perhaps the largest single factor in the absence of wide spread quality volunteer programming is that agency administrators misunderstand the complexity of volunteer management. The management of volunteers is much more complex than the management of traditional human services. A number of years ago, management gurus made a not so surprising discovery. They learned that the management of human service programs is more complex than the management of traditional businesses. The reason? In a traditional business, you manage the worker and the product. The administrator has one human

factor to manage. In human service systems, there are two
human factors--the worker (professional) and the client.
The management of human service systems is more complex because you have two human factors to which the professional
must relate. In volunteer programming, we have a third human factor--that of the volunteer.

Adding volunteers into any service system further increases its complexity. This creates a need to put the best
management expertise in the driver's seat when volunteers
are involved. Volunteer programs must have high priority
if they are to be successful. What usually happens is the
opposite. Agency administrators often put the weakest people in volunteer management. Then when the volunteer effort
falters, they wonder why.

SOCIAL TRANSFORMATION: THE MISSION OF GOD

Purpose. The purpose of this paper is, as a part of a continuous process of self-examination, to review where we've been in the last twenty years and to write a biblical view of social transformation, drawing on the papers that have been written for Consultation '83.

The Road We Have Travelled. Twenty years ago there would have been no felt need among evangelical Christians, and especially *Western* evangelical Christians, for this kind of conference. We have travelled a long way since the Berlin Congress on World Evangelization seventeen years ago. In the eight years between Berlin and Lausanne, we came to know one another. Lausanne 1974 was a watershed year for those concerned about our Christian response to human need. There has in the last ten years been a dramatic increase in the number and scope of evangelical "Relief and Development Agencies." CRESR sharpened the focus of the relationship between evangelism and social responsibility last June, and we are struggling at Consultation 83 to understand "Social Transformation" in relationship to God's redemptive mission.

Defining Social Transformation. What are God's intentions for His church? This paper will define "intentional social transformation" as a process of external intervention intended to enable the people to become better than they were before.

What Is God's Intention for the World? God's intention for the world is that the world should be redeemed, that His kingdom should be established. He has chosen to do this through the death and resurrection of His Son. God's instrument in the world is the church. It is the church which is the sign of the kingdom. The church is to make disciples of all nations, teaching them to both announce the kingdom and to live out the ethics of the kingdom. The context will decide whether evangelism or social responsibility is given priority in a given situation.

How Do We Respond to God's Intentions? The church is a community of gathered communities, not a group of individuals. The church has a mission to move out of its own environs to regions beyond. The Bible indicates no limitation on the local community's response to its environment. Widows, prisoners, poor, naked and hungry are all objects of concern. In Paul's writings and ministry we see social transformation taking place through a process of external intervention.

The Role of the Holy Spirit. Even as the Holy Spirit was active in the book of Acts, we need to discover that the Holy Spirit is active in all we do.

Mission: A Biblical View of Social Transformation. Christians are commanded to intervene in the behalf of others. The implications are that we, the people of God, must be transformed ourselves before we can help others. We need to present our bodies a living sacrifice by having our minds renewed (Romans 12:1,2) even as we are about the business of "doing good to all men."

EDWARD R. DAYTON is Vice-President for Mission and Evangelism of World Vision International and Chairman of the Strategy Working Group of the Lausanne Committee for World Evangelization.

SOCIAL TRANSFORMATION: THE MISSION OF GOD

Edward R. Dayton

THE ROAD WE HAVE TRAVELLED

This paper is part of the process of a continuous self-examination. It is important that we continually "do theology," carry out the process of biblical reflection in light of our present context. The world changes. Our own situation changes. Cultures change. We change. The gospel is always expressed within a culture.[1] It is impossible for any of us to talk without speaking and listening through cultural filters. This is equally true about the discussion on development.

It is helpful to realize that 20 years ago there would have been no felt need among the evangelical Christians, and especially Western evangelical Christians, for the conference for which this paper has been prepared. Whereas in the late 1800's Evangelicals were still actively involved in trying to set the world right, by the 1930's many Evangelicals, particularly in the West, separated themselves, indeed identified themselves, from "liberals," who were viewed as being concerned only for the "social gospel." Although a great deal of development was being carried out by Western evangelical missionaries, it was submerged under the heading of "reaching the lost for Christ." It has only been in recent years that some evangelical agencies have specifically identified their purpose as doing something called "development."

A great deal of the debate that has been carried on within the Church about the reasons for and the methods of development has resulted because different Christian brothers and sisters see the world through different lenses. Much of our debate stems from the assumption on the part of some that we of necessity must see things alike and come to a joint agreement. There is a strong feeling that, "If you knew everything I know, we would agree." As an American I believe this is a particular problem for Americans. But the Bible, history and our own experience demonstrate this not to be the case. Just as the different churches of the New Testament were permitted to work out their Christianity from within the context of their own world view, so must we permit one another to do the same. However, this should not keep us from speaking prophetically to one another. Accepting the local church in another culture does not mean to accept everything that that church does. Nor must we be naive about our own history. As George Marsden has so well illustrated in his book *Fundamentalism and American Culture*,[2] what was "an American evangelical view" in 1870, by 1925 was being described as "liberal." In 1870, most American Evangelicals held to an eschatology that was post-millenial. And, Marsden so well illustrates, one's own view of the task of the Church is greatly influenced by one's eschatology.

Furthermore, we are continually in the business of rewriting history. Speaking as an American, one has only to review the American school books of the last 150 years to see how quickly we reinterpret the same situation as time goes by. The "vicious savage" becomes the "noble savage" who is now understood as a "Native American."[3]

Our understanding of our world is greatly shaped by our own culture. I am an American. I have been brought up and educated in a culture whose values are sharply different from those of the rest of the world. It is not that American culture is different and all other cultures the same; it is only, as Edward Stewart points out, "On any culture scale, Americans seem to be at one end."[4]

Having said that, it may be helpful to realize how far we have travelled in the 17 years since the Berlin Congress on World Evangelization in 1966. When 1,000 evangelical Christians gathered from all over the world, this was the first time in history that a *world* conference had been called of those who identified themselves as evangelicals, and those who particularly identified themselves as being involved with the task of world evangelism. Berlin spent most of its time examining evangelical theology and particularly the need for evangelicals to again look out upon a world which was lost. There was a reawakened awareness as to the magnitude of the task that faced the Church. The population counter in the center of the main hall inexorably reminded us of how rapidly the world was growing and how much there was to be done. But the primary focus of Berlin was on the personal salvation of those who had yet to hear.

In the eight years between Berlin and Lausanne, there was tremendous movement in the evangelical part of Christ's Church. We had come to know one another. We knew that the church had expanded far beyond the West, and were beginning to talk to one another. We revived an interest in research in what God was doing in the world.[5] Lausanne was intended to be a congress of those actually involved in trying to reach the world. Over 3,000 people attended. But the Holy Spirit was also enlivening the minds of men and women to expand our understanding of what it meant to evangelize. The *Lausanne Covenant* greatly broadened our world view. We were called to see that the task was not confined to the sharing of information about Jesus. There was a *life* to be lived. There were commands of Christ to be followed. We saw the need for the broad redemption of the world in all of its aspects.

There were those at Lausanne who felt that the *Lausanne Covenant* did not go far enough. There were voices which called for an even broader understanding of the task of evangelization. The process of growth continued.

It is historically of interest to indicate that the year of Lausanne—1974—might also be described as a watershed year in a renewed interest by Western Evangelicals, and particularly North Americans, in social concerns. Much of this was triggered by the disastrous drought in the Sahel area of Africa. As the medium of television was used to make the need known, North American Evangelicals responded. The result was the inauguration of a number of new Christian "relief and development" agencies and the rapid expansion of those already involved, such as World Vision International. These agencies not only appeared to be taking on a new task, they also had the ability to raise large sums of money.[6] By 1981 the amount of income being received by evangelical agencies concerned for alleviating human need amounted to approximately 375 million dollars. During the same time the total income of all other North American Protestant agencies working overseas equaled 1,465 million dollars.

Evangelicals were "catching up." They were moving into an
area where Church World Service and Catholic Relief Services,
as well as other non-American agencies had been for years.
Most of them took the same approach as CWS and CRS, namely,
to draw a firm line between "evangelism" and "social responsibility." In at least one denomination of evangelical tradition, a separate agency was set up to work alongside the "mission" efforts of the agency.[7] This tremendous and rapid
growth of these agencies had numbers of consequences, all of
which had theological implications. There were those who
questioned whether it was biblical to "divert" sums from the
task of "mission" to the task of social responsibility. Many
agencies were looking for a theological justification for
what they were doing. There was a nervousness as to whether
one could have an *evangelical* relief and development agency.

But there were others who raised a more serious question.
They questioned whether the *way* that these agencies were going
about attempting to relieve human hurt and misery was biblically sound. On the one hand, they questioned the methods. On
the other hand they questioned whether these agencies are going far enough in their actions. There were calls for a deeper understanding of the *root causes* of much of the suffering
that these agencies were attempting to alleviate.

By the time of the Consultation on World Evangelization
(COWE), sponsored by the Lausanne Committee for World Evangelization in Pattaya, Thailand, in 1980, numbers of evangelical
theologians from all over the world were beginning to enunciate
clearly the need for "a theology of development." During January of that same year the Consultation on the Theology of Development had been convened by the Unit on Ethics in Society
of the Theological Commission of the World Evangelical Fellowship.[8] A major question was being addressed to those Evangelicals who were now deeply involved in this business called
"development": Were the ways these agencies were carrying out
development biblical? There was even a deeper question: Was
development itself counted biblical? The discussion at the
Consultation on the Theology of Development led to the proposal for a subsequent consultation to be entitled "A Christian
Response to Human Need." Paper writers were assigned, tasks
were given, and a program to gather case histories on how development was actually being carried out all over the world
was inaugurated. An interim discussion was scheduled for Holland, Michigan, during the summer of 1982. Meanwhile out of
COWE there developed a felt need on the part of the leadership
of the LCWE and the World Evangelical Fellowship to bring together a Consultation on the Relationship Between Evangelism

and Social Responsibility.[9] This consultation was convened
with a great deal of apprehension by many who were coming,
to quote John Stott's foreword to the report, "...with a considerable degree of apprehension. The papers and responses,
circulated in advance, had not only been critical of each
other's positions but even in some cases sharply so. How
then could we possibly expect to reach accord? Yet underneath
our natural fears there was a confidence that God could unite
us, if we humbled ourselves under the authority of His Word.
And so it proved. For me it was another dramatic demonstration of the value of international conferences...when we meet
face to face (or as our American friends vividly express it,
"eyeball to eyeball"), and listen not only to each other's
arguments but to the cherished convictions which lie behind
the arguments, then we develop towards one another a new understanding, respect and love. This is not to say that we
agree about everything (as our report makes plain), but that
our arguments are far greater than our residual differences."

The work of Grand Rapids must be seen as a major contribution to this ongoing discussion.

But the Holy Spirit and the movement of history seemed to
be moving us along at a quickening pace. When the interim
steering committee of "A Christian Response to Human Need"
met the week before the Grand Rapids meeting in Holland, Michigan and discussed with one another the work that we had done
so far, we concluded that rather than attempt to develop a
"theology of development," we should abandon the entire notion
of development! We concluded that "development" had become so
loaded with secular and humanistic freight, that it was no
longer useful to us. We struggled to find a term or phrase
that we might use to describe that particular aspect of the
church's work with which we were concerned. The best we could
do was to call it "social transformation," which, when one
thinks deeply about it, is what we are really all about.

And what is "social transformation" for the Christian? Is
it not the entire business that God is about, namely, the redemption of the world? And is not the *mission* of the Church
"social transformation" in every dimension?

Grand Rapids argued that "social responsibility" and "evangelism" were intimately entwined. They recognized that in the
Lausanne Covenant's affirmation that "In the Church's mission
of sacrificial service, evangelism is primary," they were not
referring to an invariable *temporal* priority, because in some

situations the social ministry will take precedence, but to a *logical* one.

The mission of the Church is to do all that Jesus commanded.

THE QUESTION OF HERMENEUTICS

Having completed this brief historical overview it is necessary to say a word about hermeneutics. If one believes, as this writer does, that there is continuity between the Old and New Testaments, and between the Gospels and Epistles, then one will have a view of Scripture that is different from those who deny this continuity. Since it is not within the scope or intent of this paper to develop an entire hermeneutic, I can only state my presuppositions and move on from there.

Of necessity, then, this paper will be written from a particular cultural, historical and theological viewpoint. Specifically it is the writer's view that:

1. There is continuity between the Old and New Testaments.

2. The Bible can best be understood as a history of God's relationship with humankind, particularly personified in God's covenants with Adam, Noah, Abraham, Moses and Israel and Jeremiah.

3. The "gospel" is the good news of the kingdom. The good news is that the kingdom has both come and is coming.

4. The ethics of the kingdom are applicable to the Church today.

5. The mission of the church is to announce the kingdom and to be part of God's great work of redeeming the world.

6. "Social transformation" carried out by Christians must, of necessity, carry with it a call to repentance and reconciliation with God.

DEFINING SOCIAL TRANSFORMATION

Tito Paredes defines cultural change as "any modification of the ideological, sociological, techno-economic and economic dimensions of a people, due to internal and/or external factors that are actively dynamic over time." He sees all cultures changing. Social transformation is going on all of the time.[10]

But the question before us as the Church is one of *intention*. What is it that God would have us to *do* and to *be*? How should the Church involve itself with the affairs of mankind? It is perhaps helpful to avoid biblical language and thus hopefully avoid circular definition. Thus this paper will define "intentional social transformation" as a *process of external intervention intended to enable the people to become better than they were before*.

Let us examine this definition piece by piece: It is a *process,* rather than a punctilior event. In other words, it is something which goes on in time and assumes that there are a series of consequences. (To that extent one can argue that the notion of progress is inherent in "social transformation," no matter how the phrase is used.)

It includes *external intervention*. In other words, it is assumed that if the people with whom it is concerned are left to themselves, it is unlikely that change will take place. Someone outside must intervene in order to change things from the supposedly undesirable way they would normally be. We should probably be quick to add here that the "external intervention" may well be the intervention of the Holy Spirit!

The purpose of this intervention is *to enable*. It assumes that the potential to be different, to be better, lies within the people.

The subject of social transformation is *a people*. The transformation we are talking about here is not only of the individual--it is *social*. It assumes individuals in relationship, in community. The easiest illustration is the anthropologist's island or an isolated rural community. But people also live in relationship in urban areas. Indeed, the challenge of social transformation is greater amidst exploding urban populations than in the rapidly diminishing rural areas of the world. Finally, the assumption is that the people will be *better* (by some yardstick) than they were before this intervention. Note that the definition does not define "better." As we will see, for the Christian that has to be uniquely defined for each people in their own context.

Although this definition is satisfactory from a general view of discussing the principles involved, it leaves much to be desired as a useful definition for Christians. Our task, therefore, is an attempt to pour biblical meaning into the definition.

Is "external intervention" justified? And if so, under
what conditions?

And what do we mean by "better"?

In order to arrive at the answers to these questions for
us as Christians, we will first examine God's intention for
the world. We will then look at His intention for His Church.
We will ask the question as to how we should respond to God's
intention for the world and for the Church. Finally, we will
attempt to suggest what this might tell us about a biblical
view of the mission of the church and how this mission should
be carried out.

WHAT IS GOD'S INTENTION FOR THE WORLD?

The Bible opens by announcing God's evaluation of what He
had created was good (Genesis 1:31). This goodness is vio-
lated by Adam and Eve as they break God's covenant with them
(Genesis 3). The results of this rupture in relationship are
disastrous.

> To Adam he said, "Because you listened to your wife and
> ate from the tree about which I commanded you, 'You must
> not eat of it,' cursed is the ground because of you;
> through the painful toil you will eat of it all the days
> of your life. It will produce thorns and thistles for
> you, and you'll eat the plants of the fields. By the
> sweat of your brow you will eat your food until you re-
> turn to the ground, since from it you were taken; for
> dust you are and to dust you will return." (Genesis 3:17-
> 19 NIV)

The balance of the Bible reveals God's intention for the
world, namely, its *redemption*. This redemption is at once
spiritual, physical and social.

> Then I saw a new heaven and a new earth, for the first
> heaven and the first earth had passed away, and there
> was no longer any sea. I saw the Holy City, the New
> Jerusalem, coming down out of heaven from God, prepared
> as a bride beautifully dressed for her husband, And I
> heard a loud voice from the throne saying, "Now the
> dwelling of God is with men, and he will live with them.
> They will be his people and God himself will be with
> them and be their God. He will wipe every tear from
> their eyes. There will be no more death or mourning or

crying or pain, for the old order of things has passed away" (Revelation 21:1-4 NIV).

I did not see a temple in the city, because the Lord God Almighty and the Lamb are its temple. The city does not need the sun or the moon to shine on it, for the glory of God gives it light, and the Lamb is its lamp. The nations will walk by its light, and the kings of the earth will bring their splendor into it. On no day will its gates ever be shut, for there will be no night there. The glory and honor of the nations will be brought into it. Nothing impure will ever enter it, nor will anyone who does what is shameful or deceitful, but only those whose names are written in the Lamb's Book of Life (Revelation 21:22-27 NIV).

The kingdom of the world has become the kingdom of our Lord and of his Christ, and he will reign forever and ever (Revelation 11:15b NIV).

The ultimate purpose of God for the world, as He has revealed it to us, is the Gospel. This was the "good news" that Jesus and His forerunner, John the Baptist, announced: "Repent for the kingdom of heaven is near."

This is the "good news" that God has declared His victory over the powers of sin and evil. Throughout the gospels we see Jesus in a power struggle with both Satan (Matthew 4:1-11) and with the religious rulers of the day.

Jesus entered the temple courts, and while He was teaching, the chief priests and the elders of the people came to Him. "By what authority are you doing these things?" they asked. "And who gave you this authority?" (Matthew 21:23 NIV)

The "Great Commission" is made possible because, as Jesus said,

"All authority in heaven and on earth has been given to me. Therefore..." (Matthew 28:18 NIV)

Jesus' ministry is introduced with the words:

Jesus went throughout Galilee, teaching in their synagogues, preaching the good news of the kingdom, and healing every disease and sickness among the people. (Matthew 4:23 NIV).

Matthew emphasizes this by repeating the same words in Matthew 9:35. This kingdom is to be our primary focus:

> "But seek first his kingdom, and his righteousness, and all these things will be given to you as well" (Matthew 6:33 NIV).

This kingdom has been prepared for those who do God's will (Matthew 25:24 NIV).

This righteousness is worked out in terms to their response to the world around them.

> "For I was hungry and you gave me something to eat, I was thirsty and you gave me something to drink, I was a stranger and you invited me in, I needed clothes and you clothed me, I was sick and you looked after me, I was in prison and you came to visit me" (Matthew 25:35,36 NIV).

Or to put that in contrast:

> "Not everyone who says to me, 'Lord, Lord,' will enter the kingdom of heaven, but only he who does the will of my Father who is in heaven" (Matthew 7:21 NIV).

This is the kingdom within which Abraham, Isaac and Jacob will be found:

> "I say to you that many will come from the east and the west, and will take their places at the feast with Abraham, Isaac and Jacob in the kingdom of heaven" (Matthew 8:11 NIV).

When asked what was the greatest commandment, Jesus replied:

> "Love the Lord your God with all your heart and with all your soul and with all your mind." This is the first and greatest commandment. And the second is like it: Love your neighbor as yourself. All the Law and the Prophets hang on these two commandments" (Matthew 22:37-40 NIV).

This kingdom is both a present and future reality:

> "But if I drive out demons by the Spirit of God, then the kingdom of God has come upon you..." (Matthew 12:28 NIV).[11]

Paul agrees. He tells us we have been already brought into the kingdom (Colossians 1:13 NIV).

Finally,

"And this gospel of the kingdom will be preached in the whole world as a testimony to all nations, and then the end will come" Matthew 24:14 NIV).

But the gospel takes on a fuller meaning in the writings of Paul, who assumes that his readers will understand what he means by "this gospel."

Paul tells us that it is the good news concerning God's son:

The gospel he promised beforehand through his prophets in the Holy Scriptures regarding his Son, who as to his human nature was a descendant of David, and who through the Spirit of holiness was declared with power to be the Son of God by his resurrection from the dead: Jesus Christ our Lord (Romans 1:2-4 NIV).

Paul gives us a more technical description of the gospel in his first letter to the Corinthians:

Now, brothers, I want to remind you of the gospel I preached to you, which you received and on which you have taken your stand. By this gospel you are saved, if you hold firmly to the word I preached to you. Otherwise, you have believed in vain.

For what I received I passed on to you as of first importance: that Christ died for our sins according to the Scriptures, that he was buried, that he was raised on the third day according to the Scriptures, and that he appeared to Peter, and then to the Twelve. After that, he appeared to more than 500 of the brothers at the same time, most of whom are still living, though some have fallen asleep. Then he appeared to James, then to all the apostles, and last of all He appeared to me also, as one abnormally born (I Corinthians 15:1-8 NIV).

The result of the good news is church. To quote Tite Tienou, "The proclamation of the gospel results in the creation of the church, the community of Christ. The very presence of the church in society is already the beginning of social transformation."12

God's intention for the world is that the world should be redeemed, that his kingdom should be established. He has chosen to do this through the death and resurrection of His Son. God's instrument in the world is the church. It is the church which is the *sign* of the kingdom. It is the church through which God's wisdom shall be made known:

> His intent was that now, through the church, the mani-fold wisdom of God should be made known to the rulers and authorities in the heavenly realms, according to his eternal purpose which he accomplished in Christ Jesus our Lord (Ephesians 3:10,11 NIV).

Jesus came to them and said:

> "All authority in heaven and on earth has been given to me. Therefore go and make disciples of all nations, baptizing them in the name of the Father and of the Son and of the Holy Spirit, and teaching them to obey every-thing I have commanded you. And surely I will be with you always, to the very end of the age" (Matthew 28:18-20 NIV).

The task of the Church is to make disciples of all nations, to baptize them, and to teach them to obey everything which Christ has commanded. Unfortunately the "Great Commission" has often been interpreted in a very limited sense. Even if one assumes that a disciple is "made" as soon as the acceptance of Christ is announced (a view held by this writer), we cannot escape the fact that they are to be *taught to obey* everything that Christ has commanded. Implicit in this statement is that those to whom this charge has been given are to also fol-low the commands of Jesus.

Staying within the context of Matthew's gospel, what then were these commands?

> As you go, preach this message: "The Kingdom of heaven is near. Heal the sick, raise the dead, cleanse those who have leprosy, drive out demons" (Matthew 10:7,8 NIV).

This passage is contained in Matthew's second discourse (the mission of the Twelve--9:25-10:42). It is closely coupled with Jesus' response to John's disciples:

> "Go back and report to John what you hear and see: The blind receive sight, the lame walk, those who have leprosy

are cured, the deaf hear, the dead are raised, and
the good news is preached to the poor. Blessed is
the man who does not fall away on account of me"
(Matthew 11:4-6 NIV).

In Matthew's fourth discourse (18:1-35) Jesus spells out
the ethics that are to exist within this kingdom, as he did
in the first discourse, which we call the Sermon on the Mount
(Matthew 5:1-7:27 NIV).

What we see then is that the gospel has *consequences* in
the lives of those who claim it for their own. As Karl Barth
has so aptly pointed out in his commentary on Romans, we
should not be surprised that after 11 chapters of well thought-
out doctrine, Paul turns to the consequence of that doctrine
which is ethics--how we live![13] We are to no longer conform
to the pattern of this world so that we will "be able to test
and approve what God's will is--His good, pleasing and perfect
will" (Romans 12:2). We are to fit together as the body of
Christ by using our gifts for that body. Our relationships
are to be above reproach.

Love must be sincere. Hate what is evil; cling to what
is good. Be devoted to one another in brotherly love.
Honor one another above yourselves. Never be lacking in
zeal, but keep your spiritual fervor, serving the Lord.
Be joyful in hope, patient in affliction, faithful in
prayer. Share with God's people who are in need. Practice hospitality. Bless those who persecute you; bless
and do not curse. Rejoice with those who rejoice; mourn
with those who mourn. Live in harmony with one another.
Do not be proud, but be willing to associate with people
of low position. Do not be conceited. Do not repay anyone evil for evil. Be careful to do what is right in
the eyes of everybody. If it is possible, as far as it
depends on you, live at peace with everyone (Romans 12:
9-18 NIV).

The quality of these ethics, the quality of this love is so
different that Jesus calls it a new commandment:

"A new commandment I give you: Love one another. As I
have loved you, so you must love one another. All men
will know that you are my disciples if you love one
another" (John 13:34,35 NIV).

God's intention for the Church then is that the Church act
out its citizenship within the kingdom. This acting out is

both internal and external. Internally we are to conform to the ethics of the kingdom. Externally we are to announce the news of the availability of the kingdom for all who will listen. Both are *natural* responses of Christ's disciples. No priority is given, nor intended. The fact that some evangelicals have been asking the "ultimate question" as to which has priority, evangelism or social responsibility, is philosophical interest only. When the question is asked within a real context, most of the time the answers will be obvious: The road to Jericho sets its own agenda.

HOW DO WE RESPOND TO GOD'S INTENTIONS?

We concluded the previous section by noting that "The road to Jericho sets its own agenda." We have to do theology over and over again as we are faced with new situations. But there is a need to define some basic principles within which we can share a common understanding of the purposes of the Church and upon which we can base our responses to God's initiative.

It is helpful to see that we live in an ever widening circle of relationships: our immediate family, the local fellowship of which we are a part, our neighborhood, the village, city or town within which we live, our country, our continent, our world. The demands of these relationships will necessarily vary as a function of proximity.

> If anyone does not provide for his relatives, and especially for his immediate family, he has denied the faith and is worse than an unbeliever (I Timothy 5:8 NIV).

But there is also the broader injunction:

> ...Let us do good to all people, especially to those who belong to the family of believers" (Galatians 6:10 NIV).

There is to be a continual concern for one another, and for those with whom we come in contact. The people of God are to act as citizens of the kingdom; to act as God would act, as Jesus would act. This can be thought of as the natural living out of our Christian lives.

But the Church is not a group of individuals. The Church is a community of gathered communities. And this Church has been given a *mission* to move out from within its own environs to regions beyond. There are to be those who are to be set apart (Acts 13:2 NIV) for a special service, as were Paul and Barnabas. Whereas everyday life within the community should be lived out with the purpose of doing good in whatever circumstances one finds oneself, there is another dimension, an *intentional* dimension of *going forth* to announce the kingdom, to make disciples, and to teach them all what Jesus has commanded.

The Bible indicates no limitation on the local community's response to its environment. Widows, prisoners, poor, naked and hungry are all the object of concern.

In terms of those who are to be set apart with specific intention for intervening in the lives of others, Paul's apostolic band, and the other evangelistic bands that are characterized in the book of Acts, are obvious examples of people going forth to announce the kingdom, and healing the sick and casting out demons as they went.

But it is also noteworthy how many times the Apostle Paul evidently departed from his task of verbal proclamation to one of carrying out a task of relief (Romans 15:25). Indeed, it is striking that Luke records Paul's first mission on behalf of the church as one of carrying famine relief from Antioch to Jerusalem and follows this with the commissioning by the Holy Spirit of Paul and Barnabas (Acts 11:27-30, 12-25). In other words, Paul does not seem to have any internal dilemma. Both announcing the kingdom and caring for the needs of the saints in Jerusalem have equal priorities for his time and interest. Even though he sees himself as set apart as the "Apostle to the Gentiles," he is still concerned with the needs of a Jewish church community.

Interestingly, the subject of giving financially for others is found throughout Paul's letters, for example his writing to the Corinthians about the gift he is collecting from the churches (II Corinthians 2:8,9). He also exhorts people to work so they can give.

Earlier we defined intentional social transformation as a process of external intervention with the object of enabling people to move to a condition where they are better than they were before. In all of the "external interventions" of Paul and the other apostles we can see this kind of development taking place.

Paul developed a strategy for bringing a particular message to a particular group of people.

> *As his custom was,* Paul went into the synagogue, and on three Sabbath days he reasoned with them from the Scriptures, explaining and proving that the Christ had to suffer and rise from the dead. "This Jesus I am proclaiming to you is the Christ," he said (Acts 17:2,3 NIV).

His intention was to intervene because he believed that the people he went to would be better if they knew the saving power of Jesus Christ. He intervened in sending money to the poor in Jerusalem because he believed that they would be "better" if they had famine relief. He intervened in the life of the church at Rome by giving them instructions on sound doctrine and the ethics that issue forth on sound doctrine because he believed that they would be better people if they gave heed to the gospel he proclaimed.

THE ROLE OF THE HOLY SPIRIT?

So far we have talked about the Church's response to God's intention, but part of the mystery of the Christian life and the mystery of the gospel is the intertwining of the personalities of the actors and of the Creator. Perhaps the writer of the Proverbs sums it up best when he says:

> In his heart a man plans his course, but the Lord determines his steps (Proverbs 16:9 NIV).

Jesus told us that it was the Holy Spirit who would be the primary actor in the world.

> "When he comes, he will convict the world of guilt in regard to sin and righteousness and judgement: in regard to sin, because men do not believe in me; in regard to righteousness, because I'm going to the Father, where you can see me no longer; in regard to judgement, because the prince of this world now stands condemned" (John 16:8-11 NIV).

It is the Holy Spirit who will guide us as we seek to bring glory to God.

> "But when he, the Spirit of truth, comes, he will guide you into all truth. He will not speak on his own; he will speak only what he hears, and he will tell you what

is yet to come. He will bring glory to me by taking from what is mine and making it known to you" (John 16:13,14 NIV).

This operation of the Spirit is evident all through the book of Acts. After the Spirit has come in power in Acts 2, He is promised as a gift to others who repent (Acts 2:30). The Spirit speaks in a vision to Peter (Acts 10:19). The Spirit speaks to the church in setting apart Paul and Barnabas (13:2), and guides them on their way as they go (16:6-8). In the letter to the church in Antioch from Jerusalem, James claims that "It seemed good to the Holy Spirit and to us," as he gives them instructions (Acts 15:25). Paul tells us that it is the Holy Spirit who gives appropriate gifts to the Church (I Corinthians 12).

Now this active involvement of the Holy Spirit is at once both an encouragement and a challenge. What we discover is that the Holy Spirit is involved (or should be!) in all that we do. Indeed, his involvement is so intimate that in Romans 8 Paul tells us:

In the same way, the Spirit helps us in our weakness. We do not know what we ought to pray, but the Spirit himself intercedes for us with groans that words cannot express. And he who searches our hearts knows the mind of the Spirit, because the Spirit intercedes for the saints in accordance with God's will (Romans 8:26,27 NIV).

What a fantastic statement!

MISSION: A BIBLICAL VIEW OF SOCIAL TRANSFORMATION

Whereas the world may have a desire to intervene on the behalf of others for their own betterment, Christians are *commanded* to do so. "All the world" is the object of redemption. and the Church and the Holy Spirit are the vehicles of that redemption. There have been those who have distinguished between "Great Commandment" ("love your brother as yourself") and the last Great Commission. But the Great Commission includes all of the commands of Christ.

It is time for us to recapture the beautiful word "mission" for our own use. Too long, we Evangelicals have been turned away by those who would interpret "mission" as meaning the building of God's kingdom by men and women on earth. The

Church is *sent* into the world as an agent of God's redemption. That redemption covers all of his creation.

The responsibility of each local body of Christians is to their fellowship and their community, as well as to the larger church and to the world. The very act of being a Christian assumes "doing good" to all men. Some will be gifted and called to act out their Christianity in the spontaneous ways of every day living, perhaps even within the confines of their own Christian community. Others will be gifted and called to be, at times, more intentional in the larger secular community of which they are a part: visiting widows, caring for orphans, and those in prison, seeking to change those aspects of society which oppress people--pornography, prostitution, racism, loneliness, sweatshops, false advertising. Then there will be those who, like Paul and Barnabas, have been gifted and set apart for completely intentional work, both at home and abroad.

In all this we declare that the greatest good that one can do is to so effectively and convincingly proclaim the kingdom so that others are attracted to Jesus and become His disciples. In this sense, evangelization is central to the work of the Church, not only because eternal life is of supreme importance to the individual, but because the greater number of Christians, the greater amount of good will be done to all men. But to proclaim Christ without acting as Christ is a contradiction of terms. The road to Jericho *does* set its own agenda!

The ultimate "better" is therefore to become a citizen of the kingdom and act as a community of citizens of the kingdom. The Christian goal for social transformation is therefore that people should be able to have an opportunity to respond to the commands of the gospel and live in obedience to it, *because they have had it modeled before their eyes.*

The implication of this is that a biblical view is one which is always an invitation to repent and become a disciple (one who also intervenes on behalf of the kingdom). It is not a question of *if* social transformation includes evangelization, it is a question of strategy, a question of when and how. There could well be a situation in which an entire program of development would include only an attempt in which an entire program of development would include only an attempt to encourage people to come to know Christ. On the other side of the coin, one can contemplate a situation in relationship to which verbal proclamation was impossible *for the time being.*

IMPLICATIONS

How then do we go about the business of *Christian* social
transformation? If we believe that the way we have previously carried out social transformation has actually been a dis-
guised form of Seventeenth Century humanism known as "development" what is our response? Do we design new and more effective programs? Can we create checklists for those who are
now to carry out the *Christian* social transformation.

The answer is at once simple and extremely complex: We
are called to *be* the church, the people of God and community,
as the New Testament described us to be. The question is not
what we are to *do* but what we are to be, and to become and attempt to become.

In order for the church to be "salt and light" in the world
it must first set about its own social transformation. In
order for the church to be a proclaimer of justice in the
world, it must find justice within itself.

The church too is in the process of social transformation.
We are in the process of becoming alive in the dialectic of a
kingdom that has come and is yet to arrive. We live in the
light of our own sinfulness. But somehow we must not let our
own failures immobilize us.

We need to be about the business of presenting our bodies
a living sacrifice by having our minds renewed (Romans 12:1,2)
even as we are about the business of "doing good to all men."

As Maurice Sinclair has so beautifully pointed out (see his
paper in this volume) there is a need for biblical wisdom,
wisdom which is concerned with daily living, doing as well as
reflecting. We need a biblically balanced wisdom which positively increases our anticipation of what God will do, but
which also nerves us to endure what Satan will do. For social
transformation to be brought about, wisdom is required to define the desirable state into which society should be transformed.

Continuing to quote Sinclair, "Christian action in the
world is slow burning. It hopes all things, endures all
things. There is a need for patient building, even when tackling global issues."

We are involved in a process. This paper, this consultation, the meeting of Christians "eyeball to eyeball" is all
part of our growing *into* Christ.

Our recent (and rapidly developing!) evangelical history
has brought us first a reawakening of our social responsibility; second, independent attempts to meet that social responsibility by separating physical and spiritual need; third,
a deepening understanding that if the Church is to be conformed in the image of Christ it must act Christianly in all
situations. We have no mandate to separate verbal and physical proclamation of the kingdom; and fourth, a growing understanding of the *wholeness* of announcing and demonstrating
God's redemptive purpose in the world.

BIBLIOGRAPHY

Barth, Karl. *The Epistles of the Romans*. London: Oxford University Press, 1933.

Fitzgerald, Frances. *America Revised*. Boston: Little, Brown and Company, 1979.

Ladd, George E. *Jesus and the Kingdom*. New York: Harper and Row, 1964.

Marsden, George M. *Fundamentalism and American Culture*. New York: Oxford University Press, 1980.

Stewart, Edward C. *American Cultural Patterns: "A Cross-Cultural Perspective."* Chicago: Intercultural Press, 1972.

Stott, John and Coote, Robert T., editors. *Gospel and Culture*. Pasadena: William Carey Library, 1979.

FOOTNOTES

1. Stott, John and Coote, Robert T., editors, *Gospel and Culture,* (William Carey Library, Pasadena, CA, 1979)

2. Marsden, George M., *Fundamentalism and American Culture,* (Oxford University Press, New York, NY, 1980)

3. Fitzgerald, Frances, *America Revised,* (Little, Brown and Company, Boston, MA, 1979)

4. Stewart, Edward C., *American Cultural Patterns: A Cross-Cultural Perspective,* (Intercultural Press, Chicago, IL, 1972)

5. The last attempt at research on the movement of the church in the world was done in 1924.

6. Of course, it was not only the "relief and development" agencies who had discovered ways of attracting funds through the mass media. The "electronic church" in America discovered the same response to its appeals.

7. A major exception to this was World Vision International which continued to attempt to find an integration between social responsibility and evangelism and continued to announce to itself and to others that "evangelism was the bottom line."

8. See *Evangelicals and Development: Toward a Theology of Social Change,* edited by Ronald J. Sider, Westminster Press, Philadelphia, PA, 1981.

9. See the Grand Rapids report--*Evangelism and Social Responsibility,* a joint publication of the LCWE and WEF.

10. See Tito Paredes paper in this volume.

11. Ladd, George E., *Jesus and the Kingdom,* Harper and Row, New York, NY, 1964)

12. See his paper in this volume.

13. Barth, Karl, *The Epistles of the Romans.* (Oxford University Press, London, 1933)

EVANGELISM AND SOCIAL RESPONSIBILITY

CRESR '82 Report

The World Evangelical Fellowship and the Lausanne Committee for World Evangelization jointly sponsored a Consultation on the Relationship Between Evangelism and Social Responsibility (CRESR). In June 1982, 50 evangelical leaders from all over the world came together in Grand Rapids, Michigan, to struggle with this important issue. The Lausanne Covenant made some significant statements about Christian concern for the world and our social responsibility in it. However, in the ensuing years there were some evangelical Christians who felt that the Church was giving inadequate attention to the question of social responsibility, while there were others who felt the task of world evangelization was suffering as a result of overattention to the social concerns. The CRESR conference was a result of that concern.

The Steering Committee of the present consultation have always considered that the work of CRESR would be seen as part of the ongoing discussion of the Church's effort at social transformation. The results of the CRESR conference, *Grand Rapids Report--Evangelism and Social Responsibility*, is copied here in its entirety.

We give our gracious acknowledgement to both WEF and LCWE for permission to reproduce it.

C O N T E N T S

VI. HISTORY AND ESCHATOLOGY

    A. False Dreams

    B. Differing Millennarian Views

    C. Judgment to Come

    D. The Eschatological Vision

    E. Continuity

    F. The Christian Hope

VII. GUIDELINES FOR ACTION

    A. Forms of Evangelism and Social Responsibility

        1. Social Service and Evangelism
        2. Social Action and Evangelism

    B. Agents of Evangelism and Social Responsibility

        1. Evangelism and Social Service
        2. Evangelism and Social Action

    C. The Local Church in a Free Society

        1. Intercession
        2. Love
        3. Teaching
        4. Power
        5. Vocations
        6. Groups
        7. Resources

    D. The Church under Repression

        1. Consistency
        2. Love
        3. Witness
        4. Solidarity
        5. Suffering

CONCLUSION: A CALL TO OBEDIENCE

INTRODUCTION

A. The Context of the Consultation

Jesus Christ calls all his followers to witness to him in word and deed, that is, to share his good news with others and to serve them according to their needs.

In the Lausanne Covenant, which was adopted at the end of the International Congress on World Evangelization in 1974, Paragraph 4 is entitled "The Nature of Evangelism" and Paragraph 5 "Christian Social Responsibility." But the Covenant leaves these two duties side by side without spelling out their relationship to each other, except to say in Paragraph 6 that "in the church's mission of sacrificial service, evangelism is primary."

As the years have passed, it has become increasingly necessary to complete Lausanne's unfinished business and to define more clearly what is included in "social responsibility," whose responsibility it is, and how it relates to evangelism. For many fear that the more we evangelicals are committed to the one, the less we shall be committed to the other; that if we commit ourselves to both, one is bound to suffer; and in particular that a preoccupation with social responsibility will be sure to blunt our evangelistic zeal.

So, in the conviction that evangelical Christians, who seek to live under the lordship of Christ and the authority of Scripture, and who pray to be guided by the Holy Spirit, should not be divided on an issue of such importance, it was decided to call an international consultation to study the matter. Jointly sponsored by the Lausanne Committee for World Evangelization and the World Evangelical Fellowship, the Consultation would focus on Scripture, church history, modern theologies, and the contemporary church in order to help participants understand each other better, reach a greater unity of mind, and commit themselves to a yet more active fulfilment of their evangelistic and social responsibilities.

We have not been disappointed. Fifty evangelical leaders from 27 different countries have spent a week together at Grand Rapids, Michigan. Each day began with Bible study and prayer. Eight papers, and the responses to them, have been presented to us. The issues raised by them we have discussed in both small groups and plenary sessions, and we have been encouraged by case studies from several different cultures. Throughout the week, through patient listening to one another we have grown in mutual understanding and respect. Although our agreement is not total, it is substantial, and we have been given grace to face our disagreements with charity.

This statement is a summary of the consensus which has emerged, but it makes no attempt to conceal our differences. Although participants have not been asked to endorse it individually, they thoroughly scrutinized its first draft and amended it. We now publish it with the desire to share with others the fruits of our discussion and in the hope that they will be stimulated, as we have been, to more conscientious evangelism and social responsibility.

B. Scripture and Culture

The stated goals of CRESR indicated that we would focus first and foremost on Holy Scripture. We have been determined, therefore, to let our minds be formed not by any human idiology but by the Word of God.

We have found it a struggle, however. For all of us are conditioned to some extent by the cultural environment in which we live, by our ideological settings and theological traditions, and this tends to determine what we are able to "see" in Scripture. It is not that God's Word is unclear in itself, nor that its meaning is captive to any culture. The problem lies rather within our minds as we read. The assumptions we bring with us, which are often insufficiently examined and corrected in the light of God's Word, distort our understanding of it. "Now we see in a mirror dimly" (I Cor. 13:12).

How else can we explain some of the painful anomalies that soon came to light in our discussion? To give a few examples: we heard of some Christians in a Confucian culture who, because of its assumption of the ultimate harmony of all things, have surrendered their belief in the uniqueness of Christ as Savior. Under the pressure of religious pluralism, others have fallen into universalism. In some parts of the United States there are churches which still close their doors to blacks and remain oblivious to the indignities to which discrimination has brought them, while at the same time proclaiming the love of God. In South Africa, social policy and legislation are built on the theory of the inviolable diversity of the races. Many churches, whose members are sincere Christian people, nevertheless share this view of racial irreconcilability, while continuing to preach the good news of

reconciliation. In Europe and North America, secularism--
which is a child of the Enlightenment--even has invaded the
lives of Christians and effectively banished the reality of
God from much of what they do.

It is easy to censure fellow believers in distant parts,
however, and to occupy ourselves with removing splinters
from their eyes while failing to perceive the logs in our
own. It has become apparent during our Consultation that
those of us who live in affluence do not feel the pain and
humiliation of poverty as readily as those who live among
the poor. To the former, social responsibility may remain a
topic for academic debate; to the latter, it is a self-evident Christian obligation. Yet moral blindspots are not pe-
culiar to white or black, affluent or poor, north or south.
They are a symptom of that fall in which we all have participated. It is our sin, as it comes to expression in our various cultural assumptions and tries to find justification in
them, which often blinds our eyes to what God wants us to
see in his Word. An acknowledgment of this tragic fact at
the beginning of our Consultation challenged us to listen all
the more attentively to one another and to God's Word.

I. A CALL TO WORSHIP AND THANKSGIVING

God created and redeemed our world in order to reveal his
infinite majesty and his eternal love. Therefore, the primary
sin is to refuse to honor him as God or to give him thanks
(Rom. 1:21), while the supreme duty of his redeemed people is
to worship him in humble praise and obedience. "We love, because he first loved us" (I John 4:19).

From this adoring and loving encounter with God, there immediately flows a desire to share his love with our fellow
human beings, both by telling them how God in Christ has loved
them and by serving them in deeds of mercy and justice.

Only if they are rooted in a vertical relationship to God
in worship can the church's two ministries of *kerygma* (proclamation) and *diakonia* (service) be held in proper balance and
tension. Only in this way, too, can evangelism and social
responsibility be kept from degenerating into merely human
activity and even propaganda. The mission of any church can
fall into this trap.

It is therefore urgent to heed the pre-eminent call to
worship and thanksgiving.

II. A CALL TO WORLD EVANGELIZATION

A. Contemporary Need

When we met at Lausanne in 1974, we calculated that more than 2,700 million people were still unevangelized. Now, eight years later, we believe that the number has risen to three billion, and that this comprises many thousands of people groups. We cannot think of them as statistics, however. They are human beings like ourselves. Yet, though created by God like God and for God, they are now living without God. The tragedy of this is painful, and the task of overcoming it is enormous. It calls for concerted prayer and evangelism on an unprecedented scale.

B. A Definition

But what is evangelism? This is the definition given in the Lausanne Covenant (Paragraph 4):

> To evangelize is to spread the good news that Jesus Christ died for our sins and was raised from the dead according to the Scriptures, and that as the reigning Lord he now offers the forgiveness of sins and the liberating gift of the Spirit to all who repent and believe. Our Christian presence in the world is indispensable to evangelism, and so is that kind of dialogue whose purpose is to listen sensitively in order to understand. But evangelism itself is the proclamation of the historical, biblical Christ as Saviour and Lord, with a view to persuading people to come to him personally and so be reconciled to God. In issuing the gospel invitation we have no liberty to conceal the cost of discipleship. Jesus still calls all who would follow him to deny themselves, take up their cross, and identify themselves with his new community. The results of evangelism include obedience to Christ, incorporation into his church and responsible service in the world.

We heartily endorse this statement, and we wish to emphasize that reconciliation to God lies at the very heart of the good news. Our only criticism is that the statement sounds somewhat impersonal, since neither the evangelist nor the evangelized is characterized in it as a person of flesh and blood. Yet that is what they both are, and evangelism involves a personal encounter between them. The most essential qualities of gospel messengers are loyalty to the biblical gospel and personal authenticity. They must embody the good news they proclaim. Few things repel people more than hypocrisy, and few things attract them more than integrity. As for the persons who hear the gospel, we acknowledge the need to approach them with great sensitivity. Many will already have been convicted of their sin and guilt, and it will be possible at once to share with them the good news of forgiveness. Others will be oppressed by a different sense of alienation. So we shall have to begin where they are, with their "felt needs," and then lead them to where they have to come, that is, to Christ as Savior from their deepest need--their sinful separation from God.

C. Motivation for Evangelism

There are many incentives to evangelism. To begin with, there is simple obedience to the Great Commission, and to the Lord of the Great Commission, to whom all authority has been given (Matt.28:18-20). Then there is the terrible knowledge we have that human beings without Christ are lost or "perishing" (e.g., John 3:16; I Cor. 1:18), and our earnest desire in love to reach them with the Gospel before it is too late. Another powerful motive is zeal or "jealousy" for the glory of Christ, whom God has super-exalted in order that every knee should bow to him and every tongue confess him Lord (Phil. 2:9-11).

Yet we believe that the most basic of all motives lies in the very nature of God himself, and in his saving work by which he revealed himself. We do not exaggerate when we affirm that the living God is a missionary God. He created all humankind, is "the God of the spirits of all flesh," and when calling Abraham promised through his posterity to bless "all the families of the earth."

Next, Jesus Christ during his public ministry sent his disciples to "the lost sheep of the house of Israel," and subsequently, he commissioned them to go and make disciples of all the nations. Between these two missions lay his death and resurrection. He died on the cross for the sins of the world, and was raised and exalted to be Lord. The church's universal mission derives from Christ's universal authority.

Thirdly, the Holy Spirit is a missionary Spirit, and Pentecost was a missionary event. He gave his people power for witness, as Jesus promised, and thrust them out, as Jesus foretold, to the ends of the earty (Acts 1:8).

This Trinitarian basis for mission is primary. It is the missionary heart of God himself, Father, Son and Holy Spirit.

If he yearns in his love for his lost world, we his people
must share his yearning. Commitment to world mission is un-
avoidable, and indifference to it inexcusable.

III. A CALL TO SOCIAL RESPONSIBILITY

A. Contemporary Need

We are appalled to know that about 800 million people, or
one-fifth of the human race, are destitute, lacking the basic
necessities for survival, and that thousands of them die of
starvation every day. Many more millions are without adequate shelter and clothing, without clean water and health
care, without opportunities for education and employment, and
are condemned to eke out a miserable existence without the
possibility of self-improvement for themselves or their families. They can only be described as "oppressed" by the gross
economic inequality from which they suffer and the diverse
economic systems which cause and perpetuate it.

The oppression of others is political. They are denied
fundamental human rights by totalitarian regimes of the extreme left or right, while if they protest they are imprisoned without trial, tortured, and killed. Yet others suffer
discrimination on account of their race or sex. And all of
us are oppressed by global problems which seem to defy solu-
tion--conditions of overpopulation and famine, the exploitation of non-renewable resources of energy, the spoliation of
the environment, community violence, war, and the ever-present
threat of a nuclear holocaust.

All these are rooted in the profound sinfulness of humankind, and they demand from the people of God a radical response of compassion. Only the Gospel can change human hearts,
and no influence makes people more human than the Gospel does.
Yet we cannot stop with verbal proclamation. In addition to
worldwide evangelization, the people of God should become
deeply involved in relief, aid, development and the quest for
social justice and peace.

B. A Definition

Here is the paragraph on "Christian Social Responsibility"
in the Lausanne Covenant (Paragraph 5):

We affirm that God is both the Creator and the Judge of
all men. We therefore should share his concern for justice and reconciliation throughout human society and for

the liberation of men from every kind of oppression. Because mankind is made in the image of God, every person, regardless of race, religion, colour, culture, class, sex or age, has an intrinsic dignity because of which he should be respected and served, not exploited. Here too we express penitence both for our neglect and for having sometimes regarded evangelism and social concern as mutually exclusive. Although reconciliation with man is not reconciliation with God, nor is social action evangelism, nor is political liberation salvation, nevertheless we affirm that evangelism and sociopolitical involvement are both part of our Christian duty. For both are necessary expressions of our doctrines of God and man, our love for our neighbour and our obedience to Jesus Christ. The message of salvation implies also a message of judgment upon every form of alienation, oppression and discrimination, and we should not be afraid to denounce evil and injustice wherever they exist. When people receive Christ they are born again into his kingdom and must seek not only to exhibit but also to spread its righteousness in the midst of an unrighteous world. The salvation we claim should be transforming us in the totality of our personal and social responsibilities. Faith without works is dead.

C. Motivation for Social Responsibility

Again, as in evangelism so in social responsibility, we discern the fundamental basis for our actions in the character of God himself. He is the God of justice, who in every human community hates evil and loves righteousness. He is also the God of mercy. In the first Bible study of our Consultation we read of him that, though he made the universe, he nevertheless humbles himself to care for the needy, "executes justice for the oppressed," and "gives food to the hungry." In addition, "the Lord sets the prisoners free; the Lord opens the eyes of the blind. The Lord lifts up those who are bowed down; the Lord loves the righteous. The Lord watches over the sojourners, he upholds the widow and the fatherless; but the way of the wicked he brings to ruin" (Psalm 146:5-9). We recognize that we have neither the authority nor the power to do everything God does. Nevertheless, since this text shows us the kind of God he is, and since these concerns of his were further expressed in the demands of his law and prophets, it is indisputable what kind of people we should be, seeking justice, freedom, and dignity for all, especially the powerless who cannot seek it for themselves.

It is no surprise that Jesus reflected this lovingkindness of God his Father. He had compassion on the hungry,
the sick, the bereaved, the outcast. He had compassion on
the crowds because they were harassed and helpless, like
sheep without a shepherd. And always his compassion issued
in appropriate action.

Moreover, the first fruit of the Holy Spirit is love (Gal.
5:22). It is therefore he who gives his people a tender social conscience, and impels them to immerse themselves in
humanitarian relief, development, and the search for social
justice.

Thus we find that there is a Trinitarian basis for our social duties, just as there is for our evangelistic outreach.
We who claim to belong to God and worship him, Father, Son
and Holy Spirit, must express our worship in these activities.
Orare et laborare.

IV. THE RELATIONSHIP BETWEEN
EVANGELISM AND SOCIAL RESPONSIBILITY

A. Historical Background

It appears to us that evangelism and social concern have
been intimately related to one another throughout the history
of the church, although the relationship has been expressed
in a variety of ways. Christian people often have engaged in
both activities quite unselfconsciously, without feeling any
need to define what they were doing or why. So the problem
of their relationship, which led to the convening of this
Consultation, is comparatively new, and for historical reasons
it is of particular importance to evangelical Christians.

The Great Awakening in North America, the Pietistic Movement in Germany, and the Evangelical Revival under the Wesleys
in Britain, which all took place in the early part of the 18th
Century, proved a great stimulus to philanthropy as well as
evangelism. The next generation of British evangelicals
founded missionary societies and gave conspicuous service in
public life, notably Wilberforce in the abolition of the slave
trade and of slavery itself, and Shaftesbury in the improvement of conditions in the factories.

But at the end of the 19th Century and the beginning of the
20th, the so-called "social gospel" was developed by theological liberals. Some of them confused the Kingdom of God with
Christian civilization in general, and with social democracy

in particular, and they went on to imagine that by their social programs they could build God's Kingdom on earth. It
seems to have been in over-reaction to this grave distortion
of the Gospel that many evangelicals became suspicious of
social involvement. And now that evangelicals are recovering
a social conscience and rediscovering our evangelical social
heritage, it is understandable that some of our brothers and
sisters are looking askance at us and suspecting us of relap-
sing into the old heresy of the social gospel. But the responsible social action which the biblical Gospel lays upon
us, and the liberal "social gospel" which was a perversion
of the true Gospel, are two quite different things. As we
said in the Lausanne Covenant, "we reject as a proud self-
confident dream the notion that man can ever build a utopia
on earth" (Paragraph 15).

Another cause of the divorce of evangelism and social responsibility is the dichotomy which often has developed in
our thinking. We tend to set over against one another in an
unhealthy way soul and body, the individual and society, redemption and creation, grace and nature, heaven and earth,
justification and justice, faith and works. The Bible certainly distinguishes between these, but it also relates them
to each other, and it instructs us to hold each pair in a
dynamic and creative tension. It is as wrong to disengage
them, as in "dualism," as it is to confuse them, as in "mon-
ism." It was for this reason that the Lausanne Covenant,
speaking of evangelism and socio-political involvement, affirmed that they "are both part of our Christian duty" (Paragraph 5).

B. Particular Situations and Gifts

In wanting to affirm that evangelism and social action belong to each other, we are not meaning that neither can ever
exist in independence of the other. For example, if the Good
Samaritan had been a Christian, he could not have been blamed
for tending the wounds of the brigands' victim and failing to
preach to him. Nor is Philip to be blamed for preaching the
Gospel to the Ethiopian eunuch in his chariot and failing to
enquire into his social needs. There are still occasions when
it is legitimate to concentrate on one or the other of these
two Christian duties. It is not wrong to hold an evangelistic crusade without an accompanying program of social service.
Nor is it wrong to feed the hungry in a time of famine without
first preaching to them, for, to quote an African proverb,
"an empty belly has no ears." It was similar in the days of
Moses. He brought the Israelites in Egypt the good news of

their liberation, "but they did not listen to him, because
of their broken spirit and their cruel bondage" (Exod.6:9).

There is another justification for sometimes separating
evangelism and social action, in addition to the existential
demands of a particular situation: namely, the distribution
of spiritual gifts. The church is a charismatic community,
the Body of Christ, whose members are endowed by the Holy
Spirit with different gifts for different forms of ministry.
Some are gifted to be "evangelists" (Eph.4:11), while others
are called to "service" (Rom.12:7; I Pet.4) or to "acts of
mercy" (Rom.12:8). Whatever our gifts may be, we are neither
to depreciate them nor to boast of them (I Cor.12:14-26), but
rather to use them for the common good.

The best example of the outworking of this principle occurs in Acts 6 where the apostles, who had been called to
"prayer and the ministry of the Word," were in danger of becoming preoccupied with "serving tables," that is, with caring
for the material needs of the church's widows. So seven men
were appointed to perform this social service, although Stephen and Philip also did some preaching (Acts 6:8-15; 8:5-13).
This left the apostles free to concentrate on the pastoral
ministry for which they had been commissioned, although they
also retained a social concern (e.g., Gal.2:10). Still today,
Christ calls some to pastoral, others to social, others to
evangelistic ministries; in fact, there is a wide diversity
of spiritual gifts, callings, and ministries within the body
of Christ.

C. Three Kinds of Relationships

Having seen that both particular situations and specialist
callings can legitimately separate our evangelistic and social responsibilities, we are now ready to consider how in
general they relate to one another. What has emerged from our
discussion is that there is no one relationship in which they
are joined, but there are at least three equally valid relationships.

First, social action is a *consequence* of evangelism. That
is, evangelism is the means by which God brings people to new
birth, and their new life manifests itself in the service of
others. Paul wrote that "faith works through love" (Gal.5:6),
James that "I will show you my faith by my works (James 2:18),
and John that God's love within us will overflow in serving
our needy brothers and sisters (I John 3:16-18). As Robert

E. Speer wrote about the Gospel in 1900: "wherever it goes, it plants in the hearts of men forces that produce new lives; it plants in communities of men forces that create new social combinations." We have heard of evangelists in our own day who, during their missions or crusades, actively encourage Christians (including new converts) to become involved in programs to meet specific local, human needs. This effectively highlights the serving dimension of Christian conversion and commitment.

We can go further than this, however. Social responsibility is more than the consequence of evangelism; it is also one of its principal aims. For Christ gave himself for us not only "to redeem us from all iniquity" but also "to purify for himself a people of his own who are zealous for good deeds" (Tit. 2:14). Similarly, through the gospel we are "created in Christ Jesus for good works which God prepared beforehand, that we should walk in them" (Eph. 2:10). Good works cannot save, but they are an indispensable evidence of salvation (James 2:14-26).

In saying this, we are not claiming that compassionate service is an automatic consequence of evangelism or of conversion, however. Social responsibility, like evangelism, should therefore be included in the teaching ministry of the church. For we have to confess the inconsistencies in our own lives and the dismal record of evangelical failure, often as a result of the cultural blindspots to which we have already referred. This has grave consequences. When we do not allow the Word of God to transform us in all areas of our personal and social life, we seem to validate the Marxist criticism of religion.

Secondly, social action can be a *bridge* to evangelism. It can break down prejudice and suspicion, open closed doors, and gain a hearing for the Gospel. Jesus himself sometimes performed works of mercy before proclaiming the Good News of the Kingdom. In more recent times, we were reminded, the construction of dams by the Basel missionaries in Northern Ghana opened a way for the Gospel, and much missionary medical, agricultural, nutritional, and educational work has had a similar effect. To add a contemporary western example, a recent crusade in an American city was preceded and accompanied by a "Love in Action" program, with the evangelist's encouragement. Several "social uplift" groups cooperated and were able to extend their ministries to the inner city poor. As a result, we were told, a number of people came under the sound of the Gospel who would not otherwise have come to the crusade.

Further, by seeking to serve people, it is possible to move from their "felt needs" to their deeper need concerning their relationship with God. Whereas, as another participant put it, "if we turn a blind eye to the suffering, the social oppression, the alienation and loneliness of people, let us not be surprised if they turn a deaf ear to our message of eternal salvation." We are aware of the danger of making "rice Christians," that is, of securing converts only because of the physical benefits we offer. But we have to take this risk so long as we retain our own integrity and serve people out of genuine love and not with an ulterior motive. Then our actions will be "not bribes but bridges-- bridges of love to the world."

Thirdly, social action not only follows evangelism as its consequence and aim, and precedes it as its bridge, but also accompanies it as its *partner.* They are like the two blades of a scissors or the two wings of a bird. This partnership is clearly seen in the public ministry of Jesus, who not only preached the Gospel but fed the hungry and healed the sick. In his ministry, *kerygma* (proclamation) and *diakonia* (service) went hand in hand. His words explained his works, and his works dramatized his words. Both were expressions of his compassion for people, and both should be of ours. Both also issue from the lordship of Jesus, for he sends us out into the world both to preach and to serve. If we proclaim the good news of God's love, we must manifest his love in caring for the needy. Indeed, so close is this link between proclaiming and serving, that they actually overlap.

This is not to say that they should be identified with each other, for evangelism is not social responsibility, nor is social responsibility evangelism. Yet, each involves the other.

To proclaim Jesus as Lord and Savior (evangelism) has social implications, since it summons people to repent of social as well as personal sins, and to live a new life of righteousness and peace in the new society which challenges the old.

To give food to the hungry (social responsibility) has evangelistic implications, since good works of love, if done in the name of Christ, are a demonstration and commendation of the Gospel.

It has been said, therefore, that evangelism, even when it does not have a primarily social intention, nevertheless has a social dimension, while social responsibility, even when it does not have a primarily evangelistic intention, nevertheless has an evangelistic dimension.

Thus, evangelism and social responsibility, while distinct from one another, are integrally related in our proclamation of and obedience to the Gospel. The partnership is, in reality, a marriage.

D. The Question of Primacy

This brings us to the question whether the partnership between evangelism and social responsibility is equal or unequal, that is, whether they are of identical importance or whether one takes precedence over the other. The Lausanne Covenant affirms that "in the church's mission of sacrificial service evangelism is primary" (Paragraph 6). Although some of us have felt uncomfortable about this phrase, lest by it we should be breaking the partnership, yet we are able to endorse and explain it in two ways, in addition to the particular situations and callings already mentioned.

First, evangelism has a certain priority. We are not referring to an invariable *temporal* priority, because in some situations a social ministry will take precedence, but to a *logical* one. The very fact of Christian social responsibility presupposes socially responsible Christians, and it can only be by evangelism and discipling that they have become such. If social action is a consequence and aim of evangelism (as we have asserted), then evangelism must precede it. In addition, social progress is being hindered in some countries by the prevailing religious culture; only evangelism can change this.

Secondly, evangelism relates to people's eternal destiny, and in bringing them Good News of salvation, Christians are doing what nobody else can do. Seldom if ever should we have to choose between satisfying physical hunger and spiritual hunger, or between healing bodies and saving souls, since an authentic love for our neighbor will lead us to serve him or her as a whole person. Nevertheless, if we must choose, then we have to say that the supreme and ultimate need of all humankind is the saving grace of Jesus Christ, and that therefore a person's eternal, spiritual salvation is of greater importance than his or her temporal and material well-being (cf. II Cor. 4:16-18). As the Thailand Statement expressed it, "of all the tragic needs of human beings none is greater than their alienation from their Creator and the terrible reality of eternal death for those who refuse to repent and believe." Yet this fact must not make us indifferent to the degradations of human poverty and oppression. The choice, we believe, is largely conceptual. In practice, as in the public ministry of Jesus, the two are inseparable, at least in open societies, and we shall seldom if ever have to choose between them. Rather than competing with each other, they mutually support and strengthen each other in an upward spiral of increased concern for both.

E. Some Examples

The three relationships between evangelism and social responsibility need not occur in isolation from each other. Instead, they often blend together in such a way that it is difficult to distinguish them. This was made clear to us as we listened to a number of case studies.

The "Precious Jewels Development" project in Cebu City, Philippines, is a many-pronged effort by Christians to serve their neighbors, improving their means of local livelihood, offering education and child care, developing a nutritional program, and giving emergency relief. In one respect, it is simply an expression of love, the natural consequence of the knowledge of Christ which the Gospel has brought. In another it has been a bridge to evangelism. Non-Christians "opened themselves" to Christians. Their reserve was melted, and they became ready to hear the Gospel. Thus, social service, evangelism's consequence and bridge, also became its partner God himself was loving them, one of them said, through the preaching of the Gospel and the meeting of their practical needs.

Another project in the Philippines ("Project Gamtabeng") has come to the aid of a hill tribe whose very existence was threatened by urbanization and industrialization. Medical, agricultural, and educational development have gone hand in hand with evangelism and church planting. A convert summed up the Project's aims by saying"Through Project Gamtabeng, I became an heir to my Father's heaven and earth."

We also heard about some nomadic Maasai people of Northern Kenya who had come to Christ. Amidst dancing and singing, they were being welcomed into the church by the Anglican bishop. As they celebrated, however, he noticed that half of them were either blind or nearly so. "This convinced me," he said, "that we cannot evangelize the spiritually blind and

leave them in their physical blindness." Immediately, therefore, a health care program was developed.

Next, we were told of an Indian couple, both doctors, who
have labored for more than 20 years in Jankhed, Maharashtra.
They trained despised outcaste widows in the elements of pre-
and post-natal care, proved their credentials as healers by
establishing a small operating theater, and taught out of
the Gospels how Jesus gave dignity to women. As a result,
child mortality has been reduced almost to zero, social justice has increased and fear has diminished, and many people
in seventeen villages, which for 50 years had not responded
to the Good News, now are turning to Jesus.

In addition, we learned about the Voice of Calvary ministries in Mississippi, where for 22 years the Gospel has been
shared, and the physical, spiritual, economic, social, and
material needs of people have been met. Evangelism, community development, and racial reconciliation through the church
have gone hand in hand. The reason for this holistic ministry is that its pioneer came face to face with the cycle of
poverty in which the people were trapped. They were so preoccupied with the struggle to survive, that they could not
attend to spiritual realities. It would have been almost impossible to offer Jesus Christ to them and ignore their other
needs. So the Gospel of love is verbalized and actualized
simultaneously.

V. THE GOOD NEWS OF THE KINGDOM

Having suggested three ways in which evangelism and social
responsibility are related to one another, we come to an even
more basic way in which they are united, namely by the Gospel.
For the Gospel is the root, of which both evangelism and social responsibility are the fruits. As Good News of God's
love in Christ, the Gospel demands both to be preached and to
be lived. Once we have come to know it, we are obliged to
share it with others and to "adorn" it by good deeds (Tit.
2:10).

So what is the Good News? No simple answer can be given,
since a variety of models is developed in the New Testament.
At this Consultation, however, we have concentrated on two
comprehensive models. We have thought of the Gospel both as
"good news of salvation" (Eph. 1:13) and as "good news of the
Kingdom of God" (Matt. 4:23; Mark 1:14,15; Luke 4:43).

A. Salvation

We all are agreed that salvation is a broad term in the sense that it embraces the totality of God's redemptive purpose.

It begins with *new life*. Through the substitutionary death and historical resurrection of Jesus, the individual believer is "ransomed, healed, restored, forgiven." Saved from guilt and the judgment of God, he or she is adopted into God's family as his child.

Salvation continues with the *new community*. For salvation in the Bible is never a purely individualistic concept. As in the Old Testament, so in the New, God is calling out a people for himself and binding it to himself by a solemn covenant. The members of this new society, reconciled through Christ to God and one another, are being drawn from all races and cultures. Indeed, this single new humanity--which Christ has created and in which no barriers are tolerated--is an essential part of the Good News (Eph. 2).

Thirdly, salvation includes the *new world* which God one day will make. We are looking forward not only to the redemption and resurrection of our bodies, but to the renovation of the entire created order, which will be liberated from decay, pain, and death (Rom. 8:18-25). Of this cosmic renewal the resurrection of Christ was the beginning and the pledge.

Having agreed on these three dimensions of salvation (personal, social, and cosmic), we went on to pose a further question: Is salvation experienced only by those who consciously confess Christ as Lord and Savior? Or is it right in addition to refer to the emergence of justice and peace in the wider community as "salvation" and to attribute to the grace of Christ every beneficial social transformation? Some of us do not find salvation-language inappropriate for such situations, even when Christ is not acknowledged in them. Most of us, however, consider that it is more prudent and biblical to reserve the vocabulary of salvation for the experience of reconciliation with God through Christ and its direct consequences. None of us would dream of following those who have portrayed Hitler's Germany or Mao's China or Castro's Cuba as having experienced "salvation." All of us are united in wishing to honor Christ as universal Lord.

B. The Kingdom of God

It is well known that Jesus came preaching the Kingdom of God. According to the Synoptic Gospels, the Kingdom was the major theme of his sermons and parables. Although "the kingdom of God" is largely replaced by "eternal life" in John's Gospel and by the lordship of Christ in Paul's letters, so that we recognize the diversity of salvation models and wish to avoid committing ourselves exclusively to any one of them, nevertheless the Kingdom is a richly suggestive concept, with significant applications to the modern world. Hence, our decision to focus on it.

The Kingdom of God is the rule of God, and the whole Bible declares that God is King. As the Creator, he is both King of nature (sustaining what he has made) and King of history (ordering the life of nations). "The Lord reigns" is a frequent shout of joy in the Old Testament, expressing Israel's confidence in the providential rule of God over the world. Over themselves Israel knew that Yahweh reigned in a special way. For even after the people had demanded a king like other nations, Israel did not cease to be a theocracy. Yet her kings were only a poor approximation to Yahweh's ideal of Kingship. So he began to promise through his prophets that one day he would send his own king, anointed with his Spirit, to reign in righteousness and peace over all peoples and for ever.

"The time has come," Jesus announced as he began his public ministry, "the Kingdom of God is near. Repent and believe the Good News" (Mark 1:15). Thus Jesus brought the Kingdom with him. "Eschatology invaded history." "The person of Jesus and the presence of God's Kingdom are inseparably connected." Only those enter it who humble themselves like a little child and are born again.

The Kingdom of God is both a present reality and a future expectation. As a present reality, now that Jesus' physical presence has been withdrawn from the earth, his Holy Spirit establishes it in the lives of his people. For the king must never be thought of apart from his subjects, the messianic community, over which he rules. Moreover, his rule takes the form of both total blessing (salvation, in fact) and total demand (obedience and service).

Christians often have debated the relationship between the church and the Kingdom. We must not identify them, but we must not separate them, either. The church is the community

in which God's kingly rule is revealed, which therefore witnesses to the divine rule, and is the firstfruits of the redeemed humanity (James 1:18). It therefore lives by new values and standards, and its relationships have been transformed by love. Yet it continues to fail. For it lives in
an uneasy tension between the "already" and the "not yet,"
between the present reality and the future expectation of
the Kingdom.

C. The Signs of the Kingdom

Evangelism is the proclamation of this Kingdom in the fulness of its blessings and promise, which one participant also
called "salvation." Moreover, Jesus did more than preach the
Kingdom; he demonstrated its reality with "signs of the Kingdom," public evidence that the Kingdom he was talking about
had come. We believe that signs should validate our evangelism, too, and we have spent time discussing what they
should be.

Since "the reason the Son of God appeared was to destroy
the devil's work" (I John 3:8), he inevitably came into collision with the prince of darkness. The signs of the Kingdom
were evidences that the devil was retreating before the advance of the King. As Jesus put it, once the strong man has
been overpowered by the Stronger One, his possessions can be
taken from him (Matt. 12:29; Luke 11:22).

The signs reflect this. We list them in approximately the
order in which they appeared, although this is not necessarily an order of importance.

The *first* sign of the Kingdom was (and still is) Jesus
himself in the midst of his people (Lk. 17:21; Matt. 18:20),
whose presence brings joy, peace, and a sense of celebration
(John 15:11; 16:33; Mk. 2:18-20).

The *second* is the preaching of the Gospel. There was no
Gospel of the Kingdom to proclaim until Christ arrived. Now,
however, that he has come, the Good News of the Kingdom must
be preached to all, especially to the poor (Lk. 4:18, 19;
7:22). The preaching of the Kingdom points people to the
Kingdom itself.

The *third* sign of the Kingdom was exorcism. We refuse to
demythologize the teaching of Jesus and his apostles about
demons. Although the "principalities and powers" may have a
reference to demonic ideologies and structures, we believe

that they certainly are evil, personal intelligences under
the command of the devil. Demon possession is a real and
terrible condition. Deliverance is possible only in a power
encounter in which the name of Jesus is invoked and prevails.

The *fourth* sign of the Kingdom was the healing and the
nature miracles--making the blind see, the deaf hear, the
lame walk, the sick whole, raising the dead (Lk. 7:22),
stilling the storm, and multiplying loaves and fishes. We
all agree that these were not only signs pointing to the
reality of the Kingdom's arrival, but also anticipations of
the final Kingdom from which all disease, hunger, disorder
and death will be banished for ever. We also agree that God
is still free and powerful and performs miracles today, especially in frontier situations where the Kingdom is advancing into enemy-held territory. Some of us think we should
expect miracles as commonly as in the ministry of Jesus and
his apostles (e.g., John 14:12), while others draw attention
to the texts which describe these miracles as authenticating
their unique ministry (e.g., Heb. 2:3,4; II Cor. 12:12).

A *fifth* sign of the Kingdom is the miracle of conversion
and the new birth. Whenever people "turn to God from idols,
to serve the living and true God" (I Thess. 1:9,10), a power
encounter has taken place in which the spell of idols, whether traditional or modern, and of the spirits has been broken.
God's power for salvation is displayed in the Gospel (Rom.
1:16), and converts who have been rescued from darkness to
light and from the power of Satan to God (Acts 26:18) are
said to have "tasted...the powers of the age to come" (Heb.
6:5).

A *sixth* sign of the Kingdom is the people of the Kingdom,
in whom is manifested that cluster of Christlike qualities
which Paul called "the fruit of the Spirit." For the gift of
the Spirit is the supreme blessing of the Kingdom of God.
Where he rules, love, joy, peace, and righteousness rule with
him (Gal. 5:22,23; Rom. 14:17). Moreover, love issues in
good works. Thus, if the Gospel is Good News of the Kingdom,
good works are the signs of the Kingdom. Good News and good
works, evangelism, and social responsibility, once again are
seen to be indissolubly united.

The *seventh* sign of the Kingdom, we suggest, is suffering.
It was necessary for the King to suffer in order to enter into his glory. Indeed, he suffered for us, leaving us an example that we should follow in his steps (I Pet. 2:21). To suffer for the sake of righteousness or for our testimony to Jesus, and to bear such suffering courageously, is a clear sign

to all beholders that we have received God's salvation or Kingdom (Phil. 1:28,29; cf. II Thess. 1:5).

D. The Extent of the Kingdom

If these are the signs of the Kingdom, manifesting its present reality and pointing forward to its final consummation, how extensive is the Kingdom they signify?

In one sense, as we have seen, God's rule extends only over those who acknowledge it, who have bowed their knee to Jesus and confessed his lordship (Phil. 2:9-11). These God "has delivered...from the dominion of darkness and transferred to the Kingdom of his beloved Son" (Col. 1:13). Apart from them, the whole world is "in the power of the evil one," its "ruler" and "god" (I John 5:19; John 12:31; II Cor. 4:4), for "we do not yet see everything in subjection to" Jesus (Heb. 2:8; cf. Ps. 110:1; Acts 2:35).

Yet in another sense, the Risen Lord claimed that "all authority in heaven and on earth" had been given to him (Matt. 28:18). For God already has "put all things under his feet and has made him head over all things for the church" (Eph. 1:22). His titles are "King of kings and Lord of lords" and "the ruler of princes on earth" (Rev. 1:5; 19:16).

How can these two perspectives be fused? How can Christ claim universal authority if the whole world still lies in Satan's power? The answer is that over his redeemed people Jesus is King *de facto*, while it is only *de jure* that he is presently King over the world, his right still being challenged by the usurper. We should reserve the expression "the Kingdom of God" for the acknowledged rule of Christ, since this is the new thing he inaugurated at his coming, while referring to the more general "sovereignty" of God over all things.

It is important to maintain the tension between what Christ rules *de facto* and *de jure*. For if we assume that all authority has in fact been given to him, we shall not take seriously the evil powers which have not yet capitulated. If, on the other hand, our horizon is bounded by the community in which the King is consciously confessed, we may be tempted to dismiss the rest of the world as beyond redemption. From these extremes of naive optimism and dark pessimism we return to the radical realism of the Bible, which recognizes both the defeat of evil and its refusal to concede defeat. This

double conviction will persuade us to work hard in evangelism
and in the quest for justice, while at the same time putting
our whole trust and confidence in God.

During the interim period between the two comings of
Christ, between his victory over evil and evil's final capi-
tulation and destruction, what should be the relations between the Kingdom community and the world?

First, the new community should constitute a challenge to
the old. Its values and ideals, its moral standards and relationships, its sacrifical life style, its love, joy, and
peace--these are signs of the Kingdom, as we have seen, and
present the world with a radically alternative society. All
our words of love and deeds of love must express our whole-
hearted submission to the Lord of love himself.

Secondly, as the world lives alongside the Kingdom community, some of the values of the Kingdom spill over into society as a whole, so that its industry, commerce, legislation,
and institutions become to some degree imbued with Kingdom
values. So-called "Kingdomized" or "Christianized" society
is not the Kingdom of God, but it owes a debt to the Kingdom
which often is unrecognized.

The "overspill" model has its limitations, however, because it pictures the two communities as independent of one
another, like two vessels standing side by side, the contents
of one spilling over into the other. The salt, light, and
yeast metaphors which Jesus employed are more dynamic, since
each implies the penetration of the old community by the new.
The light shines into the darkness, the salt soaks into the
meat, the yeast causes fermentation in the dough. So Jesus
intends his followers neither to withdraw from the world in
order to preserve their holiness, nor to lose their holiness
by conforming to the world, but simultaneously to permeate
the world and to retain their Kingdom distinctives. Only so
can they share the good news with credibility. Only so can
they be effective agents for cultural, social and political
change. Indeed, as "the Lord blessed the Egyptian's house
for Joseph's sake" (Gen. 39:5), so we believe he blesses the
world through the ministry of, and for the sake of, his redeemed people.

Meanwhile, we do not forget that God is directly at work
in his world, apart from the agency of his people. In his
common grace he continues without intermission to sustain

the earth and its creatures, to grant life and health, to
give sunshine and rain, to maintain the cycle of the seasons,
to cause the ground to be fruitful, to preserve society from
disintegration, and to give to all humankind (who bear his
image and have his law written in their hearts (Rom. 2:14,
15) a certain appreciation of justice, freedom, beauty, dignity, and peace.

While we gladly recognize these works of God in the world,
both directly and through his people, they are not what Jesus
meant by his Kingdom. It is, therefore, our urgent responsibility to summon all people in Christ's name to turn and humble themselves like little children, as we have sought to
humble ourselves, in order to enter the Kingdom and receive
its priceless blessing, the salvation of God (Matt. 18:3).

VI. HISTORY AND ESCHATOLOGY

We devoted a whole day of our Consultation to "history
and eschatology," that is, to the relationship between *on the
one hand* what we do now in the historical process and what
God began when the Kingdom was inaugurated, and *on the other*
what God is going to do on The Last Day when he ushers in the
fulness of the Kingdom.

A. False Dreams

We saw our study as being all the more important because
we human beings are inveterate dreamers. We cannot live only
for today; we must have some hope for tomorrow which will sustain us in our pilgrimage. Consequently, like the pseudo-
prophets of the Old Testament, we have a constant tendency to
fabricate false dreams, visions which come out of our own
minds, and not from the Lord.

We have been conscious of the special need to distinguish
between the social responsibility to which we as Christians
are called, its reasons and its content, and that which modern ideologies have generated. Both dogmatic and Messianic
Marxisms for example, proclaim a bogus milennium, which recognizes neither the Creator of the world, nor his Christ, and
yet anticipates that by changing social structures, frequently
by violent means, they will by human effort alone bring about
a fully just and perfect society. A program for change such
as this, because it denies the stubborn reality of evil and
ignores our deepest human needs, is bound to end in failure,
even in disaster.

We also reject the Messianic Western dream which aims at
erecting a counterfeit materialistic Kingdom. We recognize,
of course, the divine command to subdue the earth and harness its resources for the good of all. But selfish secular
materialism pursues its own economic growth irrespective of
the need to conserve the environment and to serve the development of the poorer nations. It is characterized by self-
absorbed individualism and insensitive affluence, which are
incompatible with Christian--let alone truly human--values,
and which unwittingly foster increasing inequality between
the rich and the poor.

Again, we cannot join those who call for a new political
world order based on a new world religion concocted from a
synthesis of all religions, as the only means of escaping
from the threats of global calamity. We, too, recognize with
sober realism the terrible potential for destruction in human
life. But we are convinced that only the power of God manifest in the forgiveness and recreative power of Christ can
restore to us that order, meaning, freedom, dignity, and
responsibility which the world so desperately needs.

It was, therefore, with relief that we turned from all
ideological substitutes to the authentic Christian hope, to
the vision of the triumphant return of Jesus, and of the
Kingdom he will consummate, which God has revealed to us in
his Word. Our concern was to relate this hope to history,
and to our concrete duties within history. In particular, we
asked ourselves whether there is any connection between our
eschatological outlook and the attitude we adopt towards
evangelism and social responsibility. We are conscious that
more biblical study and historical research are needed before
we will be ready to handle this question with more confidence.
For the present, we feel able to contribute only tentatively
to the debate.

B. Differing Millennarian Views

To begin with, we thought about the millennium and about
its influence on Christian behavior at different periods of
church history. We tried to discern whether there is any cor-
relation between the three traditional varieties of millenni-
alism and the vigor of social action and evangelism in the
history of the church. Without doubt, our understanding of
the millennium affects the way in which we view the world.
The degree of hope which we sustain seems to be proportionate
to the degree to which we see the Kingdom of God as an already
present reality or as a largely future expectation.

Since all three views of the millennium were represented
at our Consultation, and since we desired to give one another
liberty on this matter and not to convert one another to our
own position, we moved on from our millennarian differences
to seek a common eschatological motivation for evangelism
and social responsibility. Of course, Christians are given
in the New Testament many different reasons and motives for
good living and good works, which we did not consider. The
following eschatological incentives were put forward.

C. Judgment to Come

The first was judgment. A great deal of teaching by Jesus
and his apostles linked present responsibility and future
judgment. Jesus told us to be alert, sober and busy in his
service, because we do not know when our Lord will come. But
we do know that when he comes he will call us to account (e.g.,
Mk. 13:33-36; Lk. 12:35-40; Matt. 25:14-30).

The conscientious dedication of the apostle Paul to evangelism seems to have been related directly to his sense of
accountability. "Knowing the fear of the Lord," he wrote,
"we persuade men." "Men-persuading" is a clear reference to
his evangelistic methods, as we know from the Acts, and "the
fear of the Lord" to appearing before Christ's judgment seat,
of which he has written in the previous verse (II Cor. 5:10,
11).

The same motivation can sustain us in our works of philanthropy, as is evident from the sheep and the goats passage
which we studied together one morning. In this solemn description of the day of judgment, the "sheep" or the "righteous,"
who are "blessed" and welcomed into the Kingdom, are those
who have ministered to Christ in the hungry and thirsty, the
naked and sick, the strangers and the prisoners. The "goats,"
on the other hand, who are "cursed" and dismissed to eternal
punishment, are those who have failed to minister to Christ in
the needy. Whether Christ's "brethren" are his followers in
general, as other passages seem to indicate (e.g. Matt.12:46-
50; Heb. 2:10-18), or in particular his messengers, as may be
suggested by the "cup of cold water" passage (Matt. 10:9-15;
40-42), or may include the rest of needy humankind with whom
Christ humbly identifies himself, the principal message is the
same. As the rest of the New Testament teaches, the dead will
be judged "by what they have done" (e.g. Rev. 20:13), and our
deeds will include either the loving service to those in need
or a scandalous indifference to their plight. There will be an
acid test whether we are true believers, or unbelievers.

Neither of these two passages of Scripture possibly can mean that we can gain entry to heaven by our good works. To interpret them in this way would be to turn the Gospel upside down. What they are emphasizing is that though we are justified by grace alone through faith alone, we shall be judged by those good works of love through which our secret faith is made public.

D. The Eschatological Vision

We are united in rejecting utopic visions, which are dreams of human accomplishment. The eschatological vision is totally different, however, because it is a revelation of what God himself is going to do in the end. This vision can give both direction and inspiration to our present duty. We do not of course presume to imagine that we can do now what God will do then. Nor will every part of the final state have a counterpart now (e.g., there will be no marriage then).

Nevertheless, the glimpses God has given us of the end disclose the kind of community life which is pleasing to him. Twice Peter tells us "what sort of persons" we ought to be in this life on account of what is going to happen at the end. He likens the coming destruction of the present evil order to the flood, except that it will be by fire instead of water, and urges us in consequence to "lives of holiness and godliness." Then he passes from the destruction of the old order to the creation of the new. He argues that because in the new heavens and the new earth "righteousness dwells," therefore we must be zealous to be found by Christ "without spot or blemish, and at peace." In other words, because righteousness and peace will be characteristics of the eternal kingdom, we need to pursue them in the Kingdom's present manifestation (II Pet. 3:1-14).

We believe that, in a similar way, the vision of the countless multitude before God's throne, redeemed from every nation (Rev. 7:9), who will constitute the final fulfilment of God's promise to give Abraham a countless posterity (Gen. 12:1-3), should be a powerful incentive to us to obey the Great Commission to go and make disciples of all nations,and to seek to make our churches a foretaste of the heterogeneous heavenly community.

If that aspect of the eschatological vision is a stimulus to evangelism, others should prove a stimulus to social action. If in heaven they will "hunger no more, neither thirst any more" (Rev. 7:16), should we not feed the hungry today?

And if in the end "they shall beat their swords into plough-shares, and their spears into pruning hooks, neither shall they learn war any more" (Micah 4:3; Is. 2:4), does that not mean that war is incompatible with the perfect will of God? Not that the state can now discard its responsibility to enforce justice and order (Rom. 13:1-4), any more than we can expect lambs and lions to lie down together now. But does not Scripture tell us that, even if (as some Christians have always believed) war may be in some circumstances the lesser of two evils, we all still should seek to be peacemakers?

In these ways the eschatological vision can direct and motivate our Christian action, while at the same time we must never forget the fallenness of this world or the wickedness of the principalities and powers.

E. Continuity

The words "continuity" and "discontinuity" have kept recurring throughout our Consultation. That is to say, will the final Kingdom enjoy some continuity with its present manifestation, or will the future be discontinuous with the present, so that nothing will survive the judgment except those who by God's sheer grace are the heirs of his Kingdom?

We have not been able to reach complete agreement on this matter. Some of us, vividly aware of the evil of this present age and of the glory that is to be revealed, emphasize the destructive nature of God's judgment and the newness of his new creation. Others of us believe that, just as after the new birth we are not a different person but the same person remade, so the universe is going to experience a new birth (*palingenesia,* Matt. 19:28). That is, God is going to re-create it, and not create another universe *ex nihilo.* Indeed, Paul likens the pains of the created order to the birthpangs of the new (Rom. 8:18-25; cf Mk. 13:8).

We all believe this about our bodies, for the principle of continuity is evident in the resurrected body of Jesus. Although, as Paul expresses it, our new body will be as different from the old as a flower differs from its seed, nevertheless there will be a continuity between the two (I Cor. 15:35-46). And later he grounds his argument for sexual self-control and a right use of our bodies not only on what they are (members of Christ and temples of the Holy Spirit) but on what they are going to be: "The body is not meant for immorality, but for the Lord, and the Lord for the body. And God raised the Lord and will also raise us up by his power" (I Cor.6: 12-20). On this double resurrection, of the Lord Jesus and of our bodies, the apostle bases his plea for purity.

We are on more uncertain ground, however, when we ask how many of our present works will be carried over into eternity. Certainly evangelism has eternal consequences, since converts receive God's free gift of eternal life. So does our teaching, if we build with "gold, silver, and precious stones" upon the foundation of Christ (I Cor. 3:10-15). But what about our social activity? We are told of those who "die in the Lord" that "their deeds follow them" (Rev. 14:13; cf. I Cor. 13:13). We also are told that the kings of the earth will "bring their glory" into the New Jerusalem, and that they will "bring into it the glory and the honor of the nations," while what will be excluded is everything "unclean" (Rev.21: 24-27). This has seemed to many to teach that whatever is beautiful, true and good in human cultures, once purged of everything which defiles, will be consummated in the final Kingdom. Those who have the assurance of this continuity find a strong incentive to social and cultural involvement.

F. The Christian Hope

In whatever more precise ways we may formulate these motivations of judgment, vision, and continuity, we all are agreed that our Christian hope focuses on the personal, visible, and glorious return of our Lord Jesus Christ, on the resurrection from death, and on the perfected Kingdom which his appearing will bring. Also, we all are agreed that we are to live our lives and do our works in the conscious expectation of his coming. This confidence will make us committed to world evangelization (Matt. 24:14), "zealous for good deeds" (Tit. 2:13,14), faithful to one another in the fellowship (Heb. 10:25), and courageous in suffering (II Tim. 4:6-8; Rev. 2:25). With great firmness we therefore reject what has been called "eschatological paralysis." On the contrary, before the Lord comes, and in preparation for his coming, we are determined to get into the action. This is to "live anticipatorily," to experience the power, enjoy the community, and manifest the righteousness of the Kingdom *now,* before it is consummated in glory.

VII. GUIDELINES FOR ACTION

Much of our debate has been at a theological level, for we have felt the need to wrestle with the issues which relate to salvation and kingdom, history and eschatology. Nevertheless, our theologizing all has been with a view to determining what practical action we should take to forward the mission which God has given us. In particular, we have considered in what forms our evangelistic and social concerns should be expressed, what agencies should undertake the work, and how different political and cultural situations will affect it.

A. Forms of Evangelism and Social Responsibility

We all have been familiar for years with different forms of evangelism (personal evangelism, local church evangelism, mass evangelism, cross-cultural evangelism, etc.). But we have been less clear about the different forms in which our social concern should be manifested. Throughout our Consultation we have spoken of "social responsibility," "social ministries," "social assistance," "social service," "social action," "social justice," and (as in the Lausanne Covenant) "socio-political activity." We believe that a failure to define these terms has contributed to the continuing suspicion which surrounds every Christian activity described as "social." It may be easiest to divide our Christian social responsibility into two kinds, which for simplicity's sake we will call "social service" and "social action," and which can be distinguished from each other in several ways:

Social Service	Social Action
Relieving Human Need	Removing the Causes of Human Need
Philanthropic Activity	Political and Economic Activity
Seeking to Minister to Individuals and Families	Seeking to Transform the Structures of Society
Works of Mercy	The Quest for Justice

In making this necessary functional distinction, we recognize that in practice it is not as neat as it looks. On the one hand, social action of a political kind lacks integrity if it is not supported by a personal commitment to social service.

On the other, some works of mercy have inescapably political
implications--for example, teaching the oppressed to read
and write, visiting a banned person in South Africa, or sending food to Poland or North Vietnam.

1. Social Service and Evangelism

The first of these two kinds of ministry is universally
accepted as a Christian obligation; there is nothing controversial about it. Just as we are called to personal evangelism, so we are called to personal service. Jesus, we are
told, both "went about...preaching and bringing the good
news," and "went about doing good" (Luke 8:1; Acts 10:38).

All Christians should follow his example,--although, to
be sure, our way of sharing the good news may not be only by
preaching. Both personal evangelism and personal service are
expressions of compassion. Both are forms of witness to Jesus Christ. And both should be sensitive responses to human
need. The evangelist seeks to discover the principal point
of felt need--for example, a sense of guilt or shame or fear,
moral failure, personal loneliness, a lack of self-worth or
significance, domestic unhappiness, a hunger for transcendence, lack of education, social repression, or demon activity. Similarly, a person's social needs may range from the
physical (food, clothing, shelter, or health care), through
the psychological (anxiety, alienation, emotional unbalance)
to the economic (poverty, illiteracy, unemployment). Even in
welfare states there always are areas of human need which government and voluntary agencies do not fully cover, and which
Christians can take the initiative to meet.

"Development" should be put into a separate category, but
it probably should be bracketed with philanthropic service,
even though some community development projects embrace a
whole village, town, or district. It is very welcome that
many welfare agencies have expanded their emphasis in recent
years from aid to development, and many medical missions from
curative medicine to community health. To help people learn
to help themselves not only makes better sense economically,
but it also is more conducive to human dignity. It is important, therefore, to ensure that self-help programs genuinely
enable people to stand on their own feet and are not devious
paternalistic ploys to reinforce dependence, even subservience.

If Christian people are to get involved in humanitarian
service, whether in the form of helping a neighbor or of

sharing in an aid or development project, considerable sacri-
fices in time, energy, and money will be needed. We see this
whole area of service as an important challenge to our self-
centered, self-loving "me generation."

2. Social Action and Evangelism

The other kind of responsibility is the quest for social
justice. It looks beyond persons to structures, beyond the
rehabilitation of prison inmates to the reform of the prison
system, beyond improving factory conditions to securing a
more participatory role for the workers, beyond caring for
the poor to transforming the economic system (whatever it
may be) and the political system (again, whatever it may be),
until it facilitates their liberation from poverty and oppression. Such social changes often necessitate political
action (for politics is about power), and some evangelicals
fear it because they imagine it will entail civil strife and
even revolution. But this is not what we mean by "socio-
political involvement." We are thinking rather of political
processes which are consistent with biblical principles--
such as the rights of the individual and of minorities, respect for civil authority, the welfare of the whole community,
and justice for the oppressed.

The Bible lays great emphasis on both justice (or righteousness) and peace. For God is the author of both, and both
are essential characteristics of his Kingdom. We, therefore,
who claim to be members of his Kingdom, must not only seek
justice for others but must "do justice" ourselves (Mic. 6:8),
in relation to our family, our fellow workers, and any servants or employees we may have. In the same way, it is not
enough to "seek peace and pursue it;" we must also ourselves,
so far as it depends on us, "live peaceably with all" (I Pet.
3:11; Rom. 12:18). This applies to churches as well as individual Christians. If discrimination and disunity are tolerated in the church, how can we denounce them in the nation?
Conversely, it is churches which visibly demonstrate the
righteousness and peace of the Kingdom which will make the
greater impact on our world. The salt must retain its salt-
ness, Jesus said; otherwise, it is good for nothing. (Matt.
5:13).

B. Agents of Evangelism and Social Responsibility

One of the points of tension emerging during the Consultation has concerned the allocation of responsibilities. Granted
that evangelism and social concern/action are Christian

responsibilities, who is responsible for what? What should be undertaken by individual Christians, what by groups, and in particular what is to be the role of the church as church?

1. Evangelism and Social Service

We agree that alongside personal evangelism there should be personal social service. Individual Christians should be involved in both, according to their opportunities, gifts, and callings.

The parallel is similar in the local church. Just as each local church has an inescapable responsibility before God to bring the Gospel to all the people who reside and work in its neighborhood, so the social needs of the neighborhood should be a special concern of the local church.

There is an important place for both church groups and para-church groups. We shall have more to say about the former when we come to our section on "The Local Church in a Free Society." Para-church organizations, both for evangelism and for social responsibility, have an indispensable part to play in Christian outreach, especially if they specialize in kinds of ministry which no church can manage on its own, and provided that they accept a measure of responsibility to the churches.

2. Evangelism and Social Action

Does social action belong to the mission of the church as church, or is it the prerogative of individual believers who make up the church, and of groups?

We have no doubt about individuals and groups. The church should encourage its members to become conscientious citizens, to take the initiative to found and operate social programs, to inform themselves about political issues, and to advocate or dissent according to their conscience.

Since individual action usually is limited in its effects, however, Christians also should be encouraged to form or join groups and movements which concern themselves with specific needs in society, undertake research into social issues, and organize appropriate action. We welcome the existence and activity of such groups, for they supplement the church's work in many important areas. Christians also should be encouraged to participate responsibly in the political party of their choice, their labor union(s), or business association(s), and similar movements. Whenever possible, they should form a Christian group within them, and/or start or join a Christian party, union, or movement, in order to develop specifically Christian policies.

From the activity of individuals and groups, we come back to the church. Should the church get involved in politics, or keep out? Some argue that churches which engage in socio-political action, especially on controversial issues, lose members and missionaries, because the action stirs up controversy. Others counter that different factors like theological liberalism and loss of confidence in the Gospel are the real cause of dwindling numbers.

This issue is not only pragmatic, however; it is essentially theological. Behind the debate lie our differing ecclesiologies and, in particular, our differing understandings of the relationship between church and state, between the Kingdom of God and what has been called the "Kingdom of Caesar." At least three traditions on Christian political involvement, all deriving from the European Protestant Reformation, have been represented in our Consultation. All agree that the Kingdom of God is distinct from the political realm. One sees the Kingdom as *opposed* to that realm and pleads for a Christian community witness independent of political institutions. A second tradition sees the Kingdom as *separate* from the political realm, though parallel to it, and urges that Christians participate in that realm, though as citizens (not as church members) guided by Christian moral principles. The third tradition sees the Kingdom of God as penetrating and *transforming* the political realm; it argues that political involvement belongs to the witness not only of Christian individuals and groups but also of churches.

This discussion is far from being irrelevant to evangelism. People's hearts often are opened to the Gospel when they see that we genuinely care for them as persons rather than merely as souls. When they perceive that the Gospel is about the mercy and justice of God which were reconciled at Christ's cross, and see his mercy and justice still active in the situation today, they are likely to be the more ready to come to Christ.

C. The Local Church in a Free Society

In spite of our differing theological and cultural backgrounds, on account of which some of us assign social action
(of a political kind) to individuals and groups rather than
to churches, all of us agree that the church has definite
evangelistic and social responsibilities. This applies especially to the local church, which should be committed to
the total well-being of the community in which is permanently
situated. Some of these duties belong to all churches, others only to churches in a free or open society. We shall
have more to say in the next section about the particular
case of churches under repression.

1. Intercession

"First of all," wrote Paul to Timothy, "I urge that sup-
plications, prayers, intercessions, and thanksgivings be made
for all men, for kings and all who are in high positions,
that we may lead a quiet and peaceable life, godly and re-
spectful in every way. This is good, and it is acceptable
in the sight of God our Savior who desires all men to be
saved and to come to the knowledge of the truth" (I Tim. 2:
104). Thus does the apostle give priority to prayer among
the church's public duties, in particular prayer for the civil authorities, and he goes on to link it to both peace and
salvation.

We are convinced that the living God hears and answers
the prayers of his people, that by prayer we can enter into
the unseen spiritual conflict and bind Satan in the name of
Christ, and that there is special power in corporate prayer
when "two of you (or more) agree on earth about anything you
ask" (Matt. 18:19). Yet we are ashamed that our practice
falls far short of our principle. Often the pastoral prayer
in public worship is brief and perfunctory; the petitions are
so imaginative and stale as to border on "vain repetitions;"
and the people doze and dream instead of praying.

We resolve ourselves, and call upon our churches, to take
much more seriously the period of intercession in public worship; to think in terms of 10 or 15 minutes rather than five;
to invite lay people to share in leading, since they often
have deep insight into the world's needs; and to focus our
prayers on both the evangelization of the world (closed lands,
resistant peoples, missionaries, national churches, etc.) and
on the quest for peace and justice in the world (places of
tension and conflict, deliverance from the nuclear horror,

rulers and governments, the poor and needy, etc.). We long
to see every Christian congregation bowing down in humble
and expectant faith before our Soveriegn Lord.

2. Love

If evangelism and social responsibility are twins, their
mother is love. For evangelism means words of love and social service/action means deeds of love, and both should be
the natural overflow of a community of love. We do not think
the local church can reach out to its neighborhood with any
degree of credibility unless and until it is filled with the
love of God.

This love will manifest itself first in the *philadelphia*
("brotherly love") which binds Christian brothers and sisters
together. Such a loving fellowship has great evangelistic
power. For it is only when we love one another, as Christ
has loved us, that everybody will know we are his disciples
(John 13:34,35). Further, the invisible God who once made
himself visible in Christ now makes himself visible in us,
if we love one another: "Nobody has ever seen God; but if we
love one another, God abides in us and his love is perfected
in us" (I John 4:12).

But the love of God cannot possibly be bottled up within
the Christian community; it breaks out in compassion for the
world. It yearns for the salvation of sinners, so that
Christ's lost sheep may be gathered safely into his flock.
It yearns also to alleviate the material needs of the poor,
the hungry, and the oppressed, so that if we close our hearts
against the needy, we cannot claim that God's love abides in
us (I John 3:17). Love for God and love for neighbor belong
inextricably together, as Jesus taught (Mk. 12:28-34; cf.
I John 4:19-21).

We are convinced that the Christian impact on society
(both evangelistic and social) depends even more on quality
than on numbers, and that the distinctive quality of Christians is love.

3. Teaching

Every Christian congregation, of course, should be preaching and teaching the Gospel, year in year out, in season and
out of season, with biblical faithfulness, contemporary relevance, and urgent boldness. We believe the church languishes

enever the Word of God is neglected, and it flourishes when-
ver it is honored. We desire to call our churches back to
blical preaching for both evangelism and edification.

But we have to teach our people the law as well as the
spel, that is, obedience as well as forgiveness, the moral
emands of the Kingdom as well as its gift of salvation. Indeed, it is the calling of preachers, like Paul in Ephesus,
"not to shrink from declaring" to the people "anything that
is profitable," indeed "not to shrink from declaring to them
the whole counsel of God" (Acts 20:20,27). This will include
rebuking evil in all its ugly manifestations.

Thorough teaching of the Word of God is even more important in our day, in which many Christians are bewildered by
contemporary problems. They read about them in the newspaper
and hear about them on radio or television; shall such topics
then be excluded from the pulpit? We are not now referring
to issues which are controversial even among Christians (we
will come to these in the next paragraph), but to fundamental
modern challenges to the teaching of the Bible. People need
help to resist the pressures of secular thought and to take a
firm stand on the moral principles of Scripture. So we must
help them to discern the moral issues in each question, to
understand them and to hold them fast. In addition, they
need to be made aware of how the socio-political and legisla-
tive processes work, and to have their confidence raised that
they need not be the helpless victims either of an evil status quo or of revolutionary destruction, but can be active as
society's salt and light in the fight to protect or to introduce Christian ethical values. This kind of consciousness-
raising is particularly important for those church members who
are community leaders, opinion formers, and decision makers--
for example, parents, teachers, journalists, and politicians.
In a democracy (in which government depends on the consent of
the governed), legislation depends on public opinion. Our
Christian responsibility is to get into the public debate a-
bout current issues, boldly affirm, practice, and argue what
the Bible teaches, and so seek to influence public opinion
for Christ.

How, then, shall we handle controversial topics? Many
voices during the Consultation have urged us to be cautious.
Modern problems of personal and social ethics (which are often
inter-related) are legion: abortion, euthanasia, genetic
engineering, homosexuality, racism, castism and tribalism,
sexism, human rights, environmental pollution, ideologies,

polygamy, economic inequality between and within nations, terrorism, war, nuclear disarmament, and many more. To some of these ethical questions the biblical answer is clear, and in most others a plain biblical principle is involved: here, then, the teaching of the church should be unequivocal and unanimous.

Yet, highly complex issues remain. So then, whenever the Word of God speaks clearly, the church must speak clearly also, as for example did the German Confessing Church in the Barmen Declaration of 1934, and the Norwegian Church while Norway was under German occupation in World War II. If such speech is condemned as political, we need to remember that silence would be political, too. We cannot avoid taking sides. But when the teaching of Scripture seems unclear, and human reason has to seek to develop a position out of biblical principles, then the church should make a pronouncement only after thorough study and consultation.

When the church cannot agree on an issue, then the issue cannot be dealt with in the name of the church; instead, Christian individuals and groups should handle it. The church also should be sensitive to anything (such as a divisive controversy) that would weaken its evangelistic outreach. But when the church concludes that biblical faith or righteousness requires it to take a public stand on some issue, then it must obey God's Word and trust him with the consequences.

We heard from the pastor of a black church in New England that their resolve to address themselves to social issues has greatly increased their evangelistic witness. Their procedure is one of thorough consultation, in order to ensure unity rather than division in the congregation. First, the pastor makes a presentation on some issue to his deacons, next the deacons take it to the church council, and then the church council refers it to the church members. At each successive stage, agreement is sought. The result has been that the church has wider opportunities for witness because it has become known as a socially concerned church, and so evangelism and social action have had a multiplying impact on one another.

All of us are agreed that a local church should not normally engage in partisan politics, either advocating a particular party or attempting to frame political programs. We also are agreed, however, that the local church has a prophetic ministry to proclaim the law of God and to teach justice, should

seek to be the conscience of the nation, and has a duty to
help the congregation develop a Christian mind, so that the
people may learn to think Christianly even about controversial questions.

4. Power

All of us agree that God gives power to his people--power
for holiness, power for witness, and power for courageous
action in the name of Christ. We all also agree that, in
his sovereignty and his grace, God endows his people with a
wide variety of spiritual gifts for service. Some of us lay
particular emphasis on supernatural "gifts of healing," "the
working of miracles" (I Cor. 12:9,10), and the casting out
of demons, while others prefer to emphasize non-miraculous
social gifts like contributing to the needs of others, giving
aid, and doing "acts of mercy" (Rom. 12:8). All spiritual
gifts, whatever their nature, should be exercised with compassion under the anointing of the Holy Spirit and for the
common good. They can meet social, physical and emotional as
well as spiritual needs, contribute to the well-being of society as well as of the church, and, authenticating the Gospel, draw unbelievers to Christ.

5. Vocations

All Christians are called to both witness and service.
Whenever the opportunity is given, we have a privileged duty
to speak for Christ and serve our neighbor. In addition to
this general Christian calling, however, each of us has a
special vocation. We already have written about the diversity
of gifts, leading to a diversity of ministries, in the Body of
Christ.

The local church (especially its leadership) has a responsibility, therefore, to help its members (especially its young
people) to recognize their gifts and so discover their vocation. Some churches set up a "vocation group" for those of
its members who are wanting to discern God's will for their
lives, in order that they may pray together, seek advice and
investigate a variety of possibilities.

On the one hand, the local church continuously should keep
before its membership the possibility that God may be calling
some of them to a full-time Christian ministry as cross-
cultural missionaries, evangelists, pastors, teachers, or
church workers of some other kind. And the local church
should give its members opportunities to test their vocation

in evangelistic missions, house-to-house visitation, youth outreach, Sunday school teaching, and in other ways.

Full-time Christian ministry is not limited to these areas, however. Although it is a great and sacred calling to be a missionary or pastor, we must not thereby imply that other callings are "secular." There is an urgent need to encourage more of our Christian young people to respond to God's call into the professions, into industry and commerce, into public office in the political arena, and into the mass media, in order that they may penetrate these strongholds of influence for Christ. And whatever our church members' vocations are, we need both to help train them to serve there as Christians and to support them in their service.

This brings us back to evangelism again. For in order to make an impact on our society for Christ, we need more Christians to permeate it as his salt and light; otherwise, our effectiveness will be very small. But in order to send more Christians into the world, we must win more people for Christ and disciple them. "Our dire need," one of our groups has written, "is for an army of Josephs, Esthers, Daniels, and Nehemiahs, who will have a determining voice in the affairs of our countries."

6. *Groups*

Just as there are special vocations, so there should be specialist groups in every church. For it is certain that the local church as a unit cannot possibly engage in all the activities it is being urged to undertake. Therefore, it must delegate particular responsibilities to different groups.

To begin with, there should be evangelistic groups, all trained for evangelistic outreach, one perhaps maintaining regular door-to-door visitation in the district, another organizing and maintaining a Christian coffee-bar or infiltrating a non-Christian one, another serving as a music group or witness team, another arranging evangelistic home meetings or home Bible studies or prayer groups. As the church responds sensitively to the evangelistic needs which it perceives in its community, appropriate new groups constantly can be brought into being.

In addition, the church needs social service groups. One may organize literacy classes with an ethnic minority, another may visit senior citizens or hospital patients or prison

inmates, another may initiate a development project in a local slum area, or found a cooperative with the poor, or a
club with delinquent youth, while another may offer citizens'
advice or legal aid to those who cannot afford to pay for it.
Again, the possibilities are almost limitless.

Thirdly, the local church may decide to form one or more
social action groups, if this is compatible with its understanding of the church's role in society. Such groups doubtless would devote a good deal of their time to study, in
which they may seek the help of experts. They might take up
a global problem, in order to educate themselves and (if
given the opportunity) the church. Or they might address
themselves to an ethical issue like abortion. If they reach
a consensus and are able to carry the church with them, then
no doubt their study would lead to action, whether in terms
of political lobbying or non-violent protest or joining in
some national demonstration. An alternative to church groups
is the encouragement of church members to join non-church
groups.

Whatever action a group takes, however, it would have to
be clear itself and make clear to others whether it is operating on its own or has the backing of the church. All these
groups--for evangelism, social service, or social action--
need to relate closely to the church, reporting back regularly and seeking advice and support. In this way the ministry
of the church can be diversified greatly.

7. *Resources*

The evangelistic and social work of the church depends on
money as well as people. How much of its income each local
church decides to allocate to evangelism, and how much to social responsibility, will depend on its particular circumstances. This will have to be settled by prayerful consultation and not by a simple formula, and it will be related to
what other churches, government and voluntary agencies are
doing.

Each local church needs to remember, however, that it is a
manifestation in its own community of the universal church of
Christ. Therefore, it has an international as well as a local
responsibility. The world-wide Christian community should
seek to develop a true "partnership...in giving and receiving"
(Phil. 4:15). That is, gifts should flow in both directions,
so that every giver is also a receiver, and every receiver a

giver. For example, one church might send financial help to another, and in return receive a visit from an evangelist or Bible teacher of the other church. Such reciprocal Christian ministry can be extremely enriching and should be fostered by mutual discussion of needs and resources.

The context for Christian thinking about resources should be the forecast that by the year A.D. 2000 the world's population is likely to exceed six billion people. This will dramatically increase the numbers of both unevangelized and needy people. Meanwhile, a comparatively small number of Westerners, who live around the North Atlantic, continue to consume a disproportionate percentage of Planet Earth's natural wealth.

If Christians are going to take seriously the double challenge to take the good news to all nations and to enable the poor to become self-reliant, a major redistribution of resources will be necessary. We are not now pronouncing on the controversial macro-question of how to redress the economic imbalance between rich and poor nations. Rather are we wanting wealthy local churches to remember that millions of poor people in the world are their Christian brothers and sisters. The Christian conscience cannot come to terms with the fact that they live and die in poverty, while so many of us enjoy an affluent lifestyle.

We still are committed to Paragraph 9 of the Lausanne Covenant, which commented that we cannot attain our goals without sacrifice and then went on: "All of us are shocked by the poverty of millions and disturbed by the injustices which cause it. Those of us who live in affluent circumstances accept our duty to develop a simple lifestyle in order to contribute more generously to both relief and evangelism." We are not naive enough to imagine that the world's problems will be solved by such action. But we believe that a Christian lifestyle of contentment and simplicity fulfils the teaching of Scripture, expresses solidarity with the poor, and releases funds for evangelistic and social enterprises.

At present, only a tiny fraction of our total Christian resources is being applied to any kind of mission, evangelistic or social. The strongest argument for sacrificial giving was the one Paul used when appealing to the Christians of Corinth to be generous: "For you know the grace of our Lord Jesus Christ, that though he was rich, yet for your sake he became poor, so that by his poverty you might become rich"

(II Cor. 8:9). Our Lord is generous; his people therefore must be generous, too. And the place to learn generosity is the local church.

D. The Church under Repression

There are many settings in the world where today's church is like the early church, where it suffers from harassment or active persecution. We have thought particularly about churches repressed by Marxist, Muslim, or extreme rightist regimes, or by state-related churches. In such situations, it has been suggested to us, the church always has faced three temptations--to *conform* (tailoring the Gospel to the prevailing ideology), to *fight* (losing its identity by resorting to worldly weapons), or to *withdraw* (denying its mission, betraying its calling, and losing its relevance). It also has been pointed out to us that there were three similar options in our Lord's Day, represented by the Sadducees (the compromisers), the Zealots (the freedom fighters), and the Pharisees and Essenes (the escapists), and that these three groups formed an unholy alliance against Jesus, finding him a greater threat than each other.

Our brothers and sisters in repressive situations have recommended that, resisting these three temptations, the church should develop a critical involvement in society, while preserving its primary allegiance to Christ. Such a church will have little opportunity to preach openly or to exert a social influence, because it has been pushed to the margins of society and has no apparatus of power. The following guidelines for evangelism and social responsibility have been proposed:

1. Consistency

Above all, the church must be true to its Lord, a Christ-centered community, and so it must establish the credibility of its witness. There must be no dichotomy between its profession and its practice. For being precedes acting, and seeing must accompany hearing.

2. Love

Churches under duress should remember the evangelizing power of a Christian community of love which, even when public worship and witness are forbidden, can bear its testimony by deeds of love. Each local church needs to be a model of just structures, harmonious relationships, and modest lifestyle.

The people of God need also to remember that their "enemies,"
who persecute them, are persons in whom is the image of God
and for whom Christ died, and that a person is more important
than the ideology he holds. By the grace of God, they will
be enabled to love their enemies, as Jesus taught.

3. *Witness*

Even under persecution, God opens spaces for his people
to live and share the Gospel, especially in personal evangelism, and to demonstrate that the "new man" of Marxist expectation can be created only by Jesus Christ. God will give opportunities also to serve human need. Even though centrally-
planned economies in some countries have succeeded in abolish-
ing extreme poverty, there still remain pockets of deep human
need--the disillusioned, the elderly, the lonely, and the neglected minority groups. Christians will gladly love and
serve them.

4. *Solidarity*

When the church has to act, especially in some kind of
protest, who will take the initiative? It is too risky for
pastors, and individuals are too weak. So members of the
Body of Christ must stand together, the local church for local issues, and the national church for national issues, knowing their legal rights and defending them (like the apostle
Paul), and witnessing together to Christ.

5. *Suffering*

What if church and state appear to be on a collision course?

The general teaching of Scripture is plain: the institution
of government has been established by God; citizens are required to be subject to it--to obey the law, pay their taxes,
fulfil their civic duties, and seek the good of their country.
Indeed, Christian people should encourage the state to perform
its Godgiven duty to reward those who do right and punish
those who do wrong (Rom. 13:1-7; I Pet. 2:13-15; cf. Jer.29:7).

What happens if the state abuses its authority, however,
and either forbids what God commands or commands what God forbids? The principle is clear. We are to obey the state
(whose authority comes from God) right up to the point where
obedience to it would involve us in disobedience to him. In
that extreme circumstance alone, it is our Christian duty to
disobey the state in order to obey God.

This has an evangelistic implication. It was when the Sanhedrin forbade the apostles to preach in the name of Jesus that Peter said, "We must obey God rather than men," and "We cannot but speak of what we have seen and heard" (Acts 4:17-20; 5:27-29). Those of us who live in free countries are in no position to tell our brothers and sisters in totalitarian situations how they should respond to government attempts to silence them. We do not think they necessarily should defy the authorities with the outspoken boldness of the apostles. They may consider it wiser at least in many cases to bear testimony more by deed than by word. On the other hand, they will be unable to give the state complete allegiance in this matter, since witness to Jesus is an inalienable part of our obedience to him.

Turning to social action, the Bible records a noble succession of men and women who risked their lives by courageously defying a human authority in the name of the God of justice. We have been reminded of Nathan, who confronted King David over his adultery with Bathsheba and his murder of her husband; of Elijah, who denounced King Ahab for annexing Naboth's vineyard by having him assassinated; of Daniel and his friends, who between them refused either to worship an image or to stop worshiping the true God; of Queen Esther, who dared to present herself, though unbidden, to King Ahasuerus in order to plead for her people unjustly condemned to be massacred; and of John the Baptist, who told King Herod that his marriage to Herodias his sister-in-law was unlawful, and who lost his life as a result.

With these biblical precedents we should not be surprised that they have their modern counterparts. Three African examples have particularly impressed us. When the President of Chad, in the name of cultural revolution, tried to force Christians to submit to pagan initiation rites, some compromised, others were killed, and the church leaders were unable to act in unison. A single layman, however, wrote an Open Letter to the President to explain why he could not submit, even if it meant that he must die. His letter was received and respected.

Although Kenya does not fall into the category of a repressive dictatorship, and Christians (who are in the majority) enjoy freedom, yet the church has on occasions suffered and has taken a firm stand against injustices. In 1969, some Kikuyu leaders tried to unite their tribe by requiring an oath of loyalty to it. Many Christians refused to take the oath because, they said, their supreme loyalty was to Christ, and their next loyalty was to their nation, not their tribe. Some were killed. So a group of church leaders went together to President Kenyatta, and as a result the oathing was stopped.

That confrontation with a President was successful. Another, in the neighboring country of Uganda, led to tragedy, although God turned it to the church's good. During Amin's reign of terror, the House of Bishops of the Anglican Church of Uganda wrote him a joint letter to complain of the cruelty and malpractices of his soldiers, and of the total disregard for human life in the country. Archbishop Janani Luwum was summoned to appear before an assembly of leaders and soldiers, and then was falsely accused, mocked, and shortly afterwards assassinated. The other bishops stood in solidarity with him at this time of suffering.

These examples of courage have challenged us greatly. We believe that such confrontations should be reserved for extreme situations only and that in such circumstances church leaders, if possible, should act together and only after the most thorough consultation.

Nevertheless, there are occasions of moral principle in which the church must take its stand, whatever the cost. For the church is the community of the Suffering Servant who is the Lord, and it is called to serve and suffer with him. It is not popularity which is the authentic mark of the Church, but prophetic suffering, and even martyrdom. "Indeed all who desire to live a godly life in Christ Jesus will be persecuted" (II Tim. 3:14). May we be given grace to stand firm!

CONCLUSION: A CALL TO OBEDIENCE

We have come to the end of our Report. It has been a great joy for us to be together for this week. Despite our different backgrounds and traditions, we have deeply appreciated one another and the rich multi-cultural fellowship which God has given us.

We have talked, listened, pondered, debated, and prayed. We also have warned one another of the dangers of such prolonged analysis, categorization, and reflection while outside-- beyond the delightful campus of the Reformed Bible College where we have been accommodated so comfortably--are living those lost, oppressed, and needy people about whom we have been speaking.

Now the time has come for us to stop discussing them and start serving them, to leave "the mountain of glory" and descend to "the valley of problems and opportunities" (about which Bishop David Gitari preached during our opening service of worship).

Jesus our Lord is calling us to put into practice what we have written, and to determine afresh by his grace to reach all peoples with the Gospel. Challenged by the humility of his Incarnation, inspired by the love of his Cross, relying on the power of his Resurrection, and eagerly awaiting the glory of his Return, we are resolved to obey his call. We hope that others who read our Report will be moved by the same Lord to the same resolve and the same obedience.

We request the Lausanne Committee for World Evangelization and the World Evangelical Fellowship, who jointly sponsored our Consultation, and other bodies of like mind, to call Christians and churches around the world to a more costly commitment to the lost, the needy, and the oppressed, for the greater glory of God, Father, Son and Holy Spirit.

Grand Rapids, Michigan
26 June 1982